Luis Gerónimo de Oré

NEW HISPANISMS
Cultural and Literary Studies

ANNE J. CRUZ, SERIES EDITOR

Luis Gerónimo de Oré

*The World of an Andean Franciscan
from the Frontiers to the Centers of Power*

Noble David Cook
with Alexandra Parma Cook

LOUISIANA STATE UNIVERSITY PRESS
BATON ROUGE

Published by Louisiana State University Press
lsupress.org

Copyright © 2024 by Noble David Cook and Alexandra Parma Cook
All rights reserved. Except in the case of brief quotations used in articles or reviews, no part of this publication may be reproduced or transmitted in any format or by any means without written permission of Louisiana State University Press.

DESIGNER: Isabel Weber and Michelle A. Neustrom
TYPEFACE: Arno Pro, text; Luminari, display

All maps created by Greg Cook.

JACKET IMAGES: Portrait of Luis Gerónimo de Oré, ca. 1600. Courtesy of the Convent of San Francisco of Lima, Peru. Photograph by Noble David Cook. Map of the Western Hemisphere by Jacob van Meurs, ca. 1650.

LIBRARY OF CONGRESS CATALOGING-IN-PUBLICATION DATA

Names: Cook, Noble David, author. | Cook, Alexandra Parma, author.
Title: Luis Gerónimo de Oré : the world of an Andean Franciscan from the frontiers to the centers of power / Noble David Cook with Alexandra Parma Cook.
Description: Baton Rouge : Louisiana State University Press, [2024] | Series: New Hispanisms: cultural and literary studies | Includes bibliographical references and index.
Identifiers: LCCN 2023020131 (print) | LCCN 2023020132 (ebook) | ISBN 978-0-8071-8012-9 (cloth) | ISBN 978-0-8071-8105-8 (pdf) | ISBN 978-0-8071-8104-1 (epub)
Subjects: LCSH: Oré, Luis Jerónimo de, 1554–1630. | Franciscans—Peru—Biography. | Intellectuals—Peru—Biography.
Classification: LCC BX4705.O55 C66 2024 (print) | LCC BX4705.O55 (ebook) | DDC 271/.92092—dc23/eng/20230802
LC record available at https://lccn.loc.gov/2023020131
LC ebook record available at https://lccn.loc.gov/2023020132

IN MEMORY OF GREG COOK

Contents

LIST OF ILLUSTRATIONS xi
LIST OF TABLES xiii
ACKNOWLEDGMENTS xv
TIMELINE OF LUIS GERÓNIMO DE ORÉ xvii

Prologue 1

I. Beginnings

1. Huamanga 9
2. The First Creole Generation: Youth on the Frontier 18
3. The Oré Family: Mythohistory 24
4. Franciscan Novice in the Inca Capital 31
5. Preparations for a Religious Life: Lima and the University 37
6. Mogrovejo: Third Church Council of Lima and the Translators 45

II. Franciscan Doctrinero in the Field

7. Franciscan Dilemmas 59
8. Defender of Franciscan Rights 69
9. Doctrinero in the Colca Valley 77
10. Composing the *Symbolo Catholico Indiano* 91
11. Doctrinero in Potosí and Cuzco 103

III. Creole Friar at the Centers of the First Global Empire

    12. Assignments in Spain and Italy 111

    13. Naples, the *Rituale, seu manuale peruanum* 119

    14. Enigma of the Lost Dictionary and Grammar 126

    15. Recruiting in Spain 132

    16. Probing the Youth of a Future Saint, *Francisco Solano* 139

IV. General Commissioner in Florida's Northern Frontier

    17. Franciscan Province of Santa Elena de La Florida 149

    18. Cuba, La Florida, and Oré's First Inspection 154

    19. The Cuban Conundrum 157

    20. Second Inspection of the La Florida Missions 164

    21. Franciscan Martyrs in Oré's Account 170

    22. Franciscan Democracy: First Provincial General Chapter Meeting 179

    23. Economic and Spiritual Cost of Empire 184

V. Martyrs, Virgins, Nuns, and the Bishop-Elect

    24. Compiling the *Verdadera relación de la Florida* 191

    25. Spain Again: Marianism and the Virgin of Copacabana 202

    26. Bishop Oré: Preparations for the Voyage 211

    27. Return to the Viceroyalty of Peru 218

    28. Consecration in Lima and Preparations for Chile 223

    29. Huamanga, the Last Visit 226

    30. The Changing Face of Lima 231

VI. Creole Bishop on the Araucanian Frontier

    31. Chile Fractured: The Diocese of Santiago and La Imperial 239

    32. Foreign Threats on the South Sea 247

33. Beyond Araucania: A Pastoral Inspection 251

34. Church and State Conflict: The *Patronato Real* 259

35. The Struggle for Justice: Offensive or Defensive War 268

36. The Conflict Becomes Ugly 277

VII. Epilogue

37. Bishop Oré's Testament 285

38. Conclusion: The Legacy 289

GLOSSARY 295

NOTES 299

BIBLIOGRAPHY 341

INDEX 365

Illustrations

FIGURES

Doctrina Christiana y Catecismo, Lima 1584 48

Coporaque's church 81

Oré's 1598 *Symbolo Catholico Indiano* 90

Seville's Franciscan compound 117

Oré's 1607 *Rituale, seu manuale peruanum* 120

Oré's *Relación de la Florida,* ca. 1619 190

Oré's 1621 *Corona de la Virgen María* 206

Lima's Franciscan Monastery, 1675 233

MAPS

Arequipa to Caylloma, the Colca Valley doctrinas 66

Andalusia, researching Friar Francisco Solano's youth 134

Franciscan Province of Santa Elena de la Florida 150

Trade routes to and from the Caribbean 220

Chile, Araucania, and the diocese of La Imperial 242

Tables

First creole generation of the Oré family in Huamanga 15

Priests and Indian teachers 55

Bishops of Cuzco (1538–1638) 107

Quechua and Aymara dictionaries and grammars (1560–1635) 131

Bishops of Santiago de Cuba and Governors of Cuba, Santiago de Cuba, and Florida 159

Archbishoprics and Bishoprics, Viceroyalty of Peru (ca. 1629) and ecclesiastic income 240

Bishops of Santiago de Chile and La Imperial (Concepción) 241

Governors, Captain Generals of Chile (1592–1639) 244

Acknowledgments

Numerous people assisted in various ways over the years and may escape mention, but we are grateful to all. We thank especially the late Franklin Pease García Yrigoyen who sponsored a Fulbright Visiting Research and Teaching Fellowship at the Pontificia Universidad Católica del Perú in 1974 and 1984. Mariana Mould de Pease helped in numerous ways and recently in locating an important document we had consulted in the Biblioteca Nacional in Lima that seemed lost. We are grateful to the late Antonine Tibesar, OFM, for leads, letters of introduction, and copies of Vatican documents. He confided he had hoped to write a biography of Oré, but age and religious tasks intervened. Father Provincial José Lobatón Heredia, OFM, provided access in 1984 to the Archive of the Monastery of San Francisco in Lima where we worked with its archivist, Ana María Vega. In 2015 Miguel Costa, of the Pontificia Universidad Católica del Perú (PUCP) in Lima, provided a photograph of an unrestored portrait of Oré and in 2017 introduced us to the archive's director Abel Pacheco Sánchez, OFM, who graciously led us to specialists who were restoring several portraits, including that of Oré. Questions remain as to the original artist, the date, and even if the painting is based on a contemporary likeness.

Direct funding was limited to a research grant from the library of the University of Florida Center for Latin American Studies for summer 1989, and a sabbatical from Florida International University in Miami. Data on Oré often surfaced during various research projects supported by the Wenner Gren Foundation Fellowship for Anthropological Research, 1977, as well as a Fulbright Fellowship for research in Spain in 1990–1991, a John Simon Guggenheim Memorial Foundation Fellowship, 1991–1992, and an American Council of Learned Societies Fellowship, 1998–1999. We scoured archives and library collections on three continents. We thank the wonderful staff in the Archivo Nacional del Perú, the Biblioteca Nacional in Lima, and Lima's Archivo Arzobispal. We conducted fieldwork in the Colca Valley in 1974 and 1977. The late Maryknoll Sister Antonia Kaiser provided a place to live and work in a stone structure within the original Franciscan compound attached to Yanque's church. We read through bundles of documents, most of which are now in the Archivo Diocesano in Arequipa. In Spain the staffs of various archives were generous with their time and assistance, especially Seville's Archivo General de Indias and Madrid's Biblioteca Nacional.

We have subjected many people to our ruminations on a relatively obscure sixteenth-century friar. We are grateful to all in Peru who assisted us: Miguel Costa, Pedro Guibovich, Margarita Suárez, Liliana Regalado Hurtado, Marco Curatola, Renzo Honores, Nicanor Domínguez, and Julian Heras, OFM. Special thanks to friends in Seville: Pepe Hernández Palomo, Juan Gil and Consuelo Varela, Doug Inglis, Luis Miguel Glave, and Fernando Iwasaki. We thank Fritz Schwaller, Stafford Poole, Rolena Adorno, Michael Francis, Raquel Chang-Rodríguez, Larry Clayton, Paul Hoffman, George Lovell, and Karoline Cook. Colleagues and friends at Florida International University listened and frequently commented, especially Mark Szuchman, Sherry Johnson, Victor Uribe, Bianca Premo, Frank Luca, Judith Mansilla, Leonardo Falcón, and Jason Daniel. We thank our manuscript readers, who provided excellent suggestions, and our copy editor, Gary Von Euer, for improving and clarifying the text. We are grateful to James W. Long, acquisitions editor, Anne J. Cruz, series editor of the "New Hispanisms: Cultural and Literary Studies," and Alisa Plant, director of the Louisiana State University Press.

Timeline

OF LUIS GERÓNIMO DE ORÉ

1554	Born in Huamanga (modern Ayacucho, Peru)
1562	Huamanga, Franciscan Novitiate
1568–69	Cuzco, Franciscan Novitiate
1572	Cuzco, execution of Tupac Amaru I
1575	Lima, Franciscan monastery; studies, University of San Marcos
1580	Lima, ordained by Archbishop Toribio Alfonso de Mogrovejo
1583	Lima, Third Church Council
1586–95	Colca Valley, doctrinero in Los Collaguas
1595	Jauja, Guardian of the Franciscan doctrinas
1598	Lima, *Symbolo Catholico Indiano* published
1600	Potosí, served in an Indian parish
1603	Cuzco, served in an Indian parish
1603	Cuzco Bishop Antonio de Raya sends Oré to Spain and Rome
1604	Oré sets sail for Spain
1605	Madrid, Valladolid, Council of the Indies authorizes printing of *Rituale, seu manuale peruanum*; Oré presents Bishop Raya petitions at court of Philip III
1605	Rome, Oré as procurator of Cuzco Bishop before the papacy
1606	Alessandria, publication of *Tratado sobre las indulgencias*
1607	Naples, *Rituale, seu manuale peruanum* published

1607	Italy, Oré's dictionary and grammar of Quechua and Aymara disappear
1611	Spain, recruiting missionaries for Florida
1613	Spain, recruiting missionaries for Florida and Venezuela
1613	Investigates youth of Francisco Solano in Andalusia
1614	Madrid, *Relación de Francisco Solano* printed, prepares for La Florida
1614	Voyage to Cuba and Florida, inspects Franciscan Province of Santa Elena
1616	Oré's second inspection of La Florida, convokes first provincial chapter meeting
1617–18	Havana, completes the Florida report, returns to Spain
1618–19	Madrid, *Relación de la Florida* printed; General Chapter Meeting in Salamanca
1619	Madrid, *Corona de la sacratissima Virgen Maria* published.
1620	Named Bishop of La Imperial, Concepción, Chile
1621	Seville, sets sail for Peru
1622	Lima, Oré consecrated by Fernando de Ocampo, bishop of Santa Cruz de la Sierra
1622	Huamanga, Lima, consecrates Francisco Verdugo Bishop of Huamanga
1623	Concepción, first inspection
1625	Second Diocesan Synod, sets up Concepción seminary, adds parishes, Dutch threat
1626	Second inspection, including Chiloé Archipelago
1627–29	Conflict with Governor Captain-General Luis Fernández de Córdova y Arce
1630	Concepción, Oré dies

Luis Gerónimo de Oré

Prologue

> In this journey I have opened as far as I know, a path no one has taken before.
> —LUIS GERÓNIMO DE ORÉ, *Symbolo Catholico Indiano* (Lima: Ricardo, 1598), 65v

Luis Gerónimo de Oré (1554–1630) was a major intellect of the early colonial period in the Americas: he was multilingual, trained in Latin, the classics, theology, canon and civil law, music, poetry, and linguistics. He was largely unknown or ignored into the mid-twentieth century, save for a handful of Peruvian and Chilean scholars and religious historians specializing in the southeastern United States. Oré's years in Spain and Italy were unexplored and his contributions to the endeavor of conversion hidden. The friar came to our attention when we participated in an interdisciplinary research project on Peru's Colca Valley in 1974. We spent a week in Yanque, examining the parish archive and exploring nearby villages on each side of the valley. Returning in 1977, we dug deeply into the parish registers and other colonial-era documents, centering our research on demography and the social and economic transformations that followed contact between peoples of the Old and New Worlds. We were intrigued by Oré's work as a doctrinero in the valley in the 1580s and 1590s, especially his participation in re-inspection of the valley and its resources after one of the more catastrophic pandemics of the early colonial period. Using the parish death registers, Oré was able to denote those who died, thus protecting the living Indians from paying excessive tribute. We began to collect any information that we could on him. Meanwhile, we completed two books and several articles on the Colca Valley. In one we probed the trials and tribulations of a Spaniard who held the largest Indian grant in the valley. In the second we traced the transformations of the indigenous peoples and the Europeans during the first three generations following the arrival of the Spaniards.

Much of the information on Oré published before the 1990s was based on hagiographers, traditional biographers, historians of religion and compilers of documents. The leading historians of Peru and Chile from the late nineteenth to mid-twentieth centuries—such as José Toribio Medina, Rubén Vargas Ugarte, Raúl Porras Barrenechea, and Manuel Mendiburu—scoured documents in private collections and in Church and state archives and libraries, and uncovered some information on Oré, material that was used by scholars into the late 1900s. Prior to the 1970s Luis Gerónimo de Oré was recognized by a few Andean specialists and religious historians who realized his significance, especially for having translated the creed into Quechua and Aymara. Some late nineteenth-century historians and bibliophiles did provide brief paragraphs concerning his work. A handful of Franciscan chroniclers were more effusive shortly after his death. Historians and specialists in the Spanish period in the early southeast of what became part of the United States also recognized his significance. The problem facing historians was the difficulty in accessing his writings; his publications are rare and hard to find. His last text, an esoteric Marianist exercise, was printed in 1619.[1] Oré's only book that was published after his death was his report on La Florida. A recovered and edited text was published in Madrid by Atanasio López, OFM, in two volumes, 1931 and 1933. It was soon followed by an English translation and commentary by Maynard Geiger in 1936. The English edition created a stir in the academic community in the southeastern United States for, despite numerous errors, it provided rich information on the various indigenous ethnicities, especially in the missions established by the Franciscans. There was more interest on the Franciscan from Huamanga in Florida than in Peru. By the last decades of the twentieth century, anthropologists, archaeologists, ethnohistorians, historians, and religious studies academics were immersed in research.[2]

A second modern publication of Oré's work, a facsimile of the *Symbolo Catholico Indiano* (1598), edited by Antonine Tibesar, OFM, appeared in 1998. Oré began working on the text in the 1580s and polished it in the next decade. At the same time, he completed four multilingual texts that unexpectedly fulfilled the Inca intention of making Cuzco Quechua the standard for communication in much of the Andean world. Along with his translation into Aymara, Oré's *Symbolo* became the primary text used throughout the empire. It was not just the accuracy and beauty of the friar's translations, it was the poetic nature of key elements of the faith, providing a rhythmic musical appeal, enhanced by meshing European and Andean musical instruments. Oré moved further in the

Rituale, seu manuale peruanum (1607) as he shifted from the theological foundations of Catholicism to its implementation in the daily work of the religious in the field: confessions, penance, baptisms, sermons, communions, extreme unction, burials, all and more that needed to be explained in the Andean vernacular. Oré's two other books, a dictionary and grammar, that were authorized for printing and distribution at the same time as the *Symbolo* and the *Rituale*, mysteriously disappeared.[3]

Our investigations centered on learning as much as possible directly from Oré, using his own voice as well as the voices of those who interacted with him from youth to his final hours. A neutral viewpoint is challenging, yet we began and continued our investigations with a clean slate, sharing what we learned of his actions as we proceeded. We spent days, weeks, and months in archives trying to understand Oré's world and the religious beliefs that guided his life. About a decade ago, our database was so full that we were compelled to tell Oré's story, not just as snippets appearing in various articles, but in a full, book-length narrative of his life and times. By that time, several useful biographical sketches had been written, and thanks to the access to Oré's *Symbolo Catholico Indiano*, specialists of various disciplines began to take an interest in the friar's work. Linguists delved into his impact on stabilization of Quechua and Aymara and retention of knowledge of several other South American languages. Specialists in religious studies focused on the theological nature of the text. Oré and some others wanted to make certain that the complexity of the official creed of the Roman Catholic Church should be simple and easily understood, and he designed his books especially for the Andean peoples, frequently using autochthonous vocabularies dealing with a creator, Viracocha Pachacamac, or the feminine equivalent, fitting the duality of Andean society. More broadly, the words associated with religious articles or places, lakes, the sea, stars and moon, mountain peaks, mummified ancestors, all were *huacas*, objects of religious reverence. Oré included translations of Athanasius's *Simbolo* to avoid confusion with the complicated Nicene creed. Miguel Angel Espinosa Soria, Catalina Andrango-Walker, and to an extent Alan Durston and Bruce Mannheim, have all focused on some of the theological issues Oré wrestled with in his major texts. Nancy Van Deusen, Kathryn Burns, Ken Mills, Carlos Galvez, Peter Gose and Rolena Adorno have concentrated on the church in the Andes, recognizing the significance of religion and transculturation—positive or negative—as pillars of society.

The rich religious world of Luis Gerónimo de Oré has recently received serious attention, as has his experience in the Franciscan missions of the southeast prior to the foundation of Plymouth. While not a complete vacuum, his role in administration of church and empire has been largely overlooked. In various chapters we concentrate on these matters: chapter 1 deals with the reincorporation of the Franciscan doctrinas in the Colca Valley transferred to seculars or other orders. Another (chapter 12), centers on Oré as the legal representative of Cuzco's bishop, to secure his diocesan boundaries in an argument with the bishop of Charcas; Oré advocated before the royal councils and the papacy. In Florida the Franciscans and Oré challenged the policies of more than one colonial governor on a variety of issues. Oré argued convincingly, in letters to the Royal Council and the king, that they should take more action to defend La Florida from foreign interlopers. Oré's last years as Concepción's bishop involved constant negotiations with several governors of Chile regarding foreign attacks, and administration of the clerics in the forts. Incessant conflict with the indominable ethnicities on the frontiers put the aging friar into direct confrontation with the governor regarding the nature of war and the enslavement of indigenous peoples. In addition to the administration of state and church as we view the example of Oré, there is the question of conflict between secular clergy and religious clergy (friars) and between different religious orders. Within the Franciscan order there was the clash between a monastic life of prayer and charity or, in a time of messianism, the call to convert all before the apocalypse. We tried to flesh out the multiple challenges and successes Oré faced during his life, including his cooperation with other orders, especially the Jesuits.

As a first-generation Creole, born on the Andean frontier, his life was one of crossing borders, oceans, and seas, from Huamanga on the edge of rebellious remnants of the Inca empire to resistant ethnicities in La Florida, to indominable groups on the frontier of southern Chile, the Franciscan served church and empire. His crossings to the world of his parents and ancestors presented another frontier, the challenges of dealing with the powerful bureaucracies of Imperial Spain and the Roman Curia in Italy.

Oré's lifetime spanned a complex period in history and readers will notice significant themes embedded in chapters in the text related to time and place. The issue of slavery appears early, and impacted Oré from the time of his novitiate when he learned of the words of the Dominican Bartolomé de las Casas. Indian slavery had been abolished even earlier, but life as a tributary in the *encomienda* (Indian grant) system approached slavery, especially the *mita* (system of forced paid labor) that required labor from a certain percentage of Indians in an encomienda for a limited period of weeks. Mitayos were to be paid a stipend and for travel to and from the place of work. Oré dealt with mita service in the Colca Valley and more important in Potosí, where some Indians had to travel hundreds of kilometers to grueling work in the silver mine. The issue of indigenous enslavement pursued the friar throughout his lifetime. It was most serious at the end of his life, almost leading to his removal from the diocese of Concepción, Chile, as he confronted the continuous conflict between the various ethnicities and the outsiders. Oré arrived after one of the worst disasters and debates raged between merchants, settlers and miners, and the religious on how best to secure peace. Oré, influenced by Las Casas and the Jesuit Luis de Valdivia, was a staunch advocate of a defensive war. He opposed total war and enslavement of the Indians, arguing that a form of "defensive war" would serve better than "offensive war" to reach peace. Bishop Oré would become entangled in intense arguments with the governor that would reach the ears of the royal councils.

Hagiographers have extolled Oré's virtues, others may see him as a tool of colonialism, an agent destroying the culture of the peoples who were crushed by the Europeans. We view him as a man of his time, an exceptionally talented one, driven by his religious convictions, whose legacy continues in the Andean world—in linguistics, perhaps in music, and in a permissible religiosity—an amalgam of deeply rooted pre- and post-contact concepts. Oré experienced the complexity of the foundation and apogee of the first global empire established by Charles V, expanded by Philip II and continued through the challenging reigns of Philip III and IV. He lived in a period of almost continuous strife, epidemics, and economic crises, and all had an impact on the frontiers he navigated.

I
Beginnings

1

Huamanga

It is in Huamanga, Luis Gerónimo de Oré's birthplace, that we initiate our journey, one that carries us from the family's European origins to the friar's death three-quarters of a century later. The name given by city founders, "San Juan de la Frontera de Huamanga," illustrates its very nature. Pedro de Cieza de León passed through less than a decade after its founding by Francisco Pizarro on 9 January 1539, and suggests the name came from "a pueblo the Indians had named Huamanga."[1] Other accounts provide alternative sites including Quinua, located three leagues from the city's final position. Moves were common, as places that initially seemed ideal for settlement were abandoned as weaknesses appeared. The *cabildo* (city council) record is clear. On 25 April 1540 the settlers refounded Huamanga in its present location: "They transferred the said villa from where it was to the site of Pucaray and they founded and populated it because it was much better there."[2]

During its long history, Huamanga was often at or near the center of conflict. Its location as a crossroads contributed to frequent confrontations. It is also near the route from the highlands to the edge of the Andean slopes leading into the Amazon basin. For a decade and a half, combined threats of indigenous rebellion and civil war between the Spaniards posed a constant threat for the city's settlers. In 1586 Huamanga residents helping prepare a geographical report on the province explained that the city's name connoted the frontier with the Inca who had retreated deep into the Andean mountains.[3] Almost three centuries later the last major battle during the Wars of Independence from Spain was fought nearby in the fields of Ayacucho. The colonial city of Huamanga was renamed Ayacucho to commemorate that victory.

Oré's father, Antonio de Oré, was a prominent member of Huamanga society. He was not part of Francisco Pizarro's original force, but he figured among

Peru's earliest settlers. The Orés came from the Canary Islands, providing them some experience in the formation of empire when the Spanish extended their influence into the Atlantic, subjugating the Guanche, the original non-European inhabitants of the islands who centuries before migrated from the northwestern coast of Africa. Indeed, the nature of conquest and control, the administration of the islands, and even the economy of the Canarys served as models for colonial administration in Spanish America. Years later, Friar Luis Gerónimo's brother, Licentiate Francisco de Oré, claimed in his service report to the Crown that their father Antonio "served His Majesty illustriously in the conquest and pacification of those Realms. . . ." According to Miriam Salas de Coloma, their grandfather was one of those fighting to suppress the Guanche.[4] In the initial decades following Columbus's discovery, many islanders with experience in warfare joined their relatives from the peninsula and embarked on ships heading to the New World. Antonio de Oré did too, as did relatives of his future wife.[5]

Antonio de Oré missed Pizarro's first booty of conquest, Atahualpa's ransom of gold and silver distributed at Cajamarca in 1533, but he arrived early enough to fight in several major battles against the Andeans, and between Spanish factions. In 1538 he fought at the Battle of las Salinas, where the Pizarrists defeated the forces of Diego de Almagro. Antonio de Oré also contributed personal resources, estimated at 10,000 pesos, to subjugate the indigenous Guancas Chupaychos in the Huánuco district of Peru's north-central highlands. On 14 January 1541, Antonio de Oré was bestowed *vecino* (citizen) status by Huamanga's cabildo and was granted a city lot above the one held by his father-in-law, Díaz de Rojas. Oré was required to enclose his building lot within a year to secure title. In September 1542, after the Battle of Chupas and the defeat of Diego de Almagro the Younger by royalist supporters, Governor Cristóbal Vaca de Castro granted Antonio de Oré the rich encomienda of Hanan Chilques. His position and wealth came also by marriage to a widow, Doña Luisa Díaz de Rojas y Rivera.[6]

Her father, Pedro Díaz de Rojas, had served in Panama with Pedrarias Dávila around 1520, and then Francisco Hernández in Nicaragua, and finally joined Pizarro's third expedition to Peru in 1531. Díaz de Rojas acted as Francisco Pizarro's silversmith and assayer and a smelter for the Inca Atahualpa's ransom at Cajamarca, and subsequently in *fundiciones* (smelting) at Jauja and Cuzco. He participated in the defense of Cuzco during the Inca siege of 1536–37.

Like Antonio de Oré, he fought for the Pizarrists in the Battle of las Salinas, and in 1539 was one of the original founders of Huamanga. Pizarro in 1541 granted Díaz de Rojas the encomienda of Quinua. As did many other encomenderos, he switched sides several times during the subsequent revolt of the encomenderos under Gonzalo Pizarro but was on the royalist side when it counted, remaining in Huamanga to protect it against the rebels. Doña Luisa's father therefore did not fight in the decisive Battle of Jaquijahuana (1548). The Crown's victory under the leadership of Pedro de la Gasca, President of the Royal Audiencia, brought temporary peace among the Spanish settlers. Doña Luisa's father benefitted from his timely loyalty to the Crown, and his house, perhaps the best in the city, served as residence for President La Gasca while he was in the city. Díaz de Rojas was a wealthy and influential member of Huamanga's elite and his widowed daughter an excellent match for Antonio de Oré. In addition to the encomienda of Quinua, Díaz de Rojas had an estate in the Yucay Valley. In 1567 he established a chapel of San Juan de Letrán in the Mercedarian Church, where he was buried in 1570. His eldest son Pedro Díaz de Rojas y de la Cuba inherited the encomienda.[7]

Antonio de Oré fought under Pedro de la Gasca against the forces of Gonzalo Pizarro, leader of a rebellion against royal authority. Shortly after La Gasca's victory a general tribute assessment of the Indians held in encomienda was undertaken. At that point Antonio held 600 tributary Indians who were required to give him 800 or 1,000 pesos plus provide service for his household.[8] He was in Cuzco on 23 April 1549 with several other Huamanga encomenderos for reconfirmation of their grants, and redistribution of the encomiendas taken from the rebels. Antonio de Oré would face one more challenge in the "Civil Wars of the Encomenderos." In 1554 he was one of Huamanga's *regidores* (councilors) opposing Francisco Hernández Girón, who from his center in the Cuzco region led another revolt against royal authority.

The Oré family as required by royal decrees of the early 1550s lived in Huamanga, the Spanish city nearest their encomienda. The family's income came from tribute and labor of their Amerindian charges, investments in nearby mines and land, as well as *obrajes* (textile factories). Antonio de Oré amassed a substantial fortune and he and Doña Luisa were recognized as distinguished members of the city's elite.[9] Cieza de León, visiting Huamanga about the time Luis Gerónimo was born, provided a detailed description. The city was on a plain, close to the Andean intermediate-level sierras at an elevation where snow was unlikely. A stream passed nearby, carrying "very good water which those of this city use for drinking." Cieza was impressed by the quality of construction: "They have built the largest and best houses in all of Peru, all of stone, brick and tile roofs, with great towers so that there is no lack of lodging." The large and level central plaza provided ideal space for public events and became the city's principal meeting place. Cieza mentioned three monasteries for friars, the *iglesia mayor* (principal church), two Indian parishes, and a hospital for both Spanish and indigenous residents. The climate seemed to the chronicler to resemble a Biblical Garden of Eden. "Neither the sun, air or dew is bad; it is neither humid nor hot. Rather, it has an excellent climate and good temperature." In the nearby countryside the Spanish, using indigenous labor, built their country houses surrounded by pastureland for their cattle.[10] Cieza noted substantial wheat production in the area and commented that the bread baked with it was "as good and excellent as the best of Andalusia."[11] Years later, Luis Gerónimo de Oré described his native city and its environs as having "the best climate and sky of all in this kingdom of Peru." Oré declared that various Castilian and Andean products abounded; there were many cattle, sheep, and goat estancias, and wine was produced locally. Further, within the district there were rich mines of mercury and silver.[12]

Antonio de Oré was active in the political life of Huamanga, serving on the city council five times. He was *alcalde ordinario* (municipal judge) at least twice, including in 1558 when Damián de la Bandera named him acting *corregidor* (provincial governor) during Bandera's absence while conducting an inspection of the district. That year Antonio secured forty *fanegas* (in volume a Spanish bushel, or a land measurement equivalent to what can be planted by one fanega of seed) of land in the Llanos of Chaquibamba, and another fifty in the forested hillsides of the Andes. In 1570 Antonio de Oré, regidor of Huamanga and acting as the corregidor's deputy, conducted an inspection of the *tambos* (inns) and roads within the city's jurisdiction.[13]

Antonio and Doña Luisa led a comfortable life and passed on an economic legacy to their numerous progeny. In addition to the encomienda of Hanan Chilques, there was a broad range of income-producing investments. Similar to his father-in-law, Antonio possessed some expertise in metallurgy and quickly turned his attention to mining. This was a wise decision given the New Laws of 1542 designed to protect against abuses of the Indian tributaries and to end the encomienda by the third generation—that is, the third transfer of the grant—thus avoiding the creation of a creole nobility. The worst abuses were curtailed, but new regulations over transfer of the grant were weakened by the encomenderos' revolt. Oré's encomienda was in the rich mining district of Vilcashuaman within the rough "boundaries" of his silver mine of Chumbilla and he used his encomienda Indians as part of the labor force. The village of Canaria was nearby and became the seat for the family's textile obrajes. The next nearest Indian village was Chincheros, where another Oré obraje operated. Adding to his investments, on the edge of the city of Huamanga at Colquepata on the Yucay River, Antonio de Oré owned a grist mill for grinding his grain and that of other wheat growers. Lower down the Yucay valley he owned coca fields, vineyards and fruit orchards. To round off his holdings, he had access to forests and grazing lands for wool production. The labor was done mostly by local Indians, largely from his encomienda. Antonio's properties included estancias and haciendas. One of his estancias was to the northwest in the mercury mining area of Huancavelica. At Chupas, some twenty kilometers south of Huamanga, he had a horse ranch.[14] Antonio de Oré held a stake or claim at Huancavelica from about 1564. The normal size of each *estaca* (claim) was sixty by thirty *varas* (measurement of length), or about 180 × 90 feet. Several Huamanga vecinos were stakeholders, and families often extended claims through relatives. One important figure was Pedro de Valenzuela, who as we will see was a relative of both Antonio and one of the supposed "discoverers" of the mines, Amador de Cabrera.[15] Miriam Salas de Coloma in studies of the economy and society of the Huamanga district characterizes Oré as an "active encomendero-vecino-hacendado and miner." But when the mercury mines of Huancavelica reached full production, Antonio de Oré and Hernán Guillén de Mendoza as the major producers of textiles in their obrajes, renounced their mining claims and shifted to supplying the miners with needed textile in exchange for metals.[16]

Antonio de Oré met Viceroy Francisco de Toledo near the beginning of the royal official's decade-long tenure in Peru. Toledo first landed at Trujillo on Peru's north coast, then made a coastal march to Lima, arriving there in November 1569. After initiating a series of administrative reforms, he left the viceroyalty's capital to begin a *visita general* (general inspection) of the realm on 23 October 1570. Viceroy Toledo resided in Huamanga from at least 11 December 1570 until the end of January 1571, and issued several decrees and ordinances. On 22 January 1571 the viceroy addressed prominent members of the cabildo, including the city's corregidor and two alcaldes, one of whom was Antonio de Oré. The viceroy pledged royal support for continuation and completion of efforts to construct an Indian hospital and a convent for nuns. Toledo departed Huamanga for Cuzco and reached the old Inca capital by 15 March 1571.[17]

The Oré family grew. In a period of premodern medicine half of the children born died before reaching puberty, yet an amazing number of the Oré children survived to adulthood. It was a rare year that Doña Luisa, was not pregnant, for in over twenty years (1540–68) she bore at least sixteen children. Spacing of the children indicates that wet-nurses, probably from the family encomienda of Hanan Chilques, nourished the couple's infants. The Oré offspring spent their infancy between the city of Huamanga and the village of Canaria, where the family's textile factories were located.[18] In the geographical survey of the Indies ordered by Philip II and carried out in the 1570s and 1580s, inspectors found that the Indians of the villages and neighborhood of Huancapi and Colca spoke both Quechua and Aymara, and in the area of the family's obrajes, the Chilques, Condes y Pabres ethnicities, their workers did also. The linguistic competencies of several Oré children are best explained in this fashion, for their nursemaids and their first companions were the mothers and children of the Andean highlands. The fact that the Oré encomienda and obrajes included both Aymara and Quechua speakers provided the Oré brothers who became *doctrineros* (priests in an Indian parish) the opportunity to be fluent in both Andean languages long before they went to Cuzco or Lima or entered the church.[19]

The *mayorazgo* (entailed estate) that constituted the bulk of the family's wealth, passed to the eldest son Don Gerónimo de Oré around 1576, following the father's death. Antonio noted in his will that the details of the distribution of the estate were stored in his desk. In his testament Antonio de Oré ensured that his eldest son received the legally allotted share of the estate, and he was given an additional emolument to serve as patron of the Convent of Santa Clara. But most importantly, Don Gerónimo received his father's encomienda of Canaria.[20] Don Gerónimo was born about 1541 and married Doña Aldonsa de Azevedo y Guevara around 1585. The couple had at least five children before he died in 1592.[21] His widow Doña Aldonsa returned to Lima, leaving her children behind in the care of Don Gerónimo's brother-in-law Pedro Fernández de Valenzuela. His guardianship was legalized, and Pedro de Valenzuela administered the estate left by Don Gerónimo for the children, including the ten percent of the annual revenues that were to be sent to their absent mother.

FIRST CREOLE GENERATION OF THE ORÉ FAMILY IN HUAMANGA

Parents
    Antonio de Oré (d. ca. 1576, married ca. 1540 Doña Luisa Díaz de Rojas y Rivera, d. 1586)

Children
    Don Gerónimo de Oré (ca. 1541–1592, 1585 married Aldonsa de Azevedo y Guevara)
    Don Cristóbal de Serpa (b. ca. 1543)
    Doña Ana de Serpa (1544–1589) [Sor Ana de Espíritu Santo]
    Doña Leonor de Tejada (1549–1623) [Sor Leonor de Jesús]
    Doña María de Oré (1549–1599) [Sor María de la Concepción]
    Doña Inés de la Encarnación (1553–1614)
    Doña María de Oré "la menor" [María de Oré de la Purificación]
    Don Gonzalo de Oré
    Fr. Antonio de Oré, O.F.M.
    Fr. Pedro de Oré, O.F.M. (b. ca. 1545)
    Fr. Luis Gerónimo de Oré, O.F.M. (1554–1630)
    Fr. Dionisio de Oré, O.F.M. (b. 1559)
    Licenciado Francisco de Oré, clérigo presbítero (ca. 1568 - d. before 1630)
    Father Juan de Oré, S.J.
    Doña Florencia de Tejada
    Doña María Padilla

Note: There are possible errors in family data. BNP: Z328, Z330, C341; Córdova y Salinas, *Chronica franciscana* provides information on the children who entered the church.

Don Gerónimo had inherited the encomienda of Hanan Chilques, in the "second life." There were charges that he had mistreated his indigenous labor force. If the allegations were proven accurate the encomienda could revert to the Crown and be reallocated. Don Gerónimo's oldest son, born about 1586, was named after his grandfather, Antonio. He married Doña Mariana Pissaro de Orellana, thus linking the Oré family to another distinguished line. At least five of Don Gerónimo and Doña Aldonsa's children survived to adulthood.[22] One son, Gaspar de Oré, became a Franciscan friar. Daughters Doña Juana de Estrada and Doña Catalina Juárez y Acevedo entered the Convent of Santa Clara in Huamanga. The second, known as Sor Catalina de Oré, was the convent's abbess in 1636.[23]

Control over Don Gerónimo's estate led to contentious legal wrangling between heirs in the early seventeenth century. As in many complicated and lengthy legal disputes, the documents provide historians rich information on dates, the founder of the estate's service to the Crown, and the careers of descendants. The large family, with an inadequate income to support all members, led to frequent petitions to the Crown for additional rewards. The viceroys had given Don Gerónimo twenty-five Indians exempt from paying tribute or serving in mines, and he had eighty indigenous youths for his textile factory in Chinchero. In the legal papers collected against Don Gerónimo, he is charged with exploiting his tributaries, which he denied, arguing that "the said Indians eagerly worked in my obraje because the work was light, and they stayed in their land and they were well-treated and the pay was good." Don Gerónimo insisted that the obraje did not violate the law because "only *sayales* and *jergas* (both are types of rough cloth) were woven which were never taken to Spain or elsewhere, but were used here where it is necessary and very convenient for the consumption of wool and the universal good of all the people of the district and where the youth and old Indians, incapacitated (by their age) and unable to work in anything else earned enough to eat."[24] In the bundle of papers there is a copy of Viceroy García Hurtado de Mendoza's recognition of the earlier grant of Viceroy Martín Enríquez, and also the Viceroy Count of Villar's grant of a *mita ordinaria* of "eighty *muchachos*, twenty-five *viejos* and twenty tributary Indians for the service" in the obraje. The Count of Villar's grant is especially informative regarding the nature of the labor force. Two-thirds of the *muchachos* (literally young males under eighteen) were between the ages of ten and fourteen, and one-third of the *viejos* were age fifty and above. They had to be paid for their daily labor, have the assistance of a clergyman, and receive food as earlier stipulated.[25] Despite the supposed good treatment of these men postulated by Don Gerónimo de Oré, it is hard to imagine how ten- to twelve-year-olds, essentially locked in the cloth mill, could have been as content as he claimed.

The second son of Antonio de Oré, Cristóbal de Serpa, born around 1543, entered the mercury mining business in Huancavelica. As far as is known he never married, but took as his concubine Doña Luisa Mullomarca, a *cacica* (female village leader) from the Oré family's encomienda of Canaria with whom he had at least two boys, Adriano and Luis.[26] Such a relationship was not uncommon. Nicanor Domínguez suggests that a nephew of the Oré family, Don

Jerónimo de Oré, had a daughter with "Doña Clara Coya native of the city of Cuzco and descendant of the Incas."²⁷ Jane Mangan traces the trajectories of numerous Spanish and Andean stable relationships, some bonded by marriage, others not, during the first decades. Huamanga, Cuzco and Arequipa were centers for these relationships and their mestizo offspring transformed colonial Andean society.²⁸

The family's third child, Doña Ana de Serpa, was born in 1544, and when she entered the convent took the name Sor Ana de Espíritu Santo. Three other daughters who also became Sisters of Santa Clara were born before their brother and future bishop, Luis Gerónimo. Twins Doña Leonor de Tejada and Doña María de Oré came in 1549; the last child, Doña Inés de la Encarnación, was born in 1553. (See table on page 15). Whether by true conviction or from fear of eternal damnation in an age of faith, the elder Antonio de Oré stressed his family's religious education, and contributed to the church with numerous charitable bequests. There was no absence of churches in Huamanga as the Oré family grew, along with the city. The principal parish was established in 1540, and initially served as refuge in case of an Amerindian attack on the frontier settlement. The Mercedarian monastery was also laid out the same year, a Dominican monastery followed in 1548, and the Franciscan monastery in 1552.

Although Saint Jerome was the spiritual patron of the Oré family, Antonio and Doña Luisa and their offspring were staunch supporters of the Franciscan order. The family legacy was linked to the wealth that could be passed on to subsequent generations, and with each new child, the wealth was diluted. In contrast to most northern European countries Spanish laws provided for a relatively equitable inheritance, except when the child entered a religious order and renounced his or her share. The Laws of Toro issued by the Spanish Cortes in 1505 deal with family and inheritance, and the rules were closely followed during the next two centuries.²⁹ This foundation of Castilian family law flowed directly to the Spanish Indies and was largely maintained under the Hapsburgs. Five Oré daughters entered the convent, with adequate dowries to sustain them during their lives, and the four sons who became Franciscan friars gave up their inheritance. Another son became a Jesuit and another a member of the secular clergy. The bulk of the estate fell to the eldest son, Don Gerónimo, who inherited the mayorazgo. We are uncertain of the fate of the two other sisters.

❦ 2 ❧

The First Creole Generation

YOUTH ON THE FRONTIER

Early in the seventeenth century Franciscan Friar Diego de Córdova y Salinas began to prepare a history of his order in Peru. He discovered substantial material in documents, but the richest testimony came from fellow Franciscans as he probed their recollections. In his final work Friar Diego wrote about several members of the Oré family. One of his most loquacious witnesses was Friar Diego Sánchez, who probably knew the family best, and in the early 1620s provided his accounts of the four Oré siblings who entered the Franciscan order. The elderly friar remembered Pedro de Oré, who distinguished himself as a missionary in the Peruvian doctrinas; later he was custodian of Tierra Firme and guardian of the Franciscan Monastery in Panama. Dionisio de Oré served in many Andean doctrinas, including Cajamarca, and as his brother Luis Gerónimo, had been a doctrinero in the Collaguas, and later Cuzco. Friar Antonio de Oré spent many years in church service as well. But the most famous in Friar Diego Sánchez's time was Luis Gerónimo. The Oré brothers were well prepared for their task: they learned Latin from their father and were taught to play the organ and the *tecla* (a keyboard instrument similar to the harpsichord). Friar Sánchez praised the Orés as excellent singers of the *canto llano* (plainchant), stressing that Pedro and Luis Gerónimo had such wonderful voices that "they could have sung in the Cathedral of Toledo."[1] The Franciscans recognized and extolled accomplishments of fellow Franciscans, but it is rare for a religious to highlight actions of members of other orders. Dominican friar, chronicler, and later a bishop, Reginaldo de Lizárraga is an exception. He traveled through Huamanga one or more times and began composing a general description of the viceroyalty in the 1590s. He completed it when he was in his seventies. Under orders of Cuzco's bishop, he conducted a pastoral inspection that led him to the city of Huamanga, perhaps in mid-1602. Lizárraga spoke highly of the Oré brothers: "Four of the males are friars of the Seraphic Order of Saint Francis, the three are very good preachers, both for Spaniards as for Indians. All four men live today as marvelous examples of Christianity and virtue to whom the order has extended honorable offices and gave a very good account of them."[2]

Little is known of the childhood of Luis Gerónimo and his siblings. Expectations for children and their education were based on social and economic status.[3] In Iberia it was typical for the boys of a well-to-do family to study with a tutor, perhaps a clergyman, as might some of the daughters. But Huamanga was a frontier city, and fortunately the Oré parents were capable of teaching, not just reading and writing and some mathematics, but also elements of church doctrine. Young Luis Gerónimo and most of his brothers and sisters learned Quechua and probably Aymara from the indigenous servants and their families in their extensive household.

In the sixteenth and seventeenth centuries there was considerable debate over the impact of using wet-nurses, particularly if they were of lower socioeconomic status and especially if they were of different ethnicities. Rebecca Earle points out that many at the time were convinced that the use of wet-nurses by Creoles led to absorbing the characteristics of the Indians, or Africans, who served their families. Based on the humoral theory, children are influenced by their environment, the climate, or the food they eat. In Juan de Pineda's view, mother's milk ingested by the baby was influenced by her humors, the good as well as the bad. Such concepts were widely held, and as Earle and Joanne Rappaport point out, Lizárraga expressed grave concern about the upbringing of creole children. Lizárraga railed that part of the problem in the Indies was that "at birth the poor child is given to an Indian or Black woman, a drunkard, dirty, a liar, to raise him with all the other good inclinations we have said, and he is growing up, already a lad, with little Indians (*indezuelos*); How will this boy turn out? He will take the inclinations that he suckled in the milk, and will act as those he associates with, as we experience daily." He continued, "He who is nursed on lying milk becomes a liar. He who drinks drunken milk becomes a drunkard, and thieving milk, a thief."[4] As noted earlier, Lizárraga's account of the Oré children, as "examples of Christian virtue," contradicts these extreme views; one wonders if Lizárraga realized they too must have had indigenous wet-nurses and were raised by them.[5]

Luis Gerónimo's formative years in Huamanga were strongly influenced by the religious instruction of his parents, clerics, and the Franciscans, yet his initial understanding of Andean beliefs was provided by contact with indigenous children and their elders. His knowledge of autochthonous religiosity came from the Andeans of his father's encomienda and household. As an intelligent and curious youth, it is unthinkable that he and his siblings were unaware of the Taki Onqoy movement sweeping the Andes in the mid to late 1560s, for the cult was centered near the family's holding in the *corregimiento* (Indian province) of Vilcas. There are numerous interpretations of the movement, as noted by Jeremy Mumford. Some view it as a reaction against the conquest and forced labor system inflicted by the outsiders. Others stress it was a revivalist movement similar to what occurred in nineteenth century North America, since singing and dancing, a "dancing sickness," was an integral part of the ritual of its leaders culminating in an ecstatic state of being and belief of their invincibility against the European gods. The Andean concept of cycles of creation and destruction, a *Pachacuti,* with the destruction of the outsiders contributed to its rapid spread as Sabine MacCormack points out. Juan Carlos Estenssoro Fuchs sees the relationship to Christian thought as the Andeans digested and reworked what they were told by the doctrineros. Some, however, viewed it as more of a creation of Spanish clerics competing for preferment, or as way for some encomenderos to be stripped of their holdings to benefit challengers in a competition for authority and prestige.[6]

It is uncertain who first uncovered the movement; some believe it was Luis de Olivera, curate of the doctrina of Parinacochas, others argue it was Cristóbal de Albornoz. Albornoz, born in Spain around 1530, spent his first years in America in New Granada, finally reaching Peru in early 1567. He was named *visitador eclesiástico* (religious inspector) of the diocese of Cuzco. In 1568 he inspected the Arequipa district, then Huamanga the following year. There in the countryside he uncovered the "sect and apostasy of Taquiongo."[7] A more thorough investigation of Huamanga began on 8 March 1570. Luis Gerónimo was about sixteen years old and must have known of the proceedings. Several witnesses in the investigation knew the Oré family. They included Guardian of the Franciscan monastery Antonio de Almonacid; *vicario*[8] of the convent of Santa Clara, Franciscan Francisco de Zamora; and Bartolomé Berrocal, the notary of Huamanga's principal church. They were involved in Albornoz's original visita and provide detailed information about the movement. The investigation was a concern for the Orés because the places most "infected" included the encomienda of Yauyos of Captain Francisco de Cárdenas, and the "pueblo of Allauca of Antonio de Oré."[9]

Luis Gerónimo's father Antonio, who self-reported his age exceeded fifty, was one of the witnesses. Antonio's father-in-law Pedro Díaz de Rojas also testified in the investigation because his encomienda of Quinua, according to priest Pedro del Prado, was the first inspected.[10] The encomienda at the time of Toledo's visita general held 884 tributaries and a total population of 5,141 Andeans.[11] Prado stated that "Pedro Díaz de Rojas who lives near this city discovered in it one hundred fifty *hechizeros* [shamans] and other abuses and evils that existed among the natives, and he punished them."[12] The priest indicated that Albornoz executed the visita "with care and diligence inquiring into ancient and erroneous evils and superstitions." Antonio de Oré's testimony parallels other witnesses, though less detailed than some clerics who provided specific information on the practices. Oré asserted that it was common knowledge in Huamanga that Albornoz and Gerónimo Martín had discovered a "large number of *huacas* [any object of veneration] and at the same time I heard many people say, one of whom was Father Friar Francisco de Zamora, vicario of the nuns [Clarisas] of this city, that they had burned and destroyed them."[13] Zamora, at the time of the inspection was in the encomienda of Juan Velásquez Vela Núñez, and verified that Albornoz "discovered many idolatrous male and female Indians who practiced the sect and apostasy that they call Taki Ongo, and by another name, Aira." He gave special credit in the visita to "Father Gerónimo Martín, one of the most important translators for the natives of this kingdom."[14]

Gerónimo Martín was vicario in Diego Gavilán's encomienda. He testified that because he was "a good translator and having been raised from childhood in this kingdom and knowing the dispositions and manners of the natives . . . Cristóbal de Albornoz wrote to me three or four times, begging me to join him." Father Martín accepted, "recognizing it would be for the service of the Lord" and joined the effort, inspecting Oré's Indians and others.[15] Priest Cosme Vélez de Mazuelos stated he was present during the inspection of Antonio de Oré's encomienda and several others. He verified the linguistic expertise of Gerónimo Martín and reported he witnessed him conducting Mass and speaking and organizing religious processions for the Indians. Mazuelos lauded the efforts of Father Martín and inspector Albornoz in convincing the Andeans to "denounce themselves and the huacas and ancient temples they had and ask for penitence for their errors." Father Martín's description of the cult is one of the most detailed. He notes its followers rejected God and his commandments and did not adore the cross, Christian images, or enter churches or confess to priests. Instead they fasted according to their traditional "customs from the time of the Incas, not eating salt, ají, or corn. They did not copulate with their wives, and they offered llamas and alpacas as sacrifices to their huacas."[16] The priest later recorded other sacrifices such as gold, silver, birds, and guinea pigs.[17] He believed that the principal huacas of Titicaca, Tiahuanaco, and others that were venerated in Inca times continued to be adored. "The tricksters and teachers" were proclaiming that "these huacas are defeating the God of the Christians and very little remained to defeat him." Further, these "tricksters" told their followers that if they venerated the huacas and conducted their ceremonies they would be successful in their business and they and their children would be healthy, and their harvests bountiful. But the reverse would occur "if they did not venerate their huacas and conduct the ceremonies and sacrifices." More frightening if they did not do so, "they would die and their heads would walk on the ground while their feet would be up." Furthermore, "some would turn into guanacos, deer and vicuñas and other animals and they would be stripped of cognition." Perhaps the most dangerous concept for the religious was that "the huacas would make another new world with other peoples." Such a belief was appealing to the Andeans, for deeply imbedded was the concept of the Pachacuti, the ending of one age with its destruction and then creation of a new one. It was evident to all that the arrival of the Spanish had destroyed their world, literally turned it upside down and these "messengers" sent by the huacas were promising a return to a better world. As Father Martín pointed out, "their priests, falsifiers and teachers told with great conviction these things and more to the Indians, hoping they would believe what they heard and be certain that it was the truth."[18] He added, if Cristóbal de Albornoz had not discovered the movement, it "would spread throughout the entire kingdom."[19] Albornoz uncovered many huacas, and punished "the criminals, fortunetellers, augers, shamans and those married within the prohibited first and second degrees [of consanguinity]." During his inspection of the doctrinas he found that some clerics also committed crimes and he punished them and removed them from their parishes.

The world that Luis Gerónimo and his siblings knew during their formative years was far from stable. They were the children of conquest, the first creole generation. Their parents married the year Huamanga was founded, and Luis Gerónimo's oldest brother was born the following year, 1541, the year of Francisco Pizarro's assassination. The family's encomienda of Hanan Chilques was of average size for the region.[20] The city of Huamanga was rising, literally from the ground up. Recently distributed autochthonous Andeans were beginning to feel the weight of the yoke of colonialism. The indigenous people resentful of foreign domination and regimentation resisted. Although resistance was more open in the nearby eastern lower elevation slopes leading to the Amazonian rainforest and in the isolated places of the high Andean puna and in the hidden valleys, it also existed in the encomiendas of powerful settlers. As the creole generation grew, pressures on the Amerindians mounted, especially as their numbers continued a downward spiral and their world seemed to be disintegrating. The Taki Onqoy movement provided the spiritual escape. By returning to the old ways they would be liberated, and they would revive their earlier world, the one before the hated invaders stripped away their huacas. The experiences of the Oré children were embedded as they developed into adulthood; the approaches the first creole generation took to deal with the challenges were as varied as the individuals themselves.

❦ 3 ❦

The Oré Family

MYTHOHISTORY

The mythohistory of the Oré family in Peru evolved over decades as it grew in several directions. At the trunk we start with Antonio de Oré and his wife Doña Luisa Díaz de Rojas y Rivera, whose achievements were propagated largely by their eldest and youngest sons, Don Gerónimo and Licentiate Francisco as they attempted to secure rewards, a common practice in the expanding state and church bureaucracies under the Hapsburg monarchs. The major branch in the exultation of the family lineage is the "miracle" of the foundation of the Convent of Santa Clara. Another shoot in the family myth revolves around the Oré daughters who became nuns there. Luis Gerónimo de Oré, who widely disseminated knowledge of the family in his first book, the *Symbolo Catholico Indiano,* contributed to the myth.

Years after the convent was established, Luis Gerónimo published a brief account of its foundation. The initial part of the *Symbolo* includes a geographic and historical narrative of the viceroyalty and its peoples for use by future missionaries. Following his description of the mines of mercury and silver in the Huamanga region he stated,

> God furnished Antonio de Oré, my father, a vecino of this city, a mysterious mine in the villages of the Indians of his repartimiento and encomienda from which he extracted all the silver needed for the founding of the convent of Santa Clara. He erected it at his own cost from its very foundations, or better said that God endowed him with the mine which always gave its fruit while the work continued. Once the convent was completed the mine ceased, and its metal stopped and, never again was a *real* [unit of currency] extracted from it. For that reason the founders (who are four of my sisters who now thirty years

ago founded and entered it), and all the other religious of that saintly house owe it to continuously give thanks to our Lord for having built it.[1]

Others propagated the story. Reginaldo de Lizárraga began his pastoral inspection of Huamanga in the first half of 1602. Already the "mythohistory" of the foundation of the convent was flowering and Lizárraga's account of it largely coincides with Luis Gerónimo's 1598 text.[2]

Antonio de Oré and Doña Luisa were motivated by their religious faith and their desire to maintain and increase the wealth and status of their family. Remembrance, a sentiment shared by other Spaniards who settled in the New World, was another factor. Antonio and Doña Luisa successfully gained access to Amerindians, land, and political power at the local level, and took specific steps to avoid its dissipation in the next and subsequent generations. A common and prestigious way to protect wealth was to funnel some offspring into a religious occupation. Boys and girls could initiate their training early, at the age of twelve or in some cases earlier. Under a strict regimen they could be prepared to take their vows by the time they were in their late teens. In the case of male religious orders most demanded some form of "gift" or endowment for the young men, and there was a variation of the monetary equivalent of that gift, with some orders expecting a substantial amount. For the Franciscans the amount was comparatively small, and the advantage for families was that it was legally possible for the young men to waive their inheritance rights in this situation. Some monastic orders could amass substantial wealth over several decades by endowments and by investments and operation of properties they had accrued. Successful management of Jesuit haciendas, plantations, and obrajes in the viceroyalty of Peru made them very wealthy by the mid-seventeenth century. The Franciscans following the strict Rule of St. Francis in theory accepted only alms, although the "alms" could be quite large, and some of their monasteries were well furnished.

The situation was different for girls. The assumption was that convents were not self-sustaining and therefore large endowments were required for their upkeep. Kathryn Burns details this in her study of the first convent established in Cuzco, as the members of the city council decided on 17 April 1551 to secure a lot to build a convent to accommodate the young unmarried Inca women and mestiza daughters of the leading citizens, many of them of Cuzco's encomendero elite. The purpose was clear: make them good Christians who could either become nuns or marry Spanish men without encomiendas. In that way aspiring Spaniards could gain access to land and labor through marriage. The difficulty, as in the convent of Huamanga, was to locate a nun to oversee the young women. In the case of Cuzco, a "respectable" Spanish widow, Francisca Ortiz de Ayala was named by the cabildo to the lifetime position of abbess, taking the name Francisca de Jesús. For the first years it operated more as a *casa de recogimiento*—a secluded community of young women under her rule—and was not yet recognized as a convent.[3] The actual foundation in Cuzco did not take place until 1558. It was highly unusual for any city council to establish such institutions. Family endowments were normally the way that convents were founded, as in the case of the Orés. By the late 1560s, with an increasing number of Spanish nuns, or culturally Spanish, we see a tendency toward a division into Clarisas of the black veil, or white. As in Spain, the black veils were professed nuns whereas the white veils were the novices, students, and servants. In the case of Lima's seventeenth-century Clarisas, they included slaves.[4]

There was no convent for Spanish elite in Huamanga, and Antonio de Oré and Doña Luisa intended to provide a convent of the Order of Santa Clara for their daughters. It required years before their goal was fully realized. The first step was to convince local Franciscans. It is difficult to imagine that the Huamanga friars would have hesitated to support their intentions. The real challenge was at a higher level where they faced both church and state officials. There was competition between religious orders and there was only a limited opportunity to convince their own leaders of both the need for a convent and its reasonable prospects for success. If there were too many convents in a colonial Spanish American city the weaker ones were often closed, presenting the delicate question of what to do with the remaining nuns. Furthermore, state officials viewed convents as a burden, for nuns too frequently pressed the Crown for financial support. Despite the obstacles, the Orés ultimately succeeded. The construction of the convent proved costly, but it was accomplished by Oré's access to Andean laborers and by income from his mining investments.

According to various accounts, as the work progressed Antonio de Oré memorized the appropriate church ritual for the convent and taught it to his daughters, expecting them to be the founders of the Huamanga house and later, alternatively, its abbesses.[5] How could Antonio secure the knowledge necessary to prepare his daughters, or did our sources exaggerate his capabilities? The best explanation might be that, with the assistance of a friar, he obtained an important document from Huamanga's Franciscan library: a printed copy of one of the manuals used for the training of young women for the religious life. Such manuals, although scarce, did exist.[6] More likely the manuals for the novitiate were also used for the nuns, for the core was similar and used regularly for both. The Clarisas followed the rules originally set up in the thirteenth century by Santa Clara of Assisi, with subsequent modifications over the centuries. The novice nun was expected to read the breviaries and recite the hours as assigned during the day. Those unable to read would recite the Paternoster at the assigned times and in a specific set of numbers. The libraries were important to the life of the convents, along with religious paintings and engravings, sculptures, and other religious objects. On 10 May 1568, Antonio de Oré signed an agreement to become the patron of the convent, and his male heirs were to assume the position after his death. In a separate agreement, Antonio and his wife established a chaplaincy of masses and endowed it with 2,000 pesos in *censos* (mortgages) on their houses on the public plaza of Huamanga, and on four city lots in front of the Franciscan monastery, plus two city half-lots adjacent to the convent. It was in an ideal location facing the Franciscan monastery, and behind it there were farm plots tilled by their encomienda Indians, and on one side was the principal street, the Calle Real. There were also agricultural properties, including a farm in Yucay producing fruit and grapes with six thousand vines already planted, and five hundred ewes.[7] The properties, if managed well, could support the original Oré nuns for decades to come.

The completed and fully furnished convent was impressive. Twentieth-century architectural historian Antonio San Cristóbal Sebastián points out that the convent's church is one of the few in Huamanga that retains elements of the sixteenth century, including its Mudejar ceilings and a Renaissance doorway, through which one the Orés must have passed frequently.[8] It is possible the young novice Luis Gerónimo witnessed the Act of Foundation of the Convent of Santa Clara prior to his departure to Cuzco to continue his training. All had to be done in conjunction with the Franciscans. It was also necessary to bring in one or more fully professed nuns of the order to set up the convent and begin training the novices. Provincial Juan del Campo asked the Presidenta Sister of Santa Clara, Leonor de la Trinidad of the Cuzco convent, to travel to Huamanga to organize the house. Sister Leonor directed the final training of novices in the rules and constitutions of the order, and took the vows of profession of the four Oré sisters the year after the convent was founded. The formal foundation of the convent took place on 16 May 1568. It was a major event for the city and surrounding countryside: "The vecinos and residents celebrated all they could. The bells in all the churches were furiously rung to the point of breaking into pieces, alternating with many trios of oboes, trumpets and drums that placed in the corners of the church towers, filled the air with joy and merriment."[9]

Recording directly from the foundation book of the convent, Córdova y Salinas reported that Huamanga's Franciscan Guardian Francisco de Zamora solemnly brought and placed the Holy Sacrament in the convent and celebrated the divine offices. Then in the presence of all assembled in the church he bestowed the habit to the four Oré sisters. It would be the following year, on 29 May 1569, the Sunday of the Pentecost—after completion of the testing and approval of the novices—that the women would take their vows.[10] Franciscan Provincial Diego de Medellín officiated, holding Mass after which the young sisters took the veil. The Oré daughters who professed were Ana de Serpa, Leonor de Tejada, Inés de Tejada, and María de la Concepción. Sometime later a fifth sister entered the convent and took the name Doña María de Oré de la Purificación.[11] By 1586 there were thirty Clarisas in Huamanga's convent.[12]

Antonio de Oré composed his testament in 1576 and died shortly after. The Dominican Reginaldo de Lizárraga wrote, "Our Lord conferred to the founder of this convent a death that was as his life," and added that Doña Luisa, who "was a wonderful companion to him," was at his side. Lizárraga noted that "although she saw him expire, she did not resort to exaggeration in her bereavement that others tend to do. Instead with a joyous countenance she herself shrouded his body and placed it in the casket. In her house that day one did not see tears or hear wailing, rather silence, a sadness subject to reason, with many thanks to Our Lord and in conformity with His will. If there were tears, they were pious and Christian."[13]

Several years later, Diego de Córdova y Salinas described Antonio de Oré's death, following a long illness, perhaps a stroke, that he suffered stoically. The funeral was a major event in Huamanga, and Antonio "was interred with pomp and ceremony." His four sons who were Franciscan priests, and five daughters who were nuns participated in the funeral. "Three of the sons were at the altar, one who conducted Mass and the other two served him as deacon and subdeacon, and the other one in the pulpit and the five daughters were in the choir, as angels officiating the Mass." Antonio's widow "dressed in a coarse woolen habit" dedicated herself to the church and good works for another ten years. In 1620 testimony Friar Diego Sánchez recalled Doña Luisa's determination to assure her daughters were "good Christians." The friar declared, "I saw their mother sometimes scold and reprimand them [the daughters] when they had been negligent in caring for the altars, or in other things, with such liberty as when they were being raised in her home." According to the friar the daughters, like their brothers, were taught by their father "the plainchant, [to play] the organ, and they knew the Latin language very well and with such elegance, that they understood well the Council of Trent." They took turns fulfilling the role of abbess. Eight months before Doña Luisa died, she lost her ability to speak, but remained cognizant. In Lizárraga's words Doña Luisa "died as she lived, fully content with her life."[14]

In 1602 Luis Gerónimo's younger brother Licentiate Francisco de Oré prepared his service report, inflating his father's growing reputation. By the beginning of the seventeenth century few could remember that Antonio de Oré was not at the capture and ransom of Inca Atahualpa. In his service report to the king, Francisco boasted that his father "was one of the first conquistadors and settlers of those kingdoms, and assisted in the taking of Cajamarca, and imprisonment of Atahualpa Inga. . . . and was occupied in the conquest and pacification of the Conchucos and against Manco Inga Yupanqui, who had been Lord of those Kingdoms" during the siege of Cuzco. The title of María Elena Martínez's book, *Genealogical Fictions,* is appropriate here and in similar cases where descendants needed to establish family credentials in order to secure favor, some going so far as to "uncover" links to the Gothic rulers of Castile and Aragon. Francisco claimed that Antonio de Oré was in charge of the "guard and control of the fort and frontier of the city of Huamanga," and with the arrival of Vaca de Castro his father fought valiantly against Diego de Almagro the Younger, and in the Battle of Chupas he left the field "wounded in one leg and maimed in an arm." He later fought in the Battle of Huarina and left the field "robbed of all he had with him." Antonio subsequently served President Pedro de la Gasca in the Battle of Jaquijahuana, which ended the rebellion of the encomenderos with the capture and execution of Gonzalo Pizarro. Tirelessly, Francisco goes on to include his father's participation in almost every other skirmish until his death. As with all service reports there are many questions. Did Francisco have a copy of his father's original report and how much did he inflate Antonio's achievements? Service reports are notorious for exaggerating deeds and loyalty to the Crown to advance one's career and family fortune.[15]

Over the generations the Oré family narrative, told and retold, has not been forgotten; rather the myth has grown. In the early part of the twentieth century Evaristo San Cristóval suggested that Doña Luisa succeeded "to dominate her husband, a thing that was not difficult, being as she was, a woman of great talent and of a strength and incomparable will, and it was necessary to confront the challenges her life had given, preparing for the well-being of her daughters, as she intended." The author concluded his biographical sketch with a statement that "the case of the impact of Doña Luisa was singular during this period. One might say that she was a mother of saints." By the 1960s the story of the Oré family has become a cloudy mirror's reflection of reality.[16]

4

Franciscan Novice in the Inca Capital

Royal cosmographer Juan López de Velasco reported that Huamanga in the late 1560s lacked adequate educational facilities. Luis Gerónimo and several of his brothers would have to travel to larger urban centers to complete their formal training. The two possibilities were Cuzco or Lima, both roughly equidistant from Huamanga. It was toward Cuzco that Luis Gerónimo embarked on his journey in the late 1560s or early 1570s, likely choosing the Inca "highway." Lizárraga reckoned the distance was sixty to seventy leagues, and the route alternated between Huamanga's temperate climate and frigid mountain passes, even in a single day. Young Luis Gerónimo and his party followed a trajectory that many travelers took and may have spent the first night in the unbearable cold of high elevation Tambillios de Illaguaci. His group likely passed through Andahuaylas and Abancay and crossed three major rivers, including the Apurimac, carefully treading across the famous gorge on a frightening suspension bridge constructed of Andean grass so vividly described by Thornton Wilder. Shortly before reaching Cuzco on a likely twelve-day trip, the travelers crossed the plain of Jaquijahuana, the battleground where royalist forces defeated rebellious encomenderos years earlier.[1]

Cieza de León recorded only two monasteries in Cuzco when he was there around 1549, the Dominican and the Franciscan.[2] Friar Pedro Portugués, one of the first religious to reach Cuzco in 1534 or 1535, founded the Franciscan monastery. The order fared poorly in the first land allotments. The site was on a hill above the city, but a better location was found in 1549 thanks to efforts of friars Pedro de los Algarves and Fernando de Hinojosa. who reached an amicable agreement with Juan Rodríguez de Villalobos to secure title to the plaza where the Hospital of San Lazaro stood. The structure they slowly erected largely used reworked Inca blocks and was still incomplete when young Oré entered the monastery two decades later. Viceroy Toledo's support advanced the Franciscan monastery to near completion around 1574. That structure was torn down in 1645, and a replacement erected in 1649, just a year before a devastating earthquake shook Cuzco. Subsequent earthquakes and reconstructions leave the current monastery bearing little resemblance to the one the young novice Luis Gerónimo entered.[3]

We have a good idea of the Cuzco Oré encountered when he first trod its stone streets and touched perfectly jointed Inca walls, thanks to cosmographer López de Velasco. The geographer had access to papers collected by his predecessor Alonso de Santa Cruz, Cieza de León and early geographical descriptions that Philip II had ordered to gain a better understanding of resources in his overseas kingdoms. López de Velasco completed his text around 1574, but much of his information dates from the 1560s. He recorded eight hundred vecinos residing in Cuzco, far larger than the Huamanga that the teenage novice left behind. The indigenous population of the city was much greater than that of the outsiders.[4] The Franciscan monastery held eight friars; there were also monasteries for the Augustinians, Mercedarians, Dominicans, and Theatines. There were already a nunnery and two hospitals, one for Spaniards and the other for Indians. The cathedral with various religious dignitaries and a number of canons rose on one side of the main square, near the bishop's residence. The Jesuit house and school were in a prime location on the main square. The city was divided into several parishes: San Blas, San Cristóbal, Santa Ana, Los Remedios, Santiago and Nuestra Señora de Belén.[5] In 1580 there were fifteen to twenty-nine friars in Cuzco's Franciscan monastery. When Lizárraga visited two decades later there were approximately thirty Franciscan friars.[6]

Luis Gerónimo de Oré described Cuzco based on his own recollections from early 1570s, with some updates to the early 1590s when he was completing the *Symbolo Catholico Indiano*. He called it "the most noble and grand city of Cuzco, head of all these kingdoms of Peru, the ancient court and seat of the Inca kings where the Indian nobility of Peru was and continues to reside. From this great city the Inca governed all the provinces subject to his crown, dividing them into four quarters, or districts, Collasuyo, Chinchaysuyo, Antisuyo, and Contisuyo." Oré and others who have observed the city's massive stone walls, temples and palaces, marvel at the quality of the masonry. The monumental size of the stone structures profoundly impressed the young novice. "They have an excellent fort [Sacsahuaman] of strangely hewn stone, large and incredibly heavy. It is amazing that only the force of the Indians carried them from another place without any aid of oxen or other animals. There are some stones so large that ten pairs of oxen could not move them." Oré mentioned the Coricancha, originally the Inca Temple of the Sun, appropriated by the Dominicans. His sense of wonder as he described Inca achievements contrasts with his unenthusiastic outline of the colonial urbe; in the city core stood the "cathedral church, head of the diocese, and five monasteries for monks and one convent of the nuns of Santa Clara, two hospitals, six parishes of Spaniards and Indians, and in the villages of its district there are well built and finely furnished and decorated churches."[7]

Oré's training paralleled that of other Franciscan novices of the period. Religious exercises began long before daybreak. The agenda was not far different from that instituted by Bishop Francisco Verdugo for the Huamanga College Seminary of San Francisco years later. The regimen was based on the widely adopted constitution of the Colegio de Maese Rodrigo which later became the University of Seville.[8] The day began at 5:30 A.M., when the students were awakened to dress and prepare their beds in time to be in the chapel at 5:45. The boys studied between 6 and 7, then went for communal studies until 11 A.M. Between 11:00 and 11:30 they returned to their lesson in the *canto* (liturgical singing). Lunch at noon was followed by an hour for rest, then another hour was devoted for studies. The afternoon regimen officially began at 2 P.M., as the novices gathered for communal studies. They would remain in the college, concentrating on their scriptural studies and writing their compositions. Between 8 and 8:30 they had conferences covering the subjects they had studied. Finally, supper came between 8:30 and 9:00 in the evening, followed by fifteen minutes together in the chapel when "they took their exam on their conferences." At last, at 9:15 P.M. they returned to their cells to sleep.[9]

The rigors and tedium were punctuated by occasional distractions. Public spectacles were among the major attractions for residents, and ample possibilities existed with numerous days in the religious calendar celebrated jointly by civil and religious authorities. The most important religious holidays centered on the life of Christ and the Virgin Mary. The Annunciation, the Nativity, Lent, and Easter were observed everywhere in the Iberian world. Corpus Christi was another, as were the holy days associated with important local saints. In the Andes, with constant threat of massive earthquakes, veneration of any figure that could provide protection, such as Nuestro Señor de los Milagros in Lima and Cuzco, aroused fervent devotion. Another cause for public commemoration was the birth, marriage, or death in the royal family, or the arrival of a new viceroy or bishop. There were abundant opportunities for Franciscan novice Luis Gerónimo to be present when Viceroy Francisco de Toledo attended one of the civic or religious celebrations.[10]

Other public events attracted civil and religious authorities and the populace at large. Celebrations of battle victories and the spectacle of executions filled public spaces. One of the most powerful that young Oré witnessed was the execution of Tupac Amaru I. The leader of the neo-Inca state at Vilcabamba was captured and executed after a hasty three-day sham trial. Although a cautious Dr. Gabriel de Loarte presided over the proceedings, the pressure of Viceroy Toledo was felt at all levels. The viceroy had concluded Tupac Amaru had to be eliminated regardless of the damage to the tenuous relationship between the indigenous people and Spaniards. Some officials and clergymen resisted the viceroy's stance, fearing the response of Philip II, who might be perturbed by another regicide in Andean America. Philip II's father Charles V had not looked kindly on Francisco Pizarro's execution of the Inca Atahualpa nor the execution of the Aztec ruler of Mexico by Hernán Cortéz—both considered regicide. In the hours before the execution of Tupac Amaru a tide of opposition and sympathy for the Inca grew. Numerous clerics and members of the religious orders attempted to convince the viceroy to desist, some pleading on their knees, without success. Franciscan Guardian Francisco Vélez and the order's Provincial Jerónimo de Villacarrillo pressured the viceroy to stay the execution and the developments were surely discussed in the Franciscan monastery. The execution of the Inca ruler on the principal plaza of Cuzco on 23 September 1572 was especially gruesome, a sight forever imbedded in the minds of all who witnessed it including the young Oré.[11]

There are many moving descriptions of the execution. Many chroniclers have embellished their telling and we rely on a generally accepted, plausible outline of the events. A scaffold was erected on the main plaza of Cuzco, and the Inca was bound and escorted downward from his jail on the hill above the city by the priest at the Indian hospital of Nuestra Señora de los Remedios Cristóbal de Molina, and the Jesuit Alonso de Barzana.[12] The young Inca was heavily guarded by fully armed Spaniards and approximately four hundred reliable Cañari Indians, long enemies of the Inca. He was taken to the scaffold while masses of wailing indigenous supporters crushed into the square. Tupac

Amaru silenced them and then made a statement in Quechua. According to the accounts he was fully converted to Christianity and publicly renounced the Inca religion, claiming it was a sham. Viceroy Toledo wrote to the Cardinal of Sigüenza shortly later expressing his surprise at what the Inca had done, and his belief that it would aid in the process of conversion. After his statement and the standard religious rituals, Tupac Amaru placed his head on the block and a Cañari executioner grasped his hair, and cleanly severed the head and held it high. Tupac Amaru's subjects were inconsolable, and Spaniards who had pressed for his execution may have had second thoughts. Other options existed; the Inca could have been exiled to Spain, a common approach to muzzle a conquered ruler. A further error was made when the head was displayed on a pike as a reminder of what happens to traitors, common practice in Spanish justice. But in the Andean context, Tupac Amaru's severed head became a huaca to be venerated. It took Toledo only two days to realize his dangerous mistake as indigenous multitude began traditional rituals for the huaca. The head was quickly removed and buried with the body.[13]

Young Oré, witnessing the dramatic death of the Inca ruler, was moved by the violence and the response of the Andeans. He was not alone, for Spaniards and Andeans alike were unable to forget what occurred on that day. Oré's description, published two decades later retains a crispness and abhorrence of what he and those around him had seen and heard. "They took him to Cuzco, and in the middle of the plaza crowded with a multitude of Indians and amidst incredible sadness and pain among them and the religious and the Spaniards, they cut off his head, by order of the viceroy Don Francisco de Toledo. Thus ended the Inca Empire."[14]

During his early training in the Cuzco monastery had the novice heard voices defending the indigenous people? It is likely that he did. Oré's view regarding the tragedy of the condition of the Amerindians is clearly articulated in his 1598 *Symbolo Catholico Indiano*.

> Wretched natives, what an unfortunate servile condition of the Indians! . . . Witness to this is the very halfheartedness that we see in the Indians; indeed, they regard the matter of their conversion as mere accessory, and instead, as if it were more important, they tend to their continuous occupations, work, mitas, and personal service on the roads and in the cities and other places, and in the transport of goods and carrying all kinds of things, and they never stop

during the entire year and their whole life, resulting in a great decline of this Indian nation.[15]

Although Oré did not cite Bartolomé de las Casas directly, he seems aware of the position of the Dominican Bishop of Chiapas. "I wanted to hear and follow the judgments of learned men who will understand this comparison, as I do, having done so many times." Oré then continued,

> but to follow one's own opinion and issue a new judgment, as it might seem to those unversed in the histories that I now write in favor of the Indians, it is (save for a wiser verdict) that after the noble nations of Europe, that is the Spaniards, French, Italians, Flemish and Germans, and others that with baptism have received a government to live by (*orden politico de vivir*), and after the Greeks, and some African nations, I can say that the Indian nations of Peru and Chile, Tucumán, Paraguay, and those of the Kingdom of New Granada, and of Mexico are among the most honorable and pure that exist in this world universe.[16]

Oré returns in his *Symbolo* to what he viewed as an unjust execution of the Inca Atahualpa. "From Marqués Pizarro to the last of the accomplices of this murder they paid for it with their lives, because all of them were felled by stabbings and violently, for human blood unjustly spilled clamors and cries out before God."[17] The link between injustice and restitution may have been discussed by the novices in Cuzco. Bartolomé de las Casas, even before the printing of his *Brief History of the Destruction of the Indies* (1552), was pointing out in print and in person the wrongdoing to the officials of the state and church. By the 1560s he was advocating restitution—economic—to the indigenous people for what they had lost to Spanish exploitation. The novices in Cuzco and the Franciscan friars discussed the Inca past and the Spanish conquest and settlement of the Andes because that knowledge was critical for success as doctrineros.[18]

5

Preparations for a Religious Life

LIMA AND THE UNIVERSITY

Luis Gerónimo de Oré's intellectual promise was recognized by his superiors in Cuzco and with their support he traveled to Lima to complete his education. We are uncertain of the date he departed Cuzco, but it followed Tupac Amaru's execution, and he likely arrived in the viceregal capital in early 1573. The Pacific littoral must have seemed an alien world to the highlander when he first viewed it. The coastal strip from north-central Chile to northern Peru is a desert; the Atacama is one of the driest places on earth. The coast is characterized by alternating strips of barren Andean spurs extending into the ocean, with sloping alluvial valleys between. The higher western mountain slopes feed melting glacial ice, snow, and rain to several rivers. Verdant ribbons along river edges provided an oasis environment that has sustained human settlement for thousands of years. With irrigation agriculture, pre-Columbian civilizations rose and fell. The Lima valley was one of several possible sites the Spanish could set up their center of control.

After an initial attempt to establish their capital near the great ceremonial compound and pyramid of Pachacamac, Spaniards chose the adjoining valley to its north with ample water and a safer port, Callao. The site seemed perfect when they founded Lima, the "City of the Kings," in January 1535. It was sunny, warm but not oppressively hot, and the lush green vegetation—thriving in the irrigated fields cultivated by the Indians living in small clusters—made it seem idyllic. Moreover, the wide alcove in the coastline, with fortress-like islands offshore, provided what seemed a safe haven for ships. Had the city founders first viewed the site during May to December they may have had second thoughts. A cold mist, the infamous *garúa,* could cover the sun at any moment and remain so for months. López de Velasco in the late 1560s detailed Lima's dreary weeks: "The city has become sick with various illnesses. It is suspected that they are caused by the abundance of fruits and other foods, and by the continuous fog that covers it in the winter. Thus, there are many respiratory illnesses and influenza."[1]

Oré arrived four decades after Lima's foundation and if he descended from the mountains on a clear, sunny day he might see the distant city's principal buildings and streets laid out in a grid-iron pattern, with the main plaza at the center. The earliest religious orders built their monasteries nearest the plaza, the Dominican two blocks west, the Mercedarian to the south, and the Franciscan two blocks east. Just north of the plaza the Rímac River carries life-giving water from the Andean heights. The Rímac could also bring death, for during the rainy season in the mountains the river often breached its banks, flooding parts of the city. Near its edge was the foul-smelling public slaughterhouse. Across the river lies the barrio of Rímac, then largely a district of artisans and Amerindians. On approach Oré could see a more heterogeneous populace than in the highlands where the people were mainly native Andean, European, and mestizo. Over a third of Lima's population were African slaves, with slightly fewer Europeans, and a modest number of Andeans and mestizos. There were migrants from Asia when Oré returned in the early 1620s, thanks to increasing commerce with the East Indies and China via the Spanish Philippines.[2]

Oré was impressed by "the remarkable City of the Kings,"[3] and described the thriving seat of the viceroyalty filled with houses, churches, and people of all stations. In the city center, the viceroy as well as the archbishop had their residence and the Lima cabildo shared the principal plaza, while the Royal Audiencia and the court of the Inquisition were nearby. There were five principal monasteries, four convents, four hospitals, five parishes, and "a flourishing university well-staffed by doctors, masters and licentiates in all disciplines, with three student colleges." Oré mentioned the "noble caballeros, both those wearing the habit of the military orders or others known as such." There were wealthy merchants and a substantial number of the leaders of various professions. The port of Callao, a commercial hub for all the viceroyalty of Peru, and Mexico too, was teeming with people. There were more than 20,000 slaves, and a "large concourse of Indians." The Rímac River provided water for the canals to power the grist mills and irrigate agricultural fields. There were well-built fountains, fine croplands, and gardens. "It seems this city competes with any other city of its size in the world, and even with some larger ones." Oré's comparison was based on hearsay and reading, but his enthusiasm confirms his desire to portray the viceregal capital in the most attractive light.[4]

We have no drawings of the early monastery of San Francisco of Lima, "El Convento Grande de Jesús," and it is difficult to imagine what it looked like when Luis Gerónimo arrived. The cloisters may have been of local adobe plastered over, with roofs of light timbers covered with baked clay tiles, materials that failed to resist the overwhelming forces of nature: earthquakes and floods. Andean South America, including Lima, is subject to periodic seismic movements. Time after time the city was leveled, yet as a phoenix it rose anew from dust and rubble. Today's general layout of the monastery is comparable to the original, with its vast compound covering several city blocks. Balthasar Ramírez, later chaplain to the viceroy of New Spain, visited the monastery about 1580, and characterized it as "a fine house, with very good rooms and a fine cloister and garden; normally it has from seventy to a hundred friars."[5] There was a kitchen, dining hall, medical dispensary, and storage rooms to handle the needs of friars, novices, servants, and others living and working in the "village" within the city. The best remnants of the original today and what Oré saw when he arrived are some of the imported Sevillian tiles, religious paintings, sculptures, and perhaps parts of the altars.[6] The original structures were severely damaged by an earthquake in the late 1580s. The monastery's financial records of income and expenditures before the end of the eighteenth century are missing, and we have only fragmentary information covering the construction and adornment as the monastic compound grew. A report prepared by architect Friar Miguel de Huerta in 1616–17 warned against opening up new tombs in the church's floor in the area of the main altar, because doing so would weaken the structure's columns. The central nave of the church did collapse in 1656. The building that replaced it would be recognizable today as we see in a drawing prepared in 1684. The Franciscan church and monastery were rebuilt after the 1746 earthquake, one of the most devastating during the colonial period.[7]

The young Oré coincided frequently with Viceroy Toledo while in Peru. After a brief stop on the coast the viceroy entered the highlands, concentrating on three of his major projects: the visita general including its tribute assessment of the entire viceroyalty, the reduction or resettlement of the indigenous population from the countryside into towns, and the final organization of Andean administration. Toledo was in Huamanga before traveling to Cuzco, and in early March 1573 he was in the silver mining city of Potosí, and remained there, or in La Paz, until he continued to Arequipa in August of 1575, where he resided for several months. Toledo finally arrived in Lima at the end of April 1576 and was based there until departing for Spain in late April or early May 1581. While in Lima the viceroy held court almost continuously, and Oré had the opportunity to witness many of his actions, especially during major public events when state and church dignitaries were present.[8]

Francisco de Toledo, called the "Supreme Organizer," transformed administration of the viceroyalty, bringing some stability to a contentious populace. Many of Toledo's actions had a direct impact on Oré during his life. He brought the Inquisition to Peru, and Oré was conscious of its power to censure him if he erred in his writing and teaching. Toledo introduced the Jesuits to Peru, and Oré generally cooperated with them. Toledo also contributed to the foundation of a true university in Lima. A university had been established earlier by Charles V in 1553, thanks to a solicitude of the Dominican Provincial Tomás de San Martín. It was first housed in the Dominican monastery, then transferred briefly to San Marcelo before Toledo provided the university with a permanent site and secured an endowment to support its faculty and programs. Shortly after arriving in Peru, Viceroy Toledo suggested that the university should be separate from the religious orders, and communicated his position to the king. Toledo issued his principal orders in Lima on 3 October 1576. A plot of land had been set aside for the Casa de Recogimiento de San Juan de la Penitencia for mestiza daughters of the conquistadors, and there were only two or three living there, since far more remained with families. It was in Toledo's mind a commodious place to house the university. There was ample space, plenty of water, and land, providing a suitable place where the doctors and the masters of the colleges could read and direct student studies. Toledo endowed the university with 13,000 gold pesos yearly, coming largely from tributes from encomiendas the Crown assumed when the original grant ended. Payments to the various faculties and staff were established. Toledo did provide another residence for the dispossessed mestiza daughters of the conquistadors.

The new foundational date was 25 April 1577. Viceroy Toledo entered the university and there met the rector and doctors, the university council, and many others, including students. If Oré did not attend that momentous day, he certainly heard about it.[9] The University of San Marcos, situated on the edge of the Plaza of the Inquisition, was still under construction when Balthasar Ramírez described it in 1597. At the time there were "chairs of grammar, theology, arts, scriptures, chairs of canon and secular law, medicine and Indian languages, and their annual salaries are 400 silver pesos." Ramírez lamented the original endowment was insufficient for the university to grow and that after Viceroy Toledo's departure no other person or group came to its aid.[10]

The Lima Inquisition's first victim was French Lutheran Mateo Salado in an *auto-de-fé* in 1573 while young Oré was still studying in Cuzco, but he surely witnessed the 1576 execution of Dominican Friar Francisco de la Cruz. Born in Spain, Cruz met in Valladolid Peru's Dominican Provincial Domingo de Santo Tomas and traveled with him to Peru, where he served as doctrinero in Charcas. He was shocked by Viceroy Toledo's removal of the texts of Bartolomé de las Casas and the expulsion of Dominicans from some highland doctrinas. Cruz taught at the University of Lima, where he twice served as rector; he complained about the viceroy's reduction of Dominican influence at the university. Such challenges led to Cruz being ordered to testify to Inquisitors in late 1571. The friar's responses were shocking, seemingly those of a madman, speaking through a bewitched woman who had visions of angels and saints. The friar took on the mantle of a mystic prophet, an alumbrado, and was incarcerated in the Inquisition's secret jail in January 1572 to extract further information. By January 1576 there were 170 charges against him and on 14 July he was sentenced as a heretic, dogmatizer, and teacher of a new sect positioned against the authority of the pope. He was excommunicated and burned at the stake. Pedro Guibovich notes that Viceroy Toledo used his extensive powers to corral the Lascasian supporters of Cruz, while paying close attention to the actions of Dominicans.[11] How did Oré view this process and its consequences? He was cautious in his writings, to avoid possible censure by overzealous Inquisitors, but in his later years excessive caution did not appear to influence dealings with either religious or state administrators.

Other incidents likely left an impression on Oré who was in or near Lima when the English corsair Francis Drake attacked its port of Callao on 13 July 1579. As early as the 1560s Drake, John Hawkins, and other English venturers attacked Spanish ships and outposts in the Circum Caribbean. English investors influenced by Martin Frobisher and other proponents of a sea route to Asia, with the silent acquiescence of Queen Elizabeth I, dispatched a small fleet led by Drake to secretly follow Magellan's route into the Pacific. Drake intended to establish an English base, a New Albion, somewhere along the western North American coast. He planned to fund the venture by capturing treasure, but from its start disasters, including inclement weather and enemy attacks, plagued the fleet. By the time they approached the Rio de la Plata in April 1578, the Spanish king had learned of their progress and alerted Peruvian officials. When Drake, with a reduced fleet of three vessels, arrived at the Strait of Magellan, he renamed his ship the *Golden Hind* and thanks to a shift in the winds, he reached the Pacific around 6 September and continued northward. One of Drake's ships disappeared on the passage and the other returned to England. Drake attacked (5 December) and captured a ship in the port of Valparaíso, taking supplies and silver, but the greatest prizes were the navigational charts of South America's coast and a Spanish pilot whom Drake pressed into service. As Drake sailed northward, he pillaged the poorly defended coastal settlements and seized treasure along the way. By 6 February, the English had reached Arica where they sighted horsemen prepared to defend the town, enough to convince Drake to continue northward.

Coasting, Drake's small fleet captured another ship and received news the treasure ship *Nuestra Señora de la Concepción* was in Lima's port. Arriving around midnight on 13 February 1579 Drake found undefended merchant ships, and by morning he was 1,500 silver ingots richer, plus a chest of silver coins and fine silks, but the ship with the bullion for the Royal Hacienda had already departed for Panama. During interrogations Drake learned that his friend John Oxnam was held prisoner by Viceroy Toledo. Oxnam, independent of Drake, had led the English attack across the Isthmus of Panama, built a ship on the Pacific, sailing southward and capturing two merchant ships before being taken prisoner and sent to Lima for trial. Drake initially decided to hold merchant ships as ransom for Oxnam's release. But Toledo quickly dispatched from Lima a well-armed force that marched to Callao's waterfront. Weighing unfavorable odds, Drake set sail on 14 February to intercept the silver shipment, and he ultimately captured the treasure ship on the high seas near the Cabo de San Francisco in early March 1579. The half million pesos of silver more than covered the expedition's cost. Drake continued northward, inflicting more damage to Spanish shipping along the way, before setting out to cross the Pacific. It was not until 26 September 1580 that the *Golden Hind* returned to Plymouth.[12]

The encroachment of an English heretic—nearing the edge of Potosí's silver mountain whose riches supported Spain's empire and its armies in Europe—was talked about by religious and secular authorities in Peru. Drake's venture caused an immediate reaction because Peru now faced periodic fear of attacks by foreign adversaries. The impact on Oré and other creoles of his generation was significant as they became aware of the challenges of conflict with Spain's enemies and the relation of economic, political, and religious belief systems in an increasingly complex world. How aware of the events and threats were Franciscan novices in Lima? It would have been impossible not to know of Drake's attack, for the entire coastline had advance notice, and preparations for defense were in motion. Lima's cabildo acted quickly when news of the enemy's approach came. The calm of routine meetings of the city council beginning on 1 January 1579 that dealt with various issues ranging from the grain supply, the public slaughterhouse and income sources to licenses and the sad state of the city hall building abruptly stopped between 9 February until 5 March.[13] Drake's attack on Callao on 13 February ushered in a time of crisis. Asleep and ill, Viceroy Toledo and the entire city was awoken at 2 o'clock in the morning by the clanging of church bells. Oré along with other Franciscans would have heard the alarm. The viceroy convoked a *junta* (a special committee) to meet and defend the city and its port. Callao, despite warnings, was unprepared and there was no artillery positioned to repel an invasion. Fortunately, Drake was more interested in taking a treasure ship than risking a land attack on a major city. Over the next days and weeks, the viceroy, audiencia and city council discussed the attack and response, pondering various plans on how to prepare for future attacks. Arguments over who would bear the cost caused delays and repeatedly recommendations were set aside.[14] The foreign threat to Spain and the church, especially by the English, was now imbedded in the mind of Oré and others. Some must have chaffed at the inability of the colonial regime to respond adequately to be ready for the next incursion, whether it be of English, French or Dutch.

By the late 1570s, as Oré was completing his training, Viceroy Toledo—complaining of age and illness—longed to return to his homeland. Philip II appointed as his replacement Martín Enríquez de Almansa, then viceroy of New Spain. After several delays the new viceroy finally arrived in Callao in early May 1581, and within days the new archbishop, Toribio Alfonso de Mogrovejo, arrived.[15] Named in 1580, the archbishop's departure from Spain was smoother than most; delays of months, even years were not uncommon.[16] He had lodged in Seville in the Count of Gelves's palace and on 23 August signed an agreement for the transport and security of his personal and religious objects to Nombre de Dios. Philip II had issued on 24 April 1580 an order giving the archbishop-elect the "fruits of office," a document guaranteeing his income could be used to secure advance loans to ship his goods and to cover other contingencies. Most of the objects Mogrovejo shipped were associated with his professional duties, including an *agnus dei,* a crucifix, an emerald ring, toothpicks (*mondadientes*), two thousand arrobas of olive oil, and a substantial quantity of richly woven cloth for religious vestments.[17]

When Archbishop Mogrovejo approached his destination, Lima's residents witnessed the pomp and ceremony that rivaled the grand entry of the new viceroy. The Cathedral Chapter met the archbishop at Tambillo and escorted him into the city. At the entrance to the San Lazaro neighborhood an arch was erected, and young boys in magnificent garb danced. The streets and buildings along the route were decorated and at the Plaza Mayor members of the city council, church officials, clergy, and the religious welcomed the archbishop, "and with music and cheers he was carried in his litter from there to the cathedral entrance."[18] Oré would have witnessed the archbishop's ceremonial entrance into the city or in the cathedral. Much of Mogrovejo's initial work centered on long-delayed administrative duties. The list of his achievements is formidable: pastoral inspections of the diocese, the convening of the Third Church Council of Lima, and other accomplishments that all contributed to calls for his canonization.[19] It is unknown if there was a personal relationship between the archbishop and the young Franciscan, but it was Mogrovejo who ordained Luis Gerónimo de Oré on Saturday, 23 September 1581, along with other aspirants.[20]

Oré's training at the University of San Marcos focused on the study of philosophy and theology, the religious foundations that were a prerequisite for his church vocation. In addition, he studied canon law and the basics of the legal profession, which prepared him to act as *procurador* (procurator, solicitor) for the Franciscans.[21] On 3 March 1582 Oré was ordained a deacon, the same day as Jesuit Ludovico Bertonio, a speaker of Aymara and a future compiler of grammars and dictionaries.[22] Franciscan chronicler Buenaventura de Salinas y Córdova later (1631) affirmed that Oré was one of the first creole graduates who ultimately became a bishop.[23] Luis Gerónimo was then about twenty-seven years old, at the beginning of a long and fruitful religious career. But before he was assigned to a doctrina other services were placed on his shoulders based on his linguistic abilities, his thorough knowledge of Catholic doctrine, the rulings of the Council of Trent, and his understanding of the cultures of Andean peoples.

❧ 6 ❧

Mogrovejo

THIRD CHURCH COUNCIL OF LIMA
AND THE TRANSLATORS

On 15 August 1581, three months after reaching Lima, Archbishop Mogrovejo convened a church council to be held in the viceregal capital. Such a conference was a challenging endeavor, given the distances to be traversed, sometimes thousands of miles over rugged terrain. Correspondence took months to reach the scattered dioceses over the vast realm of Spanish South America. The bishops' responses took longer, given the reluctance of some to embark on a difficult journey that might remove them from their sees for years. In several cases the diocesan see was vacant, as was true for Panama, which was also under the jurisdiction of the Archdiocese of Lima. The diocese of Paraguay was vacant, but Mogrovejo quickly consecrated Dominican Alfonso Guerra to occupy the seat. Two secular clergy were called to participate: Cuzco Bishop Sebastián de Lartaún, who reached his diocese in 1573, and whom Oré knew from the time of his novitiate. The bishop was accompanied by Cristóbal de Molina, priest in Cuzco's Indian hospital of Los Remedios and author of the *Ritos y fábulas de los Incas*. Oré knew Molina from his novitiate in Cuzco, and given their common interest in indigenous languages, they must have interacted during the council.[1] The other secular, bishop of La Plata Alonso Granero de Avalos attended, as did some members of the ecclesiastical councils from various dioceses. There were two Franciscan bishops—Antonio de San Miguel, bishop of La Imperial in southern Chile, and Diego de Medellín, bishop of Santiago de Chile—who stayed in Lima's monastery. Three Dominican bishops participated: Alfonso Guerra of Paraguay, Pedro de la Peña, bishop of Quito, and Tucumán's Bishop Francisco de Victoria.[2]

A third church council was imperative, requiring incorporation of the acts of the Council of Trent (1545 and 1563), to confront theological challenges posed by the Humanists and by Protestant reformers. The Tridentine decrees were obligatory reading for novices and elder participants who had not yet fully digested the new guidelines. The Lima council also needed to maintain translational conformity of doctrinal texts used by the orders in the doctrinas to avoid confusion. Oré had studied the Indian ordinances issued by Viceroy Toledo in the 1570s, especially those regarding villages created as part of his concept of an ideal "Indian Republic." Many ordinances concerned issues that religious authorities considered strictly within their jurisdiction—the size of parishes, the nature of marriage, the linguistic competence of the doctrineros. Toledo acted under the *Patronato Real* (royal ecclesiastical patronage), the extensive powers bestowed to the Spanish Crown in a series of papal bulls at the time of Columbus's voyages. But some of the viceroy's ordinances contradicted those of the earlier church councils of Lima, and there were inconsistencies in the rulings which raised concerns about their correct application in the field.

The excitement of Lima's religious community was palpable as the bishops with their retinues arrived from the distant dioceses. Civil authorities were equally expectant as there would be numerous religious ceremonies, many requiring their presence. They were also apprehensive because local authorities were expected to assist church council members during months of residence in the viceregal capital. Members of the religious orders would board in their respective monasteries, but accommodating the secular clergy was another matter. Major church councils served various functions, including judicial, acting as a court to try cases involving the clergy. A thorny issue arose immediately, briefly threatening the work of the council. Cuzco's Bishop Lartaún was accused of collaboration in the murder of a church canon and appropriation of some of the victim's properties. Other charges concerned his business dealings. Bishop Lartaún argued that the council lacked jurisdiction in this instance, and initially convinced all but one bishop to support him. The one who persistently pressed for a trial was the Franciscan bishop of La Imperial, Antonio de San Miguel, who soon won over other supporters. Order was restored when Archbishop Mogrovejo decided to send the documents to Rome for review and threatened excommunication of those not falling into line.[3]

The principal task of the bishops and their authorized assistants was to review the decrees of previous church councils of Lima, then those of the Council of Trent and, finally, to agree on a set of directives that would concur with the new requirements. The bishops and their assistants centered attention on the role of the clergy who were expected to set the example of a "Good Christian" to their parishioners. In addition to the relation to and the treatment of women, there were questions concerning proper dress, gambling and engaging in business. The bishops worked tirelessly during the five major sessions. The new rulings varied sharply from the first and second councils, especially in the sections dealing with pre-Christian societal and religious beliefs and customs. The previous church councils of Lima provided a surprising flexibility in permitting some autochthonous practices. Participants in those earlier councils realized they could not change all beliefs and practices too quickly without fomenting rejection and rebellion.

The final decisions of each session needed ratification by the archbishop and bishops, and at the completion all members present signed the documents. Their actions required review and ratification by the monarch and his royal council, as well as the pope and the Congregation of Cardinals. Authorization for printing and distribution of the decrees could then be completed. The process required months, even years. Archbishop Mogrovejo entrusted the Jesuit José de Acosta to act as his solicitor and carry the documentation to Madrid and Rome and to ensure final authorizations. Acosta did not depart immediately, for he and others continued work on the Spanish version of the Catechism and other materials needing translation into Quechua, Aymara, or other indigenous languages. The translations were left to the specialists, including Oré. Acosta perhaps delayed departure to avoid sailing with the fleet carrying Jesuits exiled from Peru who had been processed either by the Inquisition or were dealt with by the Jesuits for positions they had taken or questionable propositions. Some Jesuits blamed Acosta, who was a qualificator (a theologian assigned to review the writings or positions) of the Holy Office, for not providing fellow Jesuits with the defense they deserved.[4]

The rapid succession of published religious texts that are the direct result of the Third Church Council's deliberations is impressive. The first, in 1584, carries the cumbersome title *Doctrina Christiana y Catecismo para instruccion de los indios y de las demas personas que han de ser enseñadas en nuestra sancta fe con un Confessionario y otras cosas necesarias para los que doctrinan*. The text was republished many times in the colonial period. The first edition, set in print by Antonio Ricardo, recently arrived from Mexico, was divided into sections.

The initial text provided the publishing details, including authorizations; it was followed by the trilingual *Doctrina Christiana*, the *Suma de la fe Catolica*, a *Catecismo breve para los rudos y ocupados*, a *Plática breve*, a *Silabario*, and a *Catecismo mayor para los que son más capaces*, and then *Anotaciones o esclios sobre la traducción*. The keys for conversion lie in the two catechisms, the short

Doctrina Christiana y Catecismo, Lima 1584. Title page of *Doctrina Christiana y catecismo para instruccion de los indios*. Lima: Antonio Ricardo, 1584. Courtesy of the John Carter Brown Library. CC BY 4.0.

one for the initial converts, or those still with imperfect knowledge of church doctrine, and the second directed toward those well conditioned to become part of the new religious order.

The following year Antonio Ricardo printed an equally hefty text that covered gaps remaining for the religious to use in their ministry: *Confessionario para los curas de indios, con la Instrucción contra sus ritos y Exhortacion para ayudar a bien morir, y Suma de sus privilegios, y forma de Impedimientos del matrimonio*. This work, later printed in the original trilingual, or separately in Quechua or Aymara editions, served as a manual for the religious still struggling to improve their own skills in Andean languages. The part stressing the need for the clergy to understand indigenous religious belief and practice well enough to accurately probe the confessants, is influenced by the writings of Polo Ondegardo. A third Ricardo volume published in Lima in 1585 completes the principal work of the Lima council: *Tercero cathecismo y exposicion de la doctrina christiana, por sermones: para que los curas y otros ministros prediquen y enseñen a los yndios y a las demas personas conforme a lo que en el Sancto Concilio Provincial de Lima se proueyo*. A key purpose of this trilogy was to provide uniformity for religious indoctrination and instruction for the new converts. There were numerous manuscript versions of the catechisms floating around, and it was a priority for the Church to have one standard text compliant with the mandates of the Council of Trent. The 1585 *Tercero Cathecismo* . . . included the "Order that in these kingdoms no other Catechism or Confessional will be used . . . , and that all who will be serving in the doctrinas will have the said Catechism, Confessional and Sermons."[5] Jesuit historian Francisco Mateos states explicitly that "the translation of the two general languages of the Indians, Quichua and Aymara, were done by Father Alonso de Barzana, assisted by the Fathers Blas Valera and Bartolome de Santiago, both were mestizos; the grammars and dictionaries are also done by Father Barzana, who has been preparing these linguistic works from the time of the Provincial Congregation of 1576."[6] Mateos's assertion is misleading; the translations were done by a heterogeneous group of religious linguists.

Blas Valera (1544–1597) is one of the most controversial Jesuits of the period. Much of the information on his life and writings has been destroyed or hidden during investigations of fornication and his religious thought by the Inquisition. Valera was born in Chachapoyas, studied in Trujillo, and became the first Jesuit mestizo in the Andes, shortly after the arrival of the order in Peru. From

1570 he served in various highland locales as a teacher and translator from the Audiencia of Lima to Potosí. He wrote and translated vociferously, but it is almost impossible to determine if he "borrowed" from others. Virtually all his texts are missing, and we have only parts integrated into Inca Garcilaso de la Vega's *Comentarios reales de los Incas,* and some manuscripts that were used in the work of Giovanni Anello Oliva and Fernando de Montesinos. Shortly after the Third Church Council, Valera was examined by the Inquisition and later held by the Jesuits for four years, followed by house arrest until 1594, when he was sent to Spain, where he died in 1597. Various texts were attributed to Valera, and some may have been forged. There is no doubt that Valera was one of the translators of the Christian doctrine and other religious texts for use in conversion of the Andeans. Other translators at the Third Church Council took the same course, but there was strong resistance by many theologians who reviewed the texts, arguing that indigenous words should not be used for the word of God, the Holy Trinity, and so forth. Sabine Hyland stresses Blas Valera's intentions to guarantee the true meaning of Andean words or phrases that were proper definitions of Christian concepts. Valera's definitions often exceeded what Christian theologians accepted. In one case he wrote that Viracocha was the equivalent of Christ.[7] The debate continues. Alan Durston has questioned the attribution to and veracity of Valera as author of the *Relación de las costumbres antiguas de los naturales del Pirú* that Hyland used.[8]

Historians often attribute authorship of the final version of the texts of the Third Church Council of Lima to Jesuit José de Acosta. The fact that the commission met in the Jesuit College led many to assume the council was solely a Jesuit undertaking, and Acosta did carry a copy of the *Decrees of the Third Church Council* to the king and the pope. Cardinal Alejandro Perelli de Montalto sent a letter to Archbishop Mogrovejo from Rome in October of 1588, reporting that Pope Sixtus V met with Father Acosta. At the meeting Acosta delivered both the decrees and a letter from Archbishop Mogrovejo. The pope sent the decrees to be reviewed, and after adjustments the examiners verified that the work met the guidelines established by the Council of Trent.[9] Indeed, Acosta was the strongest voice in concluding theological arguments in Lima sessions, and he shepherded the decrees through the labyrinth of the royal and papal bureaucracies. He was the facilitator, but not the sole individual responsible for the results of the council. In his letter (Madrid, 23 April 1589) to Fernando de Vega y Fonseca, president of the Council of the Indies, Acosta pressed for authorization to print the decrees. In a meeting with the president, Acosta detailed what had transpired in Rome. He noted that after the Lima council reached its conclusion, "because everywhere there was displeasure with the reform of the customs, some of the clergy rebelled and brought suit against the bishops, even placing appeals" and they forced a review by the Royal Council. With additional minor modification Philip II, with the advice of the council, sent the document to Rome for confirmation. There the Congregation of Cardinals examined the texts and after a few modifications recommended enactment. Acosta asked for an order to be issued to print immediately. Philip II finally granted authorization in the Escorial on 18 September 1591. The intention was to distribute copies to all the diocesan churches in the Archdiocese of Peru.[10]

Acosta's role in successfully guiding the results of the Third Church Council of Lima through the maze of the Spanish and Vatican bureaucracies is admirable. But the other half of the Lima council's endeavor was to provide a translation of a body of religious texts for use in the doctrinas. Translations were a joint effort. Archbishop Mogrovejo established a commission composed of members of the religious orders in Peru: Dominicans, Franciscans, Mercedarians, Augustinians, and Jesuits. Given the several hundred pages covering all the elements needed for successful work in the doctrinas, in three languages, the most convincing attribution for authorship is *the Commission,* its participants toiling jointly. Historians continue to debate who was most important in the preparation of the translations. Each order has its proponents, and religious chroniclers stress the contributions of their own order, often ignoring the work of the others.

In sheer numbers the Dominicans dominated the assembly. Whatever their affiliation, all participants would reflect on the contribution of Domingo de Santo Tomás, whose foundational dictionary and grammar in Spanish and Quechua were published in 1560.[11] Similar to Bartolomé de las Casas, he was born in Seville and professed in the Colegio of San Pablo (1520); the two men frequently corresponded. Santo Tomás sailed with other Dominicans to Peru in 1540 and in Lima helped found the University of San Marcos. He was the first to hold the Chair of *Prima Teologia.* Late in 1555 he returned to Spain to recruit new missionaries, report on conditions in Peru, and publish his work that was already circulating in the Andean doctrinas in manuscript form. With the printing of fifteen hundred copies of the two volumes in 1560, he was ready to return to Peru, arriving in 1562. When the Bishop of Charcas died, Philip II presented Domingo de Santo Tomás as his replacement; he was consecrated by Archbishop Jerónimo de Loayza in 1563. After participating in the Second Church Council of Lima in 1567, Santo Tomás returned to his diocese, where he died on 28 February 1570. Although his dictionary and grammar were widely consulted, they centered on the language and its varying dialects he learned in a limited region from coastal Chicama to Chincha and highland Conchucos to Huaylas.[12] By the time of the Third Church Council it was clear that the narrow texts of Santo Tomás required replacement.

Various Quechua and Aymara catechisms in manuscript form circulated in the years prior to the Third Church Council. Each order used their favorite version. These texts must have been reviewed in the Third Church Council and then integrated into the final catechism.[13] Oré followed the deliberations of the council, either by being present or by hearing reports brought back to his monastery. Meals were eaten communally as the friars sat in a great hall and listened to the evening's lecturer. One would expect the two Franciscans who attended the sessions on a more regular basis, Commissioner Jerónimo de Villacarrillo and Marcos Jofré, guardian of Lima's monastery, would have spoken.[14] Likewise the reports of the Franciscan bishop of La Imperial, Antonio de San Miguel, must have been contemplated. He was among the more active bishops in the sessions. Born in Spain in 1521 he traveled to Peru around 1550 and eventually became the guardian of the Franciscans in Cuzco and was a founder of the hospital in Cuzco. By this time, he became a key proponent for protection of the Amerindians and argued for restitution to those victimized by the encomenderos and others. In 1563 San Miguel was named as the first bishop of La Imperial in southern Chile but did not reach his post until 1568. He inspected his diocese between 1571 and 1574, and quickly learned the depth of the conflict between the Spanish and the Mapuche. Bishop San Miguel consistently argued that the only solution was by negotiation and peaceful coexistence, a position military officials and settlers resisted. Working closely with Archbishop Mogrovejo during the Third Church Council, he was a strong advocate for justice for the Amerindians and punishment of clergy and civic officials who strayed outside the bounds of Christian teaching. Oré learned much from his example and followed a similar path when, decades later, he became bishop of La Imperial.[15]

The oldest Franciscan participating in the council was Diego de Medellín, bishop of Santiago de Chile, born in 1496. Medellín arrived in Peru around 1545 in the era of the Gonzalo Pizarro revolt. He completed doctoral studies in Lima at the University of San Marcos. Medellín was Guardian in the Lima convent in 1564 and participated in the Second Church Council in 1567–1568. In 1573 Philip II presented him as Santiago de Chile's bishop; his appointment was finalized by a 1577 papal bull. A staunch defender of the indigenous, Medellín once remarked that the so-called legal "*defensores de indios*" were more their "*destructores.*" On his return to Chile after the Third Council, the indefatigable bishop ordered the Catechism to be translated into Mapuche.[16]

Oré played a role in the Third Council, especially in the translation commission. According to Rolena Adorno, Guaman Poma de Ayala, in his section on the Third Church Council, named some of the churchmen who participated in the sessions. Adorno suggests Guaman Poma might have been there and perhaps was consulted as one of the translators too. Or he learned from others as he was compiling his massive letter to the king. Adorno points out: "Yet his references to one of the council's principal theologians, the Jesuit José de Acosta, as well as to Luis Jerónimo de Oré, a Franciscan priest from Huamanga, and the secular priest and author Miguel Cabello de Balboa, evoke them not as persons whom he had met or worked for but rather as authors of the books they had written (and therefore he has read)."[17] Alan Durston doubts that Oré was active in the council, suggesting he was too young and that he was not named in the records of the council. Yet there is additional evidence confirming Oré's participation.[18]

Oré, conversant in the languages and cultures of the Andean highlands, and well aware he was destined to serve in the Franciscan doctrinas, closely followed developments that would likely impact his future work. He knew the regulations of the two previous Lima councils and the steps necessary to modify them based on changing conditions. According to later testimony of fellow Franciscans in Lima, Oré, whose thorough knowledge of Quechua and Aymara was well known among his peers, participated as translator in the Third Church Council. In 1620 Friar Diego Sánchez, who as we saw earlier knew Luis Gerónimo and his family well, told the chronicler Córdova y Salinas, "When they held the Lima Council one of those assigned to prepare the catechism and sermons and other things the Council had mandated for the doctrine of the Indians, was Father Friar Luys [*sic*] de Oré, and afterward he composed a book in the language of the Indians which is used by almost all the doctrineros in this kingdom."[19] Another friar corroborated Sánchez's testimony. Friar Bernabé de Fuentes testified that "in a Provincial Council that was celebrated in this city, they strongly agreed that the Christian doctrine should be translated into the vulgar languages of the Indians so that they could learn it with more facility and dominion. Friar Luis Gerónimo de Oré was one of those named to take part in it and he worked hard and did great service to Our Lord. It continues in print along with many other works that the said Friar Gerónimo de Oré has published."[20]

Around 1901 a researcher located a document at the Archivo Arzobispal in Lima. It listed the theologians participating in the Third Church Council of Lima and their status.[21] It is part of a package of papers prepared by the Conciliar Secretary Licentiate Bartolomé Martínez Menacho on 25 July 1583. The document is titled *Teologos Consultores del Concilio* and it names those who were summoned to attend the sessions of the council. In the first place were those with status of "Título Permanente," the provincials of the religious orders: Dominican Bartolomé de Ledesma, Franciscan Juan del Campo, Mercedarian Alonso Enríquez de Almendáriz, Augustinian Luis López de Solís, Jesuit Baltasar de Piñas, and Lima's Cathedral Canon Doctor Antonio de Molina. Others called to participate were clerics on the Royal Council, select priests and chaplains and, "mostly, the religious and creole doctrineros or '*lenguaraces*' [someone who knows several languages] of any community or title." It is in the list of priests conversant in indigenous languages that we find "Fr. Luis Jerónimo de Oré, franciscano y natural de Huamanga." [22]

As the men labored for weeks to prepare the religious texts that were authorized and published, they established lasting relationships in some cases. As in all groups there were disputes during their deliberations, which may have led to lifetime animosity. Oré was acquainted with Franciscan Provincial Juan del Campo (1527–1584), a respected theologian, strong in defense of the Andeans and the religious orders on issues relating to the Patronato Real, a position Oré championed during his career. Campo also served on Viceroy Toledo's commission to prepare the Indian *Ordenanzas*, and throughout his career traveled extensively. He was buried in the Franciscan monastery in Lima and Jesuit José de Acosta "pronounced the oration during the funeral rites."[23] It is possible Luis Gerónimo de Oré was present.

Oré's closest associate during the council may have been Hernando Trejo de Sanabria, a Franciscan with a similar background. Both were born in 1554 to

PRIESTS AND INDIAN TEACHERS			
Don Juan de la Roca	Doctor	Lima	Student, University of Lima
Fr. Alonso Pacheco	Augustinian	Lima	Student, Colegio San Ildefonso
Fr. Francisco Maldonado	Mercedarian	Cuzco	—
Fr. Gaspar de Villarroel	Augustinian	Quito	Student, Colegio San Ildefonso
Fr. Luis Gerónimo de Oré	Franciscan	Huamanga	—
Fr. Hernando Trejo de Sanabria	Franciscan	Paraguay, Asunción	—
Fr. Antonio de la Parra	Dominican	Loxa, Quito	Student, Colegio San Ildefonso
Fr. Alonso de la Cerda	Dominican	Lima	Student, Colegio San Ildefonso
Fr. Salvador de la Ribera	Dominican	Lima	Student, Colegio San Ildefonso
Fr. Bernardino de Cárdenas Ponce	Franciscan	La Paz	—
Juan Pérez Menacho	Jesuit	Lima	Priest
Fr. Domingo de Valderrama	Dominican	Quito	Student, Colegio San Ildefonso
Don Carlos Marcelo Corne	Cleric	Trujillo, Peru	Student, Colegio San Martín

Source: Jesús Viscarra Fabre, *Copacabana de los Incas. Documentos auto-ligüisticos e isografiados del Aymáru-Aymára* (Laz Paz: Palza Hermanos, 1901), ftn. 40, 28–29.

elite Spanish settlers—Trejo in a small settlement in an area between Paraguay and Brazil, or in the city of Asunción. Young Trejo was sent to Lima to study in the Franciscan colegio and was ordained in 1576. In 1589 he was elected the order's provincial, the first creole graduate of the University of San Marcos to hold this post. Philip II named him bishop of Tucumán in 1592 where he remained until his death in 1614.[24] In 1590 Provincial Trejo would be directly involved in the controversial removal of Franciscan friars from their doctrinas. His position was in conflict with that of Oré, as we will see later in the text.

Another participant of the Third Church Council, Mercedarian Provincial Alonso Enríquez de Almendáriz, was one of the Teólogos Consultores del

Concilio. Enríquez de Almendáriz and Oré coincided not just in Lima but in places as diverse as Rome, Andalusia, and Cuba. One of the principal missions of the Mercedarian Order was freeing Christian captives taken and enslaved by North African corsairs.[25] Mercedarians were well equipped to travel, communicate in multiple languages, and execute substantial monetary transfers. Enríquez de Almendáriz, born in Seville in 1551, had reached the Americas by 1574, was a doctrinero in Chuquiabo (in today's Bolivia) and in 1578 he was assigned to inspect the diocese of Quito, then went from Puerto Viejo to Manta and was next assigned Comendador of Cali in southern Colombia, before becoming Comendador of Trujillo, bringing him nearer Lima.[26] During the Third Church Council, Enríquez de Almendáriz reviewed and approved theological rulings. Throughout his long career, he traveled several times between the Indies and Spain, and on 1 November 1610 the king named him Bishop of Cuba. Before embarking on his journey, Enríquez de Almendáriz finalized the paperwork for travel to the Indies at the Casa de la Contratación in Seville. There is a strong possibility that Enríquez de Almendáriz and Oré met while in Spain, probably not for the first time, because Oré was just completing research into the Andalusian youth of Francisco Solano and beginning his recruitment of missionaries for La Florida, then under the diocese of Cuba.[27]

The church in the Indies was not of a single voice. There was a wide divergence of viewpoints, and during the sessions of the Third Church Council of Lima heated arguments and animosity were manifest. Yet in the end Archbishop Mogrovejo adroitly brought the council to a successful close. Important reforms were instituted to improve the quality of the clergy, to limit their economic activities, to make certain they or substitutes were available to perform the sacraments, to maintain higher standards of behavior, and to ensure the doctrineros knew the language of their charges. Oré's participation in the activities of the Third Church Council had an impact on the friar's subsequent religious and civic life. The participants were both creoles and peninsulares and although their ages varied, it did not impact their contributions, especially in translations into indigenous languages. There was a sense of purpose as the council began, and a concern for success. Many of the men Oré met at the council were already or would become major figures of the church in following decades, and the relationships Oré developed in Lima would be relevant to future interactions on three continents. The stage was now set, and Oré was prepared to begin his mission as a doctrinero in the Andean highlands.

II

Franciscan Doctrinero in the Field

7

Franciscan Dilemmas

From the beginning of their presence in the New World the Franciscans were of two minds. On the one hand, some friars wished to follow their Rule as laid out at the foundation of the order: an austere life of prayer, charity, and service based not on rich endowments, but rather on alms to sustain a simple existence. As Julia McClue points out, the actions of Franciscans in the Americas and into Asia were predicated on foundations established in the thirteenth century, based on the life and teachings of St. Francis and his followers. Francis's position resembled that of the earlier Spirituals who rejected the material world, stressed poverty, and rejected the role of the papacy. The Spirituals challenged the official church, believing it was filled with greed and corruption and was not needed for salvation. Whereas some Spirituals were burned as heretics, Francis tied his teaching closely to the Gospels and avoided a direct challenge to the papacy. In 1223 he secured approval for the Franciscan Rule by papal bull (*Regula bullata*). Francis was strict on the rule of poverty and rejected property, seeing it as the source of evil. Nor did he view the convent as something to possess and embellish. The Franciscan theologian Bonaventure of Bignoreggio, Minister-General from 1257–74, wrestled with the issue of material things and postulated there were four categories of temporal goods: ownership, possession, usufruct, and simple use. For the Franciscans the simple use was most appealing because it came closer to their ideal. In 1279 Pope Nicholas III solved for a time the issue (*Exit qui seminat*) whereby the papacy "owned" on behalf of the Franciscans.

For Franciscans, movement from place to place as the early apostles was the ideal way to avoid being encumbered by property. The New World would later provide, especially initially, Franciscans the opportunity to replicate their vision of the lives of the apostles, traveling from place to place, surviving by the goodwill and gifts of food and drink given by the peoples they encountered as they brought the Christian message, or so they thought. Not all followers agreed, and given the almost democratic structure of decision-making there were disputes and fragmentation. Unfortunately for the Franciscans, in a papal bull of 1323 (*Cum inter nonnullos*) Pope John XXII denied the poverty of Jesus, and the next year, condemned the position of the order (*Ad conditorem cannonum*), and forced the Franciscans to accept the ownership of property. But the link uniting the Franciscans was their stress on poverty. In 1517 the papacy issued *Ite vos*, confirming the split between the Conventual Franciscans, who were under the Minister-General, and the more rigorous Observant Franciscans under the Vicar-General. The Franciscans in Spain tended to be more aligned with the original example of Francis, and by 1502 "houses of recollection" had been established by rigorous "ermetic Franciscans." These isolated monasteries provided space for meditation and were scattered in Andalusia, as Oré discovered during his research on the youth of Francisco Solano.[1]

Guided by the teachings of St. Francis, friars during the early years of the order were compelled by the idea of the Second Coming and the scriptural mandate to bring everyone under the Christian fold before the Last Judgement. The Americas provided massive numbers of peoples who required conversion, an opportunity for the religious orders since there were too few secular priests to meet the need. As the church and Crown surveyed the substantial number of religious available in the monasteries scattered throughout Spain, they chose to tap into this pool to assist in conversion and pacification. The Franciscans recruited for the Indies reached the Andes a decade or more after Mesoamerica. That prior experience provided a cautionary tale for their efforts among the peoples of Andean South America. While adequate documentary records for Mexico exist, our knowledge of the first generation of Franciscans in the Andes is meager and comes tainted through the lens of hagiographic scripts. Several of the initial friars reaching Peru had served among the Nahua and Maya and were aware of the pitfalls. For over two decades after the capture and execution of Atahualpa the religious faced indigenous resistance in addition to internal strife between early settlers fighting over the spoils of conquest. As a result, early conversions were hasty and superficial. The Inca for decades before European arrival subjugated dozens of ethnic entities practicing their own beliefs. Subjugation required acceptance of Inca political and religious superiority, but not rejection of ethnic belief systems. Andeans expected the same from the Spanish, that conquest required acceptance of the cult of the conqueror, and simultaneously continuation of their original belief systems. The autochthonous attitude frustrated the Franciscans, and many were disappointed by the uneven results of their work to implant a faith untainted by deep rooted Andean concepts.[2]

Just as there was internal debate over the role of the order in the New World, so too there was the question of the appropriateness of using mendicant friars instead of secular clergy to bring Christianity to the Amerindians. The evangelical Franciscans stressed the need to valiantly propagate the faith, and extolled the reward of martyrdom. Friars who committed to teaching the Catholic doctrine were generally more dedicated than seculars to their principles and the need to be well versed in indigenous languages. The secular clergy later argued the opposite. The religious orders, especially at first, received the support of both Crown and Councils. Expenses were less for the friars than the seculars and more importantly, there was initially an insufficient number of seculars to minister to the scattered, isolated villages.[3]

The Franciscan order held regular general chapter meetings to assess the status and progress of their work. Houses that could send representatives did, while others, too far distant, sent reports. One of the earliest chapter meetings that included reports from friars in Peru was held in Toulouse in May of 1532. It was at this session that German Friar Nicholas Herborn was elected General Commissioner for the Order in much of northern and western Europe, as well as the Spanish and Portuguese Indies. While in Toulouse, General Commissioner Herborn collected information directly from friars or from reports, and wrote a letter to Franciscans in Cologne about the American missions, intending to recruit other friars. While early, the letter points to the Crown's interest in engaging the Franciscans as part of royal policy to extend the realm overseas. "The Emperor has commanded that no religious other than Franciscans of the Observance should go to these peoples for they [the Franciscans] do not possess gold or silver and even, according to their rule of life, they own nothing."[4]

Juan Focher's work provided a useful guide and rationale for Franciscans to invest their talent in the missions of the New World. His *Itinerario de Misionero en America,* printed in Seville in 1574 by Friar Diego Valadés, would have been available to novices and friars in the Andes shortly thereafter. Focher solved the persistent problem of worldly possessions, by arguing that money was initially a necessity as friars traveled in the New World. Further, worldly possessions and money were legitimate because there was scriptural proof in the Gospels, especially if they were held in common, as was true during the early efforts in the Americas. Focher pointed to the indigenous communities as an example, arguing that they shared what they had with all, thus resembling the Franciscan ideal. Unfortunately, the practice legitimized religious expropriation and administration of indigenous goods, and was condemned by Dominican Friar Bartolomé de las Casas and most other Franciscans. In Mexico Franciscan Friar Bernardino de Sahagún, for example, viewed America as a Garden of Eden where there was no property and all shared and lived in a state of innocence and natural law, as did Christ and the apostles.[5]

It was only later that Franciscans began collecting systematic testimony on their history in Peru, and it was as much the result of external prodding as it was for their own interest. Coinciding with the Third Church Council of Lima, the order's General Francesco (Annibalae) Gonzaga sent a request from Spain to the Franciscan monasteries around the globe to provide information on their activities, past and current. Gonzaga was preparing a general history of the order, especially in the Indies, and indicated the reports were for a manuscript, "*De origine ordinis Serafici.*" The final four volumes, printed in 1587, carried the title *De origine Seraphicae Religionis*. . . .[6] Franciscans in Lima complied at least partly, and sent their report to Spain and Rome in 1585.

Oré must have heard older friars speak of the experiences of the earliest Franciscans as they discussed the report before it was sent to Gonzaga. Four decades after the Franciscans arrived much had been either forgotten or embellished, but the report informed Oré and other friars of the Franciscan endeavors and their impact in the previous decades. Oré would have searched for any information on Franciscan work in the Colca Valley, for by 1585 he expected an assignment there. According to testimony, the first Franciscans reached the Colca Valley around 1544. The report portrays Friar Juan de Monzón as a "saintly vagabond," traveling from province to province, instructing the Andeans in unlikely spots, often in the open air in modest plazas of the small population clusters scattered throughout the realm, or in *tambos,* the way stations constructed in Inca times. The Franciscans sought to emulate Christ (*imitatio Christi*) and by preaching outdoors they were consciously recreating in their New World missions the experience of the early Christian church. Chronicler Córdova y Salinas related that Monzón converted countless Andeans and burned and destroyed idols and huacas. Perhaps Monzón was invited to the

Colca Valley at the beginning of the 1540s by encomenderos required by royal decrees to bring Christianity to their tributaries.[7] Monzón was accompanied by Friar Juan de Chaves, who according to the history of the order, "walked daily long distances, because he was extremely poor . . ., with this apostolic zeal he baptized with his own hands in the Pacajes, Collaguas and Cajamarca provinces more than ninety thousand souls."[8]

The exact nature of the introduction of Christianity in the Colca Valley is shrouded in mystery, but the Franciscan doctrinas there were formally organized in 1561. Friar Jerónimo de Villacarrillo, who Oré knew from his novitiate, had traveled to Peru with Friars Monzón and Chaves. Villacarrillo was a vocal opponent of Gonzalo Pizarro, leader of the revolt of the encomenderos, whose commander, Francisco de Carvajal, threatened to strangle the outspoken friar to silence him. According to a Franciscan witness, the Collaguas hid Villacarrillo to protect him around 1547. After he became General Commissioner of the order in Peru in 1560, he named four Franciscans to initiate a permanent mission in the Colca Valley. The doctrineros were directed by Friar Pedro de los Ríos. Coporaque, a principal Inca center in the valley, was the first seat of Franciscan activities.[9]

The Franciscan presence in select provinces in the early years seemed more permanent by the mid-1550s and became more firmly institutionalized in the next decade. Steven Wernke has located and excavated some of the chapels and small churches of the Colca Valley constructed prior to Viceroy Toledo's consolidation of dozens of hamlets into larger doctrinas. Wernke points out that five sites were significant for Inca religious and administrative matters, but only Yanque and Corporaque were left after the Toledo *reducciones* (re-settlements). In both cases the larger new churches, with the edifices on the central plaza of the village, were constructed on top of Inca or earlier ceremonial sites.[10] By the time Oré began work in the doctrinas in the 1580s, little remained of the earlier Christian religious structures. According to Franciscan chronicler Diego de Mendoza, Franciscan efforts in the Collaguas began to bear fruit in the 1560s. The monastery of Yanque and the doctrinas of Coporaque, Achoma, and Chivay, as well as Callalli, with the doctrinas of Tuti, Tisco, and Sibayo, were founded. Conversions accelerated as the majority of the people were baptized and married. The prominent physical symbols of the ancient beliefs—the funerary mummy bundles, the idols, the *apachitas*—were destroyed by the early Spaniards, but the majestic volcanic peaks of Collaguata and Hualca Hualca—the mythical origin of the Collaguas and the Cabanas ethnic groups—remained untouched by the cross of the intruders.[11]

Yet despite externals, the permanency of the doctrinas was a festering issue within the Franciscan order. Personal positions waivered, and Franciscans in the field knew success would ultimately result in their removal from the doctrinas and a return to cloistered life. Initial moves in this direction came in 1560 when General Commissioner Luis Zapata took steps to return friars to their monasteries, unleashing profound discontent. Friar Juan de Revenga, who arrived in Peru around 1546, became so indignant that he wrote the monarch. In his letter (25 June 1566) he complained about the unfolding crisis and emphasized the intensity of disagreement as friars debated their order's role in the Andean world. Revenga complained that after Zapata arrived, he "sowed discord and fire, in such manner that there is much grief," and lamented that "[before] the friars were essential in all, working hard planting the doctrine..., requiring great effort and sweat." Moreover, Zapata shamefully aimed barbs at "honorable" missionary friars. Revenga called Zapata "a wolf... in sheep's skin" and charged that he was "robbing all the older friars who were here of their honor and reputation." Revenga urged the king to aid the earliest friars, those with the best command of indigenous languages, and asked him to order that they be returned to the doctrinas.[12]

Franciscan Commissioner Villacarrillo, who had initially supported the friars' work in the doctrinas, in 1569 decided the task in many provinces was complete and recalled the Franciscans to the cloistered life of prayer and contemplation.[13] The indigenous people were unaware of the historic nature of the order, and as the Franciscans were abandoning Cajamarca doctrinas to transfer them to the seculars there was an outcry from the populace. By coincidence as the move was underway the newly appointed Viceroy Toledo arrived at the port of Paita on the north coast. Distraught Cajamarca Indians sent a delegation to express their grievances and press for the return of the friars. Once Toledo reached Lima, he went to the Franciscan monastery and conducted an inquiry. Moved by the testimony, he ordered the friars to be returned for as long as necessary to secure a complete and convincing conversion.[14]

The Franciscan work in the Andean doctrinas was disrupted again in 1581, the year Viceroy Toledo returned to Spain, when General Commissioner Villacarrillo again recalled the friars to their convents. The Andean doctrinas, especially those with significant populations and material resources, were appealing to the secular clergy. Collection of the fees for sacraments provided an incentive for unscrupulous clerics. The Collaguas doctrinas were especially rich, and the seculars fought to gain them for themselves. What happened in the viceroyalty of Peru followed the pattern set in central Mexico. Conflict between the seculars and religious was less pronounced in places where the size and wealth of the indigenous populations were reduced and had no appeal for the seculars.

The arrival of the new viceroy, Martín Enríquez, along with the almost simultaneous appearance of Archbishop Mogrovejo, provided a window of opportunity for Commissioner Villacarrillo. His declarations were surely debated in Franciscan monasteries throughout Peru, especially in Lima, where Oré was at the time. The lack of adequate record-keeping by the Franciscans leaves much to speculation, but the debates within the cloistered halls continued, sometimes whispered, at other times openly discussed. Far from Lima events taking place in the Andean countryside soon impacted the Franciscans as well as the viceregal court, the Audiencia, and the archbishop. The voice of the Andean peoples could be heard even across the Atlantic at court and in the Council of the Indies. Complaints against abuses by the secular clergy who assumed Franciscan doctrinas came quickly and were strong enough to elicit a royal response to the entreaties of the indigenous.

It is in this context that Oré was assigned to serve in the Colca Valley. The choice to send the young friar to the Collaguas was not accidental. Oré had legal training and could act, if necessary, as procurator representing the Franciscans. That qualification proved useful throughout his life. When he reached the valley, he immediately faced the challenges of seculars who refused to give up their lucrative doctrinas despite orders from the Crown on behalf of indigenous residents. It would require months, leading into years before Oré, as an effective procurator, could maneuver successfully through the defiance of the seculars.

The rich Colca Valley, located between Cuzco and Arequipa, was known as the *corregimiento* (Indian province) of Los Collaguas. Although the geographical boundaries of the first Indian grants to settlers were imprecise, by the time of Pedro de la Gasca's division and tribute assessment in 1549 the province was shared by five Spanish encomenderos, each with his own tributaries. Francisco Pizarro granted as encomienda the demographically and agriculturally rich upper half of the Colca River section to his brother Gonzalo in early 1540. The lower parts had been distributed to other encomenderos

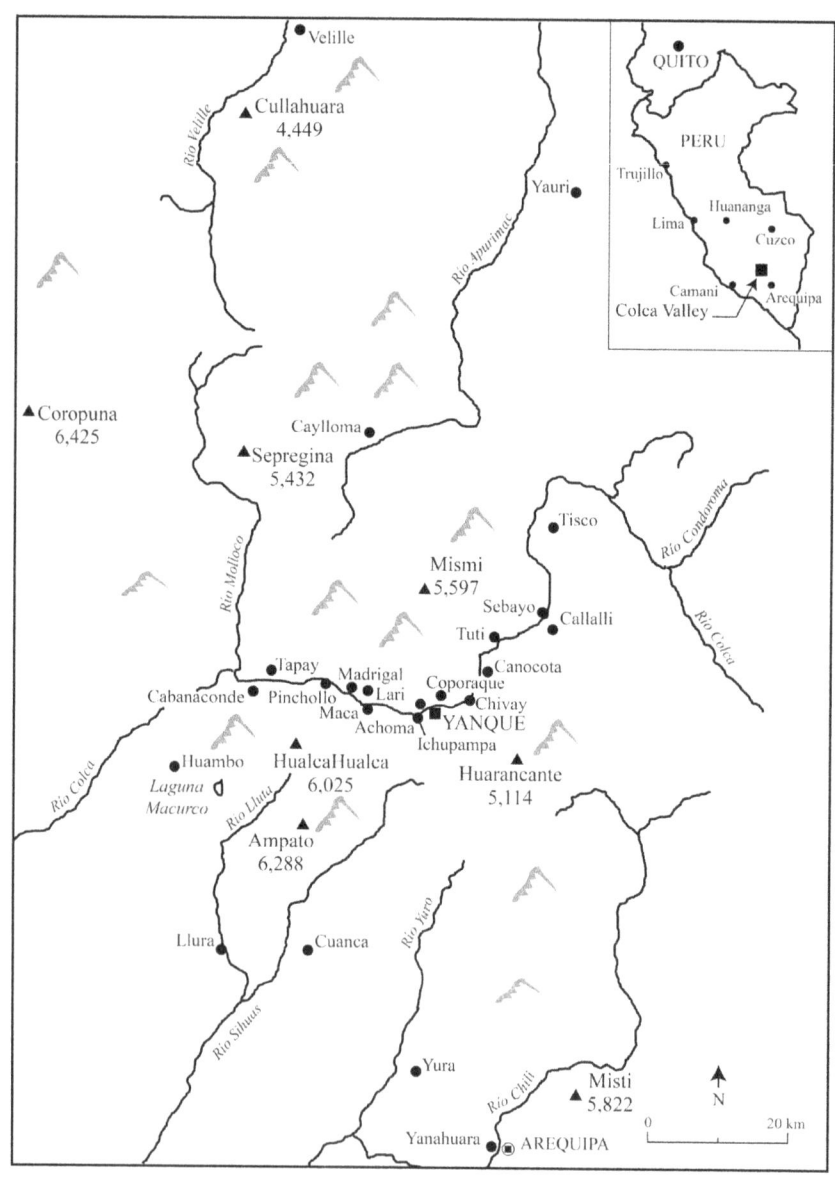

Arequipa to Caylloma, the Colca Valley doctrinas

earlier. Following the unsuccessful revolt against the New Laws of 1542, Gonzalo Pizarro lost his valuable encomiendas, land, city properties, mines, and his head.[15] His encomienda of Yanque Collaguas was stripped from him and his heirs and granted to Francisco Noguerol de Ulloa for his services to the Crown in the conflict. But Noguerol had his own legal problems, including charges of bigamy and illegal shipment of silver to Spain. He returned to Spain in the mid-1550s to face justice and never went back to Peru. After a period of imprisonment and a series of trials, he settled with his second wife in Medina del Campo. During these years he continued to collect tribute from his encomienda of Yanque Collaguas and assets in Arequipa. That ended when Viceroy Toledo took over the grant and incorporated it into the Crown.[16]

The Colca valley with its rich agricultural resources and the puna above supported an ample population. There were earlier descriptions and rough counts of the tributaries, but the first detailed and trustworthy evidence comes from Viceroy Toledo's 1570s general inspection and tribute assessment. The corregidores simultaneously implemented Toledo's policy of *reducciones*, the forced resettlement of indigenous people into Spanish-style villages. By then the Franciscans served several doctrinas in the upper valley from their initial headquarters in the village of Coporaque. The new towns were laid out in a Renaissance-style gridiron pattern: a central plaza with a church (and monastery in this case) on one side, and the house of the chief administrative official, the corregidor, on another. Streets and the town blocks were of similar dimensions, and the compounds with homes and agricultural structures, as well as an open space within the walls for cooking, were comparable. The houses were constructed of local stone, some volcanic in origin, and their roofs were covered with thatch. Fresh water was carried in channels from either the Colca River, or most commonly in the valley, from springs and streams formed by melting ice on the high Andean peaks towering above.[17]

The doctrina was the basic administrative unit for conversion and indoctrination of indigenous villagers throughout Hispanic America and varied in the number of parishioners and in geographic extent. Both doctrineros and Spanish settlers believed that with proper instruction, Christianity would be firmly implanted. The ancestral beliefs of the Andeans had to be torn out and eradicated as rapidly and completely as possible. The propagators of the faith conducted their work with fervor, initially relying on mass baptisms, then constructing churches, often on the sites of indigenous shrines. Conversion of the

Andean peoples, even if superficial, was achieved in a single generation, or at least some so argued.[18]

The task of Christianization of the indigenous population of the Colca Valley was shared by the secular clergy and the religious orders. Initially, Franciscans were in the upper part of the valley and the secular clergy were concentrated in the lower part, in the two encomiendas composed of largely the Cabanas ethnicity. The cleric was to receive "payment" of three *fanegas* of maize monthly, three *cargas* of potatoes and two *ovejas* (probably llamas or alpacas). He should also receive five poultry (likely chickens or ducks) weekly, twelve eggs on Feast Days and a daily large pitcher of *chicha* (indigenous corn beer), firewood, and fodder for livestock. In addition, the encomendero had to provide a stipend for the cleric.[19]

The majority of the Andeans of the upper Colca Valley accepted the Franciscan friars and Christianity, yet they maintained various practices and beliefs of their ancestors. The inhabitants of the valley respected the dedication of the friars and were struck by the little importance they gave to what seemed to drive other Spaniards, the desire for wealth. As we see in chapter 8, in this region and period Andeans living in the Franciscan doctrinas of Yanque Collaguas believed they would fare better with the Seraphic friars than under the seculars or other religious orders. Although Franciscans in the core of the heartland of the Quechua- and Aymara-speaking Andes were usually held in high esteem, that was not true of every Franciscan mission in the New World.

8

Defender of Franciscan Rights

Franciscan General Commissioner Villacarrillo transferred administration of the Colca Valley doctrinas to the bishop of Cuzco and the secular clergy in 1581. It was not long before the villagers who had been under Franciscan care began to protest, first to Lima and then to Spain. The pressures they brought on royal and church officials—in a series of letters prepared by the kurakas in the name of their people—dragged on for months. It was several years before their entreaties bore fruit. In January of 1586 the principal indigenous leaders affirmed:

> The Franciscan friars founded the churches in the province and they taught the law of Our Lord in the doctrinas from the time of their conversion until about two years ago when they [the friars] left their doctrinas and returned to their monasteries by order of their Commissioner Friar Gerónimo de Villacarrillo. The Indians were much affected by this, so much so that they daily weep for the fathers of Saint Francis. And they are so attached to them and so deeply love and adore them, that they have tried with all their might to get them to return to their doctrinas. In the place of the friars have come the clerics of the order of Saint Peter; they are not as accepted as the friars.[1]

The Colca Valley kurakas lodged serious accusations against the clerics, alleging that they had participated in commerce in *ropa* (cloth) and *cestos* (bags or baskets), and forced the Indians to transport wine and livestock. Furthermore, the clerics demanded large fees for the Holy Sacraments. This was not the first nor last time the practice surfaced. Abuses were even worse earlier, when ecclesiastical control over the clerics in Indian doctrinas was weak. On 19 June 1552 Charles V wrote the bishop of Cuzco that he had received notice that some clerics in the diocese collected exorbitant sums for the sacraments. Charges were so high for burials that the Andeans reverted to earlier practices burying in the countryside, even in the ancient flexed position. Such practices were precisely what the church wished to avoid by burying the dead within church buildings as commonly done in early modern Spain.[2]

The Franciscan return to most of their doctrinas of Yanque Collaguas in the Colca Valley was largely uncontested. But there were exceptions. In two cases the transition required more than diplomacy, and violence erupted. In December 1585 kurakas of Los Collaguas complained to corregidor Juan de Ulloa Mogollón that the Franciscans had still not returned to the province. A year later (15 September 1586) Oré, then the Franciscan procurator for Los Collaguas, under the direction of Guardian Luis de San Gil, presented a demand before Alonso Osorio, corregidor and *justicia mayor* (chief justice) of Arequipa. The new viceroy, the Conde del Villar, had issued the order for the Franciscan return and Oré asked the Collaguas Corredgidor Ulloa Mogollón, to comply with the order.[3]

One of the villages where the Franciscans encountered resistance to their return was Lari in the middle valley. Priest Hernando Medel argued that the doctrineros of Lari had to be assigned by the bishop. Oré, as procurator, argued before the corregidor that this was not done before and requested him to enforce compliance according to the spirit and letter of the law. Arequipa's corregidor agreed, but Medel refused to abandon his parish and Lari remained in the hands of the secular clergy for another four years. The pressure to return the Franciscan doctrinas in the Colca Valley to the order continued yearly until on 20 March 1590 the new viceroy García Hurtado de Mendoza ordered their return. Twelve men were named for the enterprise, in keeping with Franciscan tradition. They included Guardian Pedro Ramón and friars Luis Gerónimo de Oré, Bernardo de Navarrete, Martín de Prado, Lorenzo Martínez, Antonio Ruiz, Hernando Martínez, Antonio Carranco, Jerónimo de Tapia, Martín de Urbina, Francisco de Zamora, and Pedro de Orobio.[4] Finally, on 10 July 1590 Oré led a contingent of Franciscans to meet the new corregidor of the Collaguas, Captain Gaspar Verdugo, and act.

In the name of the new Franciscan Guardian, Friar Pedro Ramón, Oré as the solicitor moved to take possession of Lari. He presented Viceroy Hurtado de Mendoza's decree ordering the doctrinas be transferred to the Franciscans. As customary the decree was read in the presence of the corregidor and the then cleric of Lari, Andrés de Arana. The corregidor swore to comply, but Arana, in a delay tactic, responded that he would execute the mandate but needed a copy of it to prepare his reply. Undeterred, the friars demanded that the priest immediately leave his church and residence. The cleric refused, insisting he had the right to remain and displayed an official letter of presentation to the doctrina. Arana positioned himself firmly at the door of his residence, then locked it. While the friars discussed the situation, the doors of the Lari church abruptly opened and the friars rushed in. After praying, the friars went to the sacristy, but Arana blocked its door. Meanwhile a small group of friars discovered another entrance, and from there they entered the adjoining residence of the cleric. They then closed all the doors, rang the church bells, then returned to open the doors in a ceremonial act of possession. In spite of Arana's protest, the corregidor confirmed the Franciscan recovery in accordance with the viceroy's provisions.[5]

The next day the Franciscans along with local officals marched to the neighboring villages of Maca and its *anexo* Ichupampa. Both doctrinas were under secular cleric Juan de Camargo. The pro-Franciscan indigenous majordomos, who held the keys to Ichupampa's church, opened its doors and the friars flowed in, rang the bells, and performed the act of possession. In Maca the royal decree was read to curate Camargo. He defended his right to the doctrina, arguing that he should not be expelled without a legal hearing. The corregidor responded simply that he was executing royal orders. Franciscan Antonio Ruiz took charge of the church of Ichupampa and Friar Martín de Picado of that of Maca. On 12 July the remainder of the Franciscan group went to the village of Tuti in the upper part of the valley. There they read the order to cleric Adrián de Asperamonte. He replied he would obey but would appeal the order because he should not be dispossessed without a hearing. The next day the Franciscans occupied the church of Sibayo, an anexo of Tuti. The final testimony and account of the return of the Franciscans to the Collaguas doctrinas was compiled in the village of Yanque on 14 July 1590. Various witnesses concurred that the Andeans cried for joy as the Franciscans reassumed their religious tasks in the valley.[6]

The forceful restitution of the Franciscans to doctrinas in the Colca Valley failed to bring an end to the conflict between seculars and religious. Worse, there was now an open breach between the order and Cuzco's Bishop Gregorio de Montalvo, who sided with the secular clergy. The bishop stressed that the

Council of Trent decreed that the doctrine was to be taught by parish priests because they were better prepared than friars to administer the sacraments to the Amerindians, who were "natives of such deficient intelligence and of such a depraved nature."[7] The bishop believed that the friars used their own unauthorized works in the catechism, causing confusion and damaging the faith. He protested to Franciscan Provincial Hernando de Trejo and ordered his secretary, Bachiller Lezo, to meet with Trejo who was in Huamanga at the time. At the meeting on 13 November 1590 Lezo pressured Trejo to remove the Franciscans from three doctrinas so the seculars could return. Trejo's solicitor, Matheo de Recalde, replied the same day, emphasizing that the Franciscans returned to the province at explicit order of the viceroy. Recalde admitted that Villacarrillo earlier removed the Franciscans from the province because at that time there were not enough friars competent in the language, particularly given that the Collaguas Quechua was of "extraordinary quality." Recalde pointed out that during the administration of Viceroy Conde del Villar, and a new Franciscan General Commissioner in Peru, restitution of the doctrinas had begun. He emphasized that the Franciscans had relinquished some of the best parishes in the realm, and that his order had no intention to remain in them forever. Yet the king wished to have friars in the doctrinas. After all, he was sending them to the Indies at his own cost. Recalde further argued that the Council of Trent had not specifically prohibited Franciscans in indigenous doctrinas and suggested it would be easy to transfer the three dispossessed clerics elsewhere. Moreover, the cost of friars as catechizers was half that needed to maintain the secular clergy. Notwithstanding the arguments Recalde and Trejo, ostensibly subjecting themselves to the authority of Cuzco's bishop, concluded that "for the tranquility of the friars it would be beneficial to leave these [doctrinas] and all the others that we have." And true to his word, Provincial Trejo ordered the Franciscans to leave from other doctrinas in the diocese of Arequipa.[8]

During the arguments a new Franciscan Commissioner arrived, and his reaction was rapid. On 20 October 1590 Antonio Ortiz wrote the king emphasizing the friars needed to abandon their Indian doctrinas: "In my judgment having our friars in the doctrinas is neither expedient for the conscience of Your Majesty nor that of the bishops, nor for the good of the Indians, nor for the perfection of the friars." The Andean population was under the jurisdiction of the bishops and they should have control over their doctrinas. There should be priests and their term should be long in order to fully understand their

Defender of Franciscan Rights   73

parishioners. Commissioner Ortiz insisted that in the doctrinas friars faced daily situations contrary to the precepts of their order. His only cure, as he put it, was to remove them.[9]

But the battle was not over. After a rapid journey from Huamanga, by mid-December 1590 Franciscan solicitor Friar Matheo de Recalde reached Lima and pressured government officials to secure copies of all documentation relating to the Franciscans in Los Collaguas. In April 1591 officials in Lima authorized retention of the Collaguas doctrinas that were under the control of the Crown and simultaneously recognized the right of the friars to administer the sacraments. Here, as often occurred, the thorny issue of Royal Patronage arose, and the Crown reiterated its control over the staffing of the doctrinas in royal corregimientos—not bishops. On 2 September 1592 Recalde requested that the Royal Chancellery send him copies of the royal decrees referring to the Collaguas. On 25 November 1592 the Council of the Indies Justice Baltasar de la Cruz wrote Doctor Pedro Gutiérrez Flores recommending that for the wellbeing of all Indians of Los Collaguas and Cabanaconde they should be restituted to the Franciscans.

An assembly of *definidores* (members of the governing body) was held in the Franciscan monastery in Lima. The friars, including Pedro de Oré—Luis Gerónimo's brother—congregated with General Commissioner Antonio Ortiz, decided to send a representative to Spain to settle the issue. They chose the solicitor Friar Recalde to present their position to the papacy, the king, and the Council of the Indies, and to the General Commissioner of the Indies. The friars prepared a detailed *"Memoria e Instrucciones . . ."* (10 December of 1592) to guide Recalde to successfully petition, and he was to deliver letters and other materials prepared by the friars. His instructions were explicit. One of Recalde's tasks was to request free importation of two *toneladas*[10] of "books for the Divine Offices and for administration of the Holy Sacraments to the Indians, such as manuals for baptism, psalm-books for Mass, choir books, choir manuals and other items relating to the divine cult." This effort to secure critical religious texts was part of the friars' intent to assemble an adequate library that would permit the Franciscan novices to study under their own teachers rather than in Dominican or Jesuit schools.[11]

On 22 November 1593, Philip II examined the materials Recalde presented and wrote that the Council of the Indies had reviewed the bishop's attempts to name secular clergy to the Collaguas and ordered the Franciscan friars to retain their doctrinas. Another order issued the same day confirmed the right of the Franciscans to administer the sacraments in the doctrinas. Two weeks later on 6 December 1593, the king (referring to Recalde's petition) ordered that anything given to the Franciscan order in Peru in the missionary activities should be given as alms and not a stipend, "for the security of their conscience."[12] In addition, the monarch affirmed that Franciscan friars had toiled in the valley from the inception, and both the Quechua and Aymara supported the friars' work. The king returned to the policy of Viceroy Toledo, who during his visita general confirmed Franciscan jurisdiction over the encomiendas of Lari and Yanque Collaguas. The king reiterated that Franciscan General Commissioner Villacarrillo ordered the friars to relinquish their doctrinas, and the secular clergy had assumed them, but they were not as well loved as the friars. Further, Philip II referred to the pastoral inspection of Archdeacon Pedro Muñiz of the Cathedral of Cuzco. During the course of the inspection, the archdeacon discovered that "in the one year that they were there, [the seculars] caused the Indians much harm with their dealings and by charging excessive fees for baptizing and marrying them ... that he [Muñiz] concluded that all were simoniacs and ordered them to return to the Indians more than six thousand pesos that they had usurped during that year." The findings of Archdeacon Muñiz led the king to order the *fiscal* (crown prosecutor) of the Royal Audiencia of Lima to initiate proceedings against the culpable priests and remove them from their doctrinas.[13]

It is unclear exactly when Luis Gerónimo de Oré departed the Colca Valley, but if he first began his tenure around 1584, by 1593 he would have served three trienniums, near the maximum one would be assigned to the same doctrinas. By 1595 or slightly before he may have returned to Lima to begin his assignment in Jauja, close enough to the city to allow him to attend important discussions and provide a voice in the continuing controversies elsewhere, especially in Los Collaguas. The conflict between seculars and regulars persisted, especially in the middle valley in and around Lari. As new bishops, viceroys, and commissioners of the Franciscan order wrestled over who would administer the doctrinas, the indigenous leaders continued to fight to keep the friars in the valley. It is likely Oré was in the Franciscan monastery in Lima during part of 1598 when these disputes were aired. His first major manuscript was in printer Antonio Ricardo's hands and to avoid errors it was important to review page proofs in a timely manner.

As the wrangling over the doctrinas continued, the Franciscans held another Lima Chapter Meeting of the Province during the term of General Commissioner Juan de Montemayor. During the discussions a group including Luis Gerónimo's older brother, Friar Pedro de Oré, stressed the order's conventual role. Pedro de Oré was one of the men who signed (30 April 1600) a letter to the monarch pointing out that for a long time many of the friars as well as the bishops "greatly desired that the religious who occupied the Indian doctrinas return to their monasteries and leave them to the clerics, who rightfully held them." The friars wrote there was now an "abundance of poor clerics" and the land was vast and populated and the seculars were needed to administer in the countryside. Further, many seculars now knew the indigenous languages well and asked the bishops to assign them doctrinas. Yet the bishops "cannot accommodate them because the doctrinas are filled by the friars." The Franciscans pressed the monarch to release them from the doctrinas for "the spiritual quietude of the friars, and so that the poor clerics would have something to do, and with that, the arguments and discord over jurisdiction would cease." At the end of the letter the Franciscans requested the king to enforce the rule that inspections in the doctrinas be conducted only by the bishops, or by inspectors of their own orders, not seculars, to avoid discontent.[14] Friar Pedro de Oré, the eldest of Luis Gerónimo's Franciscan siblings, had also served in Peruvian doctrinas, and his shift in opinion regarding the role of the friars was not unique, for many others changed their view as conditions in the field changed. And as we shall see, Friar Luis Gerónimo also struggled with this question.

In keeping with church practice, inspections were frequent. A new bishop of Cuzco, Antonio de Raya Navarrete, reached his diocese late in 1596 and soon ordered an inspection of the Colca Valley doctrinas including Madrigal, served by cleric Francisco Lorido Flores. The inspector concluded that the priest "used his office in the said villages with love and charity." There were subsequent inspections in 1607 and 1610 and the priest was again deemed "exemplary." But two years later Licentiate Pedro Fernández Barrias conducted a secret inspection with a strikingly different result. In the October 1612 inquiry Lorido was found guilty on two charges. He was frequently absent and failed to designate someone to provide the sacraments of baptism or confession "in cases of necessity," that is, imminent death. The priest was fined for not "teaching to his flock the Catechism of the *Santissimo Sacramento* composed by the Father Friar Luis de Orue [*sic.*]," that Cuzco's Bishop Raya had mandated. He was ordered to use it from then on. Why had Lorido failed to use Oré's *Symbolo catholico indiano*, a text by then widely used in Andean doctrinas? Might there have been a personal vendetta, given Oré's actions in the attempt to take back the doctrinas lower in the valley? In the end the inspector ruled that Lorido had performed well, and noted that through the cleric's work, the church of Madrigal was "the richest and best served in all this province." Lorido in 1615 requested a better appointment and succeeded.[15]

The wavering between the two positions came to an end as Pope Paul V in 1614 established the new diocese of Arequipa, with clear assignments in the Indian doctrinas. In the Corregimiento of Los Collaguas there were sixteen doctrinas—eight were retained by the Franciscans and the secular clergy received the rest.[16] Tension between the secular and regular clergy persisted. Contrary to all efforts, the divided jurisdiction of the Colca Valley extended into the eighteenth century, when the friars finally left the doctrinas. Luis Gerónimo de Oré's endeavor to keep the doctrinas in Franciscan hands, though ultimately unsuccessful, showed that the young friar was adept at handling such thorny issues as the relations between seculars and regulars and signaled to his superiors that he could navigate even the most intractable situations. Oré's work in the Colca Valley was critical as his career unfolded. He had gained experience as a procurator and an adroit administrator. Oré's activities in the valley were decisive, and the experience would serve him well in subsequent years as he confronted religious and political functionaries, even at the highest levels of the social order.

9

Doctrinero in the Colca Valley

Oré's principal goal during his tenure in the Colca Valley was to achieve a more "perfect" conversion to Christianity. He spent several years as a doctrinero in the region and employed much of his time catechizing and teaching in Quechua and Aymara, the two principal languages of the Colca Valley. He carefully explained to often incredulous audiences the sacraments of confession, baptism, marriage, and extreme unction. He deepened his understanding of the Andeans so that as confessor he could probe their secrets to ferret out and help eliminate what the church considered idolatries. The theological issues may have been complicated for the peoples of the valley. Clerics followed the rules articulated in the Second Church Council of Lima (1567–68). They tried to baptize newborns within eight days, recording the date of baptism, age of the infant, legitimacy status, and the names of parents and godparents and recorded similar information on marriages. Influenced by the shock of the Taki Onqoy movement, the Council began a crackdown on Andean practices, including the head binding of children. They called for destruction of the huacas—the mummy bundles of ancestors—and fought to end the practices of folk medicine. As an inducement for the Andean population to be "good Christians," church fathers allowed *borracherías* (drunken fiestas) following a baptism, but with a caveat: non-Christians were prohibited from participation.[1]

One wonders what the Cabanas and the Collaguas really thought of Christian concepts, such as the original sin, the Virgin Mother of Christ, and the Holy Trinity. The autochthonous peoples of the valley were familiar with other belief systems, given the century-long introduction of the cult of the ruling Inca as the sun and his sister-wife as the cult of the moon, and the Inca setting aside land and labor to sustain the local temple and religious authorities. The

Collaguas and Cabanas recognized potential benefits by accepting the new invader's cult if it did not interfere with their own ancestral practices. They could benefit by cooperation rather than resistance. Local leaders expected that they or their sons might be sent for training and become important in the administration of the realm. Under the Inca a daughter or sister might become a wife of the Inca himself or become one of the "virgins" of the moon. Oré recorded that Mayta Capac, the Inca conqueror of the valley's peoples, married the daughter of the local kuraka. Might they expect a similar relationship with the Europeans? Partly yes, perhaps explaining why many Andean ethnicities seemed to accept outside control with relative ease. Some examples justified their decision. Francisco Pizarro, Hernando Pizarro, Juan de Betanzos, and Captain Sebastián Garcilaso de la Vega all united with women of Inca lineage.[2]

When Friar Villacarrillo sent the four Franciscans to the valley in 1560, the hamlet of Coporaque became the center for the order's work. It was a significant site the Inca used as the center for their administration. Coporaque lies on the Cuzco side of the Colca Canyon, and there were warm springs on the valley floor near the edge of the river. (See map on page 66). The church bells of Coporaque, originally cast from the brass believed to have plated the Inca temple, could be heard across the canyon. The clanging of the church bells represented the power of Christianity, the call to meet, the religious hours and festivals, and the sacraments from baptism to death. Coporaque changed markedly from 1560 to the mid-1580s when Oré arrived. The upheaval, or "Pachacutec," unleashed by Viceroy Toledo's forced settlements (*reducciones*) in the mid-1570s was transformational. Coporaque's size had increased with the resettlement of seventeen nearby *ayllu* groups (units composed of close kin descending from a common source). The Inca temple stones served in construction of the church and monastery, and new household compounds were built on streets extending from a central plaza facing the church. Coporaque's broken topography prevented Spanish imposition of a perfect grid iron pattern. But Yanque, across the river on a more level platform, permitted a larger town and a sizeable population. Unfortunately, some of the best agricultural land was used for streets, houses, the plaza, and church. Before the Spanish arrived, the people built their residences on rougher terrain, leaving greater space for crops—maize, potatoes, quinoa, various types of legumes—watered by the irrigation channels. In some regions the resettlement was violent and met with resistance, in other areas the process, though painful, was accepted and a Christian body politic was possible. The result as the decades wore on was transculturation, a concept articulated by Cuban sociologist Fernando Ortiz. Perhaps in the Colca Valley the pressure of the kurakas representing their people to return the Franciscans as doctrineros made a difference in the outcome. Demand for a perfect, immediate conversion could be disastrous, while a lenient approach may lead to a hybrid Christianity. Indeed, the topographical, ecological, and cultural diversity of pre-Columbian America provides keys to understanding the outcome. Micro-ecological and cultural niches characterize the Andean World. There is no single theoretical model that can apply to the whole in this complex setting, although "transculturation" encompasses the unfolding process best.[3]

Initially, Coporaque became the center of administration for the Spanish, but the foundation and expansion of Arequipa to the south led to a shift. The city's growth was fueled by the Crown mandate that encomenderos live in the nearest Spanish administrative center, not their encomiendas. Later, the creation of the diocese of Arequipa also shifted the Franciscan headquarters from Coporaque to Yanque, the largest Colca settlement. The majestic snow-capped peaks of Hualca Hualca and the volcanic cone of Ampato, venerated by valley peoples for centuries, can be seen from both villages. The Yanque church and compound was more spacious than Coporaque's, and although the church has been rebuilt several times after earthquakes and other disasters, some parts remain from the time of Oré's tenure. The doorway from the guardian's quarters to the street and the cloister with the carving over the lintels appear to date to the sixteenth century. Yanque's church was one of the three largest in the valley, and its altar stood at the end of the nave facing the rising sun, appropriate for Christian and pre-Christian concepts. Construction was carried out by the local peoples, overseen by the religious and secular officials. There was little need to quarry stones, and a sizeable amount was transported from the pre-Hispanic hamlets abandoned during Viceroy Toledo's resettlement.[4] The ornamentation of the churches came from various sources. Some gifts were made by the monarch, more were donated by encomenderos and their families, hoping that "good deeds" might reduce their time in purgatory. Indigenous artisans were occasionally paid for their work. Lari *urinsaya* carpenters received 128 pesos from corregidor Lucas de Cadabal for their woodwork in various churches in the early 1580s, and there are other records of Cadabal's stewardship of cash and gifts to the valley churches.[5]

The axis of the Coporaque church aimed toward Cuzco and varied from most of the valley churches which followed an east-west axis. Remnants of Inca temples were integrated into the Christian church, an appropriation and likely a reminder of their linkage with autochthonous beliefs. The open plaza on the western side, on a level stretch several steps above the main square of Coporaque, provided space for open-air Masses. A chapel on the plaza's western side, perhaps first dedicated to Santa Ursula, was in use by 1565. The first church was devoted to San Sebastián, but under Villacarrillo in 1569 it was rededicated to Santiago. The Franciscans also oversaw construction of a bell tower. Small cloister cells for the friars were hastily erected on the east side of the church. An Indian school and hospital were included in the compound and were fully functioning in the 1580s.[6]

It was in the church of Coporaque that Oré fulfilled his daily sacramental duties, in addition to which there were other tasks, including the instruction of the children, and keeping track of the Indian hospital. Children were for doctrineros the key to success in their efforts in America. Their elders had grown up in an earlier world, and the depth of their pre-Christian beliefs could not be accurately measured. Those Christianized frequently fell back into their ancient practices, whereas children were viewed as *tabula rasa* more likely to become good Christians. Oré frequently mentioned music in the *Symbolo* and emphasized the need to teach the youngsters in the schools to acquire best the new faith, in contrast to their elders who were influenced by ancestral beliefs. He believed that one way to capture the children's interest was to teach them the songs of the church. In chapter thirteen of the *Symbolo,* "On how one should pray and sing in the choir, and how one should know the doctrine," Oré explained the benefit of teaching music to the children and the way indigenous parishioners came to learn as the children sang. Recent musicologists have focused on the Franciscan use of music in the indoctrination process, as we shall see later.[7]

Oré also touched upon punishment as a teaching tool, in keeping with rulings of the Third Church Council. The doctrineros of recent converts should exercise care that the children "learn and study the doctrine," and "to rigorously examine each ayllu and section at least once a year during Lent, on the Sunday of the week when they confess, punishing by public penance those who do not know it." Did Oré advocate corporal punishment? John Charles suggests he might have. He notes that Oré's *Symbolo Catholico Indiano* "endorses the 'humane and charitable rigor' of routine discipline, students no doubt resented the church officials who submitted them to floggings."[8] What punishment is to be meted out? For the kurakas, alcaldes, and *principales* (community elders)

Coporaque, the early center for the Franciscan Colca Valley doctrinas, 1974. Cook Coporaque's church with remnants of the Franciscan convent on the right and to the left an open plaza with the Chapel of Santa Ursula facing the church. On the left by the steps up to the church is an Inca wall. Photograph by Noble David Cook.

and their wives, the punishment consisted of washing and sweeping clean the church. For the commoners there were harsher penalties, in accordance with Spanish concepts of the relation between social status and appropriate punishment for breaking the "laws." Punishment based on societal position was typical in early modern Europe and was also practiced under the Inca, though it differed significantly from the European model. Oré advocated that, "regarding the rest of the Indian villagers who are ordered to be whipped, it should be with humane firmness and benevolently, so that the punishment is not excessive, nor so insignificant that they laugh at it. Rather it is done to correct them, and the intended result is obtained, that they know the doctrine." He cautioned "moderation should be maintained in all the occasions that might require castigating the Indians. They should do it as fathers, who are loved rather than feared as judges." Oré argued that schoolchildren should be examined for the knowledge of the doctrine often and those who still did not know it should be punished, "with the moderation, firmness and mildness required by their tender age." Although today *any* physical punishment is considered excessive by educators, it was the norm in previous centuries. Oré, aware of human frailty and lack of patience among the clerics teaching the neophytes, issued a warning to prevent excessive punishment.[9]

Oré was involved not only in the operation of the Indian school but also the hospital of Coporaque, which was supported by an annual levy of one tomín each per tribute-paying Indian, as part of the assessment. The salary of the physician, who was likely a barber, and the costs for medications were paid from this source; according to the records of payments for both, the hospital did function in the valley, even if imperfectly. Several devastating epidemics passed through the Andes in the sixteenth century and Toledo's resettlement contributed to the high mortality by concentrating into large towns people who before had lived scattered throughout the countryside. Denser population made transmission of contagious diseases easier. The major disaster occurred when not one but several epidemic waves passed through simultaneously. Smallpox, measles, influenza, and possibly typhus devastated vast areas of Andean America, from today's Colombia to Chile. The number of deaths was staggering enough to force a detailed census to recalculate tributes in hard-hit areas, including the corregimiento of Los Collaguas. On 13 August 1591 Oré participated in the reinspection of Coporaque, and prepared for Corregidor Gaspar de Colmenares a "Report and enumeration of the Indians who died during the general sickness of smallpox and measles." It was important to confirm the number and names of dead tributaries because there was pressure from encomenderos and the corregidor to keep the number of tribute-paying Indians high to maximize incomes. A 30- to 40-percent drop in the number of tributaries would place a major burden on remaining Indians, so an accurate count was critical, and the Franciscans did their best to provide correct figures.[10]

Oré's personal experience of aiding the ill and the dying may have contributed to his views on timing the administration of extreme unction. Oré wrote that if too many simultaneously became ill a priest could with the same act confess all. If too many were dying the doctrinero could give extreme unction, praying for all of them and their souls "in the plural." When they died "the church bells should toll, and on dying they should not carry them wrapped in *mantas* [blankets] but should place them on biers and [the priest] should honor the bodies of his parishioners, accompanying them with the cross and the chanters and bury them."[11]

Illness, whether sudden or chronic, was not the only cause of death among the villagers. Lightning strike on the high puna or slipping off the edge of the Colca canyon or even murder were not uncommon causes of death. In the case of the massive number of deaths during an epidemic Oré used the "Brief exhortation for the Indians who are already very near the end of life, so that the priest or someone else helps them in the good death." It was simple and quick without the standard series of steps required under normal circumstances. The second form is more complete, and akin to those in European manuals. With ample time to prepare for death there are several sequential stages in the process, beginning with the confession, followed by restitution, a last will, communion, extreme unction, and the final statement of faith.[12] In the Indian doctrina a confession of faith was designed to test the depth of belief in the Christian God and the dying person was to agree that "all the others that your ancestors worshiped were demons, were fake and false gods; and thus you reject them, and take them as a lie."[13] Autochthonous Andean burial practices varied depending on the local environment and custom. In the Colca Valley the body was wrapped in a flexed position and placed, along with gifts, in a cave or even in stone niches in agricultural terraces. The doctrineros, realizing the significance and danger of such practice, strived to bury the dead in the churches, hoping to assure a more rapid and permanent acceptance of the doctrine. That way the Christian churches became new huacas and the ancestors could be remembered.[14] Social condition here as in Spain delineated burial placement in the church. The principal community leaders, the kurakas and their families were buried nearest to the main altar and the common folk under the floor of the nave.

Another key element in smoothing the process of instilling the new faith in the Andean community was the confraternity (*cofradía*), an old European religious institution; some were open to all, some limited to a special group, such as by occupation. In the Colca Valley where the concept of halves (*sayas*) was imbedded, each half could have its own confraternity and its own patron saint and feast days. Prior to the arrival of the Europeans the basic Andean *ayllu*, a unit composed of close kin descending from a common source, served the group by providing food, labor or aid in times of sickness or death. But as the *ayllu* came under pressure with the demographic catastrophe, the confraternity became a substitute. Among the most popular confraternities, as in Spain, were the *Santíssimo Sacramento* (The Blessed Sacrament) and the *Ánimas del Purgatorio* (Souls of Purgatory). Both men and women participated and ideally the members met frequently, initially in the presence of the doctrinero. As confidence in successful conversion grew, the religious allowed members to gather and discuss matters of concern such as the celebration of the patron saint of the church and the confraternity, repairs and maintenance of the church, the purchase of a new chalice, or for the celebrations of Holy Week or Corpus Christi.[15]

Doctrineros struggled to eradicate lingering preconquest religious concepts, a formidable challenge in a world where virtually everything could be a huaca, an object of worship. Lightning, a volcano, a spring, a lake, the sun, the moon, other heavenly bodies, unusual stones, or carved stones, ancestors, all could be venerated. During those years, a variety of factors coalesced that contributed to indigenous reaction against the new order. There are numerous examples of attempts to extirpate "idolatries" in Andean America that spanned the colonial period, including during Oré's tenure in Coporaque. In the Colca Valley cases of idolatry were uncovered during the *residencia* of Corregidor Lucas de Cadabal, an administrative inquiry by which the work of officials was investigated at the end of their assignment, and usually led by their replacement. During Cadabal's residencia numerous people testified in January 1584 to his "good works." Local surgeon Manuel de Caravajal stated that Cadabal had learned that Indians entered the burial chambers of their ancestors and conducted their old rites. He chastised the perpetrators and ordered that the bones and huacas be removed and burned. Kurakas and several Indians of Lari witnessed the corregidor's campaign against idolaters: ". . . four or five which he discovered in our pueblo he seized and castigated, and banished them from this province." Sebastián Durán, cleric in Caylloma lauded Cadabal: he "was especially diligent in extirpating idolatries and witchcraft. . . . He came to know which Indians were practitioners, and in what places, and in order to extirpate and verify it, he had gone even to the punas and other inhospitable parts at great personal risk."

Don Diego Coro Inga, the village scribe, knew the details of Cadabal's investigation, and his successor's preparation of the geographical reports commissioned by Philip II in 1586. Don Diego was one of the translators and informants for the geographical reports and the 1591 census. He provided information on the valley's past that Oré used in his *Symbolo Catholico Indiano*. Oré probably first met Don Diego Coro Inga in Cuzco and was collaborating with the well-educated scribe and schoolteacher. In his testimony for Cadabal's residencia Don Diego confirmed the corregidor strove to "extirpate and destroy the idolatries, learning who had been engaged in them and in witchcraft, and in that fashion had uncovered the idolaters and shamans. He castigated them and exiled them from the province. He had burned and buried the idolatrous objects so that never again would there be memory of them." Another witness, Francisco Hernández, testified that he, the corregidor, and other Spaniards conducted a search for idolatry in the Collaguas and discovered a shaman who had fooled "puna herdsmen and residents of Lari and Cabana, and many others in the province. . . . He convinced them that atop a snow-capped peak named Curiviri there was a great toad he called Ampato, and that this toad was god, and he defecated gold." The witness verified Cadabal took the shaman to the mountain and destroyed the objects.[16]

The "cult" of Ampato was typically Andean and made perfect sense to the peoples living in its long shadow. Ampato's towering, massive glacial summit served as a place where gifts, including human sacrifices could be placed. Ampato, and similar natural huacas scattered throughout the Andes, could never be obliterated by the Europeans, nor could the celestial bodies. But human huacas, the mummy bundles of ancestors could be broken, burned and scattered. Folk religiosity and practices continued despite efforts by Oré and other religious in the valley to eradicate them, some, such as the *apachitas* (cones of small stones picked up along the way and deposited at critical spots along paths) persisted even to the present. The candles or offerings at church chapels in the valley venerate the saints, but they could also be offerings to ancestors.

During the following decades there were extended campaigns against idolatry in the Andes, causing fear and discontent within the indigenous population as well as some elements in the church who viewed various leaders of extirpation as ambitious seekers of recognition and advancement. It reached a point where the Council of the Indies investigated and ordered Lima's archbishop to correct the situation. The only true way to eliminate autochthonous beliefs was by "the example of good living of the ecclesiastics, especially three types of people, the doctrineros, visitadores, and preachers. If any of these are evil doers, the Indians will not be able to distinguish the true Christian life, and truly the devil's idolatries will be confirmed."[17]

One event during Oré's work in the valley that certainly did not provide a good example for the indigenous people, was a convoluted episode involving a cleric, a deputy corregidor, a constable, a Black slave, an Indian concubine, and arguments over the estate of a corregidor. It was a "notorious and public" case that did not reflect well on the church. The inquiry into the events in the village of Yanque originated in Lima as part of an extensive investigation in 1588 led by the inspector Inquisitor Doctor Juan Ruiz de Prado into the scandalous behavior of Lima inquisitor Antonio Gutiérrez de Ulloa.[18] The inquisitor was accused of forcing women into having "carnal relations" with him and having "raped 70 virgins." This sexual predator paraded through Lima's streets in fine clothing accosting women, many of them married, while they gathered with their friends in public places. The inquisitor kept concubines and fathered several children. If true, no woman seemed safe in his presence. The inquisitor inherited the estate of the corregidor of Los Collaguas, Juan de Ulloa Mogollón, and to collect it he named as his commissioner Licentiate Alonso de Valencia, a priest in the Colca Valley. Some of Ulloa de Mogollón's property was deposited with court officials because the corregidor had stolen between eight to ten thousand pesos from the community chest of the Collaguas Indians (*caja de la comunidad de los Indios*) and the money needed to be restituted. According to the complaint of Arequipa corregidor Alonso Osorio, the Inquisitor's commissioner Licentiate Valencia forcibly removed the property in the name of the Inquisition and the money was never returned to the indigenous communities. There were other complaints about Valencia's overstepping his authority, and rumors that he might be "*de los prohibidos,*" of Jewish or Muslim ancestry, thus not qualified to hold any post with the Inquisition. As a result, an inspector was sent from Lima to investigate, and he questioned several witnesses including the Franciscan guardian of Los Collaguas, Friar Pedro de San Gil, resident in Yanque, and Friar Luis Gerónimo de Oré, then doctrinero of Coporaque.

Friar San Gil traveled to Arequipa to testify on 28 June 1588. The 43-year-old Franciscan guardian related that he heard that Licentiate Valencia had a commission from Lima inquisitor Antonio Gutiérrez de Ulloa to collect the property of the deceased corregidor of Los Collaguas. Friar Pedro did not witness the altercation between the deputy corregidor Alonso de Zavallos and Licentiate Valencia, but he heard about it because everyone was talking about it. The deputy corregidor along with the constable Cristóbal Fajardo went to Valencia's house in Yanque "to remove from the licentiate's house an Indian woman because, they said, she had committed a certain crime and she was the licentiate's concubine."[19] This upset Valencia, who grabbed a halberd, and along with his black slave brandishing a sword, they ran out to defend the entrance. The skirmish was a spectacle witnessed by anyone who happened to be nearby. To protect the woman, Valencia "sent her to Cuzco with one of his yanaconas." That did not deter the intrepid deputy corregidor Zavallos and his constable who intercepted the fugitives, took the indigenous woman into custody and brought her back to Yanque where the Franciscan guardian saw her in jail in chains. Friar Pedro added that "the deputy himself told him that he had taken her away from the yanacona."[20] One of the accusations against Licentiate Valencia was that he overstepped his authority by issuing excommunications and here the Franciscan guardian spoke from personal experience. Valencia, furious at the deputy corregidor and his constable, promptly excommunicated them. He issued and signed a written document that, according to Friar Pedro, stated, "consider Alonso de Zavallos and *fulano* Fajardo publicly excommunicated by the Holy Inquisition."[21] He brought the paper to Friar Pedro and asked him to post it on the door of Yanque's church and ordered him not to allow the two men to attend mass. Oré happened to be in Yanque and saw the document also. There were rumors in the village as to the licentiate's motives for excommunicating the two officials, including strong words exchanged between Zavallos and Valencia, who threatened excommunication, at which point the deputy corregidor shouted, "Why do you threaten me in this manner since I am not the Muslim or Jew,"[22] words that the licentiate, who himself was under a cloud of being "one of the prohibited ones," saw as a grave insult.

Oré, then aged 34, traveled to Arequipa with the Franciscan guardian and testified on the same day. Oré knew Licentiate Valencia had been assigned by the Inquisitor Gutiérrez de Ulloa to act as his commissioner in the Colca Valley and heard about most of the incidents that Friar Pedro had testified about. Initially, Oré believed that Valencia was fully empowered to act in anything involving the Inquisition, but soon learned that Valencia was only commissioned "for one specific issue, which was the collection of the estate of Juan de Ulloa Mogollón,"[23] the corregidor who had compiled the detailed geographical report of the province of Los Collaguas in 1586. Oré was surprised to hear from the new corregidor of Los Collaguas, Garci Mendez de Moscoso, that Ulloa de Mogollón left all his estate to the Inquisitor without providing the customary masses for his soul. Oré believed that Valencia overstepped his authority in threatening and issuing excommunication, since he was only commissioned to collect the late corregidor's estate. Oré heard all the stories about the conflict including that someone told him, he did not remember who, that "the delinquent Indian" in Valencia's house "had some papers of the Holy Office and they were saying how is it possible that he would entrust papers of the Holy Office to an Indian."[24] Oré did not opine on the issue but earlier the guardian, Friar Pedro, had testified that he had actually asked Valencia about it. The licentiate's evasive answer convinced the guardian that this rumor was untrue, especially since deputy Zavallos told him that when he searched the Indian's house, he did not find any Inquisition documents. Oré, who must have been concerned about the behavior of the Spanish officials in full view of the indigenous villagers, told the inspector that he and Friar Pedro "tried to make peace between the licentiate and the deputy." The two friars approached licentiate Valencia to reason with him and he replied that if "the deputy destroys or gives him the charge against his black slave, then he will destroy what he had written against the said deputy and his constable."[25] Oré added that he did not know "if he destroyed them or what he did with it."[26]

Oré testified that he had asked Valencia if he had been given power to issue excommunications. The cleric replied that regarding "collection of that property he could excommunicate and arrest." Oré snapped back, "What does the collection of property have to do with excommunicating for removing the delinquent from his house." Valencia retorted "well, I can say that fifteen days ago I gave the Indian a leather bag with the papers of the Holy Office." But Oré was not fooled, noting that "given the disgust with which he said it, I do not believe that the said Indian had such papers." Both friars heard that ultimately the deputy corregidor and the constable were absolved after about six months of excommunication, though Oré was not sure who did it. Oré subsequently saw Deputy Zavallos, "who was very happy saying that he had been absolved and publicly heard Mass."[27] The last issue that there were complaints about, particularly by the corregidor of Arequipa, Alonso de Osorio, was the question of Valencia's punishment of the indigenous people of Los Collaguas. Osorio heard from his deputy, Alonso de Zavallos, that "the Indians of that province were complaining about the said Valencia who gave them double whippings telling them that he did it for the Holy Office."[28]

Both Franciscan friars seemed unaware of any abuse. Friar Pedro said he heard about it but never saw it himself. Oré simply stated that "he does not know about it, nor has he heard it said."²⁹ These curt answers leave one wondering how much of this accusation was true, given its source. Or were whippings so common, that the Spanish officials and the friars did not think Valencia's treatment of the Andeans was unusual or excessive? The two friars also did not pass any judgement on Licentiate Valencia, a priest, keeping an indigenous concubine: not a good example for the Andean parishioners and yet, according to Guaman Poma de Ayala, a common grievance. Perhaps, the lack of outrage by the two friars is due to the nature of the questioning, where only straightforward answers were expected.

The successes and failures in Oré's and his fellow Franciscans' efforts in the valley in the last decades of the sixteenth century must have been discussed in the periodic gatherings of the order during provincial chapter meetings. Unfortunately, no record of those sessions has been located, but as we shall see in a later chapter centering on the Franciscan missions in La Florida, their discussions were frank, with full and open debate of all that had taken place as the friars evaluated their activities and searched for answers on how to improve their work. It is likely that some Franciscans would confess that their knowledge of indigenous languages was insufficient, and that more study of Quechua and Aymara was needed. Oré shared with the valley doctrineros his manuscripts— the dictionary and grammar and the religious texts in translation—that he had worked on during his tenure in the Colca Valley. When Oré left the valley, he carried with him four almost complete manuscripts, nearly ready for review and possible publication.

SYMBOLO
CATHOLICO INDIA

NO, EN EL QVAL SE DECLARAN LOS
myſterios de la Fe contenidos enlos tres Symbolos Catholicos, Apoſtolico, Niceno, y de S. Athanaſio.

CONTIENE ASSI MESMO VNA DESCRIP-
cion del nueuo orbe, y delos naturales del. Y vn orden de enſeñarles la doctrina
Chriſtiana enlas dos lenguas Generales, Quichua y Aymara, con
vn Confeſsionario breue y Catechiſmo dela communion.

TODO LO QVAL ESTA APPROBADO POR
los Reuerendiſsimos ſeñores Arçobiſpo delos Reyes, y Obiſpos
del Cuzco, y de Tucuman.

COMPVESTO POR EL PADRE FRAY LVIS
Hieronymo de Oré, predicador dela orden de ſant Franciſco, dela
prouincia delos doze Apoſtoles del Piru.

SANCTA MARIA SVC.

CON LICENCIA.
Impreſſo en Lima por Antonio Ricardo. Año 1598.
Acoſta de Pedro Fernandez de Valençuela.

Oré's 1598 *Symbolo Catholico Indiano*. Title page of *Symbolo catholico indiano en el cual se declaran los mysterios de la fe contenidos en los tres symbolos catholicos, apostolico, niceno, y de S. Athanasio. Contiene asi mesmo una descripción del nuevo orbe y de los naturales dél. Y un orden de enseñarles la doctrina christiana enlas dos lenguas generales, quichua y aymara, con un Confesionario breve y Catechismo de la Communion [...] Compuesto por el padre Fray Lvis Hieronymo de Oré, predicador de la orden de San Francisco, dela provincia delos doze Apóstoles del Pirú / Con licencia. Impresso en Lima, por Antonio Ricardo. Año 1598*. Biblioteca Nacional de Chile memoriachilena. Patrimonio Cultural Común.

10

Composing the *Symbolo Catholico Indiano*

The religious and linguistic impact of Oré's *Symbolo Catholico Indiano* and his other Andean texts is receiving increasing scrutiny by linguists and theologians. The attention is centering on the challenges of translation of religious doctrine and the nature of religious transformations. Oré's works and a handful of others had an impact on "fixing" Quechua and Aymara as the general languages throughout much of the core of the Andes, alongside the newly imposed Spanish. Critical linguistic analysis is best left to disciplinary specialists. We also leave the critical examination of the religious interpretation of the texts to theologians and instead concentrate on Oré's endeavor for doctrineros to be conversant in indigenous languages. We also explore the challenges he faced to secure publication, and the reception and dissemination of his work.[1]

The answers to the questions posed by Oré's collective work relate to his novitiate and his nearly three trienniums (1586–95) as doctrinero of Coporaque and Yanque, performing the routine tasks of a parish priest in the Colca Valley and acting as legal representative of the order.[2] This was not the restless frontier of early Huamanga, or Cuzco, where other Europeans provided security. Here he was one of a dozen or so Spaniards—eight to twelve Franciscans and one *corregidor* and his household—living in a sea of some fifteen thousand Andeans recently forced to abandon their small hamlets and construct and live in European-style villages. The friar's "personal flock" was about a thousand souls. Oré was the outsider and perhaps more alone among the "others" than he had been at any time in his life to this point. While imparting his religious vision to the Collaguas he was finalizing his principal texts, making additions and corrections. He was simultaneously perfecting his fluency in Quechua and Aymara. His tenure in the Colca Valley was advantageous because the Corregimiento of Los Collaguas included both Quechua and Aymara speakers. One of his most important local informants was Don Diego Coro Inga, Coporaque's scribe and schoolteacher, with whom he conversed frequently about the language, the people's past and early beliefs, and the education of children. Before Oré departed the valley around 1595 he had completed the final drafts of the *Symbolo Catholico Indiano*, the *Rituale, seu manuale peruanum*, texts of primary importance for the missionary efforts in Andean America, plus the lost manuscripts—his dictionary and the grammar of Quechua and Aymara.[3]

The origins of the *Symbolo Catholico Indiano* and the *Manuale peruanum* predate their printing by a decade or more. The exact moment when Oré decided to shoulder the task may never be known, but he may have recognized its importance early on, still in Huamanga, as he observed religious indoctrination of the Indians of his father's encomienda. Given the terrible and confusing quality of some of the sermons and the explanation of faith, despicable in the characterization of Guaman Poma de Ayala in his letter to the king, Oré understood the need for texts in indigenous languages to aid the doctrineros in their work. In August of 1587 Franciscan procurator Matheo de Recalde composed a report to Philip II on the order's work and noted that Friar Luis Gerónimo de Oré "had compiled a copious dictionary and grammar and two other books of sermons in both the two general languages, Aymara and Quichua." Recalde elaborated that they were useful for teaching the doctrine and in conversion of the Indians and asked the king to grant license to print the texts. More important for Oré's future, Recalde suggested that if there were no place in Peru to publish, Oré should receive license to travel to Spain and there print it. Recalde also asked the monarch to issue a royal order for the viceroy to assign those who were knowledgeable in the languages to examine the works and then inform the Council and approve the texts and document the need for them.[4]

After leaving the Colca Valley in 1595, Oré returned to Lima where he was assigned his next post as guardian of the Jauja missions in the central highlands directly inland from the capital. While in Jauja Oré could make necessary revisions to his manuscripts and oversee the complex process of securing authorizations and funds for the printing. He could supervise publication of the *Symbolo Catholico Indiano*, the first of his manuscripts to be printed just three years later. It was in Jauja's Franciscan monastery that Oré signed his dedication of the *Symbolo* on 18 April 1596 to Pedro Ordóñez Flores, the Apostolic Inquisitor of Peru and a member of the King's Council. It seems Oré discussed this possibility with Juan Gutiérrez Flores, the Inquisitor's brother and *alguacil mayor* of the Holy Office, and Doctor Pedro Gutiérrez Flores of the King's Council and the Council of the Indies.[5]

The work needed approval by a commission to ensure nothing contrary to the faith or the Crown was included. Viceroy Marqués de Cañete established the commission with instructions to review the manuscript along with Oré's *Sermones del año* and an *Arte y gramatica en romance y en las lenguas generales deste reyno quechua y aimara*. Tucumán's Bishop Hernando de Trejo noted Oré's work was already being used extensively in manuscript form in the dioceses of Cuzco and Tucumán and recommended its publication in Lima on 6 December 1595. But it would be the linguists and censors who would review and approve the text's accuracy in translation. On 13 July 1596 Cathedral Canon Alonso Martínez, an examiner of Quechua and Aymara in the diocese, reported he had scrutinized the manuscript, made a few corrections, and found it to be accurate in matters of the faith. He concluded the translation was excellent and the explanations more complete than any other, and that it should be authorized and used everywhere the languages prevailed. In Cuzco, Master of the *lingua franca* Pedro Baptista Solís and Juan Gómez de León jointly endorsed the text. In Lima, Master Friar Juan Martínez, Chair of Quechua at the University of San Marcos, concluded on 14 March 1596 that the work would benefit both the Indians and the doctrineros and should be in print. Luis Gerónimo's older brother Pedro de Oré, commissioner of Tierra Firme and guardian of the Franciscans in Panama, had arrived in Jauja before September 1595 and because of his linguistic expertise, he evaluated the translations. On 8 September 1595 Friar Pedro praised his brother's work stating, "As a man who for thirty years preached to the Indians because I know their language, both in Cuzco [Quechua] as well as in Charcas [Aymara], and in all the other monasteries of this province where I have served, I declare that I view these works as most useful and beneficial for both the curates as well as the Indians because the doctrine is most needed, and hence they will gain clarity of the things of our Faith and sacred religion." Friar Pedro added, "It is composed in a very pleasing language, clear and accommodating for the Indians' understanding." The recommendations are followed by an epigram in Latin composed by Juan de Vega, teacher of the *lingua franca*; a sonnet by Dominican Prior of the Parinacochas monastery, Gerónimo de Valenzuela; and subsequently a laudatory "*declaración*" in Quechua and its Spanish translation by Alonso de Inojosa. Viceroy Marqués de Cañete, signed the authorization in Callao on 4 April 1596 but the text was not printed until 1598, and taxed by the new Viceroy Luis de Velasco.[6]

Oré designed the *Symbolo Catholico* for new doctrineros, especially those fresh from Europe. He believed a description of the environment and the nature of the indigenous peoples and their past would provide new doctrineros a basic understanding of the challenges they faced. Early in the text Oré included a brief geographical and historical sketch of the viceroyalty, based mostly on published books, citing those he consulted. He incorporated material from chronicles of the history of America, including the general survey of Gonzalo Fernández de Oviedo y Valdés, Agustín de Zárate's history of Peru's conquest, the text on the Civil Wars by Diego Fernández, as well as the religious texts of Jesuit José de Acosta, specifically *Natura Novi Orbi....*[7] Oré also relied on the work of Cristóbal de Molina and his knowledge of Inca religious practices. He incorporated into the *Symbolo* one of the prayers to Viracocha, the creator of the world in the Inca universe, that Molina collected and possibly shared with Oré while they both participated in the Third Church Council in Lima.[8] Oré composed his narrative without verifying the verisimilitude of his written sources, making his brief historical sketch less valuable. He relied on other doctrineros and indigenous informants throughout the manuscript, including Don Carlos Inga, grandson of Huayna Capac, who "I knew and interacted with in Cuzco."[9] Oré consulted the Franciscan archive and library in Lima, and other libraries as he composed the religious sections of the *Symbolo Catholico*. But he missed some information, to the chagrin of some. Felipe Guaman Poma de Ayala, who had used and cited the *Symbolo* in his *Nueva Corónica y Buen Gobierno*, complained that Oré ignored, or missed the long list of native rulers of the Andes that had been kept for generations, as reported by Guaman Poma's father and dozens of elderly *quipucamayos* (record keepers on multicolored knotted strings). That genealogy was a key element in the indigenous chronicler's claims of nobility and request for offices.[10]

Oré, as other religious translators of widely spoken indigenous languages, faced the challenge of what constitutes the best model to use. Language variation in large populations distributed over vast and rugged terrain is common, as pronunciations of the same word differed from one place to another. Oré, cognizant of the difficulty, concluded: "Regarding Quechua, the general language in all this kingdom, the city of Cuzco is the Athens, which is spoken there with all the rigor and elegance that one can imagine, as Ionic is in Athens, Latin in

Rome, Castilian in Toledo; such is the Quechua language in Cuzco. But in the other provinces the greater the distance from this city, there is more corruption and less elegance in the guttural pronunciation and periphrasis particular to this language, not well understood by some who boast about speaking it."[11]

In the case of Aymara, he noted that "in all the provinces subject to Chuquiapu the Indians speak the Aymara language with much elegance, and there is a large number of Indians who communicate in this language from Cuzco and all the provinces under its jurisdiction, in the direction of Arequipa and Chuquiapu, and from there to Charcas." Oré warned that Aymara was more difficult for the translators than Quechua. "Regarding the Aymara language there are views as to where it is best spoken, and both coincide in being artificial and filled with words that the synonyms of the nouns and verbs make them difficult to know. On the contrary sometimes the lack of the words that correspond to Spanish words requires one to use circumlocutions and homilies in the translations."[12] Oré's goal was the most accurate translation to the indigenous languages, one that would best convey the teachings of the Catholic faith in the Indian doctrinas.

The religious sections of the *Symbolo Catholico Indiano* make up the core of Oré's contribution, and he stressed throughout the work that evangelization of indigenous people could not succeed without the ability to communicate basic tenets of the faith in their own languages. In Spanish, *símbolo* also means creed, a statement of the fundamental belief, of faith. Oré explained that the Nicene Creed, the Athanasian Creed, and the Apostles' Creed were the most widely used in Spanish churches. As Alan Durston points out, it is possible that Oré used *symbolo* in his title because of his respect for Luis de Granada (1504–1588), one of Iberia's foremost Dominican theologians, author of dozens of religious texts aimed at all sectors of society. Oré referred to the Dominican in various works, and likely found in chapter 5 of Granada's *Introducción del símbolo de la fe* (1583) justification for using Granada's concept of the Creator, God of the moon and planets and stars, and the sea, water, and hot and cold seasons. These concepts could be integrated easily into the world view of the Andeans. Granada's *Vida de Maria: vida y misterio de la Santisima Virgen* may have influenced one of Oré's later books, for he, like Granada, wished to reach the common folk.[13]

The earliest attempts to convert and baptize the indigenous people were fraught with misunderstandings. Many religious orders developed their own form of Christian doctrine, and there were subtle but significant variations in the translations. One of the aims of the Third Church Council of Lima was to establish a uniform, carefully worded translation of the Christian doctrine to be used for evangelization throughout the realm.[14] Almost by default, the standard form became Cuzco-based Quechua. The Europeans adopted, then completed, a policy of linguistic imperialism initiated by the Inca. John Charles suggests the working model the Third Council used for the *Doctrina Christiana* was that presented in 1576 by Jesuit Alonso de Barzana to the order's Second Provincial Council.[15] Charles also believes that Blas Valera "occupied a privileged position to sway the direction of Third Council language policy." Charles admits that "the extent of his influence cannot be fully determined."[16] Much of the problem lies in the fact that many of Valera's writings survive thanks to Inca Garcilaso de la Vega who reproduced sections. Although Garcilaso indicates his source, he is strongly committed to the idea that the Inca and their civilization were superior to other Amerindian cultures. Garcilaso's comments on the quality of the Quechua spoken by the Inca parallel Oré's. The mestizo author had a copy of the *Symbolo Catholico Indiano* when he was finalizing his *Comentarios reales de los Incas*.[17]

A key factor compelling Oré to provide a complete manual for doctrineros was to ensure they knew Andean languages. The sacraments and their understanding were critical for salvation, and as Gabriela Ramos points out, "Confession heard by a priest who had not understood what the penitent had to say was unacceptable to a considerable sector of the clergy. This is clearly illustrated by the assertion of the Friar Luis Jerónimo de Oré, who echoed the position of the Cuzco diocesan synod of 1591."[18] Regina Harrison has indicated that Oré "edited the confessional text written by the Third Lima Provincial Council, keeping those questions and exhortations that were most useful for the conversion of the indigenous Andeans."[19] She also finds that Pablo de Prado, a Peruvian Jesuit who perfected his fluency in Quechua while studying in Juli, published in Lima in 1650 (first published in 1641) a short confessional in his *Directorio espiritual en la lengua española, y quichua general de Inga*. Prado used "some devotional passages from Oré's *Symbolo*."[20]

In a section of the *Symbolo* on the administration of the sacraments, Oré remarked:

> there are entire books written in all the languages about the definition and distribution of the sacraments, and of the substance and form and administration

of each one. I do not intend to treat them now because their proper place is in the *Manual Peruano* with the necessary translations that I have done, that upon approval by the archbishop and other most reverend bishops of this kingdom and with license to print it given by the viceroy, I will attempt that after it is seen and polished, it will come to light jointly with the sermons for Sundays and the feast days of the entire year in Spanish and both general languages."[21]

Oré stressed the characteristics of a good doctrinero working among the Andeans: "The priest has to possess disposition, age, Christian zeal and courage" and must understand his various responsibilities, and "accept the curacy with all these obligations." He warned that if the doctrinero "does not intend to fulfill them he will give account to God, and he would do well to renounce the doctrina so that the prelate can provide another qualified minister for it."[22] Oré exhorted the doctrinero "for God and for his flock, bring the heart burning with the fire and flames of charity." He emphasized the importance of knowing indigenous languages well enough to effectively confess his charges, and points out that "Navarro,[23] and Medina, write in their *Sumas* that he who confesses in a language he does not know or understand commits a mortal sin."[24]

As Oré continued his analysis and argument he pointed out that the rule for use of the vernacular in the missions is in the Ordinances and Constitutions of the Apostolic Chancellery. He referred to an apostolic judge Luis Gómez, bishop of Sarno, who posed the question, "if someone partly understands a language, and partly not, does it satisfy the Apostolic Rule? He responds that it does not satisfy it," and noted, "One should also understand it and use it [the vernacular] in the parish churches."[25] Oré hinted at what he later would do: recruit in Spain new doctrineros from the religious orders. He believed that when there is an insufficient number of priests to minister to the Andeans scattered throughout the countryside then, if there were qualified religious in the convents, they should, by Apostolic concession, be entrusted with the task.[26]

Oré confessed that composing his text was difficult and lengthy, "From the sermons in the general languages and other activities and vigils that I have studiously written laboring day and night over the space of many years, and that I continue to perfect, with all this I hope to serve and benefit the priests of this kingdom."[27] He issued a common cautionary note, admitting he erred, as all humans, then apologized, hoping readers would excuse any imperfections. He was cognizant of the significance of what he had attempted: "In this journey I have opened as far as I know, a path no one has taken before."[28] Oré declared: "I am very disposed to receive the correction and modification from anyone who is able to provide it and understands it; subjecting myself above all, with my heart and soul, and capturing the knowledge, thoughts, words and writings in Latin, Castilian, Quechua, Aymara, and in all the other languages that I will speak, write, teach or preach, to the censorship and correction of Our Holy Mother Church."[29] Our cautious friar was making certain to secure official approvals guaranteeing he would not fall under the close scrutiny of inquisitors. Oré's cautionary note and his voiced apologies for his insufficiencies do not obscure a marvelous intellect that interacts comfortably with major figures of Antiquity and Spain's Golden Age.

Oré stressed throughout that his endeavor is for the benefit of the Andeans "whose conversion is my highest wish," and with this desire that "I dare to bring to light some of my own works in verse principally for the glory of God, but also for the use by the Indians and for the benefit and aid of the religious of our Seraphic Order, and other clergy whose hands this humble work might reach."[30] Poetic forms could be translated into Quechua and Aymara to aid conversion. There were indigenous poets too, whose names seem to have been forgotten until recent centuries. Martin Lienhard points out that the oldest known religious poets in the Americas date from the sixteenth century, and "Although we know the names of colonial authors of such poems or prayers, including Luis Jerónimo de Oré, Juan Pérez Bocanegra and the Jesuit Pablo Prado, Andean Catholic poetry tends to become anonymous in its passage from the notebook of one scribe to that of another and from writing to orality (song) and vice versa."[31] Margot Beyersdorff notes Oré's exceptional talents: "For the purposes of evangelization, Oré composed a series of canticles (*cánticos*) that provided choir masters with the language to convey biblical history and precepts to the neophytes of the mission in the form of chant (*canto llano*)."[32]

Subsequent to his introduction highlighting the value of the poetic form for conversion, Oré moved to the issue that has sparked the interest of musicologists and students of the process of religious conversion for decades: the nature, spread, and impact of European music in the early colonial Americas, and conversely, the contribution of autochthonous music. Oré advocated that the *Symbolo Catholico Indiano* should be available in the parishes and the doctrineros should use it, "so the Indian chanters of the doctrinas offer praises to Our Lord daily during the week, singing one of the hymns and religious *cánticos.*" These would follow the religious calendar as recorded in Oré's text. The friar then shifted to the group he considered of paramount importance for successful conversion: "The school children and the parish youth are nourished with such pure and beneficial milk, and they will be weaned from their own superstitious songs, so dangerous and contrary to the Catholic faith, and to honest and laudable customs."[33]

As testimony to the veracity of his statements, Oré boasted that "As has been seen by experience in the Province of Los Collaguas and in the Valley of Jauja, and in the Province of Vilcas, and in other places where this *Symbolo Catholico* has been used, the Indians, attracted to the affection and devotion of these canticles, frequent the churches and strive to be present to receive the doctrine and catechism, whose explanation is the content of these *cánticos*." Oré added that because these canticles have been so useful for spreading the Catholic doctrine "the prelates have ordered me, and other religious and other people who have seen it, have begged me to publish this *Symbolo*." He continued that the simple yet "true" faith as described in the biblical texts, had to be explained plainly to the neophytes to attract and persuade them to forsake their old ways. They had to be convinced that the Andean religious concepts, the "sun, moon and the stars, and the high snow-capped peaks, and the volcanos and huacas, are not gods (as they in their gentility and idolatry adored them as such), rather they are the creatures of the highest God."[34]

Church historian Rubén Vargas Ugarte highlighted the significance of Oré's verse: "Luis Jerónimo de Oré has left us in his *Símbolo Cathólico Indiano* and in his *Rituale, seu manual peruanum,* some of these *cantares,* whose memory has never been lost." Oré's musical legacy continued after his death in the texts of other translators, for example: "Juan Pérez Bocanegra in another work of identical topic also includes some of them and other devotional prayers widely extended among the Indians." Vargas Ugarte noted the desire in the religious orders to employ children, especially at first, to serve as auxiliaries in catechizing. The Dominicans focused on the schools and stressed learning Spanish so the youth could soon become teachers, while the Franciscans tended to teach in indigenous languages in the churches and plazas using tools such as allegorical painting, engravings, and music to spark the interest in understanding and truly believing the doctrine.[35]

Oré focused on the virtue of presenting religious texts in verse and set to music. The Spanish word (from Latin) comes from *canto* (chant or canticle), liturgical singing, and cántico (canticle) refers to a song, in some poetic structure that Oré summarized, that was used in the churches of the Old and New Worlds. Oré emphasized that the mysteries of the faith had been presented as hymns composed in Latin by Saint Ambrose and initially introduced in the cathedral of Milan by Saint Gregory [the plainchant, *canto llano*, integral to the Latin Christian Liturgy], Hilary, and the Roman Christian poet Prudentius,[36] as well as "in Castilian and in Tuscan, and in the other tongues of the nations." Oré was fully conversant in the rhyme schemes and noted that they exist in "various verses and compositions in octaves, sonnets and tercets, songs and in other meters that encompass Latin, Italian and Castilian poetry." He emphasized that all are useful for the indoctrination.[37]

In the subsequent three pages Oré examined various forms and uses of the music, citing both classical and Church authorities. In what today might be considered a break in the "normal" order, he explained his decision: "It seemed to me useful and necessary to situate this introduction before the *Symbolo* so that the order and method of indoctrination are not confused, and all the subjects are distributed by their assigned times and hours. Thus, it will be easier to carry it out smoothly and continue to do so." Oré insisted that this order and "uniformity of the manner of teaching" should be followed because "it has been authorized by learned men, experienced in the doctrinas, and trained in teaching it [the doctrine]. They approved it as the most condensed and useful that has been produced up to this point."[38]

Oré noted that his work has already been used in some provinces in manuscript form, by both friars and clerics. The *Symbolo* or creed was translated from the Latin text of Saint Athanasius. Oré's translation into the Andean languages was, as he wrote, read and corrected by "those most knowledgeable" and "as it is at present it was approved by priests and religious of the order of Santo Domingo and Saint Augustine, ideally suited men, and religious of La Merced and the Company of Jesus, the best translators in this land, secular highlanders and learned Indians and all of them agreed that it was a most precise translation." Oré admitted that "In poetry one may exercise more liberty" yet he insisted that he "always attempts to follow the correct word and meaning. And when it was not possible to follow the text to the letter, there will never be a lack of understanding its meaning."[39] Oré had some family assistance in his translations: "The most difficult terms and words I have translated consulting the opinions of my brothers Friar Pedro de Oré, Friar Antonio de Oré, and Friar Dionisio de

Oré, who as is well-known in this entire land, are knowledgeable and capable translators and preachers for Indians and Spaniards."⁴⁰

Oré's manuscript was printed in 1598 by Antonio Ricardo. In contrast to Mexico, which boasted a printing press as early as 1539, Peru lacked one until the time of the Third Church Council. Antonio Ricardo, from Turin in the Italian Piedmont, arrived in Mexico in 1577. He had close links with the Jesuits, who offered him space for his printing equipment in the College of San Pedro y San Pablo in Mexico City. Jesuits in Lima persuaded Ricardo to come to the Peruvian capital, and he arrived there in 1581. At first the printer was housed in the Jesuit college, awaiting authorizations to practice his trade. The Church Council of Lima pressed for publication of its critical religious texts but needed royal approval. The royal *cédula* (decree), addressed to Peruvian viceroy the Conde del Villar, was issued in Spain on 7 August 1584. Meanwhile, in Lima the Jesuits were moving ahead, and preparations began even before final authorization arrived. A shorter and important text was printed for distribution throughout the viceroyalty–the *Pragmática de los Diez días del Año,* the full notice that the old Julian calendar was to be corrected to the new Gregorian one. Hence the *Catecismo* issued by the Third Church Council was not the first work published in Peru, rather this new regulation preceded it by months.⁴¹

Oré's *Symbolo Catholico Indiano* was printed "at the cost of Pedro Fernández de Valenzuela," brother-in-law of Luis Gerónimo's older brother Gerónimo. What could have prompted such a move? Salas suggests he was a common soldier, of lesser social standing than the Orés. Although he had become wealthy, it was largely from non-elite labor, administering and operating the cloth factory of Chincheros. The marriage alliance with the Oré family had provided a narrow avenue to the upper levels. Under the terms of the guardianship over his nephews following the death of his brother-in-law Gerónimo de Oré, he was to receive one tenth of the income of the estate as compensation. By 1592 Fernández de Valenzuela became the alcalde of the Hermandad of Huamanga and a year after he funded publication of the *Symbolo* he became a *regidor* of the city. He was its solicitor in 1602, and in 1604 its *alcalde ordinario*. He operated a mine in Huancavelica and continued to administer the estancias and obrajes of Gerónimo's minor children. The encomienda Indians labored in the obrajes, and complaints against the administrator were frequent.⁴² Fernández de Valenzuela used sponsorship of publication of the *Symbolo* as part of his attempt to open new doors for public office and the respect he desired.⁴³

At the end of the *Symbolo Catholico Indiano,* Oré declared: "The author promises that for the better understanding of this *Symbolo* and for the interpretation of the most difficult terms in the language, a copious *Arte* [grammar] and *Vocabulario* [dictionary] in the two languages and in Spanish will be printed along with the other sermons promised in the introduction of this book."[44] We will explore the fate of these volumes during the friar's journey in the Old World.

❦ 11 ❦

Doctrinero in Potosí and Cuzco

As Oré's service in the Colca Valley came to an end some nine years after he first entered it, he must have reflected on his accomplishments. His victory as procurator in helping the Franciscans return to the valley, and his daily work as doctrinero, must have given him ample satisfaction. Baptisms of newborns and the teaching of children would have been gratifying. Singing and training the musically adept in playing the instruments, including perhaps using Andean musical instruments, eased the process of transculturation. At the same time, the discovery of idolatries surely caused him some consternation as to the lasting impact of his efforts.

His next assignment, as guardian, led him to Jauja, an important center on the highland route linking Quito and Cuzco. In 1600, following Jauja, Oré was serving in one of the Indian parishes of the booming silver mining center of Potosí, at the time one of the largest cities in the western world, approaching 160,000, compared to London's 130,000, and Seville and Florence's 150,000 about a decade earlier.[1] Balthasar Ramírez, a cleric and administrator of Potosí's hospital, described the city and mine not long before Oré arrived. There were in all fourteen Indian parishes, each with its church and residence for a curate. Each parish in theory held 800 Indians, based on periodic inspections, and each clergyman received the stipend of one hundred silver pesos. The cost of living was high because the city's altitude—almost 13,500 feet above sea level—required that almost everything be imported, from food and wine to lumber, tile and bricks for construction, and charcoal for cooking and heating. Ramírez claimed the Hospital of Santa Veracruz, where he was administrator for ten years, was constructed and supported thanks to his own diligence. It normally handled 120 or more, mostly indigenous patients, and "the building is low and modest, as are all the others in Potosí, because the severe cold and high cost does not allow for very tall or wide buildings."[2]

Oré provided a brief description of Potosí. His initial impression echoes others who have traveled there—the penetrating cold. He was impressed by the city's size given its climate, suggesting there were "more than one hundred thousand Indians in this seat, both residents in those seven parishes and the migrant mitayos for labor in the mines." He asserted the mine "has been God's treasury, and with it all of Europe has been enriched," noting that it provided "immeasurable wealth" for Spain. But what had it done for the Indians? "The light of the Catholic Faith" was his answer. Oré, as other contemporaries, suggested that the Andean peoples received all the elements of "civilization." Those of noble blood had gone to the Indies and brought with them the "serious and important books of the most learned authors, as daily come to light in all the faculties and the divine and human sciences." Further, "every year large fleets of many ships arrive loaded with people and precious merchandise of all kinds." Oré pointed out the fruits and vegetables, the wheat, and the European livestock that were introduced to America, "and as great as these are, there is nothing that Peru sends back to Spain, if not the fruit that is extracted from the innards of this rich mountain of Potosí, that these same fleets that bring all that has been said, carry from there three or four million ducats every year. With that Peru is content and Spain paid."[3]

While in Potosí, Oré's powerful sermons attracted the attention of numerous people, including a peripatetic Hieronymite friar, Diego de Ocaña. Born in Spain around 1570, Ocaña traveled throughout the viceroyalty of Peru from 1599 to 1606, and subsequently Mexico. He was propelled by the dream of fostering the worship of the Spanish Virgin of Guadalupe in the Indies and to support its main shrine in Extremadura, Spain. In addition to his religious obligations, Ocaña was a talented painter of illuminated manuscripts in the active scriptorium of the monastery in Guadalupe.[4] Ocaña recalled, incorrectly, that he reached Potosí on Saturday night, 18 July 1600. Despite the incorrect date, he resided in the city until late October or early November 1601, mostly in the Franciscan monastery. It was in this setting that Oré and Ocaña first met and conversed. Ocaña was not a shy man, and he detailed all aspects of his mission and travels. He claimed he distributed *estampas* (small prints) of the Virgin of Guadalupe and made certain that images of the Extremaduran Virgin were prominently displayed in the places he visited. Ocaña helped found a confraternity of Our Lady of Guadalupe in Potosí and "with zeal and excitement" he painted an image of the virgin "with such perfection and the same size as the one in Spain." The friar decided to place it in the Franciscan monastery, "because they gave me a place at the main altar above the sacrarium, and because in this monastery there is more devotion than in the others, and because these friars cannot have income." Ocaña wanted to ensure that any alms collected by the majordomos of the confraternities would be sent to Spain for the worship of the Virgin in Guadalupe. He stressed that there would not be any expense with his image, because unlike a statue requiring sumptuous clothing, he painted the virgin "with so many pearls and pieces of gold superimposed that it is more uncommon than if it were a sculpture."[5]

Ocaña provided a colorful description of the image's reception by the public, including a procession through the streets for general recognition of the Extremaduran Virgin and its intended devotion in the Andes. It was during this time leading up to the event that Oré and Ocaña, who were close in age, became more acquainted. Oré's middle name, Gerónimo, and the fact that the family's patron saint was Saint Jerome must have intrigued the Hieronymite Ocaña. After the painting was completed the town criers notified the populace of the impending procession. The painting was moved first to the Dominican monastery and then to the Franciscan with great festivities and the participation of both religious and secular authorities.

When the solemn procession reached the entrance of the Franciscan church it was greeted by the assembled friars, including one must think Friar Oré, who later delivered a sermon honoring the Virgin of Guadalupe, to Ocaña's delight.[6] The image made its way toward the main altar, amidst prayers, singing, and dancing. Ocaña praised the graceful dancers "in richly adorned and costly garb, with so many ornaments and jewels, that it was something to behold." He added, "they were all very expert instrumentalists, and while playing they danced with such grace that the dances went on for an hour and a half without them tiring or tiring those who were watching." The eight days of religious celebration of the Virgin of Guadalupe in the Franciscan church included daily High Mass with organ music. In between the Masses "many principal ladies remained in the church" which stayed open until late at night. The people of Potosí participated in the festivities by attending Mass and, once they were outside the church, enjoying "the refreshments they had bought in the confection shops."[7] As he completed his narrative of the installation, benediction, and miracles attributed to his image of the Virgin of Guadalupe, Ocaña refered to the "Very reverend Father Friar Luis de Oreé [sic]" who "preached the miracle to all the Indians in their own language." Ocaña himself reported the miracle of his image of the Virgin saving six indigenous miners who were trapped and believed dead. The wives of the trapped miners came to the church of San Francisco accompanied by other indigenous women "crying and shouting to Our Lady of Guadalupe, begging her to save their husbands and bring them out alive." Ocaña added that the Indians thought his image of the virgin, which he "painted a little bit dark" was "prettier than all the other images and they loved her because she was their color." Ocaña was particularly pleased that Luis Gerónimo de Oré "every Sunday that he preached to the Indians, he would relate to them one of the miracles included in the Book of Our Lady of Guadalupe." At the end of the *octavario* "the image was placed at the main altar, above the sacrarium where it now is, much venerated."[8]

As we have seen, Luis Gerónimo consulted with his older brother Pedro de Oré regarding the translations in the *Symbolo Catholico Indiano,* but they did not always agree on policy concerning the role of Franciscans in the isolated Andean doctrinas, or the nature of the Andean population. Both brothers attended the Third Church Council in Lima and both were in the Jauja monastery in 1595. In 1583 Friar Pedro was guardian of Potosí's Franciscan monastery for more than three years, and at the council provided information on the condition of Indian miners in Potosí that would be important in developing policy for the council and the Crown, regarding mitayos, and *mingas* (independent indigenous workers). Pedro de Oré also reviewed a report by Carmelite Friar Juan de Valenzuela, a member of the theological committee of the Third Church Council, who provided a similar evaluation. The independent Indian workers in Potosí engaged in commerce with silver ore taken directly from the mines or with stolen low-grade silver ore scraps. Mine operators and treasury officials, cognizant that the Crown stood to lose a substantial portion of the royal *quinto* (one-fifth), challenged this growing business. Indigenous miners worked in dangerous conditions as they secreted the ore. Pedro de Oré affirmed that he and others knew that almost all the Indians were involved in this business and virtually everyone in Potosí was complicit, buying and selling. Pedro de Oré's assessment of the Andeans differs from his brother Luis Gerónimo's: "It is certain that the Indians have few scruples in stealing because of their imperfect faith and little fear of God, and the little understanding they have."[9]

BISHOPS OF CUZCO (1538–1638)	
Fr. Vicente de Valverde	1538–1541
Fr. Juan Solano, O.P.	1544–1561 or 1567
Dr. Sebastián de Lartaún	1573–1583
Fr. Gregorio Montalvo, O.P.	1589–1592
Fr. Luis Quesada y las Heras, O.S.A.	1594–1594
Dr. Antonio de la Raya	1595–1606
Dr. Fernando González de Mendoza, S.J.	1610–1617
Lic. Lorenzo Pérez Grado	1620–1627

Note: All dates given are approximate.

Luis Gerónimo de Oré departed Potosí after three years, and reached Cuzco around 1603. Cuzco's Bishop Antonio de Raya Navarrete posted him at an urban Indian parish, not dissimilar to the one he had held in Potosí. It was the same parish that Alonso Martínez, who had evaluated Oré's *Symbolo,* occupied until his recent death.[10] Here too Oré's persuasive preaching style led to local fame. Chronicler Diego de Córdova y Salinas remarked: "Whatever village or doctrina that he arrived at, whether that of a cleric or of a friar of another Order, they would allow him to teach and catechize their parishioners."[11] Córdova y Salinas extolled Oré's linguistic aptitude. "As a larger planet he exceeded his brothers with the marvelous gift he had in learning and speaking many and varied Indian languages of diverse nations and provinces."[12] Bernabé de Fuentes related that Raya's decision to grant the friar an Indian parish "had never been done before, nor seen in this realm ... so that he might preach in all the Indian parishes that there are in the city of Cuzco, as he has done already, with such notable concourse of them, and he was preaching to the greatest number in the cemeteries because they could not all fit into the churches."[13] While in Cuzco Oré was said to have taught the other religious there Quechua and Aymara, and "had been named *Lector de Lenguas,*" using the *Symbolo Catholico Indiano* as well as various sermons he had composed that would later appear in another of his publications.[14] Raya may have learned about Oré from Archbishop Mogrovejo and other clergymen, or the *Symbolo* reached his attention, because it was used in the doctrinas. In 1604 Raya named Oré priest of the Indian Hospital de Los Remedios, where years earlier Cristóbal de Molina served. But his term was brief. On 31 January 1604 Oré presented to Bishop

Raya his unpublished manuscripts: a *sermonario*, a manual for the administration of the sacraments in the Indian languages, and an *arte y vocabulario*, and petitioned permission to travel to Spain to print the works. Raya, impressed by the erudite Franciscan, appointed him to travel "to Spain with license from the prelates, and letters for the King and His Holiness [the Pope], in which it would be asked for the said friar Luis Gerónimo de Oré to be accepted as his coadjutor."[15]

As word spread in Cuzco of Oré's assignment in Spain many were eager to employ the friar's talents on their personal behalf at the royal court. On 19 January 1604 more than twenty "Incas of Cuzco" granted a full power of attorney to Oré and three prominent mestizos. One of them, Inca Garcilaso de la Vega was already in Spain; Don Carlos Melchor Ynga, at the time a vecino of Cuzco, and Don Alonso Fernández Mesa, both also sons of a Spaniard and a mother of the Inca royal lineage. The twenty-plus men who gave the power of attorney shared descent from one of the ruling Inca lineages. A few days later, on 26 January 1604, the Incas of the parish of San Gerónimo extended a similar power to the same men. In both cases the purpose was to obtain *mercedes* (rewards) from the Crown that had been largely taken away by Viceroy Toledo three decades earlier. They requested freedom from payment of tribute, a privilege they argued that they deserved as members of the royal family and as local lords. They also requested any other privileges befitting their status, including freedom from personal service, and the right to petition secure testimony on their behalf. The first group also solicited remuneration for the services they and their ancestors had provided the Crown. Nicanor Domínguez suggests that Oré transferred the powers to either Don Melchor Carlos Ynga or to Don Alonso Fernández de Mesa, probably while in Valladolid in March 1605.[16]

III

Creole Friar at the Centers of the First Global Empire

12

Assignments in Spain and Italy

One could not have a more distinguished advocate than Cuzco's Bishop Antonio de Raya Navarrete. Born around 1536 in the Andalusian city of Baeza, he studied theology, canon, and civil law at the University of Bologna and received his doctoral robes in 1561, later becoming its rector. The bishop participated in the Council of Trent and held several posts including inquisitor in several dioceses in Spain before his appointment as Cuzco's bishop in 1594. A staunch defender of the Jesuits, he established the Colegio of San Antonio Abad in Cuzco, the Colegio de la Compañía de Jesús in Huamanga, and authorized the foundation of the Convent of Santa Catalina in Arequipa.[1]

On 28 January 1604 Raya, in the presence of a notary, secretary, and witnesses, stated that he had appealed to the pope and was now requesting that the king, as the patron of the diocese of the kingdom of Peru, allow him to send a bishop *in partibus* (one assigned to assume designated tasks normally performed by a bishop) to assist in confirming and inspecting the diocese. Raya nominated previously, at different times, two Dominican friars for the task, but:

> Presently he names and named Father Friar Luis Hieronimo de Oré, a Priest of the Franciscan Order and native of these kingdoms who knows very well the Indian general languages of Quichua and Aymara, and in whom converge many other elements of virtue, erudition and age, so that His Majesty is served to name and present to His Holiness any one of them and principally the said Friar Luis de Oré for the said task and thus he can provide order and exercise all the pontifical duties when and how the said proprietary Lord Bishop orders and entrusts him and under his direction and order and in no other manner.

Raya added that should Oré be granted this dignity he would need support to sustain him. He suggested, by the rights conferred by Royal Patronage, that part of the revenues assigned to Cuzco's diocese could be applied, and recommended that 500,000 maravedis yearly be allotted to Oré. Bishop Raya pointed to the normal stipend established for participants of provincial church councils as one of the sources already in place to support Oré. A copy of the commission was also sent to the king's ambassador in Rome and to important figures in Seville, Valladolid, and at court.[2]

There is also a copy of Bishop Raya's authorization for Oré to travel to Spain to publish his works. Raya noted in 1604 that Oré, *lector* (reader) of theology and preacher in Cuzco's Franciscan monastery, had presented three books for review to secure license to publish. The titles vary slightly from one reference to another. One was the *Sermonario de las Dominicas y fiestas del año* in Spanish, Quechua and Aymara. Another was a *Manual* to administer the sacraments "with the necessary things" for the doctrinero in the field "translated into the said two languages," and then an *Arte y Vocabulario*. Oré notified the bishop he was prepared for departure to Spain with royal license to travel and to print his works. Oré knew full approval for publication was needed and feared that no one would be available in Spain qualified to review the Andean language texts. He therefore asked Raya to send locally the manuscripts to be evaluated and approved by men "learned and knowledgeable in the said languages."[3] The bishop charged Sebastián Ramos, Dominican reader of theology, to review the Spanish text. Juan Pérez de Bocanegra, curate of the parish of Belén in Cuzco and a specialist in Quechua and Aymara, was to validate the accuracy of the three book-length manuscripts. The men expeditiously reviewed and endorsed Oré's texts, noting that they are "extremely necessary and useful" for the clergy as well as the indigenous parishioners. Raya certified that "the said books are examined, seen and approved by the examiners named by us" and asked the king to issue the license for printing. In his letter of presentation Raya stressed the importance of the books for the "natives of this kingdom, as has already been shown with another book by the same author," the *Symbolo Catholico Indiano*. The bishop added that after Oré's *Symbolo* was published, "the *sinodales* (those assigned by a bishop to examine the canonical correctness of the parish clergy) of this diocese ruled and ordered the priests to use it for teaching the Indians the doctrine."[4]

Raya issued his order on 31 January 1604. Assuming Oré was in Cuzco at the time, he must have quickly departed for Lima, taking with him the manuscripts and authorizations as well as his appointment documents. While in Lima, Oré completed his affairs and set sail for Spain, probably his first sea venture. We have no record of the date of his departure. The initial leg of the journey from Lima to Spain was relatively quick, given the prevailing winds and the strong Humboldt Current sweeping them northward. They may have stopped in Ecuador's port of Guayaquil, then skirted the Ecuadorian and Colombian coasts, and finally reached the Isthmus of Panama. Oré may have spent several days in the Franciscan monastery in Panama City, perhaps seeing one of his brothers there before beginning the overland trek across the isthmus to Portobello on the Caribbean coast. From there he would take the first ship available to sail to Cuba. He resided in the Franciscan monastery in Havana and finalized preparations for the Atlantic crossing to Spain. We know that Oré reached his destination by March of 1605 because that month publication of his *Rituale seu manuale peruanum* was formally authorized by the Council of the Indies in Valladolid.[5]

Seville was strikingly different from the cities of the Andean world Oré left behind. Its population size, four times as large as Lima's, and its cosmopolitan nature had to have impressed the friar. He must have admired Seville's massive Cathedral, its Patio of Oranges and Giralda, the ancient Muslim prayer tower overlooking the city and adjoining countryside, and the imposing Alcazar palace. The Seville Oré discovered was filled with merchants and manufacturers, most associated with the Indies trade. There were ship repairs and provisioning to be done on the banks of the Guadalquivir River. There was a gunpowder factory to provide the firepower for the defense of the fleets. Most important for the Indies trade was the Casa de la Contratación where ship's passengers and cargo were registered, taxes and fees collected, and its commercial court adjudicated. Virtually all the religious orders were represented in Seville with hundreds of friars and nuns in their respective monasteries and convents. One of the largest was the Monastery of San Francisco, located on the side of the Renaissance style city hall, constructed during the reign of Charles V.[6]

During his brief stay in Seville or later in Madrid, Luis Gerónimo met his youngest brother, Licentiate Francisco de Oré. Born around 1568, Francisco went to Spain about 1582 to further his studies. There was good reason to be concerned about his future. His oldest brother received the encomienda, the second son the mining operations, and four brothers entered the Franciscan order. His oldest sister had married and received her dowry and his other sisters became nuns. Francisco's best option was a religious vocation, and he likely completed the licentiate and priesthood by the end of the decade. It was difficult for a creole to secure a good position in Spain, so his intention shifted to the Indies. The recommended course of action was to cultivate connections at court and present a report of his and his family's services to the Crown (*relación de méritos y servicios*). Competition for rewards was pronounced, and some contracted a genealogist to draw up a document to support their cause.[7] It is possible that Francisco's brother Friar Pedro turned to him regarding various transactions, including one in 1590 to act as a representative to help secure travel authorization for another Oré brother.[8] Success for Francisco de Oré came slowly, and it appears he was more inclined to conduct business than God's work. Some transactions did not go smoothly. Francisco was engaged in a lawsuit in 1600 with Alonso de Cuenca, shipmaster of *Nuestra Señora del Rosario*, regarding nineteen silver bars shipped from Peru to Spain. Francisco acted as an agent in Spain for family members and other Peruvians. We find him in Seville in 1607 taking legal action in the Casa de la Contratación to secure payment from the estate of a deceased Peruvian.[9]

It is unclear if Luis Gerónimo met his brother at this time. The pressing assignments by the bishop of Cuzco led to a swift overland trip to the royal court and Council of the Indies, at the time in Valladolid. He would likely take the route north through Extremadura, the homeland of many Peruvian conquistadors and early settlers. He may have stopped briefly at the Shrine of the Virgin of Guadalupe, keeping in mind Friar Ocaña. He then forged on to Salamanca and its renowned university. To reach Valladolid he headed toward Zamora, or angled northeast to Medina del Campo where Francisco Noguerol de Ulloa, recipient of Gonzalo Pizarro's Colca Valley encomienda settled after returning to Spain. From there it was only a short distance to Tordesillas, and finally Valladolid.

Oré was in Valladolid by early March 1605, when by recommendation of the Council of the Indies, Dominican Friar and Predicador General Pedro de Paredes reviewed Oré's substantial text "with the necessary translations to the four general languages of Peru." He determined that the translation captured the true meaning of the terms and praised Oré's linguistic skills: "It is a work worthy of the esteem afforded to its author in that kingdom, because he is one of those who knows, pronounces and writes them best." Paredes concluded that the doctrine presented is "plain, serious, important, useful and beneficial for the curates and parishioners of those such remote places, where there are not enough men who know it and they lack the books to teach them."[10] Finding nothing contrary to the doctrine of the church, he wrote his approval: "It seems to me (lest there be a better judgment) that license to print it can be given, and that the book will be well received because of its urgent necessity in those provinces, and the saintly zeal of its author." Paredes signed his recommendation to publish on 22 March 1605 in the Dominican monastery of San Pablo in Valladolid.[11]

Oré's first visit to Spain lasted less than a year, from early 1605 until he reached Rome just before December. While in Spain Oré, as representative to the court of Philip III, presented Cuzco Bishop Raya's legal position regarding the jurisdictional boundaries of his diocese in the dispute with the Bishop of Charcas. There were other duties—Oré reported on the situation in Peru to the Franciscan General Commissioner of the Indies and other friars. The position of a Franciscan General Commissioner for the Indies dates from the reign of Ferdinand and Isabel and the early settlement in the Caribbean, and papal donation giving supervision over the church to the Spanish monarchs (Patronato Real). Following the conquests of Mexico and Peru, and realizing the enormous task of converting millions of indigenous people, the ecclesiastic bureaucracy expanded alongside that of the state. In the Franciscan structure, with the increasing number of provinces and custodies, and their provincials and custodians as local administrators there was need for overseers in charge of the larger units—a Commissioner General of Peru for example. In the context of the entire structure as it evolved in Spain, there was the General Minister of the Order who resided at court, but also traveled throughout Spain to supervise the Iberian Franciscans. The increasing complexity and size of the church in the Americas and the need to have someone in Spain to oversee those efforts and meet regularly with the Council of the Indies and the Casa de la Contratación regarding the movement of alms for Franciscans going to and from the Indies, led General Minister Friar Cristóbal de Capitefontium to request Philip II in April 1572 to name a Commissioner for the Indies based at the court in Madrid. The position was authorized at the 1583 Franciscan General Chapter Meeting in Toledo followed by subsequent reaffirmations by the General Assembly of the Franciscan order in Rome.[12]

The snippets of documents we have of Oré's orders and itinerary fail to provide all the information needed for a full account. There are several reasons why important documents are lost to us. The Franciscans seemed less interested in recording their activities than other orders. Furthermore, the sprawling Franciscan monasteries were easy prey in times of conflict. Their vegetable gardens, kitchens, and infirmaries provided appealing barracks for soldiers. The War of the Spanish Succession at the beginning of the eighteenth century was costly, but the Napoleonic invasion in the nineteenth century was devastating. Franciscan papers served a variety of functions for foreign soldiers, including lighting fires. The suppression of the Jesuits in the late eighteenth century, and limitations on other orders with fewer than 12 *profesos* led to further loss. The 1836 *desamortizaciones* of Juan Álvarez Mendizabal ended in a massive breakup and appropriation of the assets of Spain's monasteries. The Carlist Wars, then the Spanish Civil War caused further loss or scattering of the rich Franciscan legacy, including valuable documents.

Once Oré completed his assignments and obtained authorizations to publish his texts, he traveled to Italy to report to the pope and to fellow Franciscans. There were several possible ways to reach Italy from Castile. An overland trek through southern France was unlikely, given time restraints facing Oré, but the passage by sea would be quicker and safer. Oré's working agenda was already full. Bishop Raya's appointment included salutations for the pope, and Oré delivered them. On 3 December 1605 Pope Paul V issued an order directly related to Oré's presence in Rome. On that day, the indulgence *De salute Dominici gregis,* was granted to all who in the Lima Cathedral participated kneeling during the *Salve* and the *Litanias*. Historian Vargas Ugarte believes Oré may have composed the document, which originated in the actions of the Third Church Council of Lima two decades before, and the *Consulta o Ritual de la Iglesia Metropolitana de Lima*.[13] Vargas Ugarte adds, as the procurator of the bishop of Cuzco, Oré presented before the Congregation of Bishops a *"Relación del estado del Obispado del Cuzco."*[14] This report was critical for the bishop of Cuzco's defense of his diocese against boundary challenges mounted by the bishop of Charcas. With his work in Rome concluded and the papal indulgence in hand, Oré needed to secure its printing for distribution. It was not done in Rome.

At this juncture it is possible that Oré embarked on a personal pilgrimage to Assisi, the birthplace of St. Francis and nearby shrines associated with the saint's life. He might have visited the religious sites related to Santa Clara, given the Oré family connections with the Clarisa convent in Huamanga. But copies of the *Indulgencias* needed to be printed as soon as possible. It was short,

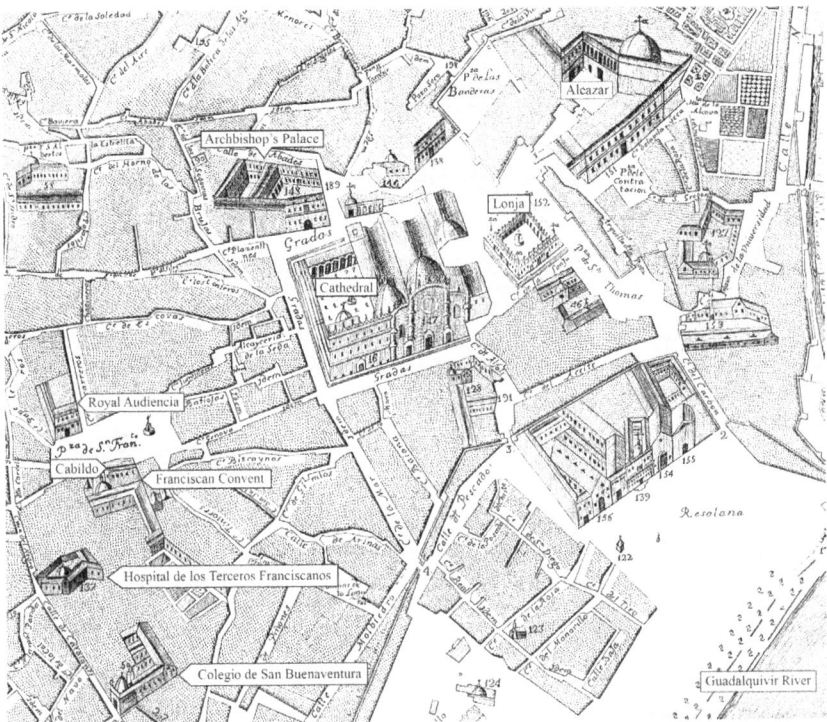

Seville's Franciscan compound. Bird's-eye view of the compound of the Franciscans near the Plaza of San Francisco by Greg Cook. From a small section of the *Plano topográphico de la M. N. Y M. L. ciudad de Sevilla [Material cartográfico] / Se levantó, y abrió por disposición del S.or D.n Pablo de Olavide, asistente de esta ciudad, intendente del exército, y provincia de Andalucía, y superintendente de las nuevas poblaciones de Sierra Morena, y Andalucía. Año de 1771*. Copy in the Bilioteca Digital Real Academia de la Historia. Creative Commons, Public Domain Mark 1.0. (CC BY 4.0)

perhaps even a single sheet, that would be placed in a conspicuous location in the church and distributed to those receiving the indulgence. Oré was usually present during the printing of his works, and it is likely that he paused in the city of Alessandria in the Italian Piedmont to oversee the printing of the *Tratado sobre las indulgencias* in 1607. Chronicler Córdova y Salinas notes that in 1607 in Alessandria, Oré printed "a Treatise on Indulgences that he wrote in Rome, in Latin, for the attention of the most illustrious Master Vestrio Barbiano, *datario* of Pope Paul V, to whom he dedicated the tract."[15] Oré's dedication to the pope's datary, a prelate presiding over requests for benefices or any other church position, including indulgences or marital dispensations that require authorization of the Tribunal of the Roman Curia, suggests that the two men established a relationship.[16] Barbiano might have provided a smooth path for the Andean friar to reach the pontiff's ear. After his relatively brief time in Rome and the northern Piedmont, Oré traveled to Italy's south, to the Spanish Kingdom of Naples. Córdova y Salinas highlights the accomplishments of the famous authors of his order—Luis Gerónimo de Oré is second on the list. He suggests that because of the Franciscan vow of poverty and the lack of printing presses in Peru Franciscans had been unable to display their erudition. The chronicler notes Oré's publications of the 1598 *Symbolo Catholico Indiano*, the 1607 "Treatise on Indulgences" and stresses the valuable *Rituale, seu manuale peruanum*, with its "many hymns of the Roman Breviary, and all the life of Christ in verse, which the Indians liked so much that they sing them in their homes and fields." Furthermore, the Andeans sang some of Oré's religious music in the churches, along with the organ.[17]

13

Naples, the *Rituale, seu manuale peruanum*

Luis Gerónimo de Oré remained in the Italian peninsula for about six years; he was in Rome by December 1605 and present in Spain in 1611. Oré's Italian trip was a time of learning, and gave him a more profound understanding of the complexities of a rapidly changing world and the challenges, internal and external, facing church and state. His tour provided ample time to complete Bishop Raya's assignments, and Raya's letters of introduction to important Jesuits in Spain and Italy were helpful during his journey. The bishop's demise on 28 July 1606 would not have been known in Europe for months and Oré might have learned of it while in Naples.

It was in Naples that Oré's most important, yet until recently overlooked work, the *Rituale, seu manuale peruanum*, was printed by Iacobum Carlinum and Constantinum Vitalem in 1607, and Oré must have been in the city to oversee the printing. Dozens of religious texts and administrative documents were published by the two master printers. Naples, just as Lima, was a viceregal capital. Spain's claims to the Italian possessions, as well as to islands and ports elsewhere in the central and eastern Mediterranean, came about through the marriage of Isabel of Castile and Ferdinand of Aragon. Naples was larger than Seville, and it was a center for commerce with the Levant and northern Africa as well as the western Mediterranean. It was also a principal center for training the Jesuits who traveled to the Indies, and it would be almost impossible for Oré not to have come into contact with them, for the Franciscan monastery and the Clarisas Convent were near the Jesuit church, school, and library.[1]

The *Rituale, seu manuale peruanum* served as a comprehensive manual for the administration of the church sacraments in Quechua and Aymara and Oré prepared it, consulting the "standard manuals" as early as his novitiate in Franciscan and other religious libraries. These included the Salamanca manual, the

RITVALE, SEV
MANVALE
PERVANVM,

ET FORMA BREVIS ADMINI-
strandi apud Indos sacrosancta Baptismi, Pœ-
nitentiæ, Euchariſtiæ, Matrimonij, &
Extremæ vnctionis Sacramenta.

Iuxta ordinem Sanctæ Romanæ Ecclesiæ.

PER R. P. F. LVDOVICVM HIERONYMVM
Orerium, Ordinis Minorum Concionatorem, & Sacræ
Theologiæ Lectorem accuratum:

ET QVAE INDIGENT VERSIONE, VVL-
garibus Idiomatibus Indicis, secundum diuersos situs
omnium Prouinciarum noui orbis Perù, aut per
ipsum translata, aut eius indu-
stria elaborata.

NEAPOLI,
Apud Io. Iacobum Carlinum, & Constantinum Vitalem. 1607.

Oré's 1607 *Rituale, seu manuale peruanum*. Title page of *Rituale, seu Manuale Peruanum, et forma breuis administrandi apud Indos sacrosancta Baptismi, Poenitentiae, Eucharistiae, Matrimonij, & Extremae vnctionis sacramenta. Iuxta ordinem Sanctae Romanae Ecclesiae. Per R.P.F. Ludouicum Hieronymum Orerium, ordinis Minorum concionatorem, & sacrae theologiae lectorem accuratum:* / Neapoli: apud Io. Iacobum Carlinum, & Costantinum Vitalem. 1607. Internet Archive, Creative Commons, Public Domain Mark 1.0.

Sevillian manual, both the old and new Mexican manuals, the one used in Portugal and Brazil, plus that used in France's Catholic churches, and perhaps in Naples, those in Italy. Oré took care not to stray from official Catholic doctrine, and received the full support of the papacy. Short versions of the basic doctrine in other languages, some no longer spoken, were included in the volume, a gem for linguists.[2] The full title of Oré's book in Latin is long and cumbersome and the thick 420-page text is even longer than his *Symbolo Catholico Indiano*. Cardinal and General Inquisitor of the Holy Office, Pompeio Arrigoni (1552–1616) provided the printing authorization. The body of the text is introduced by Friar Archangelo de Messana, the minister general of the Franciscan order. He lauds its value for doctrineros in the Andean region, and states it was in accordance with the dictates of the Council of Trent and has been authorized by Franciscan General Commissioner of Peru Juan de Venido and Juan de Cepeda, the General Commissioner for the Indies.[3]

In his short but dense introduction to the doctrineros of Peru, Oré pointed out the reasons that compelled him to prepare the volume: the absence of a brief manual for clerics in which all the important and necessary translations were available. Oré believed that a manual in the "general languages of that land, Quechua, Aymara, Puquina, Mochica, and Guaraní" was vital for the salvation of the Andean peoples, and stressed the ease with which the clerics could use it. Oré emphasized the universality of the Catholic faith and argued that all the manuals he had seen "are in agreement in the essentials of the rites, ceremonies and administration of the Sacraments, with the Roman Ritual, differing one from another only in some more or less tedious devotional texts." Oré extracted the fundamentals, "avoiding the variety and differences, and reduced it to the essential in a single *Manual Catholico Romano Peruano y Cuzquense* with the necessary translations." He aimed to have his *Manual* used in the archdiocese of Lima and the bishoprics of Cuzco, Quito, Charcas, Chuquiavo, Santa Cruz de la Sierra, Tucumán, the Rio de la Plata, "and even including Brazil, a distance of 1,800 leagues." Oré concluded his dedicatory modestly yet grandly: "I offer it to all who desire the salvation of souls," hoping the clergy would accept the *Manual* and use it in their doctrinas "enjoying the brevity into which it has been reduced, in which diverse secrets and necessary things are encompassed."[4] Many believed the *Manual* was beneficial in Europe as well, especially for priests and friars preparing to travel to the Indies. By careful study they might learn enough of the principal Amerindian languages to be ready for final language training before their examinations and appointments to the rural doctrinas. At least this was Oré's hope.

The initial thirty-three pages of the manual provide the authorized Latin text for doctrineros to use for baptism, the Eucharist or Holy Communion, penance, confession, excommunication, matrimony, and extreme unction. It is followed by the Spanish translation with detailed instructions covering the mechanics of conducting the standard rituals: the need to ensure the purity of the Holy Water, the nature of the communion wafers, the types of names to assign infants being baptized, the acceptable godparents and their duties, the types of penance, when and where to conduct the last rites, the form of religious processions, and more. Subsequently doctrineros studying the *Rituale, seu manuale peruanum* would find the texts translated into Quechua, Aymara, and Puquina. There is overlooked ethnological information throughout the book. The section on confession (pp. 140–170) is especially revealing, displaying Oré's profound understanding of indigenous norms. Here as elsewhere in the *Manual,* there are references to his earlier printed texts. "By the findings of the [Third Lima Church] Council, and by the daily experience one clearly sees the need for the Spanish priests, both regulars and the seculars who are in the Indian parishes, if they are not native to this land, to be helped with a confessional, which is why what follows is included, extracted from our *Symbolo Catholico Indiano,* approved by the Most Reverend Archbishop and the Bishops of Peru."[5] Oré did what was normal in religious writings of the period: he plagiarized himself. Religious texts requiring approval of the ecclesiastical censors could not stray from the norm. Oré's text on marriage also indicates Andean pre-Christian patterns that doctrineros could encounter.

Oré included in the last section (pp. 385–418) translations of the "Doctrina Christiana." He noted that the Quechua and Aymara translations were commissioned by the Third Church Council, and were prepared collectively by the "priests, clerics, and the religious of the Orders of Santo Domingo, San Francisco, San Agustin, La Merced and the Company of Jesus, ideal in their knowledge of them." Oré noted that the Puquina version "was largely done by Father Alonso de Barzana, the well-respected Jesuit, and after his death some items were added by the author, with the commission and approval of the Reverend Bishop of Cuzco." This is the first instance that suggests Oré had a working knowledge of Puquina. The Mochica was translated by secular clergymen and the regulars and approved by the Archbishop of Lima. The Guaraní was compiled entirely by Franciscan Friar Luis de Bolaños of the *Menores Observantes* and approved by the Bishop of the Rio de la Plata. Bolaños had arrived in Asunción in 1575 and is responsible for the first systematic work among the Guaraní. He is credited with founding numerous Guaraní missions between 1580 and 1593. Bolaños composed the lost Guaraní grammar and basic dictionary and the catechism which Oré mentioned in his *Symbolo Catholico Indiano*.[6] And finally, the "Brasílica" was prepared by the "Benedictines, Reformed Franciscans and Portuguese Jesuit Priests in Brazil."[7]

For starting doctrineros the "Brief Doctrine" in the principal languages near the end of the *Manual* was valuable. It included the Pater Noster, the Ave Maria, the Credo, the Salve, and the Fourteen Articles of the Faith.[8] The core articles—the Trinity, the Virgin Birth, and the Death and Resurrection of Christ—are included, as well as the Last Judgment. What did Quechua and Aymara speakers think of what the doctrineros tried to explain? Guaman Poma de Ayala wrote of the garbled words and total confusion caused by the teachings of certain clergy he knew. Some of the following "rules" may have been easier to digest, such as the section covering the Ten Commandments,[9] the Five Commandments of the Church, the Seven Sacraments, the Three Virtues (faith, hope and charity), the Four Cardinal Virtues, the Seven Deadly Sins, the Three Enemies of the Soul, the Four *Novísimos* (the Four Last Things: death, judgment, heaven, and hell). The next section is the translation of the General Confessional, then the *Summa de la Fe Catholica*,[10] in theory (at least) to make the Trinity more understandable to Andean neophytes. The *Catecismo Breve, y Cotidiano*[11] provides the catechism in a question-and-answer format. The Quechua and Aymara translations appear first, followed by the Puquina[12] and the text of the Mochica de los Yungas.[13] The Guaraní by Friar Bolaños follows, and it is abbreviated. At the end of the section Bolaños notes that "this copy is in conformity with the original."[14]

Oré also included a warning to the confessors of the diocese of the Rio de la Plata "concerning the things that may present the most risk and difficulty, given and ordered to avoid by the Most Reverend Señor Don Friar Martín Ignacio de Loyola the bishop of the diocese."[15] The nineteen issues identified by the bishop and the Custodian Friar Juan Descobar who both signed the original text, reveal much about the state of affairs in the region. Bishop Loyola, a nephew of the founder of the Society of Jesus, was born about 1550 and became a Franciscan. He made two voyages around the world and spent substantial time in the Philippines and China. In 1595 he traveled from Spain to Paraguay, passing through Panama and the viceroyalty of Peru before going to Chile and the Rio de la Plata. Loyola returned to Spain and in 1602 was named bishop of the Rio de la Plata, and he reached Asunción, the seat of the diocese, the following year. The bishopric covered all the territory from Paraguay, today's Uruguay, Argentina, and more. He died in Buenos Aires in 1606.[16] The nineteen orders Bishop Loyola issued could serve as a Bill of Rights for the indigenous people of his diocese if they were widely disseminated and enforced. Spaniards, especially officials and encomenderos, faced excommunication if they ignored the strict mandates. Close analysis of this text and its impact in the Rio de la Plata and elsewhere merits investigation. Here we focus on seven of the major points in the text.[17]

Bishop Loyola's instructions were directed to administrators of small ethnicities located in a wide swath of land shared by today's northeastern Argentina, southeastern Paraguay and much of Uruguay. A common characteristic was internecine conflict, fierce independence, and hatred of the Spanish and Portuguese. Loyola's first instruction was aimed at the captains and soldiers, ordering them that if knowingly involved in unjust wars and acting against the Crown's mandates, they were required to provide full restitution to the Indians "for all the harm, thefts or deaths" they were responsible for. Second, if the captains believed the war was just, but after finding the reverse was true, they had to restitute only the part that applied to them. The fifth instruction stipulated that captains and soldiers, and even the governor, who forced encomienda villager's children and women, or those not in encomienda, to serve them and "if the Indians have not committed a crime that might be punishable by taking away their children and wives" then the confessors must compel the officials to free them from their service and safely return them to their homes. The Indians were to be compensated for past grievances, and the perpetrators were told to apologize. The sixth item required payment to any of the children or elders under or over the stipulated age who were forced to provide service. Their future service was prohibited. The eighth order tackled the complex issue of raids on free indigenous peoples and selling them for service. Anyone who had "bought stolen service of the Indians" had to do penance for not only taking service extracted illegally, but also for enabling "the said robbers to persevere in their cruelties." These Indians were to be treated as free people and whenever possible returned to their land and cacique. The same obligation applied to anyone who purchased Indian service from another Spaniard, because they have "no dominion over [the Indian] and cannot take him against his will to another city or province." The next two instructions covered indigenous marriage, giving them "total liberty, because if they marry against their will" those who forced them to do so are *ipso facto* excommunicated as mandated by the Council of Trent, and those who impede their marriage would commit a mortal sin. Item sixteen specified that Indians in the repartimientos who had not received regular church services and married according to their customs "without the presence of a priest (even if they are Christians)" the marriages were valid, as they were for Spaniards before the Council of Trent. Until a priest officially married them, the couple could continue to live together because "they are not living in concubinage, nor should they be separated, if there is no other impediment." Furthermore, confessors should not absolve anyone who takes away the wives from their husbands, until the couple is reunited.[18]

Bishop Loyola's nineteen-point instructions were unlikely to have been in Oré's original manuscript—they were added later, probably in Naples. The text is strongly Lascasian, calling for better treatment of indigenous people and justice, including restitution for Spanish crimes. The relationship between native Americans and the Spanish in the Rio de la Plata region, even the very nature of the encomienda system, were both similar and different from those experienced by Oré in the Andean doctrinas. We have already noted Oré was attuned to the positions of Bartolomé de las Casas and would have found Bishop Loyola's instructions important to include in his own manual.[19]

❧ 14 ❧

Enigma of the Lost Dictionary and Grammar

Oré's residence in Naples was important in many ways. He interacted with the Jesuits, who had been active in the American missions from the 1560s. He could probe them, and read their works on the missions and the difficulties they encountered. Given their interest in translations of autochthonous languages, he could share with them his own observations on the Quechua- and Aymara-speaking regions and the challenges of working in the Andes. Oré could also learn from the detailed annual reports Jesuits received from their missions as well as their travelogues and histories of peoples throughout the Indies and beyond. He likely noted the variation in their technique of conversion from one ethnic group to another, complex because of vast cultural differences between the hundreds of ethnicities inhabiting the Americas. The Jesuit position was modified to maintain control in areas of high civilization as well as on the frontiers where resistance often led to unending confrontations. Oré departed Naples with a more global understanding. The knowledge proved important when he received new assignments in coming years.

In the last paragraph of the *Symbolo Catholico Indiano* Oré vowed to publish a dictionary and grammar in Quechua and Aymara.[1] During his Italian sojourn the manuscripts of the Quechua and Aymara dictionary and grammar that he lugged with him from Peru to Spain, then Italy, and still mentioned in the *Rituale, seu manuale peruanum,* disappear from the record. The manuscripts were prepared, copied, reviewed for publication many times, then mysteriously vanished. Had Oré lost the manuscripts, or simply lost interest in pursuing publication? There were several copies of each manuscript, given the complex set of requirements to secure authorization to print, and members of the secular hierarchy as well as other religious orders had access to the texts, since their imprimatur was needed. It was clear to all at the time that the first printed dictionary and grammar of Quechua by Dominican Friar Domingo de Santo Tomás published in Valladolid in 1560 was imperfect. Felipe Guaman Poma de Ayala later put it bluntly when he wrote that the vocabulary was "all mixed up with the Spanish language."[2] It was also obvious to speakers of Quechua that the 1586 dictionary printed by Antonio Ricardo was also incomplete and misleading.

Might Oré's manuscript dictionary and grammar have served as the foundation for other lexicographers? Oré's drafts were authorized in the mid-1590s in Peru, and the manuscript copies were surely circulating prior to this, given their significance for the religious in the field. But if someone published "his own" Quechua and Aymara dictionary that was as thorough and as excellent as Oré's reputedly was, there would be no need for his. Between authorization to print in Peru in 1598 and 1607 when he was in Naples there was ample time for other linguists to produce similar works—and they did. Juan Pérez de Bocanegra, curate of the parish of Belén in Cuzco, was one of the examiners in Quechua and Aymara assigned to review Oré's dictionary and grammar along with other of his manuscripts.[3] Lima's Archbishop Jerónimo de Loayza established a chair of Quechua for the Lima Cathedral in 1551 and Doctor Alonso de Huerta was among the first to occupy the chair. His *Arte de la lengua general de los yndios deste reyno del Pirú* was published in Lima by Francisco del Canto in 1619. The early conquistador and chronicler Juan de Betanzos who was fluent in Quechua and was married to a woman of one of the royal Inca lineages prepared his own large manuscript dictionary and other texts that he shared with members of various religious orders in Cuzco. Although never published it would be among the earliest dictionaries. Betanzos lamented that he had expended six years of "my youth" in the effort to prepare his translation, and was exhausted by the challenge, vowing never to attempt such a feat again.[4]

Oré was presumably unaware when he sailed from Lima for Europe in the first half of 1604 that Ludovico Bertonio's Aymara dictionary and grammar were being printed in Rome. Bertonio and other Italian Jesuits were assigned to serve in the viceroyalty of Peru in 1580 and on 20 September of that year the group reached Andalusia, joining Spanish Jesuits likewise destined for Peru. The fleet that included the new Archbishop Mogrovejo and the Jesuit Diego González Holguín, the future Quechua linguist, set sail from Sanlúcar de Barrameda. Coincidentally, on 3 March 1582 Oré had been ordained a deacon, the same day as Ludovico Bertonio was ordained by Mogrovejo. In addition to preparation for his priestly duties Bertonio concentrated on the humanities and excelled at composing Latin verses. In 1585 he was assigned to the Jesuit house in Juli. The Juli missions in the Chucuito region were first held by Dominicans, but Viceroy Toledo in 1577 removed them and entrusted the missions to the Jesuits. The Jesuits established a Colegio that acted as a center for linguistic and religious study for Jesuits and indigenous youth of the Chucuito reducciones. The school was normally staffed by about a dozen Jesuits. As they studied native languages they worked alongside their indigenous students. Over the late sixteenth and early seventeenth centuries other important linguists and doctrineros studied there, including Anello Oliva, Bernabé Cobo, Alonso de Barzana, Diego de Torres Rubio, and Blas Valera. While in Juli Ludovico Bertonio gradually became committed to the local Aymara and their language and served in the Andean altiplano most of the remainder of his life. In November 1593 he was fully incorporated into the Society of Jesus, and by 1595 was recognized for his work among the Aymara. Bertonio spent time in Potosí in the early seventeenth century, appearing in a list of the Jesuits there in March of 1601. He returned to Juli in 1603. This would place him in Potosí simultaneously with Oré and Diego de Ocaña.

As early as 1595 Bertonio's improving fluency in Aymara was recognized by his superiors. It appears, however, that Bertonio at first was part of a team. On 12 March the Father Provincial of Peru Juan Sebastián wrote Jesuit General Aquaviva in Rome that "the Fathers" had begun texts of sermons and other religious texts and "they have also prepared a dictionary and it seems it would be useful if it were printed."[5] Because no one was capable of reviewing the text in Italy, Father Sebastián suggested authorization should be issued for its printing in Peru. A year later, on 6 March 1596, Bertonio wrote directly to General Aquaviva requesting publication of his works, and on 6 October the general responded that he had already told the provincial that they were worthy of printing. Aquaviva on 21 October penned another letter to Provincial Sebastián authorizing publication not only of this text, "but for any other work of this nature useful for the Indians in their own language."[6] Five years went by and Bertonio's work remained unpublished. In 1601 Aquaviva wrote to him that the *Arte* (the grammar) should be published in Peru rather than Europe, "because to print it here and then send it to Peru would be too costly." But Aquaviva's warning arrived too late. By then Bertonio's manuscript of the grammar was sailing to Europe carried by Diego de Torres Bollo, who had been the Jesuit Superior of Juli while Bertonio was serving there. Now Torres Bollo (ca. 1550–1638), was traveling to Rome as the Provincial solicitor and was carrying not just Bertonio's work, but also manuscripts in Aymara and Quechua prepared by linguist Diego de Torres Rubio (1547–1638). They were published in Seville in 1603. Torres Bollo reached Peru in 1581 and throughout his life was vocal about the treatment of indigenous peoples. In 1603 he wrote to the president of the Council of the Indies challenging justifications for the Spanish conquest. In 1604, the year he returned to America, Torres Bollo published a brief history of the Jesuits in Peru and established the Jesuit Province of Paraguay that included the Guaraní missions.[7]

Two of the manuscripts Torres Bollo took to Europe may have been Bertonio's *Arte Breve* and his *Arte y Grammatica muy copiosa de la Lengua Aymara* which were printed in 1603 in Rome by Luis Zannetti. Although Bertonio was displeased with the quality of the published texts, he admitted at the end of the first part of his corrected 1612 *Vocabulario* that he frequently added material taken from the *Grammar* of Aymara from his 1603 Rome publication. But Bertonio stressed that he strove to make his 1612 edition of five texts in Aymara as free from errors as possible. On the last two pages of the second part of the 1612 text Bertonio warned the religious who were learning Aymara of the complexity of the language and culture. He wrote that he had done his best by constantly questioning native Aymara speakers and noting the differences in dialect between those living in Charcas or Chuquisaca. But even more complex was what he notes of the dialects spoken in the same village, depending on which of the three parcialidades they belonged to.[8]

Although Bertonio arrived in Peru in 1581 without training in the language, his long residence and close association with the peoples in the Jesuit missions, plus his diligent work at the school in Juli, contributed to his knowledge of Aymara language and culture. Bertonio stressed more than once that he hoped the religious would avoid the *"barbarismos"* frequently uttered by the imperfectly trained students of Aymara. He warned of the damage they could cause as new converts listened to sermons that seemed more hilarious than holy, as noted by Guaman Poma de Ayala. Bertonio emphasized he acquired the Aymara language largely in the heartland of the Lupaca. His sources for his Aymara dictionary and grammar may have included earlier manuscripts of Jesuits, or other orders although he does not cite them. However, he does give ample recognition to the Indians working in the school in his prologue in July 1611. Bertonio praised "the good abilities" of the indigenous parishioners who "have come to understand very well everything one can ask of a faithful and Catholic Christian," and added "we strive so they can write in their Aymara language, with the greatest accuracy that is possible."[9] Alan Durston notes that of the Jesuits in the Andean missions, Bertonio was one of the more apt to employ native collaborators to prepare religious texts.[10]

When Oré reached Rome, he must have learned of the printing of the early and short versions of Bertonio's Aymara texts which would have made him cautious about printing his own works. Was Oré able to compare his grammar and dictionary with that of Bertonio? Perhaps. What were his thoughts? If Bertonio's Aymara dictionary and grammar were available another was not needed, and could cause confusion. Further, the Franciscans had limited resources, but the Jesuits had assets, including access to the required printing equipment in Rome and Naples. Oré could have learned while in Naples that there was a move to authorize a Quechua dictionary and grammar prepared by the Jesuits in Juli. In Lima in the Jesuit doctrina of El Cercado, Father Juan Vázquez on 15 September 1607 approved publication of a massive Quechua dictionary compiled by Jesuit Diego González Holguín. Vázquez pointed out that the dictionary was substantially larger than any other, and a new orthography was employed to make it easier to pronounce the complex Quechua sounds that did not exist in Spanish or Latin.[11]

González Holguín's *Gramática* and *Vocabulario* "the greatest monument of the Quechua language of all times," according to Raúl Porras Barrenechea, is an impressive achievement. It is remarkable that González Holguín, who began his studies of Quechua so late, managed to produce so quickly such an excellent work in an extremely difficult language. Born in Spain about 1552, González Holguín came to Peru in 1581 along with other Jesuits. He traveled to Cuzco to study Quechua and from there he went to the Jesuit house at Juli. González Holguín worked alongside Bertonio until 1586, when he was assigned with other Jesuits to establish a new house in Quito. With this task complete in 1600 he assumed a new position as Rector of the Jesuit school in Chuquisaca. González Holguín subsequently returned to Juli as Superior until he left to set up a new Jesuit house in Paraguay. His *Gramática* and *Vocabulario* were printed in Lima in 1607 and 1608.[12]

This brings us back to Oré's dictionary and grammar. What if any is the relationship between Oré's works and those of Bertonio and González Holguín?

QUECHUA AND AYMARA DICTIONARIES AND GRAMMARS (1560–1635)	
1560	Domingo de Santo Tomás, *Gramatica o arte de la lengua general de los indios de los reynos del Peru*
1560	Domingo de Santo Tomás, *Lexicon o vocabulario de la lengua general del Peru*
1586	Antonio Ricardo, *Vocabulario y phrasis en la lengua general de los indios del Peru, llamada Quechua*
1594	Luis Gerónimo de Oré, Both the Grammatica and the Diccionario were authorized for publication in Lima
1603	Ludovico Bertonio, *Arte y Grammatica muy copiosa de la lengua Aymara*
1603	Ludovico Bertonio, *Arte breve de la lengua Aymara para introduccion del Arte Grande de la misma lengua*
1604	Dr. Fr. Juan Martínez de Oramachea, *Vocabulario Quechua*
1607	Diego González Holguín, *Grammatica y arte nueva de la lengua general*
1608	Diego González Holguín, *Vocabulario de la lengua general de todo el Peru llamada lengua qquichua o del Inca*
1612	Ludovico Bertonio, *Vocabulario de la lengua aymara*
1612	Ludovico Bertonio, *Arte de la lengua aymara, con una silva de phrases de la misma lengua, y su declaracion en Romance*
1616	Alonso de Huerta, *Arte de la lengua general de los yndios deste reyno del Perú*
1619	Diego de Torres Rubio, *Arte de la lengua quichua*
1631	Juan Pérez Bocanegra, *Ritual formulario*

The Jesuits at Juli's language school would have had access to Oré's books and manuscripts. Which Jesuits reviewed Oré's manuscripts for publication and did they pass them to other Jesuits to contemplate, and perhaps find information they might later include in their own works? At the time, "borrowing" from the good work of others was not disparaged, especially if it contributed to a quicker and more effective guide to conversion. While in Italy Oré may have realized that their translations were at least as good, perhaps even better than his own. Did the Franciscan, on seeing Bertonio's books in Rome and then learning that González Holguín had received sole authorization to print the two Quechua volumes in Lima, abandon his long effort? Unfortunately, Oré slips from sight until 1611. Was he assigned different duties while in Italy? Perhaps he needed a time for reflection and spiritual rejuvenation. The Franciscan Recoleto Monasteries would provide him exactly that, and there were many available in Italy and Spain. Oré reappears in the historical record by the latter part of 1611 with a new appointment.

❦ 15 ❧

Recruiting in Spain

Following a fruitful sojourn in the center of Roman Catholic Christendom, Oré was back in Spain. In late 1611 the Crown and General Commissioner for the Indies Antonio de Trejo appointed Oré to recruit missionaries for La Florida. Oré's first recruiting efforts for the Florida missions during late 1611 and early 1612 succeeded, and he gathered twenty-four men. It seems he resided near the court much of the time following his return from Italy. Oré's oratory was recognized long before he spoke at various monasteries in Spain. He had a special gift to engage his audience, to stimulate, challenge, even compel listeners. As he scoured the Franciscan monasteries of Castile, he convinced many friars and lay brothers to join the mission in the Indies. Oré later reported in his *Relación de la Florida* that "with the support of the President and Justices of the Royal Council I took them [the friars] to Seville to embark and they traveled in the year of 1612 to La Florida where Juan Fernández de Olivera was already governor."[1]

Oré remained in Spain and ready for another assignment. It came quickly as he received instructions to head an entirely different expedition. He presented before Seville's Casa de la Contratación a royal cédula (25 April 1613) authorizing him as commissioner in charge of the religious to lead a Franciscan group to the Province of Venezuela.[2] Casa de la Contratación officials entered into an agreement with Gerónimo de Beas, shipmaster of the *Esperanza*, to accompany the annual fleet, and on 20 June 1613 they authorized Oré to embark with the new missionaries aboard the *Esperanza*, first bound for Santo Domingo, Hispaniola. But again, Oré remained behind.[3]

The Crown recognized the value of the religious orders as part of its colonial policy to control its vast empire as the Spanish faced increasing pressure from foreign interlopers, particularly the English, in the case of Florida. The

Spanish foundation of St. Augustine in 1565 and the use of the religious to pacify the indigenous inhabitants provided a model that, although imperfect, was sustainable so long as Spanish sea power was superior to that of its enemies. With the deaths of Philip II in 1598 and Queen Elizabeth in 1603, and the arrival of James VI of Scotland to assume England's throne as James I of England, there was a shift in foreign policy more attuned to Spanish interests. It flowed into an uneasy Twelve Year Truce that lasted until 1621, though the privateers were never eliminated.[4] Franciscan attempts to establish good relations with indigenous people in Florida worked, to a degree, for they were not subjected to the forced labor systems prevalent in Peru and Mexico, nor were they granted to encomenderos and required to pay tribute. Along the Florida coast Amerindians were permitted to take the spoils of shipwrecked foreigners and were given gifts for notifying the Spanish of passing enemy ships. This was the type of relationship the Spanish often established throughout lowly populated sectors of the circum-Caribbean. The Franciscans were assumed to be ideal participants. Spanish authorities wanted to ensure that Amerindians, in part under the careful guidance of the Franciscans, were assets, and not enemies who might join the English, French or Dutch.

The cost to send twenty-five Franciscans to Venezuela in 1613 with Oré—fourteen ducats per person—was much less than that of soldiers or civilian authorities. The Crown authorized an additional payment of 5,125 ducats for transport of ten and one-half toneladas of books and vestments the friars were taking. The shipmaster was to provide four cabins for the religious, each accommodating five friars.[5] Payment for the travel was to be covered by the officials in Hispaniola or Margarita, where they were scheduled to land. Although the Crown was somewhat lax on control of religious emigrants, other travelers required authorization in order to keep undesirables—Conversos, Moriscos, Gypsies, and those whose religious orthodoxy was questionable—out of the Indies. One had to be an "Old Christian."

Oré failed to sail with this group because on 7 June 1613 the General Commissioner for the Indies charged him with an important new assignment, one that kept him occupied in Andalusia in the triangle between Seville, Córdoba, and Granada for months. The task was critical to the investigation of the youth of Friar Francisco Solano who Peruvians already hailed as a saintly man. Documentation for the opening of a process toward that end was sent from Peru to Spain; the packet needed to reach Rome quickly for consideration at the Gen-

Andalusia, researching Friar Francisco Solano's youth

eral Meeting of the Franciscan Order. Oré was to collect testimony, compile it, and print a proof that would be part of the materials necessary for a process of canonization. He now shouldered two tasks, the final preparations for the Venezuela missions and the Francisco Solano research. Oré was well enough along in recruitment to initiate the Solano inquiry on 11 July 1613. Scouring the Franciscan monasteries in Andalusia and talking about Solano's life and mission in South America meshed with his recruitment efforts.

Shortly after receiving the order to collect information on Solano's early life Oré began taking testimony in Seville. He then traveled to all the places associated with Solano, including his birthplace, Montilla near Córdoba. While in Córdoba Oré visited a fellow Peruvian, Inca Garcilaso de la Vega, already a well-known Renaissance scholar and translator and mediator between two worlds. He recently published a valuable text for potential friars being recruited by Oré: *La Florida del Inca*. Garcilaso, the mestizo son of a Spanish conquistador and an Inca princess, was born in Cuzco and was fifteen years older than Oré. Both men were practiced in the art of translation, and surely exchanged words in Quechua during conversation. Garcilaso had access to Oré's 1598 *Symbolo Catholico Indiano* and borrowed excerpts for his history of the Incas. The famous chronicler reported that Oré, "a great theologian," asked for a copy of the history of Florida so the friars "could take it along to know and have information about the provinces and the customs of those heathens. And I presented him with seven books, three were of Florida, and four of our *Commentaries*." Garcilaso noted that Oré was pleased with the gift and added his hope that "His Divine Majesty be served in aiding in this endeavor, in order that those idolaters leave the abyss of their ignorance." According to Garcilaso the two men reminisced about events in Peru. The Inca asked Oré about the fate of the skulls of Peru's notorious rebels, Gonzalo Pizarro, Francisco de Carvajal, and Francisco Hernández Girón. Oré told Garcilaso that they were kept in the Franciscan monastery along with two others, and that he would like to know which one belonged to the infamous Carvajal. Garcilaso responded that he should be recognizable by the inscription on the iron cage ordered at the time of his execution. Oré replied that the skulls were "not in cages but loose, each one by itself, without any identifying sign."[6]

During travels between Madrid and Seville, Oré continued to recruit missionaries and oversee the processing of their travel documents. They were busy months, perhaps complicated by the presence of his younger brother, Licentiate Francisco de Oré, who was preparing his paperwork to return to Peru. On 24 February 1614 Francisco presented to Seville's Casa de la Contratación a license to sail on a merchant ship. He had been appointed Canon of the Cathedral of Huamanga and was authorized to take along his young nephew Francisco de Zerpa y Padilla,[7] from the island of Gran Canaria. He was scheduled to travel with two other men also destined for Huamanga. Authorization had been issued in Madrid on 5 February, and the nephew was granted license even without testimony from his homeland in the Canaries because he was known at court thanks to his uncle Francisco de Oré and perhaps Luis Gerónimo as well.

The passenger authorization files provide more information on the background of the young nephew. A relative, Anton de Zerpa y Padilla, stated that

Francisco's father Pedro de Zerpa was a lifetime regidor and captain general of the island's artillery force. The relative testified that Francisco was about fourteen or fifteen years old and had "a thin face with incipient beard (peach fuzz). He was somewhat tan in color with a mole or two on his right cheek." Francisco's two uncles from Huamanga also testified on 1 February. Licentiate Francisco de Oré, at court in Madrid and residing on the Calle de la Puebla in the house of Catalina Gonzáles, had known his nephew and his parents, now deceased, from the time he was born. He stressed that young Francisco's parents and grandparents were "Old Christians," with no taint of Muslim, Jewish, or Converso ancestry, and were never charged by the Inquisition. Friar Luis Gerónimo de Oré confirmed all the previous testimony, adding that Francisco de Zerpa's family was "of the most honored and principal of the Canary Island." Friar Luis Gerónimo's age at the time was "greater than 44" and he resided in Madrid's Monastery of San Francisco.[8]

With all documentation and authorizations presented before the Casa de la Contratación on 23 February 1614, the required steps were complete.[9] The next day, the Casa's officials issued the requisite authorization for Francisco de Oré to sail to Peru with "his nephew and two servants together on any merchant ship."[10] There would be a total of forty-four passengers with slaves and servants boarding the *Nuestra Señora de Socorro,* part of the fleet of General Lope Diez de Armendariz.[11]

On the same day, 24 February 1614, testimony on the background of Luis Gerónimo de Oré's servant was being taken in Villacastín in the jurisdiction of Segovia. Juan Tundidor Sánchez *el mozo* (junior) who was to accompany Oré to Florida "for my service," needed license to travel to New Spain, Peru, and the Indies in general. When the testimony confirming his family's Old Christian status was completed, Oré signed the papers. Documents and witnesses established firmly that Juan Tundidor *el mozo* was seventeen years old and had "four moles between the right eye and ear."[12] Later, in Seville on 17 June 1614 Oré appeared before the officials of the Casa de la Contratación and stated he had license to travel to Florida with a servant and presented Juan Tundidor. He turned all the documentation over to the officials and asked them "to order his dispatch so he can embark with me."[13]

Earlier, Franciscan General Commissioner Juan de Vivanco had petitioned the king to grant a travel permit to Luis Gerónimo de Oré and two others to travel to the Indies. Vivanco stressed that the Franciscans had decided that for the "good administration of the region" the monasteries of La Florida and Havana should be inspected and that the visitador should be one "of authority, lettered and virtuous, and these qualities fortunately coincide in the person of Friar Luis Hieronimo de Hore [sic]." Vivanco added that Oré had worked many years in Peru, and because "he is the one who had recruited in these kingdoms the religious who have gone to that province [Florida], he had named him to inspect it."[14] Vivanco asked that Oré, given the "short time before the fleet's departure be permitted to name the person who will accompany him; after all, it is understood that he will take someone appropriate." Vivanco also requested the king to award the normal support for passage for Oré, his fellow Franciscan, and a servant. The Council of the Indies granted Commissioner Vivanco's request on 12 June 1614.[15]

At last, Oré seemed ready to sail for the Indies. Philip III in Madrid on 15 June 1614 issued a royal cédula directed to officials of the Casa de la Contratación in Seville, which they received on the 26th. "I order you to allow Friar Luis Gerónimo de Oré of the Order of San Francisco to pass to the Island of Cuba and the Province of La Florida. He goes to inspect the convents of his Order and takes along a servant for personal service, who presented to you the information taken before his local magistrate and approved by the same, that he is not married nor among those prohibited to travel there and corresponds to his physical description." The members of the Casa did not tarry; all the paperwork was in order, and the monarch stressed the urgency. There is an important issue that Philip clarified that could have stymied the operation. "Notwithstanding that the said Friar Luis Gerónimo had come from the provinces of Peru and I have ordered that none of the religious coming from the Indies can return, in this case and in the future he may, and I permit it."[16]

The final travel plans were well underway the next day. Two dispatch authorizations were completed on 27 June 1614, one as the president and officials of the Casa de la Contratación met, and based on the king's royal cédulas, they have "come to an agreement with shipmaster Sebastián de Reiçu of the ship named *Nuestra Señora de los Remedios* that is going to Havana." Oré would take with him Friar Francisco de San Buenaventura and the servant, Juan Tundidor. The passage cost was apportioned at twenty ducats per person plus 9,000 maravedís for the cost of freighting a tonelada of books and religious vestments, and 11,250 maravedís, the price for two-fifths of the cabin for the religious. They were well accommodated, considering the size of the cabin, ten feet long and eight feet wide, with ample space for the berths. According to the papers, the justices in Cuba would pay the shipmaster.[17] The same day, 27 June 1614, the officials of the Casa issued a separate authorization for Oré's servant Juan Tundidor, destined for the "Island [sic] of San Agustin de la Florida."[18]

⚜ 16 ⚜

Probing the Youth of a Future Saint, *Francisco Solano*

Oré's delay in embarking on his mission to inspect the Province of Santa Elena de la Florida prior to 1614 was, as we have seen, the result of another commission: to research the youth of Francisco Solano, a mystic and a future saint. Although the seventeenth-century world was a time in which the active intervention of saints in daily life was expected, a time in which one could witness the actions of saintly individuals, the actual ecclesiastical process by which one became a saint—and the investment of time, energy and money—was formidable. Further, new regulations were issued at the Council of Trent. Friar Francisco Solano, an active and successful missionary on the dangerous Gran Chaco frontier, died in Lima's Franciscan monastery on 14 July 1610. Within two weeks of Solano's death, Friar Miguel Roca presented a petition to the Lima Curia to open an investigation into Solano's life and miracles. With Archbishop Bartolomé Lobo Guerrero's approval the process began and by 30 August the first witnesses presented testimony before Lima's Curia. Statements were collected in Peru's north coastal Trujillo between 27 November 1610 and 20 July 1611, where Solano had also served. Reports from Ica were compiled between 19 December 1610 and 11 February 1611. Lima testimony from 200 witnesses was completed by 18 February 1611. Peruvian Franciscans hoped their delegation carrying the report with an abbreviated twelve-folio imprint would reach Rome in time for the 123rd General Chapter Meeting during Pentecost of 1612.[1]

Solicitor Friar Díaz de Navia wrote on 20 March 1611 to the Franciscan General Commissioner of the Indies, Antonio de Trejo, and outlined the events that transpired in Peru, emphasizing the importance of Solano's canonization.

He voiced his concern that although Lima's current Franciscan Commissioner General, Friar Diego Altamirano, supported the process, many friars did not. If Altamirano were replaced, the canonization process could be jeopardized. Díaz de Navia requested special authorization to continue, stressing the difficulties and mistreatment he had faced while attempting to collect information on Solano. He complained he had suffered "many hardships and persecutions from those same friars, and in particular from some guardians.... After I began making these inquiries, they have whipped me too many times. I have this count of the lashes they have given me; to this point there are eighty-seven."[2] At the same time, the solicitor noted widespread support in Lima for Solano's beatification, including that of Viceroy Marqués de Montesclaros, who promised to fund the process. Díaz de Navia emphasized the importance for full documentation to verify the reputed miracles, urging the General Commissioner to make an inquiry into Solano's background. This letter provided a pretext to appoint an agent to travel throughout Andalusia and collect testimony and prepare an account of Solano's early years.

Díaz de Navia's letter to Trejo was probably sent to Spain along with part of the first documentation collected on Solano's miracles in the viceroyalty of Peru. A second set of testimony was taken largely from Lima and Callao on the first two days of March 1611. Other testimony was recorded in coastal Santa between 14 November 1611 and 10 January 1612. A third Lima process took place between 3 November 1611 and March 1612.[3] On 24 April 1612 Díaz de Navia wrote the monarch asking for his support, reminding him of his letter sent the year before. By late 1612 or early 1613 copies of most of the relevant Peruvian documents on Solano's activities in America should have reached the office of the General Commissioner of the Indies of the Franciscan Order in Spain. They were reviewed and eventually transmitted to Rome.[4] General Commissioner Trejo took Díaz de Navia's recommendations and on 7 June 1613 in Madrid ordered Oré to collect testimony on Solano's early years. There were several reasons why Oré's superiors in Peru and Spain chose him to investigate Solano's life. He must have known Solano, only five or six years Oré's senior, as they were frequently together in residence in Lima's Franciscan monastery. But timing was probably the key reason why Oré was assigned the task. He was physically present in Spain and his reputation and experience signaled efficiency and speed, something that the Franciscans needed in order to present in Rome as complete a case of Solano's holiness as possible. Oré's close contact with the General Commissioner in the Council in Madrid also contributed to his appointment.

Oré applied himself with accustomed zeal and thoroughness. He began collecting testimony in Seville on 11 July 1613, a month after Trejo's commission. Oré traveled to the places where Solano had lived and preached, taking oral and written testimony in Marchena, Baeza, Arrizafa, Adamuz, San Francisco del Monte, Perabad, Montoro, and finally Montilla, where he finished the first part of the report on 9 August. Oré was in Córdoba on 21 October, where he met Inca Garcilaso de la Vega then returned to Montilla, Solano's birthplace, to collect final oaths of the forty-four witnesses who knew him from his youth. The material he collected, supplemented with the testimony of the bishops and archbishops of Seville, Granada, Lima, Córdoba, and Malaga, provided the foundation for Oré's 1614 (Madrid imprint) *Relación de la vida i milagros del Venerable Padre Fr. Francisco Solano de la Orden de San Francisco....*[5] One copy of his report is in the Archivo de San Isidoro (Padres Irlandeses, Rome), along with the full set of individual reports.[6] The entire "Proceso San Francisco Solano" is in the Archivo Secreto Vaticano (#1328), along with the 1610–12 and 1628–30 Lima reports collected to support the process.[7] In all there are dozens of reports, many of them prepared in the first decades after Solano's death.

Oré initiated his narrative with Solano's birth (10 March 1549) in Montilla, a town southeast of Córdoba. The young Solano studied in the town's Jesuit school but professed in 1569 or 1570 in Montilla's Franciscan Recoletos Monastery of San Lorenzo. In the subsequent nineteen years Solano served in communities in the Córdoba, Granada, Seville area. Shortly after his novitiate in Montilla he learned of the strict observance of the rules of the order at the monastery of Santa María de Loreto, near Seville, and asked to be transferred there.[8] Oré, pursuing his research on Solano, took the daylong trek from Seville to the monastery of Santa María de Loreto, just west of today's Espartinas, a comfortable trip upward from the Guadalquivir floodplain to the bluff of Castilleja de la Cuesta, and from there through a fertile, rolling plain. The sixteenth-century convent as Solano and Oré saw it was solitary, with a small austere church unlike the lavish display of the baroque one sees today. Some of the earlier structure remains. The original church is now the sacristy; the early image of the Virgin of Loreto was there, and the thirteenth century tower remains, as well as the traceable basic structure of the original cloisters. It is here that Solano's piety and self-mortification became notorious, according to testimony Oré collected. As if the cell assigned to the young Solano were not small enough, he reputedly built another himself with the help of a friend. It was even smaller, made of reddish mud and reeds. Solano trained novices in the monastery of Arrizafa in Córdoba, and later at San Francisco del Monte. He solicited alms to support Franciscan charity, and he aided the ill. The guardian at Arrizafa noted Solano's all-consuming concern for the infirm and asked him if he was neglecting his prayers. Solano replied that caring for the sick "was a precept of the Rule, and that he would rather be obeying it in assisting the ill than in his will to pray." Oré's voice as narrator is strong: "In this occasion as in many others in different places and convents he demonstrated maintaining deep within his soul the much-praised recommendation that our Father San Francisco makes in the Rule regarding the sick."[9] In addition to his exceptional piety, Solano was reputedly an excellent singer, played a simple flute and a stringed instrument, depicted in many later paintings as a violin; attributes he shared with Oré.[10]

The itinerary next took Oré to the monastery of San Francisco del Monte, five leagues from Córdoba. Oré's description of its isolation is compelling. For some it was an ideal place to escape the indecorous cities, "because it is in an isolated, deserted place, one for contemplation and the spiritual life." The site is a "craggy, bramble-filled terrain with dense mountain spurs that begin here and extend throughout the Sierra Morena. This is one of the sanctuaries of greatest devotion of our Order." It was a special place, a "Holy Mountain," for "the spiritual men who desired to exercise themselves in prayer, meditation and penitence of solitude and abandon of the world."[11] There were several nearby villages: Adamuz, Villafranca, El Carpio, Montoro, and others. In addition to celebrating masses, Solano taught the novices. Oré collected copious information on Solano's piety, extreme penitence, and mortification of the flesh which Oré notes he had maintained throughout his life.

Up to this point in the *Relación,* Oré included in the margin of the text the place where the information originated, in the general order of Granada, Montilla, Arrizafa, Seville, Córdoba, San Francisco del Monte, Malaga, Adamuz, and Perabad. He then shifted to the declaration of Friar Francisco Roldán in Seville, and then returned to Montilla. Oré's report on Solano's life was constructed and documented in a similar fashion as his later report on La Florida, printed in the same decade. In both texts he extracted the primary material, reworked it, sometimes quoted directly and at other times cited, but Oré pieced the text together into his own "history."

Oré's shift in the narrative centers on a brief discussion of the Franciscan way, and reflects his knowledge of the theological rudiments of the Franciscan founders of thirteenth century Italy. He noted the task of curing and caring for the ill and helping those in need, which consumed the time and energies of many friars. But they must always remember the importance of prayer, self-mortifications and penitence, obedience, a life of contemplation, humility, *recogimiento* (retreat), all with the purpose of coming together "in the enlightened path," as referred to by San Buenaventura in his *Teología*.[12] Oré's narrative was designed to present the Vatican theologians with the evidence of an exemplary life of extreme poverty and humility, to justify moving forward with Francisco Solano's candidacy for sainthood.

Oré noted that his depiction of Solano's youth in Andalusia is based on the five reports he collected, the last in Granada where Solano served in the Recoletos Monastery of San Luis El Real in la Zubia, near the city. Solano continued his strict regimen and served outside the confines of his monastery with the guardian's license. His caring for the ill was centered in Granada's Hospital of San Juan de Dios and he provided invaluable service to prisoners in various jails of Granada. This experience in part, Oré mentioned, was why Solano was selected to go to the New World. Before departing in 1589, Solano's route took him to his old convent of Santa María de Loreto near Seville to prepare for his journey to Peru and perhaps convince others to join him in the future.[13]

Approaching the halfway mark in his text, Oré shifted to Solano's experiences in South America. After a short rest in Lima, Solano and his group of friars continued to Paraguay. Oré describes the difficulties they encountered in their treacherous journey, as earlier friars did: "The evangelical friars of our Seraphic Order expose themselves to all these dangers to find souls and convert them to the knowledge ... giving light of the Catholic Faith to those who live in the blindness of infidelity and idolatry."[14] Oré noted that before Solano, Friar Alonso de San Buenaventura worked in the same area "to cultivate those barbaric nations." Even before him, Friar Luis de Bolaños "the Apostle of the Provinces of the Rio de la Plata because he had learned the most difficult languages of that land, had translated the Christian doctrine and Catechism of the Third Council of Lima." Oré reminded readers that "I had printed it in our *Rituale* for administration of the Sacraments, along with other translations in five different languages." He pointed out that it was Bolaños who had begun the efforts toward conversion in the region, and that his successes provided need for others to follow. Oré seems amazed that Solano, who had been accustomed to a life of the Recoletos of oration and fasting, attempted such a long and arduous journey. Oré stressed the difficulties that Solano faced, "the greatest one, which is not knowing the language of those parts," yet he managed "with some effort and study that he put into it to learn sufficiently two or three languages." Oré breaks into the narrative to inform there now existed an easier way to reach the Rio de la Plata from Lima: by ship to Chile, then cross the Andes to Córdoba and continue to the destination. Oré justified this aside, because he thought it was important to "include it and to alert so that the religious going to that province not become discouraged or abandon their vocation." Too many had died or simply had given up during the arduous trip. Oré notes another way, from Lisbon to one of three ports in Brazil, then on to Buenos Aires and up the Paraná River.[15]

By the time of his final sickness many Limeños believed Solano to be a saint. In his text Oré tackled the thorny theological issue that might stop the process altogether. In Section XIII of his *Relación,* "About the raptures and mental extasis that he [Solano] had in prayer," Oré turned to the writings of San Buenaventura in his *Teología* to place Solano's mystical experiences within the theologically permissible. It was San Buenaventura who had reformed the Franciscan order, established a new Constitution, and had rejected various theological positions of Joachim de Fiore (1135–1202) and his followers who had challenged the nature of the Trinity, the path to God and illumination, and the prophesies of the second coming. There were proponents of various paths by some of the early Franciscans working among the peoples of New Spain, as John L. Phelan analyzes in his study of millenarianism, and Julia McClure in her work. She notes, as does Phelan, that Fiore's concept of three ages, and the seventh seal to bring in a new age of peace leading to the Last Judgement, influenced Friar Mendieta and Montolinia's vision of the role of the Franciscans. San Buenaventura viewed the stigmata of Saint Francis and believed that was a sign of the breaking of the sixth seal, and he wrote they were now in the age of the spirit. Millenarian Franciscans saw their role as new apostles, a belief that would influence their work in New Spain. Oré explained the two ways of contemplation according to San Buenaventura: "one is natural, which uses the discourse of reason, whose perfection is to reach the love of God" while the other "is a supernatural and mystical contemplation that the Holy Spirit infuses into the soul with a superior light of heaven." After describing Solano's holy deeds, his penitence, prayers, and his virtues, Oré stated that Solano "at last arrived at the supernatural contemplation and had marvelous raptures and mental ecstasies, where he received hidden mercies of Our Lord."[16] At the same time Oré also stressed Solano's acts of charity after he returned to Lima. "There was nothing that produced in him a greater contentment than to visit many sick of the city and those who were in the hospitals, he made the beds, cleaned latrines and consoled them with his spiritual conversation." Solano's final sickness lasted two months, and he died on 14 July 1610, the day of San Buenaventura, which Oré found fitting, given that Solano "was very devoted to the Saint." Viceroy Marqués de Montesclaros, as well as Lima's Archbishop Lobo Guerrero and many city officials attended his funeral. Solano was interred in the chapel beneath the main altar of the church of San Francisco.[17]

No Catholic saint was canonized from 1523 to 1588, the era of the Reformation and the Council of Trent. Under pressure of internal reformers, the institutional church from 1588 to 1622 demanded compelling examples of true virtue. Peter Burke argues, "the very idea of a saint was under fire."[18] Political and religious forces within the various sectors of the church often opposed each other. After 1588 the papacy exercised increasing control over the process of beatification and canonization. Pope Urban VIII in 1628 established a waiting period of fifty years after a candidate's death. Beatification was relatively easy, but canonization was not. Disagreements over the qualities of the candidates— who were to possess the characteristics of Tridentine orthodoxy: poverty, humility, and chastity—were often acrimonious.[19] Four times as many men as women were canonized during the Counter-Reformation as in the Baroque Era. Teresa of Avila was the only Spanish woman to reach sainthood in 1622, in the same period as Felipe de Neri, Francis Xavier, Isidro the Laborer, and the founder of the Jesuit order, Ignatius Loyola. It is in this context that the long process of the canonization of Francisco Solano must be understood.[20] It was not until 27 December 1726 that Pope Benedict XIII issued the bull of canonization, *Ad fidelium Dei servorum gloriam*. The celebration of the first fiesta of San Francisco Solano took place in Lima on 24 July 1728, just under a century after Oré died. "The pealing of the bells did not cease; all were joyous with a brilliant display of fireworks, sparkling wheels, exploding rockets, and the music of trumpets, drums and oboes."[21]

Oré's modest book on Solano's life was one of many but it was the earliest and it did contribute to the desired outcome. Careful readers of Oré's report will note its weaknesses, similar to the imperfections of his subsequent report on Florida. Both were "uncooked" texts, pieced together under the pressure of time, resources, and other endeavors. It is unlikely Oré reviewed the manuscript before printing, for the episodic shifts could have been avoided and the extraneous additions could have been expunged. Oré's contribution to the Franciscan effort to secure Solano's sainthood largely ended in 1614, as copies of his *Relación de la vida i milagros* were printed in Madrid. It is unclear how many were issued, but first they were distributed to the Vatican as part of the documentation for the beatification process. Many copies were transported to Peru for civil and church authorities, and especially Franciscans. The young chronicler Friar Diego de Córdova y Salinas was especially interested as was his brother Buenaventura de Salinas y Córdova. A copyist, perhaps even Friar Diego, included it in a draft for his *Vida, virtudes y milagros del nuevo apóstol del Perú el venerable P. F. Francisco Solano*. Oré's report on Solano appears in the book almost verbatim, and unattributed, in several subsequent Franciscan chronicles.

During much of 1614 Oré traveled. His presence was required at court in Madrid, in Seville's Casa de la Contratación, and in the port of Sanlúcar de Barrameda, as he completed all the details needed before he set sail for La Florida. It was precisely during the hectic months leading up to his departure that Seville was scandalized in September 1613. According to chronicler Diego Ortiz de Zúñiga, during the celebrations of the Nativity of the Virgin Mary a friar delivered a sermon expressing "the impious view regarding the Conception of the Queen of Angels whose immaculate purity, never touched by original sin, was so firmly believed in the spirit of this city." Did Oré become involved in the commotion regarding the dogma of the Immaculate Conception that flowed into 1614? The New World reality of Cuba and La Florida that the friar would soon confront was a world apart, yet these events inspired him to write about the Virgin Mary upon his return to Iberia several years later.[22]

IV

General Commissioner in Florida's Northern Frontier

❦ 17 ❦

Franciscan Province of Santa Elena de La Florida

Before initiating his voyage to Florida Commissioner Oré prepared for his assignment to inspect the Franciscan Province of Santa Elena, which included the missions of "greater Florida" and the Franciscan houses on the island of Cuba. Inca Garcilaso de la Vega's history of La Florida was just one of the published accounts Oré examined. He read Gonzalo Fernández de Oviedo and other historians and cosmographers. He interviewed the religious of his own order and others who worked in Cuba and La Florida. His intent was to gain a better understanding of the people he would encounter: Amerindians, Spanish soldiers, clergy, and merchants. He also read recent reports and letters regarding Santiago de Cuba, Havana, and St. Augustine.

The Franciscan order came to Florida relatively late. The Jesuits were the first group charged with conversion of the indigenous peoples of "La Florida," a vast and vaguely delineated frontier extending north from the Keys at the tip of the peninsula northward as far as one could go, as the Spanish claimed by papal donation and the Treaty of Tordesillas. This "province" in the mind of the Crown reached the fishing banks of Maine and Canada and stretched westerly toward the northeastern frontier of New Spain. Florida was a critical strategic region for the Spanish. The Bahama Passage and the strong northerly flowing Gulf Stream provided the best and fastest route for the annual return of the treasure fleets to Iberia, the mainstay of the Spanish economy and a keystone upholding Spanish hegemony over the first global empire. Following concerted efforts by the French to establish a beachhead along the mid-North American Atlantic coast in the early 1560s, the Spanish reacted with a vengeance. The large fleet of 1565 led by Pedro Menéndez de Avilés swiftly attacked and de-

Franciscan Province of Santa Elena de la Florida

stroyed the French Fort Caroline outpost at the mouth of the St. Johns River and established the town and military garrison of St. Augustine. The Spanish dealt mercilessly with the French at Matanzas and elsewhere where survivors were found.

Although there was a religious presence at the settlement of St. Augustine, chaplains for the *presidio* (military outpost) and the early Jesuits, the initial Franciscan missionary effort came in 1587. Within a decade indigenous disaffection with the friars' attempts to implant a "Christian" lifestyle led to revolt. Among the Guale ethnic group in southeast Georgia and northeast Florida, several Franciscans were massacred. Undeterred, Franciscans persisted, and by

1600 they had established several missions from the area of the Mosquito Lagoon north of Cape Canaveral to the Carolinas. They designated it as the new Province of Santa Cruz, with headquarters in Santo Domingo on the island of Hispaniola. The province was large, and included La Florida, Venezuela and Cuba. But in 1609, under direction of Custodian Friar Pedro Ruiz, La Florida, Havana, Santiago and Bayamo were aggregated, and in 1612 the Province of Santa Elena was established, leaving Venezuela and Hispaniola as the Province of Santa Cruz.[1]

Secular and church officials appointed to the Indies were encouraged, indeed expected, to consult administrative papers relating to their assignment. Frequent letters and reports were sent to Spain by previous administrators, allowing new officials to develop a grasp of what they might encounter. In the case of Florida ample correspondence was available, given the peninsula's strategic importance. Known earlier, but "officially discovered" by Juan Ponce de León in 1513, it lacked precious metals and worse, it housed a hostile indigenous population offering little to settlers, except initially slaves. It was only after the French and English took an interest in establishing settlements in the 1560s that the Spanish realized that a permanent base was necessary to check the foreign threat. The primitive presidio and settlement of St. Augustine was little more than a garrison and base for the religious to direct conversion of various scattered ethnicities. Florida's coasts were low, with sandy beaches, and beyond them marshes and savannas. In places, dense mangroves along the brackish littoral posed an almost impenetrable barrier. The soil was a veneer of infertile sand covering a limestone base.[2] Given that the various ethnicities in Florida had fought each other for generations and were adept at defending themselves, Spanish military superiority was a costly fiction. Yet the indigenous population offered a fertile field for all religious dreaming of martyrdom, a wish frequently fulfilled.

One report Oré may have read was prepared by Bartolomé de Argüelles. His 1601 account would have provided Oré, arriving a little over a decade later, a perceptive depiction of what he might face. The first challenge was St. Augustine's harbor: "At the entrance of the port is a sand bar, with many surrounding shallow flats extending outward to a depth of up to twenty *palmos* (roughly the distance from the base of the palm to the tip of the index finger), and as the sand at the bottom tends to shift and form new bars, ships that surpass ninety *toneladas* (tonnage) cannot enter into the harbor except those of Flemish construction. Those ships are called *filibotes* and are flat-bottomed and can sail in shallow waters."[3] St. Augustine was a poorly staffed and equipped garrison town with insufficient infrastructure to be self-sustaining. Argüelles paints a pathetic picture: "All the surrounding area is encircled by bogs and saltwater marshes and before it on the right side are rivers and lagoons and tidal flats. What land there is holds scrubs and slash pines, worthless for building or cultivation."[4] He suggested that St. Augustine was so inhospitable that the Spanish should abandon it and set up headquarters to the north, with better soil and a dense indigenous population.[5]

In an additional account of 13 April 1601, the royal treasurer Juan Menéndez Márquez provides a glimpse of the deplorable condition of the Franciscans in the city. The port had been attacked and briefly occupied by English corsair Francis Drake in 1586. A decade and a half later, the ransacked town was not yet completely rebuilt. The fort's soldiers had worked with the confraternity of Nuestra Señora de la Soledad to establish a hospital that was almost finished, and "because the monastery of San Francisco had been burned down, the *cofrades* permitted the religious to stay in the hospital until the monastery was built." Menéndez Márquez also reported to the king on relations with the local population. "It seems that your governor has attempted to reach a peace agreement and confederation with the Indian apostates who have rebelled in the province of the Guale because of the death of the five religious."[6] In another letter addressed to the king, sent from the nearby Indian village of Nombre de Dios, Doña María Cacica thanked the monarch for the gifts given to her and other caciques in St. Augustine on 9 November 1598. She stated she was born a Christian, as was her mother, and that she and others were dedicated to the faith. She stated the governor had given her 150 ducats, half in cloth and other goods. Spanish policy to maintain peaceful relations with the local populace of La Florida, and in other "frontier" regions where similar conditions prevailed, was through gift exchange, implying a reciprocal tributary relationship, with both parties giving and receiving. It was not always successful.[7]

On 16 September 1602 Franciscan friar Blas de Montes, a seven-year resident in Florida, composed a letter to the king. Montes complained that the governor had given little support to Franciscan efforts, emphasizing that the friars had done their best against great odds. Had Oré reviewed this letter he would have found a useful description of the religious terrain ahead. "To the south side of the city there is a lagoon and flowing into it there is a freshwater river and over a distance of 24 leagues there are seven Christian villages." In all there were two hundred Christian Indians, "and the last pueblo that is some eight leagues distant from the closest of the six, has the most who need to be baptized of the five." Some of them "on this river, without the religious, received no indoctrination." Friars had occasionally made it there, but they came and went. In Guale there were more than 1,200 Indians who were aware, he said, of their previous sins (the revolt) but in the interior there were infidels, and he implored the king to send twenty-four religious. Montes further asked that a bishop be sent to confirm the prepared converts. He also appealed to the king for help to finish construction of the Franciscan convent. Some friars were still sleeping in the hospital and others in the church. Oré included Friar Montes in his report as one of the 1595 group impacted by the Guale uprising (see chapter 21).[8]

Another letter, much closer to the date of Oré's time in Florida, describes the obstacles the Franciscans faced. Lorenzo Martínez, one of the friars Oré recruited for the Florida missions, wrote the monarch on 4 September 1612, reporting his arrival along with twenty Franciscans, despite the "difficulties of the land and the dangers of the sea."[9] The newcomers quickly realized the stark reality of earlier attempts to Christianize the original peoples of La Florida. The religious of the Province of Santa Elena lamented on 16 October 1612 that although there was a great potential for conversion, the difficulties seemed overwhelming. The indigenous people steadfastly retained their old ways and every few years they moved to a new location. They could not be trusted, not even the caciques, who tenaciously defended their ancient practice of having multiple wives. Even more disheartening was the fact that they came to the friars only because of the gifts they received. There was one positive note: at that time, fifty friars were active in La Florida and some had served there as long as eighteen to twenty years.[10]

⚜ 18 ⚜

Cuba, La Florida, and Oré's First Inspection

After a three-year delay Oré, accompanied by his young servant Juan Tundidor and Friar Francisco de San Buenaventura, finally set sail for the Indies in 1614, possibly on the ship *Nuestra Señora de los Remedios*.[1] Had they been delayed in Spain until the fall they would have witnessed one of the more memorable events of the early seventeenth century, the arrival of the Japanese embassy (with Franciscan Friar Sotelo) at Sanlúcar de Barrameda on 5 October 1614. During their tour the Japanese visited the Franciscan Monastery of Loreto where Oré recently gathered testimony about Francisco Solano. Oré probably heard of this Japanese diplomatic mission when he returned to Spain in 1618 following his assignment in La Florida.[2]

Oré reached St. Augustine in late fall 1614. He emphasized that he conducted the first of his two visitas of the Province of Santa Elena in 1614, an indication that Florida was the first stop of his assignment and that he may have sailed on a packet ship rather than with the Indies fleet. Oré's first inspection of the Florida missions was rapid, and he later lamented he had been unable to see as much as he intended, partly because the population was too widely dispersed. In addition, the Florida missions comprised various ethnic entities not yet fully under Spanish control. There is little evidence that Oré's first visita was more than a cursory reconnaissance.[3]

Near the end of the printed *Relación de la Florida*, Oré detailed his two inspections. He accomplished little on his first visita and relied on the account of another Franciscan, Martín de Prieto, definidor of the Province of Santa Elena. This is the closest equivalent to a first inspection that we have, other than brief notices of it elsewhere in Oré's text. Following an oath administered by Oré in late 1616, Prieto declared that he arrived in Florida in 1605 and was based initially in the mission of Nombre de Dios on St. Augustine's edge. Prieto emphasized his successes during his 1607–1609 evangelizing efforts from the central Timucua communities westward into the land of the Apalachee. In one Timucua village Prieto was resisted by jeering and threats. The community of Santa Ana's shaman informed the friar that the cacique was old and infirm. As a youth the cacique was held captive by Hernando de Soto and because the Spaniards treated him terribly, he would never let his people be Christian. Undeterred, the bold friar entered the cacique's house. The cacique became furious and when Prieto began to speak the "word of God" the chief covered his ears and ordered him expelled from the village. As the friar was forcefully pushed out, there was a massive thunderclap and a violent blast of wind leveled the buildings, leaving only a cross and a small "chapel" that had been used for Mass. Prieto recalled, "Such was the fear that it caused all of them, that the next day the cacique sent for me to catechize him, and within six days I baptized him, and upon completing the baptism he gave his soul to God." Here and elsewhere the Franciscans employed every example of "divine intervention" to foster conversion. In what may have been a matter of life or death, luck was on the friar's side. Prieto boasted that he baptized four hundred in Santa Ana, and two hundred in San Miguel and San Francisco.[4]

Buoyed by his success Prieto continued efforts to win converts, entering Apalachee territory with Timucua assistance. He arrived at the plaza of Ivitachuco where "there were more than 30,000 Indians," and he and the two hundred Timucua accompanying him were welcomed.[5] Prieto had reported his experiences in letters to the king and the Royal Council, and to Governor Pedro de Ibarra. He noted that other friars went to the area and provided him reports that he delivered along with his own account to the next governor, Juan Fernández de Olivera. When the Timucua and Apalachee met in Ivitachuco, Prieto reported, "I discussed with them the need for peace." Despite a long cultural tradition of warfare between southeastern ethnic groups, the friar was surprised that they were amenable to his efforts. Perhaps they realized, as they faced the Spanish threat—which from the time of arrival brought death and suffering—that their own existence was in jeopardy if they continued in conflict with each other. When the cacique of Ivitachuco spoke, he marveled that he never expected to see such constant enemies come together to sit and eat, "in my plaza and house in peace. Now we will have food, now we will have contentment, now we will have, my children, tranquility."[6] Here, under Prieto's prodding the assembled chiefs authorized Apalachee chieftain Inihayca to travel with him to St. Augustine to swear obedience to the governor as representative of the king. Coming within two leagues of the city they were met by two soldiers sent to escort them, but without the friar who was responsible for the new relationship. Prieto discerned the motives of the governor, who wanted "to gain the thanks for what he had not done." Resigned to accept the governor's orders he concluded, "As poor friars of St. Francis, we hope for nothing other than the gift of heaven."[7] Prieto's report ended with a brief geographical description of the Apalachee terrain, a hundred leagues west of St. Augustine, a fertile land with fields of corn, beans, and squash.

Oré closed his transcription of Prieto's account verifying that all he said "was taken from the report that this religious gave me, although he [Oré] had a longer and more detailed one from Friar Alonso Serrano who arrived after Friar Prieto and went about preaching and planting the crosses in Apalachee territory, followed by four or five other religious who also entered the area. All indicated the Indians' desire to become Christian." Oré, reviewing the distances involved as well as the difficulties of bringing provisions to the mission, cautioned that if the Apalachee were contacted assisted by soldiers, more damage to the Franciscan mission might occur. Weapons from St. Augustine's presidio would end up in the hands of the Indians causing conflict and mistreatment. In the end armed men would have to quell the disturbances, resulting in even more harm. In the next lines Oré alternated between potential future problems and successes in evangelization of the Apalachee, people with many "dishonest and terrible vices," and mentioned the possible benefit of concentrating the Indians from small communities into towns for more effective conversion, as Viceroy Toledo had done in Peru four decades earlier.[8]

Perhaps Oré's digression is a consequence of the way his Florida *Relación* was compiled, by drafting a series of short texts, then sewing them together with occasional attempts to link them. There are other instances where Oré used this mode of narrative construction as he prepared a manuscript for printing. His initial inspection was superficial, although successful, and he left "things related to the conversion of the natives ordered and well organized." In early 1615 Oré with other friars arrived in Havana's harbor to commence the challenging work specified in the original assignment to deal with the chaotic situation in Cuba. For months Commissioner Oré was entangled "in the government of this province."[9]

19

The Cuban Conundrum

Oré faced serious challenges in Cuba. Philip III and the Council of the Indies had received many notices of conflicts on the island. Officials needed reliable information and suggestions for redress. Given the tumultuous nature of the transient population of the port city of Havana on the island's northwest coast, and Santiago de Cuba on the southeast, the Franciscans were viewed as a stabilizing influence. During his residence in Cuba, Oré prepared friars with the religious training required for the priesthood. Many of the candidates were soldiers, seamen, and transients of all types, clearly not ideally suited for service in the church, raising suspicions as to their motives. The pool was small and defective, but the need was great. Oré confronted other issues involving Franciscan endeavors in Havana and elsewhere on the island. The early history on the island of the church, and especially the religious orders, is incomplete, although recent works are beginning to clarify what has been an opaque glass.[1]

When Oré entered Havana about a century after the city's founding, the church's authority was minimal. Although a Franciscan was at work on the island in 1514, it was not until 1531 that the monastery of Santiago de Cuba was established, under the jurisdiction of Santo Domingo on Hispaniola. The Havana house was originally under administration of the General Commissioner of the Order for the Indies, then was transferred to the Yucatán, and subsequently Mexico. The Custody of Santa Elena was established during the 1609 General Chapter Meeting of the Franciscans in Toledo, then in 1612 promoted to a Province at their General Meeting in Rome.[2] When Oré arrived in 1615, Havana and the surrounding area accommodated about seven to ten thousand people. The number exploded when the fleets entered the harbor. For decades there was only one parish church and following the attack on Havana by French corsair Jacques de Sorés in 1555, it needed to be rebuilt. The Crown's primary focus in Havana was on defense, and construction moved slowly for two decades until the cathedral's completion in 1574. For many years most religious passed through the city on their way to nearby assignments or to prepare for their return home. Without a monastery Franciscan and Dominican friars were forced to rent rooms during their temporary residence. Many accommodations with beds in the city served multiple needs, and sleeping friars were often awoken by arguments over payments or by sounds of passion. Religious orders needed their own houses. The first Franciscan monastery was small, made of mud walls with a palm-thatched roof. Havana's city council recognized the need for a better structure and in 1577 the city and Franciscans joined to build a stone church. By 1580 with three thousand ducats the order raised from the community, the Franciscans secured land in a more conspicuous place in La Fuerza, and by 1584 their monastery was almost complete. Royal favor aided in speeding construction and by 1586 the Franciscan monastery was a landmark.[3]

A thin Franciscan presence extended throughout the island when Oré arrived. In the southeast Santiago de Cuba, with its excellent harbor, earlier dominated administration of the island. By the mid-sixteenth century Havana surpassed Santiago's size and importance. Competition between the two cities was continuous, and internal and external pressure led the Crown to split political administration of the island into halves. With support of Havana's Governor Gaspar Ruiz de Pereda, the warden of the Morro fortress, Juan de Villaverde Ureta was named governor and captain general of eastern Cuba in 1607. When the new governor arrived the following fall, Santiago's cathedral remained under construction, but the city already had a functioning Franciscan monastery and other principal masonry structures. Bishop Juan de las Cabezas Altamirano, a Dominican friar, reported to the king that he recently conducted an inspection of the island and that in 1608 his diocesan seat, Santiago de Cuba, had a population of at least 600 people in the city and its immediate vicinity. Applying a similar ratio range used by Alejandro de la Fuente for his estimate of Havana's population, the total number of inhabitants in Santiago may have ranged from three to four thousand. Bishop Cabezas Altamirano earlier in 1606 conducted an ecclesiastical visitation of part of La Florida: St. Augustine, the mission of Nombre de Dios and a section northward into Guale territory.[4]

Governor Villaverde died on 27 September 1612 during what appeared to be an epidemic of "fevers" sweeping the district; he was buried in the Francis-

BISHOPS OF SANTIAGO DE CUBA AND GOVERNORS OF CUBA, SANTIAGO DE CUBA AND FLORIDA

Bishops of Santiago de Cuba	
Fr. Juan de las Cabezas Altamirano, Dominican	1602–1611
Fr. Alonso Enríquez de Almendáriz, Mercedarian	1611–1623
Governors of Cuba	
Pedro de Valdés	1600–1607
Gaspar Ruiz de Pereda	1607–1616
Sancho de Alquiza	1616–1619
General Francisco de Venegas	1619–1624
Governors of Santiago de Cuba	
Juan de Villaverde Ureta	1607–1612
Francisco Sánchez de Moya	1612–1613
Juan García Nabia	1613–1618
Rodrigo de Velasco	1618–1623
Governors of Florida	
Gonzalo Méndez de Canzo	1597–1603
Captain Pedro de Ybarra	1603–1610
Captain Juan Fernández de Olivera	1609–1612
Captain Juan de Treviño Guillamas	1613–1618
Juan de Salinas	1618–1624

Note: All dates given are approximate.

can monastery in Santiago.⁵ Santiago's cabildo recommended to the Audiencia in Santo Domingo artillery Captain Francisco Sánchez de Moya to succeed to the post. He seemed an ideal candidate and was a powerful figure in dealing with local challenges. Philip II sent him to Cuba in 1597 to establish a foundry and to administer the region's copper mines, and he brought with him dozens of artisans and specialists. The Audiencia of Santo Domingo did appoint Sánchez de Moya governor of eastern Cuba, but it was temporary until ratification in Spain. Havana's Governor Ruiz de Pereda was infuriated by the appointment and pressed for reincorporation of the east.

Oré could not avoid the turbulent relationship between Governor Ruiz de Pereda and Bishop Alonso Enríquez de Almendáriz (1551–1628). Oré and the bishop were no strangers to each other. They had met during the Third Church

Council in Lima and their paths had crossed several times after. Oré had some experience with conflict between civil and religious administrators during his work as a solicitor in the Colca Valley, but that confrontation and its resolution was minor in comparison to the clash between the bishop and governor that was taking place in Cuba. For Oré this struggle was instructive, and he would find himself in a similar contest several years later when he became bishop of La Imperial in Chile.

Bishop Enríquez de Almendáriz assumed his diocesan seat, Santiago de Cuba, on 9 September 1611, and served there until 15 April 1625, when he was appointed bishop of Michoacán.[6] Enríquez de Almendáriz, appalled by the deplorable state of his diocesan seat, decided to transfer it to Havana. That move, made without authorization by higher church or state officials, led to immediate protests. The dispute centered on royal patronage, notably clerical appointments–especially military chaplains. Church expenses paid by the state made the relationship even more contentious. Further, the cathedral chapter and the cabildo of Santiago joined forces to compel the bishop's return. Santo Domingo's Audiencia also became involved. Letters from various parties reached the king and his councils with news of the bishop's excommunication of the governor. Philip III, attempting to control the situation, ordered Bishop Enríquez de Almendáriz to return to his diocese in Santiago de Cuba and to lift the excommunication of the governor.[7]

The battle between bishop and governor was ignited. On 30 April 1614 members of Santiago de Cuba's cabildo wrote the monarch thanking him for retention of the diocesan seat in Santiago. While stressing their obedience and respect for their bishop, they simultaneously emphasized the importance of following correct procedure in any important decision. Meanwhile, Governor Ruiz de Pereda sent eighty soldiers to notify the bishop of the royal provision to absolve him from excommunication, threatening to imprison him in Havana if he failed to do so. At this point there was a pause, and the bishop reached an agreement for a delay allowing him to collect papers to send to Spain to support his position.[8]

On 10 May 1614 Captain Sánchez de Moya wrote the king complaining that two earlier letters he had sent reporting his actions and the questionable maneuvers of Governor Ruiz de Pereda had not left Santo Domingo. He then updated the monarch and royal officials on more recent developments. The captain enumerated preoccupying consequences of the governor's actions:

fraud in the collection of government revenues, interference with operation of the copper mines and other areas of the economy, meddling with local administration on the eastern half of the island, and his intention to imprison members of Santiago de Cuba's cabildo and bring them to trial because of their resistance to his orders.

The captain's correspondence is important for our understanding of the state of affairs in Cuba. He believed Governor Ruiz de Pereda intended to retain governorship of the entire island.[9] Sánchez de Moya expected that Ruiz de Pereda also wrote to Philip III about these events and expressed his certainty that the governor "failed to include what I here will relate."[10] He told the king that he witnessed the bishop being oppressed day and night by guards posted around his residence and lamented he was unable to do anything about it. Frustrated, Sánchez de Moya requested that the king send a new governor to control the entire island to prevent this situation from happening again.[11]

Despite the struggles with a cantankerous governor, Bishop Enríquez de Almendáriz stabilized and improved the position of the church and clergy during his tenure. The bishop, complying with Philip III's order for a full account of events, defended his actions, and his report was ready for printing in 1619. The bishop indicated that during the first of his three diocesan inspections around February 1612, he realized that Santiago de Cuba was not the ideal center of the church. He recommended a shift to Havana where there were 7,000 "souls" (2,530 Spaniards, 4,082 Blacks) and the seat should be there "because this city is the key to all the Indies." Havana had only two older curates even though they reported many times to the Royal Council the need for more clergy. The bishop noted that under his rule the church was reconstructed and boasted an organ and choir stalls and confided that he donated 1,500 pesos of his own fine fabrics for its service. The main altar and sacristy remained to be constructed, and the bishop hinted that perhaps His Majesty could help with alms of lime, bricks, roof tiles and fine wood. He stressed the need for a second parish, which could be centered in the small church where they held Mass for the Blacks. He mentioned that there was a chapel with a chaplain for the soldiers in the Castillo del Morro. The bishop did not inspect Jamaica "because of the disputes the abbots of the island have had with my predecessors." Nor had he conducted an inspection of La Florida and noted that the costs would take two to three years to cover from his allotted budget. Further, the previous bishop had recently done so. He stated that there was no need for an

Indian doctrina in Cuba but added "except only in La Florida that has more than twenty, according to a report I have." Based on this statement, the bishop read Oré's report on Florida, as becomes more clear later.[12]

Oré conducted an inspection of the Franciscan monasteries in Cuba and attempted to correct the reported abuses. It was a daunting task, and he spent some sixteen months on the island before returning to Florida to begin his second inspection there in the fall of 1616. Oré was wedged between several competing authorities and factions, including internal dissenters among his own religious flock. There were often surprises and new challenges and Oré aimed to bring contending parties together to reconstruct amity, if it had ever existed. In some instances, his efforts to reform the most deplorable were so successful that men cast aside their old ways, studied for the priesthood and were ultimately ordained, to the disgust of some authorities.

Oré must have heard that the ships sailing into Havana's harbor in early August 1616 carried Peru's viceroy and an extensive entourage returning to Spain after a decade in South America. Havana's permanent residents benefitted from the payments for services they rendered during the weeks the fleet was moored before the travelers embarked on the last leg of their voyage to Iberia. Viceroy Juan Manuel de Mendoza y Luna, Third Marqués de Montesclaros, was born in Guadalajara, Spain, in 1571, and like many other viceroys had first served as *asistente* (governor) of Seville. Before becoming Peru's viceroy in 1606, he spent about three years as viceroy of New Spain. The Marqués de Montesclaros remained in Lima for almost eight years, completing his term in mid-December 1615. It would be almost eight months before the viceroy's party reached Cuba. His wife Doña Ana Mesía de Mendoza was frequently unwell, and the voyage from Lima to Panama was taxing. Doña Ana fell ill and died at sea before reaching Havana. The viceroy and his wife had prepared their wills in Lima on 26 September 1614. As soon as possible on arrival in Cuba, Doña Ana's will was officially opened in front of witnesses. Four men who traveled with the couple from Lima on the same galleon verified she died some fifteen days earlier and testified they saw Doña Ana's body placed in a casket, which was then nailed shut and taken to Havana for burial. In her will Doña Ana provided preferences for burial but if she died during the voyage, she left the choice to the executors of her will.

Speed was essential, given the heat and humidity of a Caribbean August, and as soon as the fleet landed in Havana's harbor the funeral and interment took place. Havana's cathedral was in no condition to accept the charge, and the second choice, the Augustinian monastery and church remained unfinished. Therefore funeral ceremonies for Doña Ana were held in the Franciscan monastery and afterward Don Rodrigo de Mendoza, nephew of the Marqués de Montesclaros, asked the notary who was present to place in testimony that he had asked "Friar Gerónimo de Oces [sic] commissioner of the province of San Francisco . . . of this island and Friar Martín de Aguil [. . .] guardian of this convent" to accept "the body of the said marquesa."[13] Doña Ana's remains would be placed in "the small niche that was prepared at the right side of the main altar" in the Franciscan church. Commissioner Oré and the Franciscan guardian agreed that the Franciscans would retain the body until the marqués, or someone authorized, could send it to Spain for final burial. Doña Ana's body needed to be identified before it was interred. There were several witnesses present, including Oré, when the casket "covered with velvet" was opened. The next step must have been quick and unpleasant, given the rapid decomposition of the body in the tropical heat. The notary duly recorded that they uncovered "a face of a body that was wrapped in a shroud of the order of San Francisco." The witnesses looked and saw that "by a nostril of a nose it seemed to appear to be a human body; and with that they closed the said casket and placed it in the said niche and closed its door." Luis Gerónimo de Oré "commissioner of this province" signed the testimony along with probably the guardian, whose signature is illegible, as is the exact date, other than August 1616.[14] Oré's role in this brief but necessary undertaking provides one of just a few glimpses of his activities in Cuba. At the time he had only two more months to complete his tasks there before sailing back to the southeastern mainland of North America. Oré left Havana in October 1616 to initiate his second inspection of La Florida.

20

Second Inspection of the La Florida Missions

Oré's primary assignment was to conduct a thorough evaluation of the Franciscan missions in La Florida, and to give a full report to his order and the Crown. Florida's Atlantic inlets are notoriously dangerous, and many sailing vessels run aground. Late season hurricanes are common; even more common are the fall storms that sweep ahead of early cold fronts. Oré described the dangerous entry in the St. Augustine harbor. Waiting for the high tide the ship had anchored outside the sandbar, but "because of the storm it became necessary to cut the cables and lose two anchors."[1] After a harrowing twenty-five-day voyage from Havana, having faced rough seas and contrary winds that blocked the entrance through the shallow, sandy, and shifting inlet, Oré and his entourage finally reached St. Augustine on 6 November 1616.

The weary passengers were greeted by Governor Treviño de Guillamas, the religious, and the soldiers of the presidio. Oré remained in the Franciscan monastery in St. Augustine for ten days while notices were dispatched to the other religious in the Guale and Timucua doctrinas. Oré, as visitador authorized by Cuba's bishop, inspected the blessed sacrament (*santísimo sacramento*) in the main church of St. Augustine as well as the baptismal font, the chrism oil, and the jar containing it. Given the reputation of St. Augustine's citizenry, Oré "published an edict against public sins existing among the presidio's soldiers." To that end and with "the permission and approval" of the governor, he named a fiscal and a notary chosen from among the soldiers. As Oré prepared to leave St. Augustine he believed that "everything was remedied that was asking to be remedied without harm to anyone." The pragmatic commissioner knew that dealing with soldiers required "caution and prudence" in order "to achieve the desired correction" of errors.[2]

Following the brief stay in St. Augustine, Oré set out with three friars to inspect the scattered missions on the vast frontier. The governor offered Oré a horse, but the intrepid friar insisted on traveling on foot "in the company of his religious," and later in a canoe to go from settlement to settlement, staying a scant average of three to four days at each mission and examining the quality of indoctrination and recording the number of Indians baptized. The only version of Oré's second visita of the missions is his report. This might not be the complete version as originally recorded, but it is the best we have and superior to the scant information about the first inspection.[3]

Travel along the coasts of present-day Florida into South Carolina was best accomplished by a canoe. When the friars departed St. Augustine, they headed on foot in the westerly direction until they reached the St. Johns River, "larger than all the rivers of Spain, France and Italy," where they boarded a canoe. As Oré and his companions paddled along the river he was impressed not only by its size but also "the groves of pines and other trees on its banks," and noted that "there are many good fish." He recorded that they traveled twenty leagues upriver and landed at the San Antonio de Enacape convent.[4] When the friars disembarked, they ordered the guardian of both missions, Enacape and Avino, to meet along with the other religious there, and the definidor. With all gathered, Oré delivered a spiritual discourse and inspected the mission. When complete he held in the monastery's communal hall a *capítulo de culpas* (meeting to discuss sins or acts of commission or omission) and charged the friars to pray for a prudent outcome in the election they were to conduct in the upcoming Provincial Chapter Meeting.[5] The same schedule was sent to other doctrinas along with notice of Oré's arrival. They were also instructed to conduct at vespers and matins the customary *suffragia* (prayers for the souls of the deceased) "to make certain Our Lord would be served in our first Chapter Meeting and election of his agent, without intervention of vice or corruption, or interference of worldly influences, or anyone's solicitations." Along with the religious of the two missions, Oré concluded with prayer and *disciplina* (submission to moral canons and practices of the order).[6]

Next, Oré examined the knowledge of the doctrine and catechism of the indigenous people. He found that most of the men and women knew it well and the children generally understood it. They not only knew the doctrine, but also assisted during Mass. Oré preached to all in the village and inspected the baptismal font and the chrismatories. He followed the same procedures in all the villages of the province and acted not only as a priest but "as an inspector of the province in the name of the bishop, with the particular commission that he had given him for it."[7]

Having completed the inspection of San Antonio de Enacape, Oré and his companions trudged toward the monastery of San Francisco de Potano. He remembered that although the land was generally level, in some parts it resembled a savanna with tall pine trees and marshes and lakes, making the journey difficult at times. They required two and a half days to reach the doctrina of Apalo where they rested, and then continued past another lake filled with fish and surrounded by tall trees. Here the specific descriptions abated, and Oré provided merely the brief order of the visitations—on to Santa Fe de Teloco, from there to the monastery of San Martin de Timucua; he was "preaching to the Indians in all these villages and examining them on the doctrine."[8] In the monastery of San Martin de Timucua, Oré assembled the mission's guardian and also the guardians of Potano and Tarihica, as well as the friars of the monasteries of San Juan de Guacara, Teleco, and Cosa, urging them to dedicate themselves to the conversion of the Indians. Oré spent three or four days in each village, conducting the inspection, examining the indigenous converts, and "writing down the exact number of baptized Christians, both those alive as well as the dead Christians."[9]

Oré soon realized, given the difficulties of travel, that it would be both impractical and costly to hold the chapter meeting in St. Augustine as originally planned. He consulted all the guardians and the local Franciscan friars, pointing out not only the obstacles facing the religious to attend the meeting in St. Augustine, but also the indigenous carriers "who would be forced to come along loaded with their books and vestments." He suggested that it might be more convenient to hold their chapter meeting in the Monastery of San Buenaventura de Guadalquini, "where the food for the Indians and the refreshments for the capitulars could be had for less cost because everything is very expensive in the city of St. Augustine." The new site would simultaneously save extra work and time because the friars could congregate in the most convenient place for the two linguistic families, the Timucua and the Guale. Oré noted the missions were referred to as the "*agua dulce* (fresh water)" and "*agua salada* (salt water)" depending whether it was near the ocean or a river. Furthermore, the mission of Guadalquini was located on the water's edge, and the two "provinces" were accessible by canoe. Once the friars resolved to proceed, Oré informed the governor and asked him to send any royal "orders, decrees or provisions" relevant to the missions that he might have received so "the religious can fulfill everything in every way."[10] Oré and the guardians wanted to ensure that the friars' conversion efforts complied with the monarch's orders. There was likely to be opposition by some friars regarding the new site for the chapter meeting, especially those already in or close to St. Augustine.

After he dispatched the missive to the governor, Oré and his secretary left the Timucuan monastery and set out for the Mission of San Juan de Guacara, some eight leagues distant. After inspecting it, they continued to the mission in Santa Cruz de Tarihica. Oré was amazed how successful the conversion efforts were in the mission. When the Franciscans had first come to the village about five years earlier "there were hardly four Christian Indians" and now there were "712 living Christians." Oré examined the village with even greater care, "because it was of Indian neophytes, recently converted." He was impressed because not only did they know well the doctrine and catechism, but "some Indians, men and women, knew how to read and write, being thirty or forty years old, and all of this they had learned in four years."[11] Oré paused here for a few days to preach, teach, and meditate.

To reach the next mission, Santa Isabel de Utinahica, Oré decided to take a rugged but shorter route through a desolate and depopulated land for some fifty leagues. The hilly terrain covered with thick live-oaks and clumps of brambles was difficult to transverse. They passed through isolated indigenous villages where according to Oré they were "received with much satisfaction and display of their desire to become Christians." They arrived in the village of Taraco "on the day of Saint Barbara (4 December) and we named the place Santa Barbara." After Oré and his group left the settlement a messenger from the village caught up with them "to ask for the name of the saint that the village would be named after once they become Christians." Furthermore, the villagers asked Oré to "provide in the meantime a Christian Indian to teach them the doctrine and catechism." Oré must have been thrilled by such enthusiasm and immediately wrote to a religious residing in Tari, who was "a very competent translator," to travel to the village and cautiously take up "the good work and fulfill the wishes of the pagan Indians."[12]

The commissioner and his companions continued, passing through several small non-Christian settlements. They "lacked food" but Oré noted that because it was Advent "Our Lord provided us with a gift of mushrooms that we collected along the way to sustain us in the shelter we made with branches to sleep in and protect us from the frigid air and the drenching downpours that soaked us to the skin and our papers as well." There are occasional glimpses of Friar Luis Gerónimo the man. Continuing toward the monastery of Santa Isabel they encountered rushing rivers so deep that they could not be forded, nor were there bridges other than "a long thick pine trunk that the Indians who accompanied me crossed running as someone who lost all fear of those dangerous passages." Oré, undaunted, but clearly apprehensive, followed the indigenous guides: "First confessing, I crossed over in the name of Our Lord and holy obedience of my prelates who had charged me with this inspection and commission."[13] Did the intrepid friar after confessing and crossing himself "lose all fear," as he lifted his robe and sprinted across the tree trunk to the other side of the raging river? Oré reached the Mission of Santa Isabel where he preached to the Amerindians and probed their knowledge of the doctrine. Next, Oré and his companions descended to "the villages of the Guale language by canoes on a river larger than the Tajo" in Spain.

Oré often compared the condition of the indigenous people in Peru to those of the Florida missions. He emphasized the desire of the Apalachee living in a heavily populated district in a radius of twelve leagues to receive the Franciscans. The Latama peoples, another sizeable population, as well as those of Santa Elena where the first presidio had been, were now ripe for conversion. The religious were filled with the spirit to assume the burden, "as oxen, reaping the multitude of the Lord." Oré lamented that the distances between the small indigenous settlements meant the friars faced difficulties to baptize and administer the sacraments. He suggested future governors should consider concentrating the Indians from several small places into one large village, as the reducciones in Peru were accomplished "by the design and resolution of the Viceroy Francisco de Toledo." That way the people would be better instructed, and it would reduce the "excessive difficulty" the Franciscans faced "with changing weather, either raining or snowing in the winter, or burning in the heat of the summer."[14] Such a policy was impractical given the natural environment and the cultures of La Florida ethnicities and was rejected.

Did Oré fail to inspect the Indian doctrinas of the island of Cuba? Bishop Enríquez de Almendáriz provided clues in his report to the king (12 August 1620), completed after Oré returned to Spain. "I say it seems there are no more Indians on this island that are true Indians, other than the few I have mentioned that are found in each village, already mixed with the Spanish." He stressed they were treated and taught as all the Spanish were. The bishop noted that in one place near Havana, Guanabacoa, the Spanish encroached on indigenous lands and advised the monarch to issue an order to secure justice for the Indians.[15] The bishop ended his missive reiterating that the only friars with indigenous doctrinas under his jurisdiction were in La Florida, "as I have said before." He continued, "according to what I have learned, they treat them well, although they take more license than they have in the administration of the Sacraments to the flock subject to the vicario who I have there."[16]

❦ 21 ❧

Franciscan Martyrs in Oré's Account

Oré's principal goal in his report on La Florida was to preserve the memory of the martyrdom of Franciscans during the Guale uprising in 1597. He was collecting information during his two inspections and at the Provincial Chapter Meeting, and in St. Augustine and Havana. Oré's purpose, similar to his *Relación de la vida y milagros de Francisco Solano*, was to provide evidence that could lead to recognition and sainthood of the martyred Franciscans. Carlos Gálvez Peña points out that Oré's incursion into martyrologies in the Atlantic world was among the earliest, superseded only by a brief mention in an anonymous Jesuit chronicle published around 1600 on the martyrdom of Father Diego de Urrea in Peru in 1596.[1] Given the competition between orders for saints and martyrs, details of their lives and the nature of their deaths needed to be catalogued. Reported miracles needed to be confirmed. Hagiographies were popular reading during the early modern period fostering their publication. Oré's manuscripts on Francisco Solano and the Florida martyrs did not need authorizations from censors to print because his reports were for internal use. Oré's narrative begins with Philip II authorizing to send twelve Franciscans to Florida missions. The recruits, largely from Castile, sailed for the Indies on 14 July 1595.[2]

Oré provided biographical sketches of each friar on the expedition, not just those martyred, stressing their spirituality in Spain and Florida. For example, Friar Blas de Montes "who was loved by everyone" received a substantial portrayal. Oré alluded to a "certain person" who because Friar Montes thwarted some of "his lascivious attempts and intentions, wanted to take revenge" and spread rumors about Montes that were "incredible in such a saintly person." The friar became ill, returned to Spain where he later died. Oré did not identify the person who caused the turmoil. Friar Pedro Bermejo served several years in Florida, and Oré met him in 1616 during his inspection in Cuba. At that time Bermejo was guardian in Bayamo on the island's east.[3] Although Oré did not mention meeting Friar Pedro Fernández de Chozas, it is possible. The friar was based at the mission in Latama when the Guale revolt erupted, and learning of the uprising he managed to notify Governor Méndez de Canzo. After the revolt he returned to Spain and provided a detailed report. In 1612 he attended the General Chapter Meeting in Rome, and later was guardian of the Madrid monastery. It is possible that Oré and Fernández de Chozas coincided before Oré's departure for Florida, or in Madrid upon his return.[4]

Friar Francisco Pareja served in Florida from the 1580s and became one of Oré's most trusted advisers. Oré described Pareja's early years in the Florida missions where "at first the Indians caused him many hardships, but he overcame all of them with much patience and perseverance." Pareja taught the indigenous people the doctrine and protected them from "the offences that the Spanish soldiers did to them." Oré observed that in the end "by the good example he has always given, he conquered the cruelty and ill temper of the Indians, turning them from wolves into sheep."[5] Pareja's fellow Franciscans in La Florida valued his work, and over the years he was elected guardian, definidor, custodian, and later, provincial. His religious texts and his dictionary and grammar in Timucua were the key to Franciscan success; they provide modern ethnohistorians valuable insight into Timucua culture. Oré noted, "In the inspection that I conducted in order to celebrate the First Provincial Chapter Meeting of this province, he was found to be a saintly man and most deserving of his election."[6] Oré saw in Pareja a man of similar interests who recognized the importance of communicating directly to the converts. With painstaking work Pareja produced various texts "in the language of the Indians which gave him advantage over the others."[7] Oré also mentiond Friar Pedro Ruiz, "priest, confessor, religious person who always gave good example to the Indians and the Spanish," and added that "during this first provincial chapter meeting that we held" Ruiz was named guardian of Havana's Franciscan monastery.[8] Friar Francisco de Avila, part of the 1595 Florida mission, was captured by the rebels. He survived and provided an account of his experiences and the deaths of the martyrs. Oré included Avila's narrative in his *Relación de los mártires*.[9]

Oré praised Friar Pedro de Viniegra, who learned the Florida indigenous languages so well, that "he knew and understood them perfectly." He lamented that Viniegra, "a very humble religious" and an eloquent preacher "was not yet a priest, able to confess them and conduct Mass, having the competence to do it and to administer the other sacraments." Other Franciscans in Florida shared the opinion and successfully petitioned the commissioner of New Spain to send an order authorizing them to ordain the friar. Oré added that after Viniegra was ordained "we have made him one of the best ministers for the Indians we have had in our time."[10] Another of the twelve was Friar Francisco de Bonilla, who after arriving in Florida was sent "with certain provisions" to New Spain and stayed there. Oré noted that Bonilla "already old, came now and was present in our Chapter meeting" in San Buenaventura de Guadalquini.[11]

When the twelve Franciscans reached Saint Augustine in 1595, they were received by the elderly Custodian Friar Francisco Marrón who had been in Florida since 1574. His memory was excellent, and Oré consulted him as he compiled his report. While writing in Cuba after his second inspection of La Florida, Oré talked to Friar Marrón who was then (in 1617) on his deathbed in Havana's monastery. Oré inquired how long he had the habit, and Marrón "replied that more than eighty years," and regarding his age, he responded "more than one hundred." Marrón, one of the few who provided a *relación verdadera* of the martyrdom of the five Franciscans, verified the narrative of Friar Avila, the only near eyewitness left to "tell us how, when and the cause why his companions were martyred." One can imagine a pensive Oré dipping his pen into the ink, as he contemplated Friar Marrón's life and composed these words: "he died twenty-two years after [the Guale Revolt] in this Monastery of Havana, and I buried him."[12]

Before Oré continued his narrative, he named seven friars who came to Florida with Friar Alonso de Reynoso between 1583 and 1589, providing a short biographical sketch of each. Some would be killed by the Guale. Friar Pedro de Corpa came to Florida with Reynoso in 1587, and according to Oré was the first one killed during the uprising.[13] The elderly Friar Juan de San Nicolás, a lay brother that Oré met "who at present lives in the monastery of St. Augustine," received special recognition. Oré related he was a simple man who found the whole of his existence in the church's work. Friar San Nicolás, when not absorbed in prayer, worked from dawn until dusk in the monastery's garden tending the vegetables and fruits and medicinal herbs. The friar, who could be seen in the streets of St. Augustine begging for alms, was admired in the presidio for his faith to such a degree that some "collected his old and torn undergarments to wrap their infants in because they treat them as if they were relics." San

Nicolás was also a sacristan in the monastery, cleaning and refilling the lamps with oil and tending to their wicks. Oré, clearly impressed by the elderly friar's piety, stressed his devotion to both the living and the dead.[14]

Friar Juan de Silva helped bring the unfortunate group of Franciscans to Florida in 1595, and later returned to Spain. Mission assignments in La Florida were made by lot after discussion of the most appropriate placement. In this case Guardian and Custodian Friar Marrón in the presence of Governor Domingo Martínez de Avendaño did the final naming. The friars were distributed to ten missions, "each one by the luck of the draw and assignment by the Superior." The missions were usually three to four leagues apart, although some were more separated, "by bad trails because of the many marshes and shallow streams so it is not easy to travel by either land or sea."[15] Within two years the Guale rose up. The apparent cause given by Oré parallels that of the earlier Jacán rebellion in the north. In both cases it was triggered by public humiliation of caciques in front of their people. The Spanish with their own deeply embedded sense of honor should have recognized this characteristic and been more cautious. The early religious in the Andean World, where the elite had multiple wives, faced similar difficulty enforcing Christian monogamy, but were at first somewhat tolerant of indigenous custom. Following the Council of Trent, the rule of church doctrine in the Andes and elsewhere was more stringently enforced. One consequence was indigenous resistance and rebellion in La Florida and in other frontier regions of the empire.

Oré's vivid description of the events as the uprising unfolded is gripping, and can be read in the original and translated in either the *Account of the Martyrs in the Province of La Florida*, edited and translated by Raquel Chang-Rodríguez and Nancy Vogeley, or the translation of the sections of the text concerning the Guale rebellion in J. Michael Francis and Kathleen M. Kole's *Murder and Martyrdom in Spanish Florida: Don Juan and the Guale Uprising of 1597*. Francis and Kole find that Oré's sources place the blame for the revolt on the shoulders of that shamed cacique of Tolomato, Don Juan, known also as Juanillo.[16] There were other reasons for the revolt than Don Juan's public humiliation: the unwanted presence of outsiders in their land, demands placed on the Guale for labor and food, lack of respect as well as the taking of slaves, all contributed to ill feelings. But the act of public shaming inflamed Don Juan, who left the mission and united with other malcontents to plan a response. The first Franciscan to die, Friar Pedro de Corpa, was killed in Tolomato, the principal indigenous village, as men in war-paint and feathers—"a sign of cruelty and killings"—entered the mission. As elsewhere, Oré employed Andean terminology to describe the weapon used to strike Friar Corpa: "They killed him with a stone hatchet that they call a *macana* or *champi* in the language of the Incas of Cuzco."[17] His head was placed on a pike on a boat-launching site at river's edge, and "two Indians took his body to hide in the forests so that the Christians do not find it, and thus it has not appeared." Oré's account of the friar's decapitation is the only one. Francis and Kole warn, "Oré's version of Fray Corpa's murder must therefore be viewed with extreme caution."[18] They were unable to discover ethnohistorical evidence that the Guale and other southeastern ethnicities displayed enemy heads in this fashion. Amerindians of the southeast would adopt this grisly European practice, having viewed the decapitated heads of their chiefs mounted on pikes. The Guale warriors expected the Spanish would be intimidated by such displays of their own prowess and pride.

From Tolomato the rebels sent a message to the Guale cacique on St. Catherine's Island[19] demanding that he kill the friars there. But the cacique, unwilling to participate, "alerted the lay brother [Friar Antonio de Badajoz], who was a translator, what was underway." The cacique suggested that he and Friar Commissioner Miguel de Auñón should escape to San Pedro Island[20] and he promised them a boat and men to take them "even though he would be risking his life." Unfortunately, Badajos, refused to believe it, declined the offer, even after the cacique repeated his warning the following day, and did not tell Friar Auñón. Oré stressed that both friars were killed by non-Christians because the indigenous Christians tried to protect the Franciscans. Oré reported a miracle in the minds of the observers. Within a few days the infidel who had killed Auñón "sank into utmost despair and hanged himself on a live-oak tree using the string of his bow, which caused much wonderment among the Indians."[21]

The last to die was Friar Blas Rodríguez in Topiqui, who was fluent in the indigenous language, and Oré provided a moving account of his tearful arguing with the rebels. Rodríguez spoke to his captors and the mission's Christians: "My children, I have no fear of death, because death of the body, even if you do not give it to me, it will come, and every hour we should expect it and in the end we all have to die. What most weighs on me is the harm to you, and that the devil has succeeded with you in doing such offense to Our God and Creator. It also distresses me that you are so ungrateful for the pains that I and the other fathers have taken in teaching you the path to heaven." Oré again recorded a miraculous occurrence. After the friar was killed "they threw his body to the birds, because the Christians did not dare to bury him. The birds did not touch him and a dog who came later, immediately died, something that was seen by everyone." An old Christian secretly took the friar's body to bury in the forest. Oré added that at the time that he was writing, "we know nothing of his bones."[22]

Oré completed this chapter focusing on one of his more important sources, Friar Francisco de Avila, the only survivor. The friar, in his mission of Ospo,[23] having heard of Friar Corpa's fate had locked himself in and attempted to dissuade the attackers. When they broke down the door, Avila fled into the darkness, disappearing into the rushes (*juncal*). But the moon shone brightly; they found him, shot him with three arrows, and left him for dead. Eventually he was taken captive and subjected to abuse and taunts. Oré marveled at his suffering: "It is incredible what this religious endured in the one year that he was captive among those barbarians; he was nude where the winter is as harsh as in Madrid and without anyone curing his wounds, without cloth for bandages, or to wrap them or bind them." Oré concluded that the friar was cured by "God miraculously and mercifully."[24] Oré included the harshness of Avila's teaching method: "He was greatly persecuted by the young men, who many times came close to killing or drowning him, because earlier, when he had been teaching them the doctrine and to read, he sometimes whipped them." At one point during his captivity the Indians decided to burn the friar, tying him to a post of resinous candlewood, with much firewood and kindling. Avila was saved by an indigenous woman whose son was held prisoner by the soldiers in St. Augustine. She released the friar from the post exclaiming "This one I have to have instead of my son, and he has to bring him to me. If I free this one from death, the governor will not order my son killed."[25]

Oré learned that Friar Avila wrote "in his own hand" an account of his captivity and before he returned to Spain gave it to Friar Francisco Marrón. It appears that Marrón made the manuscript available to Oré who used it in his own description of Avila's imprisonment. According to Oré, the Franciscan's handwritten manuscript "is stored in the archive of the monastery of Havana." It has never been found, but Oré had copied it and included it as a separate chapter of his narrative, inaccurately titled the "Account of the great hardship that Father Avila endured in the year and a half that he was in the power of the rebel Indians." The captivity actually lasted ten months. Oré felt that his own brief description did not do justice to Avila's harrowing ordeal and decided to let the friar "tell in detail his hardships."[26] Given that the original of Avila's vivid captivity narrative, reminiscent of that of Cabeza de Vaca's tribulations, is missing, Oré's inclusion of it provides a valuable source of early Florida history.[27]

Francis and Kole argue that Oré likely "consulted native informants, although he does not identify anyone in particular."[28] They also suggest that, lacking the original Avila manuscript, "It is therefore understandable why some scholars might perceive Avila's captivity narrative with some skepticism." Indeed, caution is advisable in analysis of all such "captivity narratives." As Francis and Kole indicate, Oré's text was compiled twenty years after the events. Yet, careful reading of Oré's *Relación de la Florida* provides justification for taking the text as largely accurate. Avila had used clerical immunity and refused to tell when pressed by the governor the details and names of all the Indians who had killed the Spaniards or held him captive. But sometime later while in the monastery in Havana and before returning to Spain the then Guardian Marrón pressed him to provide a full account of what he knew of the events. Marrón wanted to ensure that the details of the four friars' deaths and Avila's suffering were preserved as a record of their martyrdom. As Francis and Kole note, memories of events are modified over time. Despite these concerns Oré's copy of Avila's account held by Marrón in the monastery's archive, remains the authoritative voice in the historiography of the uprising. Francis and Kole conclude that "With few exceptions, modern interpretations of the 1597 Guale Uprising characterize the revolt as a response to Franciscan interference in Guale affairs and missionary opposition to the practice of polygamy."[29]

Francis and Kole point out that among the friars attacked by the Guale, only Avila was saved. Why was this? He was taken to the village of Tulufina, where he began his work two years earlier. A relationship already existed, and when Avila was captured, he overheard discussion of his possible use as a hostage for future exchange or ransom. The young man held captive in St. Augustine was a possible chief taken with other young men in 1595, and the Guale in 1598 demanded their release in exchange for Avila. After a period of torment Avila was allowed more freedom as the captors tried to integrate him into their society, even tempting him with an indigenous maiden. His transfer came in June 1598 when he returned to the Franciscan monastery in St. Augustine. The governor, needing information on the rebels who murdered the friars, pressed Avila for names. He refused, even after receiving authorization from his superior. Clearly, he was protecting his captors. Francis and Kole note that Oré shifted from Avila's voice to his own.[30] Avila's narrative style is dramatically different from Oré's, as is clear when Oré briefly paraphrased a part of Avila's account. At the end of Avila's main narrative, Oré added a story "that a religious gave me, who spent much time with him and talked to him before and after his captivity."[31] He told Oré how Avila's captors pressed the friar to make gunpowder and gun balls because they had captured ten harquebuses. He said he did not know how, but the captors, who had observed and learned from the friars the importance of the religious texts they carried responded, "Don't make excuses, because you do know that your books speak and tell you what you have to do."[32] When Avila replied that he has no books "because you have taken them from me" his indigenous captors brought him his books, a *Suma*, an oratorio, texts of Friar Luis de Granada, and a breviary. One might think that Avila was in trouble, but pleased to have the texts back, and after consultation, he saved their "truth" saying he could not make the gunpowder and balls for lack of the ingredients.[33] Oré included other oral testimony and written records that modified the details of the account.

Guale enmity continued into the early 1600s. Governor of La Florida Méndez de Canzo, with fresh soldiers and ammunition, plus the participation of Christian Indians, brutally suppressed indigenous resistance, destroying crops and burning villages and fields. Near the end the governor told the Indians that there would be peace only when "the head of the heir of Tolomato [Don Juan], who was the leader of those who conspired for the deaths of the religious" was brought to authorities. Various caciques rebelled against Don Juan and Oré wrote "they went against him and his Indians and killed them all, without brother pardoning brother, or cousin, relative or friend or their neighbor. With this the land was pacified, and at the end of six years following the deaths of the religious, they were brought back to our Holy Mother Church and to the service of Our Lord."[34]

With the help of his scribe Oré had a rough manuscript to carry back to Spain and report to the king and councils, the Franciscans and the papal consistory in Rome. In initial sections Oré covered the life and deaths of various martyrs–the Jesuits, Dominicans, and others–and the Franciscans. His report detailed, if imperfectly, the history of La Florida for the edification of potential religious recruits to assume their mission on the unstable frontier. The package included Ore's analysis of the threat of foreign powers and the need to take immediate action to protect Spanish sovereignty over the North American Atlantic seaboard. Oré also warned of the tensions between church and state in La Florida and the need to protect the Amerindians.

When he reached the Franciscan monastery in Madrid, he must have encountered Friar Juan de Silva, an earlier General Commissioner for La Florida who had recruited and brought the Franciscan missionaries to the Guale in 1595. Silva's amazing career spanned his initial days as a soldier who fought in the siege of Malta, in Flanders under the Duke of Alba, and later with the Duke of Medina Sidonia against England. He laid down his arms and spent twenty years as a Franciscan in New Spain and Florida. Silva published three texts describing treatment of indigenous people. He lived his last years in the Madrid monastery and became the king's confessor. Oré may have first met Silva in Spain in 1605, or when he returned from Italy to recruit Franciscans for the Florida missions. Oré would have wanted to consult him to learn from his prior experience; the two friars shared similar views on conversion and treatment of indigenous people. Silva's strongly Lascasian texts were printed later, between 1613 and 1621. In his writing Silva condemned the Spanish soldiers and settlers for the exploitation and deaths of millions of Amerindians, and like Oré argued that conversion efforts were weakened by such acts. Excessive oppression led to rebellion.[35] "In the great kingdom of La Florida it has scarcely been spoken of, and already the Spaniards have killed more than thirty thousand Indians in various entradas and discoveries that they have made."[36] Oré shared Silva's concerns. His stress on justice for indigenous people was deepening and can be glimpsed throughout his *Relación de los mártires de la Florida*.

❧ 22 ❧

Franciscan Democracy

FIRST PROVINCIAL GENERAL CHAPTER MEETING

Oré's inspection of the Franciscan missions flowed directly into the first general chapter meeting of the Province of Santa Elena. In his first visita of Florida in 1614 Oré had held a chapter meeting in St. Augustine. The principal function of a general chapter meeting of a Franciscan province was for the friars to discuss and vote on various matters, to choose new local religious leaders, and especially to select a friar to send to the Franciscan general chapter meeting in Spain. Oré wrote that during his second inspection, traveling by river, he and his team reached the Guale settlements. They first met and questioned six priests in the monastery of San José de Zapala. It was here that one of the five Franciscans was martyred in the uprising. The conduct of the visitation followed the norm, as "they held the capítulo de culpas" and completed "the prayers and disciplina as in prior meetings." A few days earlier Oré had dispatched an order and letter convening the friars of the missions in Guale territory to meet in the chapter hall at the mission of San Buenaventura de Guadalquini. They had already arrived in the meeting hall and Oré and his team joined "all the other *padres vocales* [voting fathers in a religious assembly], definidores, and guardians."[1]

They reached their destination late in the day, and after disembarking, Oré and the Franciscans processed, holding "the cross high, singing the *Te deum laudamus*" until they reached the church where "we gave thanks to Our Lord who congregated us in his name to deal with the issues related to his service." Oré noted that the reunion of the friars provided relief and consolation, because "since the first time I visited this province two years before many of them had not seen each other because they were separated and dispersed in such distant villages." On the first night the friars rested and the following day "we dealt in the *definitorio* with the reasons for the inspection and then held the capítulo de culpas" discussing their sins and their conduct in missionary endeavors. Oré's scribe wrote "so that in such a poor meeting place for the religious and apostolic event there would not be sadness, once all the obligations required in the general statutes of the order were completed, he [Oré] admitted, consoled and qualified all the vocales for the day chosen for the election."[2]

The scribe carefully recorded Commissioner Oré's actions, providing a glimpse of a proceeding normally restricted to members of the order. It was a remarkable Franciscan democratic process as they discussed their work in the mission fields, the challenges, the trials and tribulations as well as successes. It was "Sunday, the fourth day of Advent, . . . 18 December 1616. Father Commissioner, the deacons, and two padres definidores sang the Mass of the Holy Spirit," and then together in their communal hall the Franciscans initiated their meeting presided over by Oré. First, Friar Lorenzo Martínez delivered a sermon which was followed by Oré "exhorting all the voting fathers [padres vocales] to elect the one who according to the Lord they judge most suited to be the provincial and the definidores." Oré then named witnesses and a secretary, "all three highly qualified people."

On the first round of voting the friars elected Francisco Pareja as provincial. They also elected the next four definidores in accordance with the canonical order and the guidelines of the general statutes of the order. Oré ordered the cross draped with a white cloth and the tall processional candles to be brought out and began singing the *Te deum laudamus*.[3] The procession was led by the newly elected Provincial Friar Pareja, with Commissioner Oré second. The new definidores then filed in, next the definidores of the previous triennium, followed by all the religious participants by order of age. The scribe noted that "this was done punctually and expertly" as the friars filed in order from the chapter hall to the mission church. Next, Oré commanded the new provincial and definidores to conduct the capítulo de culpas, then confirmed the provincial and the others with a short discourse based on an Old Testament text with David's advice to Solomon to punish Joab and Semei (Shimei), and only to seat at his table "faithful and loyal friends." Oré urged Provincial Pareja to keep in mind that only the most deserving should be honored and admitted to the table of the dignitaries. Furthermore, Pareja should have the courage to discipline those who were unworthy.[4] Oré called Pareja "one of the religious who has contributed most to the conversion of the Indians" and noted that he had devoted more than twenty years, largely among the Timucua, wishing to reach not just those of his own doctrina but all those scattered in the province. Pareja hoped to communicate with the indigenous people not only by learning their language, but by providing texts that other friars could use. He had written and printed in Mexico the Christian doctrine, a catechism, a confessional, and other devotional treatises for use in the Timucua doctrinas. Oré marveled at the efficiency of these texts and noted that "many Indian men and women have easily learned to read in less than two months, and they write letters to one another in their language."[5]

Oré, as part of his inspection had posed questions regarding the progress of indigenous conversion and if "they live as Christians, if they confess as such and if there are reasons that they should be denied holy communion." The questionnaire Oré presented was akin to those used by bishops throughout the Spanish Americas. Oré, impressed by Pareja's written response "to some items I have proposed in writing to all the religious," included it in the *Relación* verbatim.[6] Pareja was not the only one who complied; other friars prepared and gave Oré their own responses. Manuscript copies may still exist, awaiting discovery to illuminate further the Franciscan efforts in the frontier missions. Pareja's detailed and extensive report included by Oré highlighted Franciscan accomplishments in the Florida missions. Oré noted that "the other religious confirmed it by answering as had Father Pareja," but Oré did not include the responses of the other friars in order "to avoid tediousness."[7] These few pages have provided ethnohistorians one of the clearest insights into the process and impact of the encounter between the Spanish and Timucua cultures. Pareja, Oré, and the other Franciscans who contributed to the *Relación* were most interested in the nonmaterial world, of autochthonous belief systems the religious aimed to replace with the Christian faith. But belief extended to concepts of food, illness and healing, relations between men and women, the nature of birth, of origins, of death and what followed, of creation and destruction, of the relation with animals and plants, of the heavenly bodies, and more.

There is much of interest to extract from Pareja's text, but the following sample points to the relatively rapid and "successful" transition to Christianity among the Timucua, in contrast to the Guale, the Calusa, or other ethnicities. Pareja asserted that when, as the custodian, he had examined other friars' charges he found that "among them were Indians who were well enough prepared to catechize, and Indian women who catechize other women to be Christian." Not only that, "they attend all the obligatory Masses and on Sundays and Feast Days they officiate and sing; and in some places their confraternities hold the procession on Holy Thursday." Indeed, they seemed to provide all the skills required for "good Christian citizens." Pareja claimed that "they taught each other the religious songs and to read." Even in the temporary absence of the priest who may have traveled to St. Augustine for church business or in illness, "many Indian men and women say they wished to be confessed before he left, saying they were afraid they might die before" the friar returned.[8]

Pareja did not find any reason to deny communion to the indigenous people in the missions. He stressed that "I have never found among them a hint of idolatry or witchcraft, only superstitions, [for example] saying that with this you will be cured; if you do not cure with this herb you will die. If the owl sings it is a sign that some disgrace will befall me." Pareja included a long list of superstitions but added that these have all been forgotten with successful indoctrination. There was persistent concern among the religious that drunkenness, common among some New World cultures, was a vice leading to sin. Pareja stated, "Of drunkeness there is no need to speak because their drink does not inebriate." He added that even the friars "cannot be without it" because "it is merely leaves of a tree that looks similar to the oak.[9] They are dry toasted in a large earthen pot or a wide bowl. And then water is poured in, neither too hot nor cold. There is nothing else in it, and it is useful to prevent formation of stones or sand, and to alleviate lower abdomen pains." Pareja noted the medicinal plant was so effective that it was exported to New Spain and even to Spain. Indeed, its use was known, and is mentioned in the texts of Gonzalo Fernández de Oviedo y Valdés and Sevillian physician Dr. Nicolás Monardes.[10] From the inception of settlement in the Indies, the Spaniards were interested in indigenous medicinal plants. Profits could be earned, and physicians and others from the time of the second Columbus expedition engaged in the trade and wrote treatises on the benefits of these plants. Dr. Monardes first received a sample of sassafras from a Frenchman who brought it from Florida and devoted an entire chapter to its nature and use. He extolled the virtues of the plant to ward against the plague and tertiary fevers, and as a remedy against various abdominal indispositions.[11] Monardes wrote that the Spaniards learned of the benefits of sassafras from the indigenous people. He asserted that the Spanish in Florida use sassafras water "for all types of illnesses, without making exception; rather when they are ill with any sickness that they have, sudden or long-term, hot or cold, serious or light, they all cure them with one type of water." He added that the best part is "that all are cured."[12] As demonstration of a successful cure Monardes mentioned a cleric who just returned from Florida and before he went there "urinated badly and very weakly, and was passing stones frequently, with much pain and some endangered his life." But while he was in Florida "he regularly drank the sassafras water, as others did instead of wine, and he passed many large and small stones without any suffering and afterward was healthy." He added, "many drink this water for the same reason."[13] When Pareja wrote several decades after Monardes it was clear that there was widespread use of this beneficial indigenous brew among the Europeans.

Because the time of the Christmas celebrations was approaching and the friars would be returning to their doctrinas and parishes, Oré ordered them to assemble briefly to discuss and prepare an orderly list of the doctrinas in the province. In the same way, other voting members were asked to gather separately so they could propose and discuss the appropriate time and place to meet to compose the statutes and ordinances of the province and then present them to be considered in the definitorio. The friars completed the list of doctrinas and the statutes of the province in four days. There was one more item to be addressed. Because this chapter meeting was close to the approaching date for the next general chapter meeting of the Franciscan order held in Spain, it was necessary to elect a custodian in accordance with the general statutes of Barcelona and Toledo. Friar Lorenzo Martínez, whom Oré had recruited in Spain, was elected.[14] Modern readers unfamiliar with the internal administration of the Franciscan order may be surprised by what seems to be an open democratic organization, quite distinct from the state and the secular church, with their hierarchy and authoritarian structure and decisions flowing largely from the top downward, from the monarch or pope to the underlings.

23

Economic and Spiritual Cost of Empire

La Florida was a financial sinkhole for the Spanish monarchy. There was neither gold nor silver, and the soil was of little value. There was no compliant Amerindian labor force. From the Gulf of Mexico to the Chesapeake Bay the absence of good and safe harbors limited the possibilities for large defensive fortresses. St. Augustine's foundation in 1565 required a more tractable indigenous presence in the surrounding area, not more soldiers but rather missionaries. For the Royal Treasury, it was less expensive to support one friar than one soldier. Furthermore, the Crown found that exporting friars to the Indies reduced the excessive number of religious in Spain and the church's control of land. The Crown contributed to paying the passage of friars to the Indies. The annual stipend, the *situado*, paid to the men in arms and the religious in La Florida was sent from the Royal Treasury office in Mexico and could come via Havana after payment for the soldiers and other officials there. Delays were frequent. Loss of the ship transporting the situado due to storm or piracy could cause hunger and discontent in both Cuba and La Florida. When the religious failed to receive their situado, or "alms" the required term for the Franciscans, there were disruptions in their work. But as Oré repeatedly stressed, for the friars any hardships or obstacles they faced just reinforced their mission of conversion.[1]

There were other issues requiring address prior to Oré's departure from St. Augustine. Oré had been warmly welcomed by Florida Governor Treviño y Guillamas, but the courtesy was soon tempered by conflicting interests. Successful defense and the economic costs of maintaining the presidio was a priority for the governor. Under pressure from his men the governor complained to the king that "alms" for friars were roughly equal to the annual situado for the soldiers. He contended there were too many religious, forty-three by his calculations, yet too few soldiers to defend St. Augustine and its outlying mission towns. He postulated eight to ten friars sufficed. On 12 October 1617 the governor charged: "The friars give me all kinds of trouble, trying to intrude on the royal jurisdiction."[2] Oré, familiar with tensions between the religious and government officials in the Andes, now in his administrative role faced similar issues and later would confront comparable conflicts on the Chilean frontier.

Tension between the governor and the Franciscans in La Florida was only one issue; there were internal conflicts between state officials and between religious figures as well, preceding and following Oré's tenure as commissioner. By 15 May 1616, General Commissioner of the Indies Juan Vivanco, who had sent Oré to Florida two years earlier, learned "that during the course of his inspection some things had arisen," and the king had been informed.[3] Vivanco proposed to the monarch, "for the explanation of what the said Friar Luis Gerónimo had done and for the correction of some religious," to send Guatemala's Custodian Friar Francisco Hurtado to La Florida. He had made the decision "having consulted some knowledgeable and conscientious persons" and because Hurtado, a "disinterested person" could "ascertain what had taken place and what reform was necessary." Vivanco ended his missive promising that "since it has been such a short time ago that Your Majesty made the grant to the said Friar Luis Gerónimo for the voyage [to Florida]," the Franciscan order would provide the necessary alms for Hurtado's journey.[4] The king authorized Hurtado's assignment, and he was assured of the political and economic support of the governors of Cuba and Florida. The Council of the Indies made it clear that the religious should be favored and aided in their role in the conversion of indigenous people. Vivanco never stated the nature of the "things" that Oré had found nor is it clear from Oré's report, but whatever irregularities existed required independent verification.

There was a final item. On 14 January 1617 Oré and the Franciscan chaplains serving the soldiers and populace of St. Augustine composed a letter to the king. They expressed gratitude for the years of support from the Crown and stressed the great strides they made in converting the indigenous people. They stated that Oré and the custodian of the province of La Florida, Friar Lorenzo Martínez, would give a full report of their efforts "to Your Majesty in the *Verdadera relación*" that they are taking with them. The friars added that Oré and Martínez were to participate in the Franciscan General Chapter Meeting in Spain and would press for necessary support to assure the continued success in the Florida missions. The friars continued cautiously, entering the dangerous issue of church–state relations. They praised St. Augustine's royal treasurer Juan Menéndez Márquez, asking the king to name him governor, "because it is most important to provide in this governance a person who does not impede, but rather assists by his favor and support, what the religious with their enormous and fatiguing labor are daily gaining." The friars emphasized they made the recommendation because "the one who currently holds the post has finished his term." They were taking a risky step, for the current governor Treviño y Guillamas was still in office and not ready to relinquish his post even if the friars treated him as a lame duck.[5] He remained governor for another year and a half and was succeeded by Juan de Salinas. Three days later, the friars—without Oré—composed a second and more disturbing account of their tenure in La Florida and their assessment of the province's needs.[6] Without Oré's voice they were less diplomatic in their approach, more direct and stinging in their accusations. The friars stressed their desire to fulfill "the holy intention of Your Majesty," but after several years in Florida, their original hopes to convert were dampened. Because of their situation the provincial and voting body of the province decided to make this appeal, "to avoid further aggravation with the person who governs, and the loss of so many souls because of the lack of assistance."[7] Their missive included a detailed account of the condition of the province. Noteworthy is the Franciscans' recognition of the unfolding demographic catastrophe. "We have found that in four years half of the Indians have perished because of the great plagues and contagious diseases that they have suffered . . ., in these great die-offs there have been very large harvests of souls for Heaven. There remain alive up to eight thousand Christians, more or less."[8]

The friars emphasized there were more Indians to convert—the Apalachee, Jama, Santa Helena, and those along the coast of Carlos—and they blamed governors and their "greed for amber [ambergris] found along this coast." The friars complained their missionary work along the southwest coast of Florida had been thwarted by the governors who refused to give them permission to enter in that part, because of "such diabolical and damaging greed." They pointed out the indigenous Christians would not harm the trade but could help "these interests" because they would be friendly to the Spanish sailing along that coast.[9] The friars lamented that the governors admonished them to stay near the presidio, "as if your Majesty had sent us to guard it and to be material soldiers." Nevertheless, they could not remain idle, and "with good spirit and zeal" they had entered into "the said provinces of the infidels," and because of the friars those areas now were calm and obedient to the Crown. They had built houses and churches and had come over vast distances to the presidio to plead with the governor for more religious to administer to their souls, but "return disconsolate."[10]

The friars complained to the king how "very unjustly" they had been treated by the Spaniards in the city and its fort: "They slander us, discouraging the spirit and fervor of the good religious." They lamented that they had been accused of entering the countryside in military fashion because some Indians who accompanied the friars were "carrying some harquebuses, their own," and they only used them to hunt deer or bears for food on the way. The friars asserted they were accused of carrying a military flag when it was only "a small standard to show reverently to the faithful Indians the Holy Cross that was on it."[11] They stressed that they were writing to the king because they feared that the St. Augustine officials had sent a false report about their activities and they wanted to correct the unfounded accusations. They pointed out that they had made significant strides in the previous four years, but conditions were deteriorating. Because of false rumors the soldiers were spreading—that the friars only had come to pray and say Mass rather than work with the indigenous people and deal with their needs—the Indians were losing respect for the friars. As a result, the friars feared for their safety, especially those among the Guale who remembered vividly what had happened years earlier. The soldiers had also, by their actions and mistreatment of the Indians, damaged relationships that were vital for successful conversion. Given these abuses, "fugitive Indians" returned to the hills and forests to resume their old ways "and there they die as barbarians." The list of complaints was long. The friars stressed that they had taken great pains to tell the king the true situation and the need for reform, and noted that some officials were serving their posts well, praising two men especially qualified and "very good Christians," the treasurer Juan Menéndez Márquez and the factor Juan de Cueva.[12]

Historians question if missives such as this one ever reached the king. Was it instead filed and lost in the mountains of paper of the Hapsburg bureaucracy? In this case the letter did reach official notice in Spain, as can be seen by extensive marginal annotations penned by officials reading and making recommendations. Often the items that stood out in minds of the Council of the Indies appear in the margins. First the deaths by disease of "half of the Indians," yet the Council noted that eight thousand remained. The second noted that the governor had impeded the work of the friars, because of the trade with ambergris. Following is a note on the Indians' loss of respect for the friars because they had heard they came only to pray and conduct Mass, and that Spaniards continued to enter Indian towns, committing offenses. The next note suggests interest in pursuing the issue further: "The religious are not favored in their work by the current governor, rather he says that there is no conversion of the Indians nor can one hope for it, which scandalizes the Indians."[13] The next annotation stated succinctly the treatment of the friars: "The governor insults them." The subsequent notation is recognition that the friars had spoken well of Juan Menéndez Márquez and although the factor's name was not mentioned in the letter, we see in the margin "that the Factor Juan de Cueba is a competent person."[14] The annotations indicate that the issue would be acted on: "This [correspondence] should be brought together with what the previous governor had written on the subject so that the Council could review it and act appropriately."[15] This last notation also confirms the friars' fear that the governor had written to the king. They were right to send their version of events and defend their position.

With his work in St. Augustine at an end Oré, along with other Franciscans traveling to Spain or elsewhere, took the letters, reports, and other papers and, perhaps as early as the third week of January 1617, boarded a vessel hoping for a quick sail to Cuba. Oré intended to complete his still pending task on the island, assemble his final report on Florida, and prepare for the return to Spain to attend the General Chapter Meeting of the Franciscan order for the Indies and present the report to the officials of the King's Councils. Yet several challenges remained facing Oré as he sailed southward to Havana.

V

Martyrs, Virgins, Nuns, and the Bishop-Elect

RELACION DE

LOS MARTIRES QVE A AVIDO EN
las Prouincias de la Florida; doze Religiosos de la Compañia de IESVS, que padecieron en el Iacan y cinco de la Orden de nuestro Serafico P. S. Francisco, e 'a Proui̇cia de Guale. Ponese assi mesmo la discripcion d ˙acan, donde se an fortificado los Ingleses, y de otras cosas toca˙tes a la conuersion de los Indios. Hecha por el P. F. Luys Hieronymo de Orè, Lector de Teologia, y Comissario de la Prouincia de santa Elena de la Florida e Isla de Cuba.

EL AÑO DE MIL Y QVINIENTOS Y TREze, descubrio la Costa y Tierra firme del Reyno de la Florida, primero que otro Español alguno, Iuan Ponce de Leon, Cauallero natural de la Ciudad de Leõ, Gouernador q antes auia sido de la isla de san Iuan de Puerto rico, y por auerla descubierto dia de Pasqua de resurreccion, que cayó en veynte y siete de Março, le puso por nombre Florida, porque entre Españoles este solénissimo dia se llama Pascua Florida. Hallola al Septentriõ de la isla de Cuba, y se contentò con solo descubrirla, como otros en otras partes se ocupauan en descubrimientos de diferentes islas y tierras, qual fue la isla de la Madera, por el Infante don Enrique hijo del Rey de Portugal, hombre docto y gran matematico, que por sus estudios alcãçò auer otras tierras, y a su costa hizo nauegar dende Portugal hasta aq̃lla y otras islas de aquel paraje, dõde como piadoso Principe hizo predicar en ellas la Fè de Christo, cerca de los años de mil y quatrocientos y nouenta. El qual despertò los desseos de Christoual Colon, q̃ dos años despues salio de España despachado por los Reyes Catolicos, y descubrio la Española, llamada la Fernandina, y pobló la Ciudad de santó Domingo Puerto rico y se descubrierõ las demas islas

Oré's *Relación de la Florida* ca. 1619. Copy of the first page of Luys Hieronymo de Oré, *Relacion de los martires qve a avido en las Provincias de la Florida.* Courtesy of the Department of Special Collections, Hesburgh Libraries of the University of Notre Dame.

❧ 24 ❧

Compiling the *Verdadera Relación de la Florida*

Based on internal evidence, Oré's *Relación* was pieced together shortly after his final return to Havana. It was based on his two inspections of the Franciscan missions, his personal observations and experiences, and at times it is a direct transcription of manuscripts he collected. These included state and church administrative reports, correspondence, personal memoirs, and oral testimonies Oré and his secretary recorded. He also drew on published historical accounts. The sources were biased and in some instances Oré did probe motivations and accuracy. Due to the variety of sources and lack of time, paper, and ink, the narrative is disjointed and broken into several parts. The *Relación* seems more a preliminary report, or first draft, than a polished historical narrative. There are errors throughout, yet it contains information not found elsewhere. The work is neither a "true history" nor a chronicle. Nonetheless, Oré assembled enough material to compile a brief narrative that is a standard source on early Spanish Florida, the Franciscan missions, church-state relations, and the ethnohistory of Florida's indigenous peoples.

In the initial folios Oré surveyed the discovery, exploration, and settlement of La Florida, as in his *Symbolo Catholico Indiano* for the Andes. In both Oré aimed to provide background for future religious who would be serving the indigenous doctrinas. He mentioned the major figures relevant to Florida, but often confused names. His discussion of their contributions is brief and frequently flawed. Oré relied on *La Florida del Inca*—which Inca Garcilaso de la Vega gave him when they met in Spain—as the foundation for historical background. Juan Ponce de León, the "discoverer," receives a full folio; Luis Vázquez de Ayllón receives half, covering the massacre of two hundred soldiers. Oré misnamed the explorer Francisco [Juan, sic] Vázquez de Coronado. Pánfilo de Narváez's disastrous expedition was noted, because of Cabeza de Vaca's narrative of his journey from Florida to Mexico accompanied by the North African morisco slave Estevanico. Oré wrote "Alvar Núñez Cabeza de Vaca with only three Spaniards escaped, who God had so favored that they were able to produce miracles in the name of Christ among those infidels, as Father José de Acosta had pondered in his book of the *Natura novi orbis,* and other writers."[1]

Where did Oré encounter the authors he mentioned as he constructed his text? In addition to Inca Garcilaso's history of Florida, he was familiar with most of the other books since his novitiate. Did he rely on memory regarding events and chronology as he wrote on Florida? That might explain the inaccuracies in the *Relación*. He could have read those texts while in Italy or Spain. Most of these works would have been available in Franciscan libraries, or those of the Jesuits and Dominicans. It is just as possible that copies of all the books mentioned existed in Havana, or even in Florida. The extant authorizations found in the records of the Casa de la Contratación often show on the ship manifests the large volume of books taken to the Indies with the religious.[2]

Throughout the work Oré highlighted the numerous religious who fell victim to the revenge undertaken by the indigenous people whose rejection of "outsiders" was based on the vile actions of the Spanish from the time of the earliest expeditions. In 1549 the Dominicans, led by Friar Luis Cancer, offered to bring the faith to La Florida. Oré related that on landing ashore "they began to preach to the Indians, who having learned from past experience with the Spaniards, without waiting or wanting to hear them, killed Friar Luis and the other two companions."[3] Oré briefly summarized the conflict with the French over settlement of Florida. He then turned to the martyrdom of several religious in their attempts to establish missions in the northern part of La Florida. Here Oré's narrative, based in part on Inca Garcilaso's last chapter in the 1605 edition of *La Florida* becomes garbled, suggesting Oré may have been influenced by other accounts that did not coincide with Garcilaso's version. Or Oré was simply sloppy with his details.[4] He began with an early 1570s expedition that set forth under Adelantado Pedro Menéndez de Avilés from the mission town of Santa Elena. But the actual events Oré presented are those relating to the 1561 expedition by Angel Villafañe. That group, as they were returning, entered and conducted a brief reconnaissance of a large bay that they named Madre de Dios—the English renamed it the Chesapeake Bay.[5] They took back with them an indigenous boy, related to a cacique, intending to educate and Christianize him. Baptized as Don Luis, he was captured to serve as a future translator, as were many other indigenous young men.

Oré confused his chronology further, with the adelantado bringing to Florida fifty settlers in 1577 (*sic*), then in 1578 (*sic*) eight Jesuits arrived and established a base at Santa Elena. From there two of the Jesuits went to Guale territory and another traveled north to the province of Escamacu, taking along ten-year-old Juan de Lara, son of a settler, to learn the language. Oré added that he "today lives in St. Augustine," implying that he was one of his informants. Having little success, after eighteen months the Jesuits returned to Santa Elena. One of them, Father Alamo, "came to Spain to report to the superiors about the conditions and qualities of the natives," stressing the difficulties the Jesuits faced. At the time the indigenous captive Don Luis was studying under the Jesuits in Seville. He offered to accompany a new group of Jesuits to Florida, because "with God's help and his good effort, the Indians there would convert to the Faith." As Oré briefly narrated, fresh Jesuits and Don Luis soon arrived at Santa Elena. There the adelantado provided a ship and supplies for a year and twelve Jesuits sailed north, taking with them the older brother of Juan de Lara, Alonso, and others. From here, Inca Garcilaso de la Vega's description of the events weakens, and Oré's voice takes on a more authoritative tone. Whereas Garcilaso used Jesuit Pedro de Ribadeneyra as his source for this section, Oré had more knowledgeable informants.[6]

According to Oré, reaching the Chesapeake Bay (Jacán) the ship entered one of the many rivers and traveled upstream twelve leagues to "where the Cacique Don Luis had his villages and two of his cacique brothers." The Jesuits were welcomed, and finding the site well disposed they began to set up a mission. Satisfied with apparent success, their ship returned to Santa Elena to report on a promising beginning. Don Luis, now among his own people, failed to be submissive to the Jesuits. Jesuit Superior Juan Bautista de Segura reprimanded him publicly, but the humiliation was too much, and Don Luis turned against the Jesuits. All were killed. Oré provided a vivid and detailed account of the ill-fated mission. The pages flow with ease and grace as the events unfold, not simply a tale of revenge but one of humiliation, anger, hatred, treachery, friendship, and enmity. The young Alonso de Lara was saved by Don Luis's younger brother, who secreted him in his house. When Alonso saw the carnage afterward, he tearfully convinced the cacique to permit burial of the slain Jesuits.

Oré remarked that the names of the martyred "are written in the heavens," and apologized that "in the diligent search I have made I have not been able to discover anyone's name, other than their Prelate and Superior Father Juan Bautista."[7]

Oré provides an informative narrative of the first Guale rising that broke out around Santa Elena after the departure of the adelantado for Spain in 1572, leaving administration of La Florida in the hands of his son-in-law, Diego de Velasco.[8] At the time the Guale and Escamacu were at peace, but as Oré painted it, one of the principal Guale caciques and his wife had recently converted to Christianity. This rejection of traditional beliefs caused some, especially rivals, to lose respect and secretly plan to replace the cacique. The plot was executed when a group attacked the village and during the skirmish a nephew of the Christian cacique killed him. The cacique's wife demanded revenge but lacking support from other Guale leaders she went to Governor Velasco in Santa Elena and demanded justice. The young governor was in a difficult position, wary of becoming involved in a local dispute and creating enemies. Hoping to calm tensions he called the Guale caciques, including the one who had killed the Christian, to Santa Elena to conduct an inquiry, promising safe conduct. The governor tried to placate the widow, but she was not swayed, and "with great urgency asked for justice, protesting that if it were not done, there would be among them many deaths."[9]

Governor Velasco succumbed to the widow's entreaties and the murderer was judged and executed in the presence of the caciques, who were filled with indignation and rage at the governor's broken promise of safe conduct to and from the meeting. Vowing revenge, they confederated with other Guale caciques and the Escamacu, reputed to be "very valiant, both feared and esteemed as such."[10] Some indigenous who had been serving the Spanish fled and reported what was taking place; the Spanish sent twenty-two soldiers from Santa Elena to investigate. Reaching the Escamacu village, the soldiers noted that women and children were absent, often a sign of war. They asked why they were not present and the Escamacu replied they saw the Spanish had their guns prepared and were fearful. Intending to convince them they came in peace the soldiers disabled their weapons and were given one of the huts (*bohíos*) to spend the night in. At dawn one soldier, Calderón, went into the brush to relieve himself, and saw a large group of Indians heading for the hut to attack. When the Spanish guard raised the alarm a rain of arrows pierced the bohío, killing most of the soldiers before they could prepare their weapons. Calderón fled toward Santa Elena, and soon heard two wounded soldiers behind him, one was Alonso de Lara, and they related what had taken place. Suddenly Calderón, seeing a group of warriors coming after them, shouted, "I am healthy and you are wounded, adios brothers" and took off running. He jumped into a lake and hid in the dense underbrush along the lake's edge. He stayed there until he saw the warriors triumphantly returning to their villages "with the heads of Alonso de Lara and the other companion." At nightfall Calderón began the trek toward Santa Elena. Fortunately, he was a good swimmer for he had to cross a large bay to reach the island settlement. As he was struggling out of the water, the younger Juan de Lara and other youth saw him and rushed to ask what happened. Calderón must have repeated his story more than once, probably embellishing it with each retelling. But the outline is clear, and Oré's description of the reception of the news in Santa Elena rings true, "the wailing for dead brothers, sons and husbands was great." Within days, three other soldiers were ambushed by Guale warriors, "thus all the land of the Guale was in rebellion and risen up."[11]

For a brief time in 1576, the Governor and Captain-General of Florida was Hernando de Miranda, another son-in-law of the Adelantado Pedro Menéndez de Avilés. Hoffman points out that at the time, the other son-in-law, Diego de Velasco, was lieutenant governor, and the two brothers-in-law did not get along. The settlement, already torn apart by internal divisions, edged toward chaos.[12] Oré, lacking civil records and accurate dates, again errs in chronology. Using letters and administrative documents, Hoffman notes that Governor Miranda jailed his brother-in-law Velasco for misappropriation of funds. According to Hoffman, Miranda "ordered an unnecessarily fierce revenge on the Guale for their murder of their Christian chief, commenting offhandedly that one or two dead Indians were of no concern to him."[13] In Oré's account Governor Miranda, instead of first landing in Florida went directly to Havana to collect the annual stipend, the situado, then went to St. Augustine to pay the soldiers and officials, and then continued with three ships to Santa Elena,[14] the seat of La Florida. Hoffman details the unfolding events as the ships approached Santa Elena and another fleet was arriving from Spain. Here there is closer agreement on the developments as officials set out on reconnaissance, sailing northward along the coast. With the weather worsening ten men including royal officials were set ashore. Unfortunately, as the wind grew stronger, the ships were driven out to sea. Meanwhile the ten men made their way along the intercoastal waterways toward Santa Elena and, according to Oré, all were killed by the Guale. When Governor Miranda reached Santa Elena and learned that the entire Guale population had risen against the Spanish, he dispatched a search party to find the ten men, unaware of their fate. As the group approached a Guale town they saw smoke rising "a signal among them" and within an hour twelve canoes filled with warriors arrived "and therefore they understood that the royal officials and the soldiers who went with them were dead." In Oré's account the Guale tempted the Spanish "with chickens and women" to come ashore, but they returned to Santa Elena leaving a man on shore to act as a spy. Oré added, "by now thirty-seven were dead." When the group reached the fort at night, they saw lights and dancing Indians and realized a siege was underway. When they finally entered the fort and gave the news about the killings, there was "much confusion and lamentations."[15] The siege continued for 45 days before the governor decided to send all but seventy soldiers to St. Augustine. Oré wrote that in the heat of battle the plan changed, and all boarded the ship at night, leaving the fort and all in it to be sacked by their enemies. At the end of this section Oré noted that during the uprising a French galleon named "*El Príncipe*" that had been damaged by the Spanish under Don Cristóbal de Eraso arrived. Anchored some three days off the coast of St. Augustine, the French learned that the Spanish had evacuated Santa Elena and decided to sail there to scavenge for armaments left behind. On approach they ran aground and were unable to break free. The Guale, likely with their Escamacu confederates, assaulted them and the Frenchmen who survived were enslaved.[16] Oré's account of these episodes is detailed enough to suggest that he was relying on eyewitnesses, perhaps long-term settlers. Were their recollections exact? With the passage of time memory becomes clouded, exaggerations occur, and some details are forgotten. The most impactful actions are frequently embedded in memory, and yes, the broad brushstrokes can hit close to the mark.

Oré covered the period 1577 to 1595 quickly, highlighting the Florida activities of Pedro Menéndez Márquez, the adelantado's nephew, who at the time was Admiral of the Indies fleet and the treasurer of La Florida.[17] One of his primary tasks was to subjugate the Guale and rebuild the settlement and Santa Elena's fort. After a forced weather stop in St. Augustine the Spanish continued north to Santa Elena in October 1578 and established a new fort named San

Marcos, near the one the Guale destroyed. The Spanish revenge was merciless. According to Oré, one hundred well-armed soldiers attacked and burned all the Guale villages; in one assault alone the Spanish captured and enslaved one hundred twenty. As their villages burned, "seeing themselves defeated, dead and imprisoned they submitted, confederating in friendship."[18] The Guale requested that the religious be sent to Christianize them, "and thus they were being quieted and subjugated."[19] Oré's narrative seems free of emotion as he described the aftermath of the rebellion. He displayed no concern for the human and cultural losses suffered by the indigenous peoples along the Atlantic seaboard.

As we have seen, Oré's narrative of the Franciscan martyrs began in December of 1587 as Friar Alonso de Reynoso arrived with a sweeping assignment: conversion of the indigenous in the villages of Nombre de Dios, San Sebastián, San Antonio, San Pedro, and San Juan. Oré relied on informants as well as church and secular reports and his writing became more focused and detailed. Reynoso and his companions had been in Florida years earlier, occupied in conversions in the Guale area, in Tolomato, Topiqui, Santa Elena, and St. Augustine. Their efforts were succeeding, and many indigenous accepted baptism. Unfortunately, the non-Christians "persecuted the Christians who they treated as one who treats the excommunicated, showering on them a thousand outrageous insults."[20] This situation persisted twenty years, but gradually, as more became Christian, the tables were turned and persecution of nonbelievers accelerated "in such manner that it is necessary for us religious to be the defenders and protect the *hanopircas* among the Christian Indians."[21] This is another example where Oré edges toward ethnographic comparisons. He explained that the term *hanopirca* in the Andes meant "a painted man" and referred to "infidels who for the most part, go about smeared and painted in a vermilion color, or lacking it they paint themselves with soot and charcoal. In this, the infidel and barbarian Indians of La Florida are similar to those on the other [eastern] side of the [Andean] cordillera of Peru. Both are bowmen, but there they go about dressed, or at least less nude than those here, and these have the advantage of being more warlike, and lacking the vice of drunkenness that all Indians are noted for, both those of New Spain as well as those of Peru."[22]

Oré shifted his chronology to May 1588 when Captain Vicente González sailed from St. Augustine with Sergeant Major Juan Menéndez Márquez and pilot Ginés Pinzón, along with thirty soldiers and seamen, to reconnoiter the

Chesapeke Bay to determine possible English settlement. Their large vessel had come from Spain via Havana with that specific mission, and Oré provided detail that must have come from the ship's log. When they reached Santa Elena, they found the Guale seemingly at peace, as well as at Cayagua.[23] They reached the bay in early June 1588 and continued sailing in a northwesterly direction until they encountered a spot that Captain González recognized as the place where he had put ashore the ill-fated Jesuits years earlier. They explored the bay, taking frequent soundings and measurements of latitude as they sailed in a northerly direction. They noted the topography and the variety of vegetation, from the pines further south, to the oaks and other hardwoods as the terrain became rougher. The saw deer and spotted fish in the bay, specifically shad, and in the freshwater rivers emptying into the bay trout were abundant. Oré's narrative of this expedition sporadically mentioned indigenous people. He noted that at one point "many Indians came to the beach and the one who seemed most respected had a string of noserings around his neck which appeared to be of fine gold." Oré stated the Spaniards "here captured an Indian, a boy of about fifteen years," though he did not elaborate on the reason for his capture.[24] Perhaps they hoped to train him as a translator or that he would tell them where to find gold. Oré stated subsequently that they took another captive on their return. By the end of June, they departed the Chesapeake Bay and sailed south for about two days, reaching the abandoned Roanoke colony. Oré related how the Spanish came upon a large but shallow bay and saw "a place assigned for repairing small light vessels, and on land a number of wells made of English casks and other signs of rubbish, as if a large group of people had been there." Oré estimated the English settlement at one point held "some three hundred men and more than twenty women."[25] They continued to sail southward, passing today's Charleston and the Guale territory, until reaching the island of San Pedro "which was then very populated by native Indians." There they found Friar Baltasar López hard at work and they "were well received and given refreshments" by the indigenous Christians. They anchored in St. Augustine in July, a month and a half after they set out on their journey.

Such detail was based on official reports of the reconnaissance, and Oré recognized his source: "according to this timely and carefully prepared report by Sergeant Major Juan Menéndez [Márquez], who at present is the Treasurer of His Majesty in the city of St. Augustine."[26] Oré stressed how valuable this account was, "because it is such a true and necessary description of the Bay of la Madre de Dios (Chesapeake Bay) and the ports, with the degrees of latitude and the directions of this navigational chart for when His Majesty is served to order to clean it of the thieves who have occupied it and have fortified themselves there in the course of thirty years. It seemed to me worth spending time on it."[27] Oré noted more evidence for the English presence, provided by another ship's pilot, Pero Díaz Franco, and by the Irishman David Glavid. Both separately had been captured by the English and later ended up at the ill-fated Roanoke colony. Both gave Spanish authorities accounts of what they had seen. Glavid later served as a soldier in St. Augustine from 1595 to 1600.[28]

This critical information needed to reach authorities in Spain quickly and Oré wrote that General Pedro Menéndez Márquez set out with his cousin Sargent Major Juan Menéndez Márquez. Following delays due to inclement weather, they reached Sanlúcar de Barrameda on 5 July 1589. Pedro Menéndez Márquez "went to court and reported to His Majesty about the discovery referred to." Oré proceeded, with a caveat that "as it was understood," a term he rarely used in his report, there was an agreement with the Crown "that they would return" to La Florida with a large fleet and would construct a fort housing three hundred infantry at around 35 ½ degrees, the site of Roanoke. Oré described what they intended to do and detailed their assignment, all written in the conditional subjunctive. He concluded "this plan did not take place, because another was decided instead, ordering that General Pedro Menéndez should go to Tierra Firme with two *galizabras* (small, swift ships) and in them bring to Castile the silver, gold and pearls belonging to His Majesty." Oré added, "as he did."[29] Certainly, Oré heard from soldiers and seamen, and perhaps officials, of the decision taken in Spain to build a fort at the site of an abandoned English settlement, but he did not provide sources. Hoffman scoured Spanish archives to verify if the subject was discussed at court at all and suggests that the Spanish had assigned a low priority to what the English were attempting in Roanoke.[30] Indeed, the Spanish were fully engaged in reconstructing their Armada in the months following their disastrous attempt to invade England. Sending Pedro Menéndez Márquez to collect needed silver for the treasury would take precedence over building a potentially expensive fort.

Hoffman clarifies and corrects the dating and nature of the two galizabras under Pedro Menéndez Márquez. Hoffman relates that there was concern at court in the spring of 1590 that the regular fleet preparing to sail for Tierra Firme might be unable to safely transport to Spain the desperately needed treasure.

Therefore, the king and his advisors decided to send the swift galizabras to bring back the revenue and devised a "double deception." According to Hoffman, there was a "public order" for Pedro Menéndez Márquez to take the two galizabras to La Florida "because there was news of English corsairs." Hoffman argues that Oré used in his text this order that had been devised to deceive the enemy. The galizabras would ostensibly travel with the convoy but once they were at sea, Pedro Menéndez Márquez and the two small swift ships would head for Cartagena de Indias while the rest of the fleet was to spend the winter in Havana. According to Hoffman, Menéndez Márquez left Cartagena in early July 1590 and brought the treasure to Spain in "near-record time"— less than two months—arriving at the end of August.[31] Hoffman presents a convincing case that Oré's source was the deceptive public order. But it is also possible that the original report—of the Spanish reconnaissance of the eastern seaboard and the English settlement at Roanoke—brought to Spain by Pedro Menéndez Márquez, was discussed in the Casa de la Contratación, or at court. This report could be lost in the mounds of loosely bound documents in the "*Indiferente General*" section of the Archive of the Indies or elsewhere, remaining to be discovered.

Oré highlighted important developments to about 1611, focusing on major administrators, movement of both ships and men to and from St. Augustine, and conflict between officials in the city. He also wrote on the value of additional reconnaissance of the area north of Santa Elena, potentially under English settlement. He examined the 1609 and 1611 expeditions which sailed to reconnoiter English developments. In June 1609 Governor Pedro de Ibarra sent Captain Francisco Fernández de Écija and the pilot Andrés González to investigate "the English population that is said to have settled in the bay with great fortification and a substantial group of armed men and settlers." When the two men arrived at the mouth of the bay, they saw a large ship there, and quickly returned to St. Augustine to report. Two years later two Spaniards plus an English pilot sailed into the bay and jumped ashore only to be captured by the English. It is clear Oré had access to reports on the English settlement to the north. He stated that "according to the report of those who have entered and seen the disposition of the bay that we have described," the number of English and strength of their fortifications would "require a large armed force in order to destroy them."[32] Oré detailed the English threat, the need for action, and the military strategy required to defeat the enemy. A force of a thousand men was necessary to take the fort and its soldiers. He stressed the damage that had already been done with the attacks on the Spanish in the Caribbean and Tierra Firme. Oré believed it was necessary to settle and fortify a port in the Chesapeake Bay, "with which one would quickly be able to dismantle that den of thieves." He also emphasized the importance of removing the English from "the other place they are fortifying on the Island of Bermuda."[33]

Oré spoke repeatedly of the English threat, explaining its danger and stressing the cost of inaction. "Every year enemy ships depart from these two ports of Jacán and Bermuda and sail along the coasts of the island of Cuba, Puerto Rico, Jamaica and Santo Domingo, carrying out robberies without us being able to punish them." Oré, outraged at the theft of Spanish "cowhides, wine and anything else they can pillage," pointed out that afterward the corsairs returned via the Bahama Channel, "which they now know as well as pilots with ten or twelve voyages from the Indies." He complained that "from their safe-haven the thieves return to England rich," while their victims are left poor. To persuade the Crown and the Royal Council, and to raise the passions of his readers, Oré used one of the deepest elements of the Spanish character: honor. "And above all, the reputation of the Spanish is shamed in keeping quiet and for so many years suffering so many corsairs on the look-out for places without defense, in order to enter them and carry away as much as they can, by contraband or by armed force." He concluded, that given the impunity of the corsairs, the only safe way to travel was with the well-armed annual vessels that protect the convoys.[34]

Oré's emphasis on Spain's defense of her global empire rather than protection against heresy, Lutheranism, and Protestantism is noteworthy in a man of the church; his position seems more attuned to the idea of *realpolitik* than the religious outlook of a barefoot friar. Has Oré changed since he departed the Andean doctrinas, and if so how and why? Did the realities of greed, hatred, and corruption tarnish his youthful idealism? Was his view of empire and church evolving as he interacted with others who were in positions to direct policy? Individuals in the state and religious bureaucracies recognized Oré's qualities of intellect and personality. These characteristics were essential for newer, more important tasks in the Spanish empire.

25

Spain Again

MARIANISM AND THE VIRGIN OF COPACABANA

Given the pressure of time and the availability of a printing press, the imperfections in Oré's account on La Florida are not surprising. His immediate task was to distribute the report to fellow Franciscans and Crown officials. Oré, and the custodian of the Province of Santa Elena, Lorenzo Martínez, likely reached Spain by late Spring 1618, in time to participate in the General Chapter Meeting of the Franciscan Order held in Salamanca.[1] Oré was exceptionally busy during the next three years. He advocated before the royal councils in support of the missionary endeavors in La Florida and elsewhere. His voice was respected, given his broad experience in dealing with non-Christians, and his understanding of the contentious relationship between civil and religious authorities. His tempered advocacy seems designed to convince without alienating, a character trait that served him well over the years. His knowledge of the difficult conditions in La Florida and the need to defend the area, keep it well settled, and maintain a good relationship with its indigenous population was sealed with the publication of the *Relación*. It is unclear where the *Relación* was printed. Perhaps in Salamanca where the General Chapter Meeting was held; this indeed is why a publication date of 1618 is traditionally attributed. The absence of the place of publication, the name of the printer, and the date of publication, as well as the standard authorizations indicate the intended audience. The few hundred printed copies would be distributed to Franciscan monasteries, officials in the headquarters of the order, the papal consistory, the monarch and members of the Council of the Indies, and probably missionary friars of other orders. Copies also were destined for secular officials in Cuba and La Florida.

At some moment Oré began laboring on an extensive manuscript in praise of the Virgin Mary. Oré's devotion to the Virgin developed early in his youth and is noted in both the *Symbolo Catholico Indiano* and the *Rituale, seu manuale peruanum*. The friar recognized the usefulness of the concept in indoctrination of the Andeans. The role of Jesus and the Virgin Mary in Christianity meshed with the concept of duality, upper-lower, sun-moon, and the male-female relationship as part of the nature of the official Inca state religion and was embedded in the psyches of peoples throughout much of Tawantinsuyu. Diego de Ocaña in his account of Oré's activities in Potosí lauded his devotion to the Virgin. Seville, where Oré resided on and off, was at the epicenter of the Marianist/Immaculist movement sweeping Catholic Europe. Oré's years traveling through Spain and Italy, and especially through the heartland of her cult in the cities and villages of Andalusia must have deepened his devotion to the Virgin Mary. It may have been during those years that he considered writing about her, or he might have been inspired during his stay in Naples, another center of Marianism.

Seville was at the forefront of the movement to declare the Immaculate Conception of the Virgin Mary as official church dogma. The impetus came after a scandalous assertion in 1613 by a Dominican prior that the Virgin was tainted by the original sin. The popular reaction was swift, and support of some of Seville's leading church and secular figures led the effort to appeal to the pope to sanction the purity of the Virgin Mary and her immaculate conception. Theological arguments over the virgin birth of Mary had begun earlier, but the growing impact and threat of the Reform movement throughout Europe resulted in a conservative reaction and a radical populist position to protect core elements of the Roman faith. Whereas earlier church theologians could debate the position, it was no longer possible for it was a matter of conviction, one way or the other. Seville's chronicler Ortiz de Zúñiga asserted that one could not speak ill of the matter. From the archbishop to the lowest levels of the populace there was profound agreement, and there were massive public demonstrations "in one voice the whole city detested the doubt and the doubters."[2] The position of the Immaculists was bolstered by a wealthy patron of the arts Mateo Vázquez de Leca, the priest Bernardo de Toro, and songwriter/tailor Miguel Cid. Their actions were equivalent to a publicity effort to reach the populace through massive street processions as adherents carried banners and sang songs dedicated to the *Immaculada*. Children in the streets sang: "The whole world loudly proclaims, chosen Queen, that you were conceived without original sin."³ In 1615 Vázquez de Leca and Toro took the message to court and convinced Philip III to support their efforts. That announcement led to a massive procession and ceremony in Seville on 29 June 1615, followed by dozens of others the same year. During a trip to Rome the two men pled their case to the pope and in 1617 Paul V issued a bull directed against anyone speaking publicly against the concept. Following his death in January 1621, his successor Gregory XV provided direct support, although an enforcement mechanism did not come for another four decades.⁴ The movement was not restricted to Andalusia; it was widespread in the Roman Catholic Mediterranean. Philip III's death in March 1621 did not change policy, because Philip IV "in this inherited the spirit doubled." Pope Gregory made the position official in an order of 24 May 1622 that "no one should in word, writing, in public or in secret, affirm any contrary pious opinion." The announcement was sent in an extensive papal communication directed to the cabildo of Seville and the celebrations soon followed.⁵ The Inquisition could deal with offenders.

Oré, swept up in the Immaculist fervor, wrote an ode to the "Virgin Mary, Mother of God, our Lady," and dedicated it to "the very sacrosanct Virgin, conceived without the original sin, in her image and sanctuary of Copacabana." The cumbersome full title of Oré's work reflects its religious character, and his theological position on the matter.⁶ Oré first mentioned the Virgin of Copacabana in the *Symbolo Catholico Indiano*. Its shrine was located on the shores of Lake Titicaca, "the largest fresh-water lake that has been discovered. . . . And within the district is a pueblo called Copacabana, where there have been many miracles associated with the image of the Most Sacred Virgin Mary . . . whose favors and protection had been granted especially to the Indians. . . . In all the villages and cities of this kingdom there is an image of this calling, and everywhere it has produced many miracles."⁷

Long before the arrival of outsiders, many places held special powers for Andean peoples, and among the most venerated sites were the Island of the Sun and Island of the Moon, as well as the peninsula of Copacabana, extending from the southern side of Lake Titicaca and pointing toward their shores. There was a stone idol at the tip of the promontory when the Spanish arrived, a center of veneration for the entire region. The Dominicans made the first efforts to systematically Christianize the peoples surrounding the lake but following an inspection of their "misdeeds" Viceroy Toledo ordered their removal and replacement by the Jesuits. Attempts to extirpate "idolatries" among the new Christians in the region produced questionable results but a series of 132 "miracles" recorded by Augustinian Friar Alonso Ramos Gavilán from 1582 to 1618, contributed to the site becoming a major center for Christian pilgrims. It appears that conditions created by a severe drought in the early 1580s triggered the devotion. Verónica Salles-Reese points to competition between the *anansayas* and *urinsayas* over the choice of a patron saint of Copacabana that played a role. The *urinsayas* believed Saint Sebastian would bring rains to end the drought, while the *anansayas* supported the Virgin of Candlemas (*Candelaria*). During the crisis, the kuraka of *anansaya* traveled to Potosí to meet with a relative in his ayllu (kin group), Francisco Tito Yupanqui, who was sculpting the image of the virgin for his church in Copacabana. Ramos Gavilán described Tito Yupanqui's endeavor, as he prayed to the virgin and fasted, and before he finished the work others of his saya joined to help in various ways until it was completed. Once in place the image of the Virgin of Copacabana gradually gained fame, as miracles began to be attributed to her intercession.[8]

Oré's theological text of the *Corona de la Virgen* was an orthodox work and the manuscript found sympathetic censors. The Franciscan chapter in Madrid authorized publication on 19 July 1618. Pedro Morejón, commissioned by the Royal Council, provided the Jesuit stamp of approval on August 25, and Philip III issued a ten-year license to print the manuscript on September 22. The completed version became available in June 1619.[9] General Commissioner of the Indies for the Franciscan Order Antonio de Trejo, who had supported Oré's activities years earlier, was a leading proponent of the doctrine of the Immaculate Conception and may have encouraged Oré's aspiration to compose the text.[10]

The *Corona de la Virgen* is different from Oré's other work. In his earlier texts, the *Symbolo* and the *Manuale,* he explained why he wrote, to whom the texts were directed, and what results he hoped for. Most of that is absent here. Friar Antonio de Velasco, guardian of the Convent of San Francisco in Alcalá de Henares, recommended the printing on 24 June 1618, stating "the author, in addition to his extensive knowledge, has demonstrated to be well versed in the sacred scriptures. His knowledge and his deep devotion to the Virgin Mary Our Lady, is attracting all kinds of people to her; it is sound Catholic doctrine." Oré demonstrated his devotion in his four-page "dedicatory prayer" to the Virgin. He shed the bureaucratic style of his reports on Francisco Solano and the martyrs of Florida in his ode to the Virgin Mary. "I who am the most miserable sinner of all, hope and try to come to you, because to whom can I

CORONA
DE LA SACRATISSIMA
VIRGEN MARIA MADRE DE DIOS
nueſtra Señora, En que ſe contienen ochenta
meditaciones, de los principales miſterios de la Fè: que
correſponden a ſetenta y tres Aue Marias y ocho
vezes el Pater noſter, ofrecidas a los felices
años que viuio en el mundo.

*Compueſta y ſacada de graues Autores por el Padre Fr. Luys
Geronimo de Ore Lector de Teologia de la Prouincia de los
doze Apoſtoles del Piru, de la Orden de S. Franciſco
Comiſſario de la Florida.*

DEDICADA A LA MISMA VIRGEN
Sacroſanta, Concebida ſin pecado original, en ſu
Imagen y Santuario de Copacauana.

CON PRIVILEGIO.
En Madrid, Por la Viuda de Coſme Delgado.

Oré's 1621 *Corona de la Virgen María*. Title page of Luis Gerónimo de Oré, *Corona de la sacratissima Virgen Maria madre de Dios nuestra señora, En que se contienen ochenta meditaciones, de los principales misterios de la Fé: que corresponden a setenta y tres Ave Maria y ocho vezes el Pater noster, ofrecidas a los felices años que vivio en el mundo . . . Dedicada a la misma virgen sacrosanta, concebida sin pecado original, en su imagen y Santuario de Copacavana . . . por el Padre fr. Luys Geronimo de Ore.* Madrid: La Viuda de Cosme Delgado, 1619. Courtesy of the Biblioteca Nacional del Perú.

appeal better than to you, you who are exalted above all the saints and angelic choirs." Poetically extolling Mary's virtues, "resplendent moon that lights the darkness of our night," Oré returned to his own weaknesses. "I am a completely miserable sinner, born in sins, all unclean, filled with stain and abominations, and the greater is my vileness, all the more your humility is shown, and the greater are my wounds, the more you demonstrate your power and compassion in wishing to heal me." He referred to what he faced both physically and spiritually, "the dangers of the road and navigations, trials and tribulations that I suffer," yet Oré knew she aided him on his long journey. He supplicated for "assistance with the grace of your precious Son, that you favor the conversion of the souls of the pagans in general, and in particular those of La Florida that had been entrusted to the religious, your serfs, in order that in the entire roundness of the earth, God our Lord will be known, loved and served." Nearing the end of the dedication, Oré asked Mary to, "receive this *Corona* constructed from the mysteries of your life and that of your precious Son." What does Oré mean as he constructs his "corona"? Literally it is a crown, but here it refers to the rosary prayers to the Virgin Mary. Oré requests the Virgin's aid "in order to be comforted and revived to begin to sing a new cántico in your adulation, recounting your mercy, and blessing you endlessly with all generations who call you hallowed."[11]

The overwhelming force of Marian devotion struck Oré the moment he disembarked in Spain in 1606 and grew during his travels throughout Spain and the Italian peninsula. In his preface to the *Corona de la Virgen* Oré explained the origin of the rosary prayers, miracles associated with it, and the spread of the devotion thanks to indulgences granted by various popes. Oré recounted the story of a novice who regularly made a crown of fresh flowers to place on the head of the image of the Virgin Mary. But once he professed, he was unable to go out to collect flowers for the wreath. He was distraught and while praying "with this anguish" the Virgin appeared to him and told him how he can "satisfy his devotion, making another wreath, better than of flowers, and offering it to me every day making a Crown of Angelic salutations." She specified seven prayers starting with a Pater Noster "in the memory of the joy I felt when I conceived my son, thanking God the Father for the mercy that he had granted me to be the mother of his only Son," and with that he should also say ten Ave Marias. The following six prayers all revolved around specific points in her life: visitation, nativity, adoration of the Magi, presentation in the temple, and resurrection, "the joy I felt when my Son Jesus Christ having resurrected, visited me and greeted me,"[12] and the last prayer was dedicated to her assumption.

Oré's book is the work of a mature theologian firmly on the side of the Immaculists, arguing that God in his wisdom in order to redeem humanity from the sin "that for Adam's offence all of us fall into," not only did he decide to send Jesus Christ to earth but "decided at the same time, that a short time before, a virgin would have to be born, exceeding the Angels and all other creatures in grace, purity and sanctity, in order to be the Mother of the Redeemer."[13] In Oré's retelling of the story, Mary's parents were visited by an angel sent by God to tell them that after twenty sterile years a daughter would be born. He fittingly entitled the chapter on Mary's origin: "She was conceived without the stain of original sin." He argued that God "wanting to supply the tabernacle and house where during the period of nine months his only son would have to be, he wanted that the Virgin Mary would be conceived with revelations and apparitions that the Angel made to her parents."[14] Oré depicted Mary's early years and training. His information seems based on the third-century religious writer, Saint Epiphanius (310–403), bishop of Salamis in Crete who collected early writings and wrote extensively in defense of what he viewed as orthodox. Oré, inspired by Epiphanius, described Mary's learning, reading the Hebrew scriptures, but also needlework and embroidery working with wool, linen, and silk. He portrayed her character, not dissimilar to the ideal described in *The Education of a Christian Woman* (1523) by Juan Luis Vives dedicated to Catherine of Aragon and intended for her and Henry VIII's daughter Mary. After a lengthy adulation of the Virgin's character, Oré provided a seemingly realistic physical description: "Her stature in height was barely seven and a half palms, her skin was the color of wheat, her eyes the color of gold, clear, with a placid gaze. Her eyebrows black, the nose and face moderately elongated, long hands and fingers, and finally the most beautiful soul and body of all the daughters of mankind."[15] The description of the long hands and fingers, elongated face and dark eyebrows are reminiscent of El Greco's paintings, which Oré may have seen. Oré continued for the next 150 folios writing of the life and works of Joseph, Mary, and Jesus, based on biblical and other texts. The narrative is readable and teachable, as Oré must have intended. It includes prayers and invocations, and reference to the relevant canticles appropriate in religious festivities.

At the end of the text Oré inserted in a smaller font "a prayer for acts of contrition for common sins."[16] Is this a standard three-page detailed list of the faults and weaknesses, or is Oré alluding to his own failings? Many of the sins that Oré acknowledged seem personal and specific: "I recognize my faults, and with sadness I repent, admit and confess of having exceeded in the use of bodily comforts of eating, drinking and sleeping." And elsewhere, "outside of the time for modest nourishment I have eaten and drunk unnecessarily, exceeding the quantity and quality of food more than what true and strict necessity required, counter to the poverty and austerity that is part of my profession, condition and possibility." He confessed that "by the indiscrete excessive consumption of food and drink I became ill with indigestion and weakness in the stomach, torpor, lethargy, debilitating my thinking and impeding my spiritual exercises, and after light nourishment I gave thanks, carelessly and distractedly." There is more: "I have slept more than was truly necessary and have woken up later than I should have and have planned. While sleeping I have had wanton and unchaste dreams." He further confessed that "many times I have sinned by speaking thoughtless, rash, superfluous, vainglorious, detractory, contentious, harsh, adulating, untrue, imprudent, strange, idle, hurtful, and damaging words." Beyond suspect dreams and gluttony, there is mention of maligning others. "At the same time, I have been very open to hearing from others superfluous murmurs and rumors of crimes, and indiscriminately I have told others. Many times, I have been inclined to laughter and vain joy. I know my sins, and with sadness I confess, that I am very far from the perfection of the true religious poverty that I have professed." No stone is left unturned by the friar as he continued, "I have loved, searched for, desired and had precious things, curiosities, superfluous and less fitting to holy poverty, and at present I have and possess them."[17]

Oré in the subsequent paragraph confessed: "I have not maintained perfect and whole chastity and purity of soul and body and have sinned in many ways against the obedience that I promised, and the deference owed to the Superiors." He reiterated his general weaknesses and added that he confesses to "having been delinquent in many ways against those near me, by lack of pure love for them, of reverence, suffering, congratulations, fraternal compassion, correction, of pardoning them, aiding them, protecting them, advising them and instructing them, being affable, harmonious, keeping them at peace, crying for them, and in all kinds of piety and compassion." In his final paragraph Oré was brief in his plea for redemption and promised "to correct all my faults and sins, and in confessing them completely and complying with whatever penance might be given."[18] Oré's confessions, a part of a genre among religious writers, appear to be deeply personal and provide a glimpse of the man and his perceived weaknesses. Did he really enjoy good food and drink and indulged in activities and thoughts contrary to his vows? All that the friar confessed certainly humanizes him; he was not always the serious theologian and obedient Franciscan serving his order and the Crown. He was deeply religious but struggled with worldly temptations. He emerges in these pages as a more sympathetic figure, giving us a more realistic and fuller picture of Luis Gerónimo de Oré, the man.

Oré's writing ends at this point, but the volume does not. Before the final Table of Contents there appears a text of several pages written by Friar Antonio Ortiz, who had been the general commissioner of the Franciscan order in Peru in the 1590s. Ortiz was no stranger to Oré, and the two men held diametrically opposed visions of the role of Franciscans in the doctrinas. Ortiz had arrived at his post as commissioner of the order in Peru intending to return friars from the doctrinas to the monasteries at precisely the same time that Oré was overseeing the return of the order back to the Colca Valley. Yet Ortiz's text, a concise explanation of the significance of the Mass, seems a fitting epilogue to Oré's book. The brief text stresses the need for proper preparation to ready oneself and others to participate in the Sacrament, in order that all understand the full meaning of Mass. Twice Ortiz pointed to the Mass as cure of the illnesses of the soul.[19] And that may be the explanation for Oré including Ortiz's essay following his confession of weakness, to show the path toward his own redemption and that of others, the promise that the celebration of Mass will provide "medicine to heal all the illnesses of the soul and body."[20]

26

Bishop Oré

PREPARATIONS FOR THE VOYAGE

After Oré returned to Spain from Cuba, he maintained an interest in the Florida missionary venture. Oré wrote the general commissioner of the Franciscan order at court explaining that during the First Provincial General Chapter Meeting in La Florida, the Franciscans had emphasized the need for more missionaries, given the large number of potential converts. Oré stated that the indigenous people of Apalachee even constructed a church and awaited clergy to instruct them. He requested the Crown to support and dispatch the religious that he had asked for "at other times."[1] In 1618, after the General Chapter Meeting of the order in Salamanca, Oré wrote to the king and Council of the Indies reiterating the need for more religious in the Florida missions. He noted he had collected friars in Spain to go to Florida seven years earlier and "they are actually serving to the great benefit" of the Indians.[2] Through their efforts, "a large number have received the Catholic faith and have been baptized, as I have seen with my own eyes when I was sent four years ago to serve as commissioner and visitador." Oré emphasized that while in La Florida he had twice inspected the province, exposed to "the dangers and difficulties of the Florida coast, because it was there that the Bahama Channel was most stormy, and at the entrance of the inlet into the city and port of St. Augustine." He noted the shortage of religious because "there remained no more than twenty-four priests and two young choralists and two lay-brothers, because one priest died and four young men had drowned, perishing at sea traveling to Havana to be ordained." Oré stressed the urgency of sending more religious to Florida, because "at present entire provinces ask for baptism."[3]

Officials of the Council of the Indies reviewed on 23 July 1618 along with Oré's petitions letters from Governor Treviño Guillamas and resolved to consider Oré's pleas, "since the reasons are so substantial." They informed the current governor of La Florida, Juan de Salinas, "as a person who has the case at present," and delegated him "to dispense with the matter in a way that nothing is lacking in the preaching of the gospel and the administration of the sacraments" and to assure an adequate number of religious. At the same time, the Council recognized "how important it is for the soldiers to have their situado and rations, without which they could neither survive nor provide military service," and advised the governor to proceed "so that in meeting the needs of the one, the other is not lacking." The Council, praising the governor's "prudence and care," was confident that he would act judiciously "as something that his conscience has an interest in and for the discharge of that of His Majesty." They ended asking the governor to "inform if the mission of the religious that has been requested is necessary." The Council of the Indies, despite lip service to the needs of the church, was cautious about both excessive costs and the political and operational impact of too many religious in close proximity to military outposts, particularly in unstable frontiers with recurrent warfare. Further, St. Augustine faced the ever-present threat of indigenous uprisings and foreign attacks.[4] These issues must have been on the minds of the members of the Council of the Indies when they considered the qualifications of candidates for a bishop in a similar frontier environment at the austral tip of America. Various nominations were on the list, including Friar Luis Gerónimo de Oré.

Oré's impressive career trajectory had been long noted within the Franciscan order, and his activities were known at court, especially his recent tenure as vice-commissioner for the Indies at the Council of the Indies.[5] His administrative skills evolved over the years. With the printing of his latest books, his intellectual and religious credentials were recognized in all quarters. The opportunity came with mounting pressure to replace Bishop Reginaldo de Lizárraga at the diocese of La Imperial, Concepción, in the southernmost part of Spanish America. The diocese remained vacant for over a decade following Lizárraga's departure, and in the interval was administered by the bishop of Santiago de Chile, who made strenuous efforts to retain jurisdiction and collect revenues from La Imperial, meagre though they were.

Over a century earlier the papacy granted the Catholic monarchs, Isabel and Ferdinand, several privileges, including the right to propose new bishops for the Indies. In a series of papal bulls, beginning with Alexander VI's donation of 1493 that gave them sole rights to bring Christianity to the Indies, and his 1501 Bull allowing them collection and disbursement of the church tithes, Pope Julius II in 1508 gave Spanish monarchs the power to make decisions on church and monastic foundations and distribute benefices. The church retained control over doctrine and discipline of the clergy, but in the Spanish Indies church and state were one. Thanks to this Patronato Real (royal patronage) bishops as well as archbishops and other officials were nominated by the Crown to the pope, who then gave his religious blessing. The king relied on his council to provide suitable candidates. Church officials in the Royal Council made suggestions that would be discussed in meetings to supply the monarch with a list of candidates. With the personal files of each candidate, usually three were submitted to the monarch to select from. The king, under the Patronato Real, could name someone else, but that was unlikely.

On 18 October 1618 Philip III appointed Carlos Marcelo Corne (1564–1629) to the vacant diocese of Concepción. Corne, a cleric from Trujillo, Peru, was a first-generation creole whose parents came from France. He was part of the same group of multilingual translators in the Third Church Council in Lima with Oré decades earlier. (See table on page 55). After early studies in Trujillo and Lima, he received a doctorate in theology at the University of San Marcos. Corne was unwilling to accept the post in Concepción, hoping for a better appointment. That came on 10 August 1620, when he was named bishop of Trujillo, his hometown. Corne, the first creole bishop in Peru, died on 14 October 1629, three and a half months before Oré.[6]

To finally fill the continued vacancy at the diocese of Concepción, the Council of the Indies examined four candidates and on 12 March 1620 presented to the king: Pedro de Cárdenas, who served as cleric in Huamanga for three decades; Doctor Andrés García, who held the canonry of sacred scripture of the Lima Cathedral and was rector at the city's Colegio Real; Licentiate Gaspar Sánchez de San Juan; and Friar Luis Gerónimo de Oré. After reviewing all the candidates, Philip III was impressed by Oré's broad experience and recognition as a trustworthy and dependable administrator as well as a man of letters. On 17 August 1620 the king named Oré Bishop-elect of La Imperial and the friar from Huamanga became *preconizado* (in process and expected to be named) and his files, the equivalent of a service report, were submitted to the papal consistory in Rome for final approval.[7] By normal practice a bishop needed to be in the Americas prior to his consecration. Various tasks faced Oré before he could sail from Spain.[8]

The complex bureaucracies of both Spain and the church provided an extensive paper trail that Oré could access before he departed for his diocese in southern Chile. He could scour the papers, decrees, letters, and reports of previous bishops. He could secure information from government records, especially those concerning the unending conflict with the Mapuche. The Chilean frontier was one of the most dangerous and challenging in the Spanish empire. Much of the material Oré needed was in Madrid and Seville in records of the Council of the Indies and the Casa de la Contratación. Oré must have recognized the similarities with La Florida. Each was a frontier outpost surrounded by often hostile Amerindians. Dutch, French, and English intruders threatened both areas in the early seventeenth century. The turmoil of garrison life greatly influenced both settlements.

Oré needed a qualified retinue to join him. After selecting a group of men to accompany him, Oré provided the Casa de la Contratación with copious paperwork to obtain authorization for their emigration. In a bundle of papers in the Casa de la Contratación's vast collection, we discover the bishop-elect first on a list in a small stack labeled: "Those who traveled to the Province of Chile as dependents of Bishop Don Friar Luis Gerónimo de Oré."[9] Oré presented new papers to the officials, including a copy of a royal license authorizing him to bring three religious in addition to the dependents. They were Friar Pedro Erenchun, thirty-two-year-old preacher and confessor who was "blond and of good stature"; Friar Hernando de Villavicencio, a lay-brother of thirty-four, "small in stature, a *moreno* (tan or brown) face with a scar beneath his left eye"; and Friar Francisco de Cabeza de Hierro, age thirty-six, "of small stature, his face white with a high forehead."[10]

Between 3 March 1621 and 24 March 1621, Oré was busy, frequently signing the required reports of individual applicants. On 25 November 1620 the monarch had authorized him to bring eight *criados* (dependents or servants) and three priests, Friar Cabeza de Hierro, Licentiate Juan Tello, and Licentiate Miguel Martínez. Another cleric, Andrés de Vera, native of Córdoba was named. There were four unmarried men among the dependents: Diego de Rivera and Laureano de Arteaga from Seville, plus Francisco Soler from Barcelona and Lázaro Muñoz from Madrid. Diego de Rivera, Oré's personal servant, generated a lengthy testimony with statements by eight witnesses between 20 March and 22 March 1621. Rivera was the son of Rodrigo Hernández Palmero and María del Hoyo. Why did the officials express such an interest and require extensive testimony? Perhaps it was his family's profession and place of origin. Diego's father was a silk weaver, and most of the witnesses who knew the family were involved in the industry. Gaspar Ortiz, a silk weaver in Seville, stated that one of Diego's brothers was a Trinitarian and Diego's maternal grandfather was a Commissioner of the *Santa Cruzada*. What could be better? He noted Diego's two scars: "one in the palm of the right hand and the other on the index finger of the said hand."[11] Sevillian tailor Hernán Pérez Chacón testified he had known the family in the town of Antequera and that Diego was now seventeen or eighteen years old, and "of good stature with two scars on the right hand."[12] Pérez Chacón stressed that Diego's father's family hailed from "the heartland of the Palmeros of Antequera and is very honored and respected," and there was no evidence to prohibit them from going to the Indies. Sevillian silk weaver Simón Pérez concurred.[13] The close attention to Rivera's travel application suggests concern about the possible illegal emigration of a Morisco. Antequera, in the mountains between Seville and Granada, was home to numerous Moriscos, forced converts from Islam after the conquest of Granada. Moriscos, suspected of practicing Islam in secret, were expelled from Spain beginning shortly after 1609, a process that continued for several years, and some were said to have gone underground. Casa de la Contratación officials scrutinized all migrants to the Indies, especially those whose Christian devotion was suspect. Diego's family's close ties to silk production, a profession associated with Moriscos, necessitated close examination of his pedigree. It seems all was in order and Diego de Rivera's authorization package was signed on 23 March 1621.[14]

Others in Oré's retinue were subjected to scrutiny. Eighteen-year-old Sevillian Laureano de Arteaga presented his report to the Casa de la Contratación on 1 April. His physical description may have caused concern: "On his body on the left side of his neck and the left cheek there is a scar from a pistol shot."[15] Oré inserted a note vouching for Lázaro Muñoz, Francisco Soler, and Andrés de Vera adding "because I have raised Lázaro since he was a child, and the others I know to be unmarried." Oré noted Soler was twenty-six years old, of medium stature and little facial hair, and Vera was thirty, tall and moreno. Oré declared, "I certify to your Lordship that the report that I make is accurate and if it is necessary, I firmly swear to it because they are the people that I have most need for my service."[16] Juan de Sandoval, the official reviewing additional information (3 April 1621) forwarded the documents for Lázaro Muñoz and

Francisco Soler to the Council "so that the authorization could be made." Soler was originally from Barcelona and several witnesses testified there on 24 September 1620, that his family lived in the Santa María de la Mar parish and were Old Christians. Soler was baptized in that parish church in 1594, lived with his parents until they died when he was about twelve or fourteen years old, then he left for Castile. Following the testimony from Barcelona, witnesses in Seville testified he was "of the same status as his grandparents."[17]

Lázaro Muñoz—the son of Lázaro Muñoz, a barber surgeon, and his wife Catalina López—was born in Madrid and was "of average stature, a good face with a scar from a headwound." His file included documents he had assembled earlier. On 7 March 1617 he had obtained a certified copy of his baptismal certificate from Sacristan Friar Juan Varona, of the parish of San Martín in Madrid, attesting that Lázaro had been baptized on 11 November 1596. There was also an inquiry that began on 30 March 1617 in the Franciscan monastery in Madrid and continued for several days before the testimony was completed. Oré had stated that he had raised Lázaro "since he was a child," and it is unclear whether he first encountered him in the Franciscan monastery in Madrid and brought him to Seville. Various witnesses who knew Lázaro's parents and grandparents testified that they were Old Christians.[18] Nevertheless, more witnesses in Madrid were called on 3 March 1618. Final authorizations were completed on 10 November 1620.

The request for the third dependent, Licentiate Andrés de Vera, was challenged. Sandoval wrote on 3 April 1621: "regarding the addition of Andrés de Vera, it is rejected."[19] He needed more information regarding Vera's physical description and status as an unmarried man. Frustrated, Oré replied that same day pointing out the obvious: "and because he is a cleric of minor orders and perpetual chaplain of the church of Santa Marina of the city of Córdoba and he is the one in this information," Oré continued, "he is thirty-five years old, small face, sunken eyes and a scar on his left hand. . . ." The officials deemed the information "sufficient" and Oré's request for the cleric's papers to be processed was successful.[20] Vera had given the officials information regarding the Old Christian status of his family taken in Córdoba on 23 March 1621, but it did not provide the two items that Oré supplied. All the witnesses in Córdoba swore that Vera's parents, Francisco de Vera and Ynés de la Torre, were Old Christians and that "he is not a descendant of the Pizarros nor of other of the prohibited lineages."[21] Royal officials continued to be suspicious regarding the Pizarrists,

Preparations for the Voyage

not just New Christians and other groups viewed as undesirables for passage to the Indies. Francisco Pizarro had been assassinated eighty years earlier, in 1541, and his brother Gonzalo Pizarro was executed a decade later, but an underlying preoccupation with rebellion against royal authority was perhaps more acute as the Spanish faced increasing pressure from their European enemies and internal unrest in Portugal and Aragon.

On 5 April 1621 there is a final entry on the register that covered the three friars—Pedro Erenchun, Hernando de Villavicencio, and Francisco Cabeza de Hierro—and three licentiates, Pedro Herrero, Juan Tello, and Miguel Martínez. "The said six people are to be dispatched in the company of the said bishop and the clerics in place of the dependents that his Majesty had given him license for, and in their number, and dispatch five dependents as appear in this book on folio 306."[22] The five dependents were: Francisco Soler, Lázaro Muñoz, Diego de Rivera, Laureano de Arteaga, and Andrés de Vera, who became Oré's secretary.[23] It is unclear when Oré and his retinue set sail for the Indies but it must have been on the 1621 fleet that would have been preparing for the voyage in the spring and summer of that year.

Oré and his group would be assigned space on the ship to transport all the articles required for the journey and setting up services in the diocese. The list of items Oré took along has not been located, but we do have the shipment inventory of the goods that Archbishop Mogrovejo took to Lima four decades earlier. A notarial document signed on 25 April 1580 provides a detailed list of the goods Mogrovejo shipped. It included silver jars, cups, plates, candlesticks, gilded serving bowl, serving platter and dessert plates, toothpicks, and various rings, a crucifix and an *agnus dei*. There was a generous amount of cloth, including select vestments with gold and silver thread for religious services.[24] The articles Oré, a Franciscan friar, carried onboard and destined for the poorest diocese in the viceroyalty of Peru could not match the archbishop. Yet the religious books, the administrative documents that Oré needed, the paper and ink, all the articles required for religious services, church vestments, paintings, and engravings were necessary, and he brought them along. The inventory of Oré's estate conducted shortly after his death provides a clue to some of the items he may have brought from Spain.[25]

❦ 27 ❧

Return to the Viceroyalty of Peru

In November 1620, one year before setting sail for Peru, Oré learned that a previous bishop in Chile, Friar Juan Pérez de Espinosa, when leaving for his post carried with him a manuscript book containing copies of the "Foundation of the diocese of La Imperial" as well as the *arancel ecclesiastico* (a list of charges for sacraments, the Mass, burials, and so forth) that the last Lima Council had authorized for the two Chilean dioceses of Santiago and Concepción. Oré wrote to the king that he was ready to depart and asked for a copy of the manuscript. Well-aware of potential jurisdictional disputes that faced him in Chile, he stressed that it was necessary so "that there would be no controversy when he entered the two jurisdictions."[1]

It took Oré almost three years to reach his diocese, a not-uncommon delay. Oré did not provide an account of his journey, but we can trace his route thanks to Gerónymo Pallas, S.J. Pallas set off with thirty Jesuits on 14 April 1617.[2] After stopping at the Canary Islands for additional supplies the fleet began its long voyage. Pallas and the other Jesuits settled into a routine similar to Oré's and the other religious who made the passage. Rising at four o'clock in the morning and preparing themselves for half an hour, the Jesuits spent the next hour in meditation, then recited the Canonical Hours, and later began study of "the Inca language which is the general language that the Indians of Peru speak." Pallas stated that he was "studying aboard ship, in order to be able to begin work immediately upon setting foot in those provinces."[3] Did they carry with them copies of Oré's *Rituale, seu manuale peruanum* published in Naples a decade earlier? The *Rituale* along with dictionaries in Quechua and Aymara would have been useful. The Jesuits, as the Franciscans, maintained a program of studies, examinations and religious offices throughout the day. During the voyage the passengers suffered from poor or spoiled food and water, and sickness erupted. Their galleon *Nuestra Señora del Juncal* escaped death, although most ships lost four to six passengers. They entered the Caribbean on 22 May, a rapid passage.[4]

Pallas's first mainland stop was Cartagena de Indias and he vividly described the fort, with a naval force of two galleons and numerous galleys and other craft. The Tribunal of the Inquisition, third in the Americas, was established there in 1610. He marveled at the number of ships arriving almost daily from Angola, the Congo, the Lesser Antilles and Caribbean and Gulf of Mexico ports.[5] He noted a sparse indigenous population, but a substantial number of slaves and free Africans in the city or in nearby estates. Pallas mentioned Paul V's papal bull of 16 May 1614 (by his reckoning) that ordered the Jesuits to bring the Africans to the faith by baptism and instruction in their own languages. One might expect Pallas to mention Jesuit Alonso de Sandoval, who worked among the slaves, learning their languages and cultures and composing a text for their conversion.[6] Born in Seville in 1576, Sandoval traveled to Peru as a boy with his father's family. He entered the Jesuit College of San Pablo in Lima and in 1593 became a Jesuit. It is possible Sandoval and Oré met at some point before Oré traveled to Europe. Sandoval was assigned to work in Cartagena de Indias in 1605 and remained there most of his life. His *De instauranda Aethiopum salute...*, based on years of systematic interviews of arriving slaves from Africa was completed before 1627. Pallas, considering his quick acquisition of information included in his travel account, questioned Sandoval. And it seems safe to speculate that Oré, arriving in Cartagena three years after Pallas, met with Sandoval, given their linguistic concerns and studies in Lima.[7]

After a few weeks in Cartagena, Pallas sailed for Portobelo, reaching it ten days later. The port's narrow entrance, shaped like a horseshoe with small forts on both sides, provided a modicum of protection. Pallas noted the town was poor, with outrageous prices for necessities. Most food had to be imported and housing was inadequate for permanent residents. Pallas complained, "On this occasion many fell sick, as ordinarily happens here because this land [Isthmus of Panama] is extremely unhealthy."[8] The Jesuits did not remain long, instead they continued to the city of Panama on the Pacific coast. There were two possible ways to cross from the Caribbean to the Pacific, directly by land or by taking the coast and entering the Chagres River and going upstream on river boats. This was the route the Jesuits used for the bulk of their clothing, books, and other articles packed in trunks. Both routes met at a place appropriately

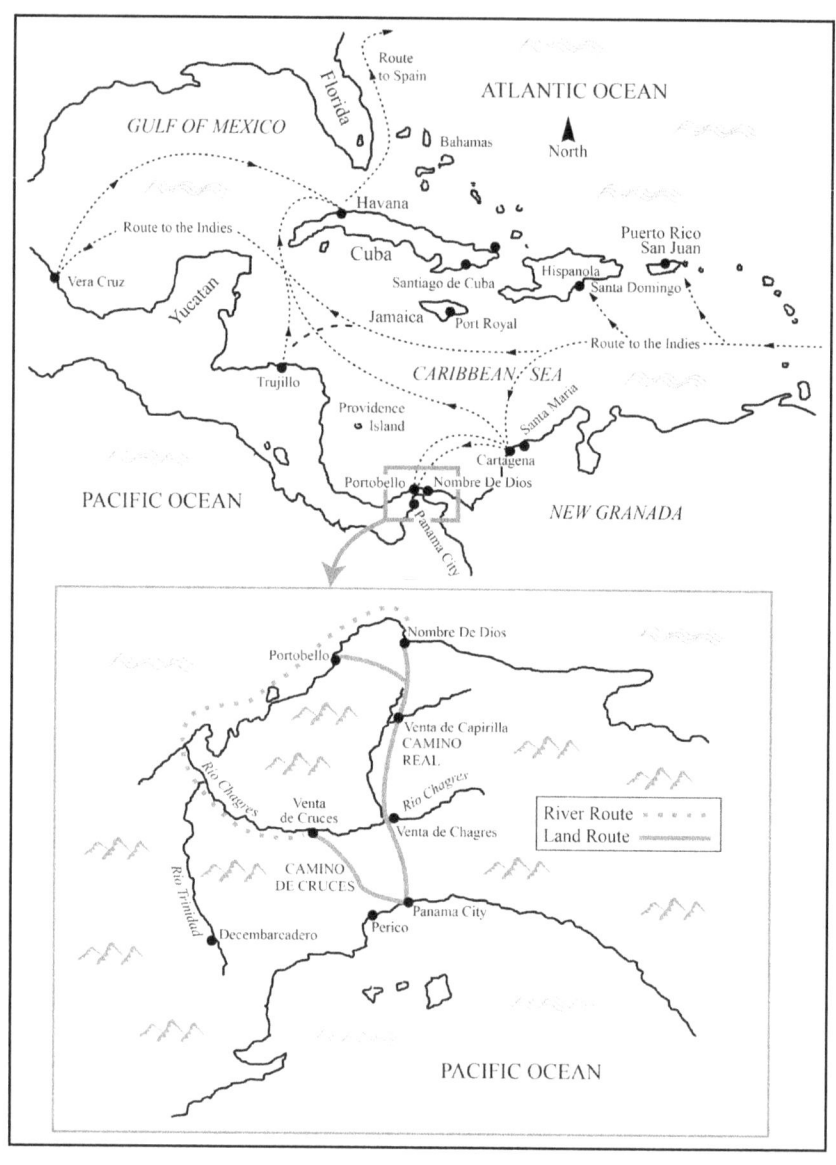

Trade routes to and from the Caribbean

named Las Cruces, where there was an inn and several palm-thatched structures, or shelters. The upriver method worked well until the lower stretches gave way to a narrower and shallower riverbed and increasing current as one rowed upstream. Dry weather, although infrequent, required the goods to be unloaded and carried overland. Torrential rains produced the reverse, increasing the possibility of small crafts capsizing resulting in loss of goods, and life. For most, the land route, taking about two weeks, was preferable. Travelers complained about the rain, mud, insects, poisonous snakes, foul food and water, and lack of a dry place to sleep. The road from Panama City to Las Cruces was paved with smooth stones from along the riverbeds, with mud and gravel in the joints, and wide enough for two carts to pass. The land route follows the river course, and the march into the interior, either walking or on horse or mule, was dangerous. Travelers often slipped and fell on rocks as they crossed the river back and forth and clamored up steep hillsides. Tired, soaked, and hungry, more fell ill daily, Pallas wrote.[9]

The city of Panama was much larger than Portobelo. Pallas complained frequent thunderstorms and high humidity made Panama "ill with fevers and tetanus, abundant flies and ants and toads and a thousand maggots, worms and other disgusting insects and reptiles that are engendered from putrefaction. There are also scorpions."[10] The Cathedral was built with wood *tablas*, although construction of a new masonry structure was underway. There were five monasteries and a convent. There were sixteen Franciscans, and in the past two of Oré's brothers had served there. Most monasteries, the hospital, as well as other buildings in Panama were wooden, given the paucity of stone. Pallas noted the transitory nature of the city and like Cartagena, neither wheat nor grapes were grown, and residents relied on maize. Pallas mentioned the fruits: bananas, guavas, pineapples, avocados, mameys, and granadillas. Reasonably priced beef was available, given an ample number of cattle, plus chickens and Nicaraguan turkeys, birds, and fish.[11]

The Jesuits embarked quickly to secure passage to Peru, something Oré would soon do. Oré carried royal orders that directed local Crown officials to cover a per diem, plus costs of transportation of baggage for him and his retinue. Pallas and the Jesuits, as Oré, brought dependents whose travel was also subsidized by the monarch. The Jesuits suffered setbacks on their way from Panama to Peru.[12] They were offered the choice of splitting into two groups and taking a merchant vessel southward or waiting for a government frigate, which needed repair and caulking before setting sail. Not wishing to separate, the Jesuits waited for the repairs to be completed. Soon after departing, the pilot realized he had not received the necessary travel documentation and had to return to Panama. Finally, the Jesuits sailed south from Panama with a good wind, but again, misfortune hit as the overloaded ship began to take on water. The pilot told the religious to pray and called his men to pump out the rising seawater. Simultaneously, the crew attempted to right the ship by shifting cargo. They aimed the prow of the ship toward the nearest land and beached it on a deserted island. The Jesuits removed the goods they carried from Rome and Naples across the Atlantic only to discover that the books, religious articles, the vestments and other items were wet and damaged, some unsalvageable.[13] After some patching the ship returned to Panama.

The normal time to reach Peru from Panama was from three to eight months. Pallas and the Jesuits with the delays took many months before they reached their destination.[14] It is not clear what conditions Oré endured during his voyage, but he was a seasoned traveler and had experienced the perils of transatlantic travel, having made the journey from Peru to Spain two decades earlier, as well as having traveled between Spain and Florida. Although we lack details of Oré's journey back to his Andean homeland, we know that his first stop was Lima, where he was to be consecrated bishop of La Imperial.

❧ 28 ❧

Consecration in Lima and Preparations for Chile

The consecration of Bishop-elect Oré was complicated by the death of Lima's Archbishop Lobo Guerrero on 12 January 1622. Conveniently for Oré, shortly before Lobo Guerrero died, he consecrated Fernando de Ocampo, OFM, as bishop of Santa Cruz de la Sierra, on 14 December 1621. Peru's new Viceroy Diego Fernández de Córdoba, Marqués de Guadalcázar, entered Lima amidst magnificent celebrations on 25 June 1622, a few months before Oré arrived.[1] In the Spanish Indies the archbishop was the usual consecrator, but the act could be performed by any available bishop. Given the absence of an archbishop in Lima, it was Bishop Ocampo who consecrated Oré. True for all high-level clergy, religious life includes frequent and often ostentatious ceremony, and the consecration of a bishop represents a major transition in one's ecclesiastical life. The ceremony normally occurred on a Sunday or on the feast day of one of the Apostles. We lack the exact account and date of Oré's consecration as the bishop of La Imperial, but we can reconstruct it based on the template of the consecration ceremony. Thanks to a letter from the Bishop-elect of Huamanga, Francisco Verdugo, we do know that the consecration took place before 27 October 1622.[2]

The bishop-elect and the consecrator fasted the day preceding the act, which takes place during Mass. There are two altars, the second one set up for the bishop-elect. Bishop Fernando de Ocampo would have sat in a faldstool to receive the assistants who presented Bishop-elect Luis Gerónimo de Oré. The bishop-elect then took an oath of obedience while kneeling before Ocampo, who would also examine Oré's knowledge of church doctrine and practice. After this the High Mass would begin. At its end, the consecrator would relate to all assembled the duties of a bishop. The ceremony would continue with symbolic transferral of authority as Oré would accept the ring of office and be anointed, all amidst prayers and singing. Oré would then receive the crosier and the Book of the Gospels. Both men would continue Mass jointly. Bishop Ocampo would bless the mitre and the gloves and give them to the new bishop. With all completed, the diocese of Concepción's newest bishop would have been enthroned, with the *Te Deum* intoned by Ocampo, followed by Bishop Oré being led around the cathedral. On returning to the altar Oré would give the final blessing and with crozier and mitre in hand genuflect toward Ocampo and chant, and after more chanting and reading of the gospel the act would come to an end.[3] The ceremony is not for the faint of body or spirit. Franciscan chronicler Buenaventura de Salinas y Córdova witnessed the consecration of Bishop Ocampo and reported that the ceremony continued throughout the day into the night, "beginning at six in the morning, and [following the consecration] the Host was elevated at 5:30 in the afternoon, continuing through Mass near the time of the evening prayers."[4]

Not long after Oré was consecrated, he left Lima and traveled into the highlands to Huamanga, to visit remaining relatives in his birthplace. While Oré was in Huamanga, the bishop-elect of Huamanga Francisco Verdugo was in Lima awaiting his consecration.[5] Verdugo, as Oré, was to be consecrated by the archbishop of Lima, but given the archbishop's death, the next choice was the bishop of Cuzco. Verdugo complained to the king that the prelate of "Cuzco is more than 150 leagues distant from this city, and if I had to travel to do it [the consecration] before him I would have to spend a great deal of time and face major expenses and risk." Since Verdugo refused to travel to Cuzco, it fell to the newly minted Bishop Oré to perform the ceremony in Lima. In the letter of 30 November 1622 Verdugo informed the king that after consultations with legal experts and Lima's theologians it seemed "that in conformity with other similar examples based on reason and law, I should and could make the said profession before the bishop who would consecrate me in order to avoid the said inconveniences in the shortest time in order to assume the government of the bishopric that has been vacant for such a long time." Verdugo stated that "because the Bishop of La Imperial of Chile is not in this city I have not been consecrated. But he will soon come in order to embark with the treasury payment that is being sent to the Kingdom of Chile."[6] Verdugo added that "when the bishop of La Imperial comes, it will all be done and fulfilled, as I have informed Your Majesty."[7]

On 20 April 1623 Bishop Verdugo informed the king regarding his consecration: "I had been presented on 27 October 1622. Because there was no bishop in this city to consecrate me, I had to wait until the one of La Imperial of Chile who was in Huamanga descended to this city to embark with the situado. After he arrived, he consecrated me on the Day of San Juan Evangelista" [27 December 1622].[8] In a letter dated 1 April 1624, Verdugo wrote that he had departed Lima for Huamanga on 1 October 1623. During his travel to the city, he conducted a thorough pastoral inspection and held confirmations along the way. Bishop Verdugo reached Huamanga on 27 November 1623.[9]

It is unclear how much the two bishops conversed, but Oré's familiarity with Huamanga could provide Verdugo with valuable insight. Two items come to mind that concerned both men. One was the nature and quality of the religious and the doctrineros, the other was language instruction. Many had argued that mestizos, fluent in both Spanish and the indigenous language, were best equipped. Having served in the Lima Inquisition Verdugo was familiar with cases of mestizo priests or friars, and the debates about their trustworthiness. Oré was sympathetic to the idea, but Verdugo became adamantly opposed. In a letter of 1 February 1626 to Philip IV, Verdugo pointed out that many viewed the mestizo children of Spaniards and Indian women as illegitimate. There were mestizo doctrineros in the diocese of Huamanga, but Verdugo refused to ordain new ones. The bishop complained that mestizos mistreated Indians, took their lands, and refused to work and "there are already so many that in a short time there will be more of them than the Indians." Verdugo grumbled that they dressed as Spaniards and exhibited their vices. He suggested a law that would turn illegitimate mestizos into tributaries, which would force them to work and live as Indians, thus increasing the tributary population and improving the economy. Verdugo's negative views of mestizos echoed the fears of many contemporaries, particularly among the clergy. The bishop warned "that with the number there are now, one fears they may commit any kind of evil. And if because of our sins there may be some civil wars here, or from enemies of our Holy Catholic Faith, we should not trust them, rather they will be the greatest enemies that the Spanish nation will have and they will lead the Indians into favoring them, which will cause great damage."[10] Verdugo's mistrust of mestizos is reminiscent of the mistrust traditionally shown toward Moriscos in Spain, whose loyalty to the state was suspect and their religious beliefs questioned. If Oré shared these preoccupations regarding mestizos, he was not as vocal as Verdugo and thus his position is unclear.

29

Huamanga, the Last Visit

Following his consecration in Lima, Oré traveled on foot into the highlands, heading directly toward Huamanga, reportedly confirming 14,000 people along the way. We do not know how long he remained in the city of his birth, but he was back in Lima by 27 December 1622. In Huamanga he visited his remaining family. His younger brother Licentiate Francisco de Oré was now canon and archdeacon in the Huamanga cathedral. At least one of his sisters of the Santa Clara convent founded by his parents survived, and there were numerous nieces and nephews.

By the time the peripatetic friar returned to Huamanga, the "fame" of his sisters in the Convent of Santa Clara was receiving wide attention within and beyond the Franciscan order. Oré must have remembered the day in May 1568, when his sisters took the habit.[1] The oldest of the family's nuns, eleven years his senior, was Sor Ana del Espíritu Santo. She lived in the convent twenty years until her death around 1589 and was thrice its abbess. In his hagiographic elegy, Diego de Córdova y Salinas extolled Sor Ana's virtues, her piety, poverty, and humility, including her cleaning and cooking for the nuns, and her intense religious exercises. The chronicler related her only clothing was her habit, "an under petticoat of grogram and a tunic of thick homespun sackcloth next to the flesh." It was the garb she lived and died in. Her bed was a rack (*barbacoa*) of wooden poles, with "only a blanket and a pillow of sackcloth." It was only during her final illness that she accepted a "small mattress."[2] Never eating meat, or drinking anything but water, her fragile and almost wispy figure was striking; "her normal diet was an *ají* mashed in water and a bit of bread as she fasted" throughout her life. According to the enraptured chronicler, Sor Ana disciplined her body until bloody and most of the time she wore cilicium, prickly hair cloth or a cut wire mesh, "which although causing much pain to her delicate body, comforted and consoled her soul, in such a way that ... she breathed the excessive ardour of divine love that burned in her heart."[3]

The long hours of meditation, prayer, sleeplessness, mortification of the flesh, and inadequate diet led Sor Ana del Espíritu Santo "into marvelous ecstasies." She became transfixed. "There were many times that she transported and elevated herself in prayer, losing all feeling, because all the forces of her soul were concentrated on her God. Living in this world, she was as if outside of it, and yet still in her own body."[4] The nuns in the convent tried "to test whether she would return from the trances, but she never made any movement." Furthermore, there were reports that "many times they found her levitated in the air above the ground during her prayers."[5] Nancy E. Van Deusen helps situate Sor Ana's "ecstatic rapture" in the world of female mystics who would communicate through their body with God, "and while in this state (which could occur only after years of careful preparation and mental prayer) they were able to access and then read the internal domain of their spiritual senses."[6] The fame of Sor Ana's piety and ecstatic elevations during intense prayer survived long after her death and her younger brother Luis Gerónimo, bishop of La Imperial, would have heard from those in Huamanga who remembered her. Córdova y Salinas, who devoted two chapters to the saintly nun, collected testimony about her around 1620, shortly before Oré's brief return to Huamanga.[7]

The nuns of the Santa Clara convent must have relayed to Oré not only family news but also an episode of just a few years earlier, when the infamous transvestite Catalina de Erauso, better known as the swashbuckling, drinking, dueling "lieutenant nun," entered Huamanga.[8] She stayed in the city several days, dressed as a man, spending hours in the local gambling house before the constable arrived and questioned her. When he attempted to arrest her, a skirmish erupted, and she escaped and hid for several days. She tried to leave the city but was discovered, and while the constable and his men attempted to apprehend her, Bishop Agustín de Carvajal took her under his protection.[9] This led to heated arguments between church and civil authorities. The bishop prevailed, perhaps seeing this as an opportunity to bring a lost soul back to the faith. With food, protection, and an open mind, Catalina gradually began to confess her past to the bishop, who was astounded, and asked two midwives and three physicians to examine her to verify her true sexual identity.[10] She was a virgin woman.

By then all Huamanga was abuzz with the strange history of the woman who escaped the convent she was sent to as a child, dressed as a man, and traveled from the Basque country to Seville, then sailed as a cabin boy to the Indies. Her life was a picaresque adventure before she was finally discovered. Bishop Carvajal arranged for Catalina to stay in the convent of Santa Clara, where she was received by the abbess and the nuns at the entrance, "bearing lighted candles."[11] Catalina stated that she stayed there for several months. When Carvajal died, the Archbishop of Lima Lobo Guerrero summoned Catalina for an examination. Her departure from the convent was memorable: "The nuns were beside themselves when they took their leave of me, and I was carried off in a litter with a retinue of six priests, four friars, and six swordsmen."[12] Catalina remained in Lima, placed in the Trinitarian convent, more than two years. When it was discovered she never professed, she was authorized to return to Spain. According to her narrative the route took her briefly to Huamanga, "to say good-bye to the nuns where I had first stayed and they kept me there for eight days with much hospitality."[13] Catalina de Erauso sailed to Spain, went to Rome and finally Naples where her autobiography abruptly ends, though not her remarkable story. She later returned to the Indies, by papal and royal dispensation continued to wear man's attire, and years later died in Mexico.[14]

While Oré was in Huamanga, there were several important items to address. It is likely one of his sisters, Sor Leonor de Jesús, was still alive. According to Córdova y Salinas, Sor Leonor was "well disposed, very beautiful and in all her actions very gracious."[15] She was also a good administrator and was abbess of the convent five times. In addition to her great devotion and religious discipline, Leonor showed "great compassion for the sick and the poor," using whatever alms her family gave her to help and cook for them. The chronicler hinted at her sanctity as he reported that when she died in December of 1623, about a year after her brother's visit, "her face remained beautiful and her body pliant, agile, tender and soft." When Oré visited Huamanga, his sister Leonor may have been ill, as she reportedly had breast cancer.[16] The abbess of the convent at the time was Doña Antonia Vela de la Cuba, and the nuns were faced with financial problems. On 7 November 1622 the abbess, along with four other nuns, "congregated together, at the sound of the ringing of the bell as we do by use and custom" to give a power of attorney "to the illustrious Señor Don Friar Luis Gerónimo de Oré of His Majesty's Council and Bishop of La Imperial of Chile," to appear before the king, Royal Audiencias and Chancelleries, and before the Viceroy Marqués de Guadalcázar. It was a standard power of attorney that covered all issues relating to the operation of the convent.[17]

Oré also reunited with his younger brother Francisco. They had coincided in Seville and Madrid and saw each other with some frequency. The now Archdeacon Francisco de Oré was serving in Huamanga's cathedral by 23 November 1618. Prior to Luis Gerónimo's arrival Huamanga's Bishop-elect Verdugo, still in Lima, had written a letter to his brother, the Augustinian Friar Diego Verdugo. The letter of 26 October 1621 was perhaps the first notification to Huamanga residents that King Philip III had died. The death of a monarch led to public mourning, soon followed by celebrations for the new king, the still minor Philip IV. On 2 December 1621 a procession that began at six o'clock in the morning ended with a High Mass delivered by Archdeacon Francisco de Oré.[18] According to Bishop Verdugo's pastoral inspection Archdeacon Oré's annual stipend was 200 pesos. He held an estate in the Yucay River valley, which provided additional income.[19]

Bishop Oré might have reflected on the fate of his siblings and relatives during his two-decade absence. His oldest brother Gerónimo died in 1592 and his children were left under the guardianship of his brother-in-law Pedro Fernández de Valenzuela, who also administered their estate. As we have seen, Fernández de Valenzuela had subsidized the publication of the *Symbolo Catholico Indiano* and Bishop Oré must have spent time with him discussing the family's business. Don Gerónimo's children would have been grown up now and Oré must have met his two nieces, Doña Juana de Estrada and Sor Catalina de Oré, nuns in the convent of Santa Clara. It is not known if he interacted with his older brother Cristóbal de Serpa or his descendants.

While in Huamanga Oré might have visited other relatives. Thanks to the pastoral inspection of Bishop Verdugo during 1624 and 1625, we can identify several family members living in the area.[20] The Guamangilla doctrina was under Father Cristóval de Oré y Azevedo, and he received the hefty sum of 500 pesos as his stipend. He administered a flock of 360 persons *de confessión*, including 210 tributary Indians. In the annex of Guayhuas y Paraca, several Spaniards including Alonso de Oré and Gerónimo de Oré owned haciendas. There were other relatives of the extensive family too, including Don Cristóval de Rojas, Don Diego de Rojas, and Doña Aldonsa de Azevedo.

Although some of the Oré family seemed reasonably well situated, the Convent of Santa Clara was not in a strong economic position. Some of the income came from Indian tribute, but with the continually declining indigenous populations that income diminished. In 1606 the Convent of Santa Clara received additional payments from the Guancas encomienda.[21] Bishop Verdugo on 1 March 1628 confirmed he had received the king's order to make certain the convents in his diocese did not accept more "novices unless they could sustain them with their income." Verdugo replied that there was presently only one convent in Huamanga, Santa Clara, which had been "founded by a vecino encomendero around the year 1568, and the founding nuns were three of his daughters who governed it until they died, the last one around 1615. And while the founder was alive, the nuns were able to get along with their incomes and the years were more prosperous and the land was filled with more Indians. But lacking them, the nuns have had, and at present have grave need." According to the bishop, despite the necessity, the nuns were admitting novices, but "with the struggle to sustain themselves, they have not invested the dowries, but spent them on food and payment of the debts." Verdugo had obeyed royal orders and stopped the entrance of new novices to the convent but added that it was time to allow new ones, but only if their dowries were sufficiently large.[22]

Oré left Huamanga having visited relatives, interacted with prominent citizens and reminisced about old times. His younger brother Francisco helped him financially by loaning him 3,700 pesos to put together the equipment necessary to take up the position of bishop.[23] It was probably a bittersweet visit as he must have been aware that it was his last trip to the land of his birth. His next task awaited him in Lima where, as we have seen he consecrated the increasingly anxious bishop of Huamanga, Francisco Verdugo. At the same time Oré was preparing for his journey south.

⊰ 30 ⊱

The Changing Face of Lima

Lima was in a process of transformation from the beginning of its Spanish foundation. Before departing for Chile Oré possibly resided in the Franciscan Monastery but given his new status he may have stayed in the nearby Archbishop's Palace. The monastery's library had grown considerably since his student days, now holding thousands of volumes, including dictionaries and grammars, around a thousand by Franciscan authors.[1] In the early 1620s the monastery resembled a bustling village. The Jesuit Pallas noted "they have remarkable studies and subjects both in the faculties as well as in the pulpit, and a good number of the laity."[2] Bernabé Cobo described the Franciscan monastery in detail. Ten to twelve years following the administration of the Viceroy Marqués de Cañete the monastery's size increased when Francisco Pizarro's *huerta* (vegetable and fruit garden) was incorporated, expanding the compound to the bank of the Rímac River, resulting in a tract of approximately four by four city blocks. The gardens and fruit trees were well laid out and carefully cultivated. The friars added an aqueduct that provided clear drinking water, for them and nearby residents. The church, with three naves, had seen considerable improvements during the administration of Viceroy Montesclaros, "because he provided the transept to the main altar of very large and handsome chapels and the wooden ceiling was renovated covering it with stucco and gilded carving. He constructed a beautiful tower for the bells" that was completed in 1624. Other additions took place that year, in part thanks to recent imports. The ornaments and precious objects of the sacristy were already of recognized value, and in 1624 exquisite cloth to cover the altar and the sacramental objects as well as a cape for the priest had been added, and at the same time a cedar pulpit—"one of the most elaborate that has been seen"—was installed. There were richly ornamented chapels in the church for four confraternities. In 1625 the chapel of the confraternity of La Concepción added "a magnificent retablo that cost 14,000 pesos, with a most beautiful statue of Our Lady, brought from Spain as a rare piece, as a work of great piety."[3] Given Oré's involvement in the Immaculist movement, it is plausible that he had brought the statue from Spain for the confraternity's altarpiece, and that he contributed minor gifts to the church. The "main cloister of the monastery is quite large and the oldest of this city, as can be seen in its construction that although strong does not have the beauty or luster of those now built. Outside of it are two or three patios, a very large novitiate, a well-supplied infirmary with its patio and separate office." The principal staircase leading from the porter's office to the choir hall and to the upper galleries, was completed in 1625, "at great expense and magnificent architecture. It is the most beautiful and grandiose in this city." Cobo observed that normally two hundred religious, not counting lay brothers, lived in the monastery.[4]

One wonders about possible interactions between Oré, now in his midsixties with two young creole Franciscan friars, brothers Diego de Córdova y Salinas and Buenaventura de Salinas y Córdova. Both were born in Lima. Diego in 1591 and Buenaventura (his name as a Franciscan) in 1592. Their grandfather was one of the original conquistadores, situating the family amidst the top of Lima's society.[5] Buenaventura graduated from the University of San Marcos, then served at Lima's viceregal court rising from a page to a councilor in the staff of Viceroys Luis de Velasco, the Conde de Monterrey, and the Marqués de Montesclaros. He did not take the habit until 1624, at the age of about 32. According to Buenaventura's 1631 *Memorial*, Viceroy Montesclaros assigned him to organize the Franciscan archive. Yet his brother Diego was already in charge of the archive's organization, according to a 1620 manuscript. It was also Diego who collected and compiled testimony of the older Franciscans about their past, as well as the miracles of Friar Solano and other members of the order, both male and female.

Unlike the meteoric rise of Friar Buenaventura, his brother Friar Diego was more methodical. His religious world was solidly rooted in Peru, especially Lima. He was for a time in charge of the studies of the novices. Historian Gento Sanz found little information on Diego in the Franciscan records in Lima; Sanz estimates he entered the order as a novice around 1606. Perhaps the reason for sparse information was that Registro 35 of the Franciscan Archive in Lima had somehow found its way to the Biblioteca Nacional. Many documents

The Changing Face of Lima

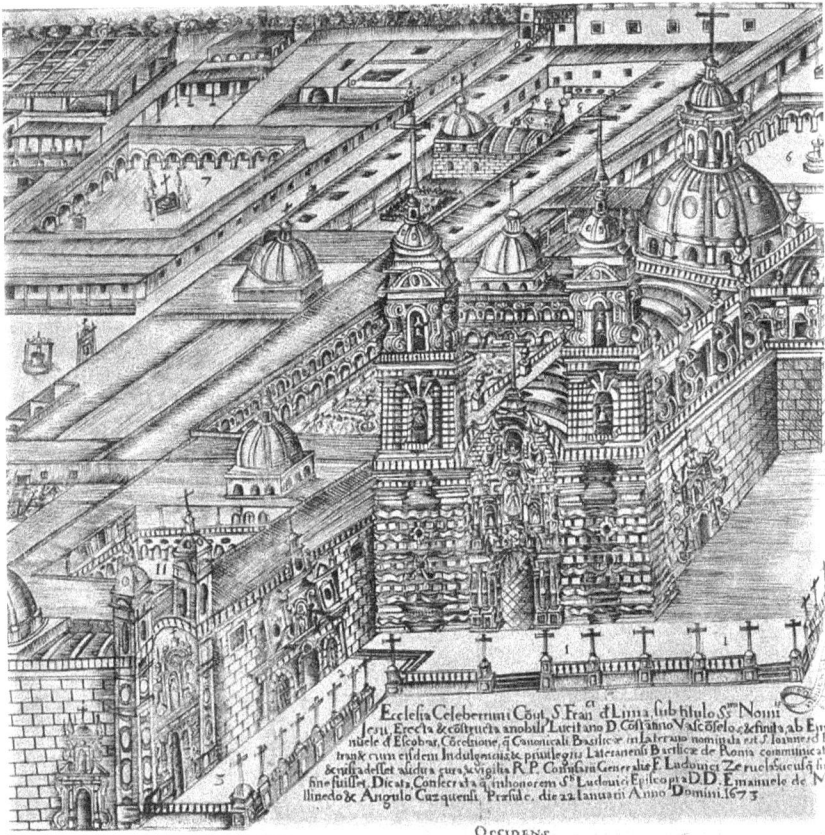

Lima's Franciscan Monastery, 1675. Partial view (adjusted by Greg Cook) of the *Templo de N. grande patriarca San Francisco de la provincia de los doze apostoles de el Peru en la Ciudad de los Reyes,* by Juan de Benavides. Courtesy of the John Carter Brown Library. CC BY 4.0.

from the Franciscan archive were destroyed. Some disappeared and sometimes reappeared in subsequent centuries. Diego wrote that he took sworn testimony from many people on the miracles associated with Francisco Solano following his death in Lima in 1610. He received the "depositions and statements of witnesses under oath" that he administered as an apostolic judge and notary "by the authority and commission" of Friar Francisco de Herrera, general commissioner of the provinces of Peru and of Archbishop Lobo Guerrero.[6] Gento Sanz notes that Archbishop Lobo Guerrero made the assignment in 1620, two years before his death, and General Commissioner Herrera had named Diego de Córdova y Salinas General Chronicler of the Province of the XII Apostles of Lima at the same time.[7]

Both Diego and Buenaventura were official church chroniclers. Both wrote extensively about Francisco Solano and provided histories of their order and its growth in the viceroyalty. Both were consumed with Baroque religious passion, magnifying "cures" into miracles, and saintly actions into sainthood, all of which led the Roman Curia to challenge some of the examples given by witnesses on Solano's miracles. Buenaventura de Salinas y Córdova did break from the mold, often to his detriment. His charges against the Spaniards—including the bishop of Cuzco and even the king—for the suffering and deaths of Amerindians led him into exile more than once. In spite of this, he was appointed General Commissioner for his order in Mexico, where he died in 1653. There is much overlap in some of the brothers' texts, a subject that historians have yet to probe sufficiently. Diego seems to have been more effective in extracting sworn testimony from witnesses and compiling the information. Buenaventura was a more florid writer, more lettered in the classics of Latin and the early church fathers and produced a richer legacy in print. Both brothers copied parts of Oré's book on the youth of Francisco Solano, but without assignation.[8]

The University had changed since Oré's student years. According to Pallas, "its large faculty assembly was one of the most important in the world because the number of doctors reaches eighty . . . with the principal professors receiving an income of one thousand pesos." In 1619 there were about three hundred students enrolled, based primarily in three main colleges. The Colegio Real, founded by Viceroy García de Mendoza, was given the name of San Felipe and San Marcos. The Jesuit Colegio Real de San Martín, founded in 1582 by Provincial Baltasar de Piñas while Oré was still in Lima, was largely for boys from elite families able to pay substantial fees, although there were twelve fellowships. The third Colegio, San Toribio, was founded by Archbishop Mogrovejo.[9] Bernabé Cobo later noted that there were numerous changes since Toledo's official organization and endowment of the university, including financing. Doctor Juan de Castro, in the name of the university, sent a report to the monarch pointing out that an earlier royal order to increase revenues by granting vacated encomiendas had not been effective. Additional income was required to pay faculty and staff. The king responded with a royal cédula on 23 November 1613 providing part of the revenue from the royal treasury accounts of the church's income, of which two-ninths was earmarked for the university. The extra income would be useful. The Toledo structures that Oré would have known before included "a medium-sized rectangular patio, enclosed on four sides by the hallways and classrooms, and a spacious chapel." Some damage to the university occurred during a major earthquake in the late 1580s. Oré must have been impressed by the new university. Cobo related chairs were made "of marvelously carved cedar for the doctors and masters and positioned by order of preeminence, and many other seats for the principal and important people who gather for literary acts that take place with great solemnity and attendance, some of them favored with the presence of the viceroy and the Royal Audiencia."[10]

Before leaving Lima for Concepción, Oré on 5 January 1623 met with a notary who recorded that the "bishop of La Imperial of Chile, at present resident in this city" transferred the power of attorney to represent the nuns of Huamanga's Santa Clara convent, especially in financials matters, to Franciscan Friar Gerónimo Serrano, who served as a general procurator at the court.[11] Signing this notarial document may have been one of the last actions Oré took before setting out on his journey south. He was leaving a prosperous viceregal capital for a land in turmoil that most officials tried to avoid.

VI

Creole Bishop on the Araucanian Frontier

31

Chile Fractured

THE DIOCESE OF SANTIAGO AND LA IMPERIAL

Oré sailed southward from Callao with Inspector General Francisco de Villaseñor, accompanied by a fleet that included three hundred soldiers sent to defend Chile against both internal and external enemies. The diocese of La Imperial had been created from the bishopric of Santiago roughly a half century earlier and there was continuing friction between the two. If the diocesan rents of Santiago and La Imperial were combined, the amount would approach that of the more lucrative diocese of Panama or Cartagena de Indias. But the five thousand pesos paled compared to the thirty thousand for the diocese of Cuzco. La Imperial was one of the most difficult in the Indies to administer. The Araucanian frontier cut through its center, dividing it in half, separated by indomitable autochthonous warriors. The ethnic groups—of various cultures and languages south of the Biobío River in Chile and other ethnicities living from Patagonia in southern Argentina to the Strait of Magellan—resisted domination and the "Arauco Wars" continued for generations. The early conflict and the heroic actions of indigenous leaders against the Spanish were memorialized in the epic poem *La Araucana*, composed by Alonso de Ercilla y Zúñiga (1533–1594), a Spaniard who fought in the battlefields under Chile's Governor García Hurtado de Mendoza from 1557 to 1559. *La Araucana*—serialized in three parts published in 1569, 1578, and 1589—was immensely popular at the time, and Oré would have read it. Its popularity influenced the terminology of the territory and its people, and only in the middle of the twentieth century was "Araucano" replaced by "Mapuche," the predominant indigenous group and language.[1]

Concepción, little more than a military fort when Oré arrived, was in the northern section of the diocese and not far from the Biobío River which

ARCHBISHOPRICS AND BISHOPRICS, VICEROYALTY OF PERU (CA. 1629)	ECCLESIASTIC INCOME IN PESOS
Archbishopric of Lima	60,000
Archbishopric of Charcas	50,000
Archbishopric of Nuevo Reino de Granada	20,000
Bishopric of Cuzco	30,000
Bishopric of Chuquiabo	16,000
Bishopric of Trujillo	16,000
Bishopric of Santa Cruz	12,000
Bishopric of Quito	12,000
Bishopric of Huamanga	12,000
Bishopric of Arequipa	10,000
Bishopric of Cartagena	6,000
Bishopric of Panama	6,000
Bishopric of Popayan	6,000
Bishopric of Tucumán	4,000
Bishopric of Paraguay	3,000
Bishopric of Buenos Aires	3,000
Bishopric of Santiago de Chile	3,000
Bishopric of La Imperial (Concepción)	2,000
Bishopric of Santa Marta	2,000
Bishopric of La Margarita	2,000

marked the boundary between Spanish and Araucanian (Mapuche) zones. The other half of the diocese began hundreds of kilometers southward and extended to the very tip of the continent into the Straits of Magellan and Cape Horn. In addition to the threat of indigenous rebellion, the small posts and missions on the exposed southern coast were easy prey for Dutch and other interlopers who dared the treacherous passage through the straits.

Oré knew the difficulties awaiting him from the numerous reports he had read. His predecessor Bishop Lizárraga described Concepción, and one wishes that Oré penned a description also. The diocese name, "La Imperial,"[2] comes from a town founded by Pedro de Valdivia in 1551 or 1552, but it was abandoned in 1558. When founded the area was heavily populated, and settlers from Santiago de Chile migrated there to take advantage of ample water and a large labor force. Lizárraga related that the indigenous people, hoping to rid themselves of the detested Spaniards, did not plant their crops one year. The consequences were disastrous, and famine swept the land. When Governor Martín García Oñez de Loyola came to Chile the tributary population of the larger encomiendas had fallen to about a thousand. The governor, nephew of Saint Ignatius Loyola, had traveled to Peru in 1568 with Viceroy Toledo. He was at the capture of the Inca Tupac Amaru in 1572 and later married Doña Beatriz Clara Coya, the Inca's niece. After he had served in Tucumán and Paraguay, Philip II named him governor of Chile, where he arrived with his wife in 1592. He intended to defeat the Araucanians from a base in Chile's south. But Spanish officials in Santiago and Lima failed to provide men and supplies for an effective campaign against a larger indigenous force. They surrounded the governor and his men at Curalaba, a small defense post between La Imperial and Angol, killing almost all the Spanish, including Governor Loyola (23 December 1598). The indigenous victory was decisive. By the time the soldiers from Concepción finally arrived and expelled the attackers the city of La Imperial was in ruins and abandoned, leaving the Mapuche holding all the territory from the Biobío River south to the Canal de Chaco.[3]

BISHOPS OF SANTIAGO DE CHILE AND LA IMPERIAL (CONCEPCIÓN)	
Bishops of Santiago	
Rodrigo González Marmolejo	1561–1564 (never assumed seat)
Fr. Fernando de Barrionuevo O.F.M.	1566–1571
Fr. Diego de Medellín O.F.M.	1574–1593
Fr. Pedro de Azuga O.F.M.	1596–1597
Fr. Juan Pérez de Espinosa O.F.M.	1600–1622
Francisco González de Salcedo	1622–1634
Bishops de La Imperial	
Fr. Antonio de San Miguel Avendaño O.F.M.	1564 (named, installed 1568–1588)
Agustín de Cisneros Montesa	1589–1596
Fr. Reginaldo de Lizárraga O.P.	1597 (named, installed 1602–1607)
Diocese of La Imperial suppressed	1608
Carlos Marcelo Corne	1618 (named but did not assume)
Diocesan seat replaced at Concepción	1620
Luis Gerónimo de Oré O.F.M.	1620–1630
Diego Zambrana de Villalobos	1633 (named, installed 1638–1653)

Note: All dates given are approximate.

Chile, Araucania and the diocese of La Imperial

There were too few religious in Chile to be effective. Santiago's first bishop, Pedro de Valdivia's confessor, was appointed in 1561, although never consecrated. Four Franciscan bishops followed between 1566 and 1622. Religious administration of Chile was split into two dioceses in 1561: Santiago in the north, and La Imperial in the south. The first bishop of La Imperial was the Franciscan Antonio de San Miguel. After serving at La Imperial he was named Bishop of Quito but died in Riobamba before he reached his diocese. Oré met Bishop San Miguel during the Third Church Council in Lima in 1583. According to Lizárraga, Bishop San Miguel was somewhat of a prophet, exhorting the vecinos to mend their ways and warning that if they failed to do so the land would suffer terrible disasters. By the time Lizárraga arrived, the many depopulated cities of the diocese provided ample proof of the accuracy of San Miguel's prediction. San Miguel was followed by Bishop Agustín de Cisneros, who administered the diocese of La Imperial for five to six years. His death led to Reginaldo de Lizárraga's appointment, which by his own account he received "without deserving it, during such a difficult time, where a man of great experience and virtue was needed to aid the poor to endure their hardship and help them in their necessities." Lizárraga lamented "this diocese is so poor that I can barely sustain myself. I do not have a house to live in, and if they did not give me two cells in San Francisco [monastery] to live in, I would have no suitable place in the entire town. With all this I have more than I deserve because if I were given what I deserve, it would be many lashes."[4]

Lizárraga thought the Mercedarians were the first to serve in the Chilean doctrinas, followed by Franciscans. He mentions several friars in the first Franciscan wave, and highlights Juan de Tobar, martyred along with two companions in 1598. Lizárraga narrates the religious and political administration of Chile from the time of Governor Loyola to about 1602, when he reached Concepción. The last two chapters of his text are relevant to set the stage for Oré's arrival. Given the almost continuous state of rebellion against the Spanish in the south, the king—aware of the nature of the death of Governor Loyola—appointed an experienced military man to the post. Alonso de Ribera arrived in 1601 and, according to Lizárraga, was a "good soldier with much experience in the war in France and Flanders." The new governor soon found the land was challenging, Concepción was surrounded by warriors and supplies were difficult to secure. Yet Governor Ribera, according to Lizárraga, "pacified and reduced the rebellious ones so that the city was able to enjoy a little peace."[5] He regained control of old forts and established new ones, garrisoned with well-provisioned soldiers. Ribera also attempted to use infantry, as in Europe, rather than predominately cavalry, with unpromising results. Any victories and peace agreements were temporary. Ribera was replaced by Alonso García Ramón, who arrived with a thousand soldiers. Lizárraga hoped for improvement, stating that if they could not find a solution, "the war is infinite."[6] Lizárraga's opinion of the "qualities of the Chilean Indians" is telling. His portrayal resembles Gines de Sepúlveda's position and he echoed the assessment of an Inca captain who called them "the most barbarian."[7]

Lizárraga's tenure ended with his appointment as bishop of the Rio de la Plata in 1607, thus opening the possibility for the bishop of Santiago to recombine the two dioceses. Consequently, the members of the ecclesiastical cabildo of Concepción on 7 January 1607 penned a letter to the king, nominating Dominican Friar Gerónimo de Hinojosa for the position. No progress was made and on 2 February 1609 the ecclesiastical cabildo, the chaplains, and the canons of the cathedral of Concepción wrote to Spain again, stressing the

GOVERNORS, CAPTAIN GENERALS OF CHILE (1592–1639)	
Martín García Óñez de Loyola	1592–1598
Pedro de Vizcarra	1598–1599
Francisco de Quiñónez	1599–1600
Alonso García de Ramón	1600–1601
vacant	—
Alonso García de Ramón	1605–1610
Luis Mero de la Fuente	1610–1611
Juan de Jaraquemada	1611–1612
Alonso de Ribera	1612–1617
Fernando Talaverano	1617–1618
Lope de Ulloa y Lemos	1618–1620
Cristóbal de la Cerda	1620–1621
Pedro Osores de Ulloa	1621–1624
Francisco de Álava y Nureña	1624–1625
Luis Fernádez de Córdova y Arce	1625–1629
Francisco Laso de la Vega	1629–1639

Note: All dates given are approximate.

need for a bishop. It seems the message did not reach the attention of the king and council until 17 August 1612.[8] Regardless of the efforts of church officials in Concepción, the diocese of La Imperial was united once again in 1608 with the diocese of Santiago under the administration of Bishop Juan Pérez de Espinosa, OFM. Historian Antonio de Egaña paints a bleak picture of Concepción at the time, reduced to "a single military chaplaincy in the middle of a warfront, with hardly any priests and weighed down by misery." It was not until Bishop Oré arrived in 1623 that the diocese recovered its independence.[9]

If Oré, while still in Spain, had the opportunity to read a letter to the king from Santiago dated 27 November 1619, the conditions in the south of Chile would have been abundantly clear. Signed by various officials and sent by order of the Dean of the Cathedral Chapter of Santiago de Chile Alonso Moreno de Zarato, the authors noted that during the first Audiencia the center of administration was Santiago, but at present Osorno, Valdivia, La Imperial, and Angola were far to the south, and much had been lost "in the general uprising by the death of Governor Martín García de Loyola." The Spaniards were unable to rebuild, "nor are their provinces at peace, nor can one hope for it by means of a defensive war and the ransom of the captive Spanish men and women has been much delayed." The costs to the Royal Treasury were exorbitant. Fearing the arrival of additional church appointees, the officials stressed there were already ten church canons in Santiago and no more were needed because revenues were lacking to support them. The stipends set aside were meagre. For example, in Santiago the dean received 1,000 pesos, but in Concepción 750; in Santiago there were 800 pesos each for the archdeacon, precentor, chancellor (*maestrescuela*), and treasurer, versus 550 pesos each in the diocese of Concepción. The four canons of Santiago received 600 pesos each, and the two canons of Concepción only 400 each. The officials requested that the diocese of Concepción be aggregated with Santiago, arguing that only one bishop was needed. This statement of the position of church officials in Santiago on the eve of Oré's departure from Spain provided a clear warning.[10]

By August 1621 church authorities in Santiago were notified that a new bishop was being assigned for La Imperial. The dean and the Cathedral Chapter on 25 August complained about the loss of income if a new bishop at Concepción were appointed, and sent another urgent testimonial to the Crown summarizing their concerns.[11] On 24 April 1623 the Cathedral Chapter of Santiago sent a report to the monarch describing the dire situation on the southern frontier as it was in 1621, at about the time news of Oré's appointment as bishop of La Imperial reached Santiago. "The rebellious Indians have had many victories, taking peaceful settlements, killing and capturing Spaniards, gaining a fort, and burning another. They are the lords of the campaign, forcing the governor to retreat from some of the presidios." The wording was alarming. "They have achieved these victories with great audacity. With their actions there is fear that the damage is irreparable because the enemy forces are so superior." As part of their strategy to prevent the loss of revenue from the diocese of La Imperial that Santiago had enjoyed, the officials stressed "that hope has been lost" that Concepción and other southern cities could survive, and that peace could be restored.[12] Oré was fully briefed on the challenges he faced from both internal and external enemies before he arrived in Concepción. He surely knew that church officials of Santiago resisted the loss of the southern benefices they had enjoyed after Bishop Lizárraga's departure. Friction between the two dioceses continued long after Oré's arrival.

32

Foreign Threats on the South Sea

Pirates, corsairs, or armed merchants who braved the treacherous Strait of Magellan or Cape Horn, became an increasing menace to the Spanish as the Potosí silver mines reached full production toward the end of the sixteenth century. The English were the earliest to successfully pose periodic threats along South America's Pacific coast, but it would be the Dutch who presented the most serious concern in the seventeenth century. The Dutch were compelled by nationalism, religion, and lucre, and the painful subjugation they had suffered under the Spanish Hapsburg monarchs. The Low Countries (Netherlands) rose against Spanish rule in 1566, initiating decades of conflict. The linkage of Spain and Portugal under Philip II in 1580 created the "first global empire" and provided enemies—the Dutch and English as well as the French—the perfect opportunity to resist. Spain, despite American treasure, could not defend its vast possessions in America, all the Portuguese commercial outposts along the coasts of Africa, and south and southeast Asia. Both the English and the Dutch looked to the seas, and both had a tradition of fishing and overseas exchange to sell goods and provide lacking commodities. Although they were competitors and were at times at war, their Protestant faith linked them against a common enemy.

The Dutch East India Company had been chartered in 1602, and the West India Company in 1621. Their fleets of well-armed merchant ships became an immediate threat to Iberian commerce and shipping in undefended ports or unsettled coastlands and islands. The Dutch needed sugar, salt for their fisheries, and dyes for their textile manufacturers. Sea salt from the islands off the coast of Venezuela, Brazil's sugar, and brazilwood for a brilliant red dye made those areas easy targets for traders and possible permanent colonies for the Dutch. The earliest significant Dutch attempt to round the tip of South America began in mid-1598 as a fleet of five ships set sail for the South Seas and reached the Strait of Magellan in early 1599. Due to the contrary winds and strong current, the ships separated. One ship stopped at Santa María Island near Concepción, another coasted along the Chono Islands. Attempting to trade, they were frequently attacked by indigenous groups.

Other Dutch ships soon followed, one reaching the Chilean coasts and attacking the Spanish position on Chiloé Island before continuing north, then westward across the Pacific to the Philippines. One of the most serious challenges to Spanish control of South America's Pacific coast coincided with Oré's assignment to La Florida. The Dutch East India Company sent out a fleet of four ships in August 1614. After stopping in the Canary and Cape Verde Islands, they crossed to Brazil and continued on southward toward the Strait. News of the fleet's movement had been sent overland to Lima, and Viceroy Marqués de Montesclaros began preparations for defense. The ships passed through the Strait and then, cruising past Mocha and Santa María Islands, they were off the coast of Concepción in early June 1615. Chile's Governor Alonso de Ribera prepared the defense. The Dutch avoided engagement here and sailed northward to attack and burn the port of Valparaíso. They continued north, landed briefly at Arica, then continued and fought a major battle with the poorly armed Spanish fleet under Rodrigo de Mendoza. It was a disaster, and several Spanish vessels sank. The Dutch might have captured the port but, erroneously believing the Spanish had it well fortified, continued up the west coast of North America, then to the Philippines and Moluccas before returning home in July 1617.

As the Twelve Years' Truce with Spain was expiring in 1621, the Dutch Estates-General chartered the West India Company and authorized it to use force, if necessary, to establish posts on both coasts of the Americas. The Company also received a twenty-four-year monopoly for governing any territories they could establish a foothold in, focusing primarily on the Atlantic seaboard. At the same time the Dutch East India Company remained interested in securing a position on the west shore of the Americas to cut off the Spanish supply of silver and crush Spain's hegemony.

On 23 April 1623 a fleet of eleven ships authorized by Count (later Prince) Maurice of Nassau, carrying over 1,600 sailors, soldiers, merchants, and others, left the Netherlands under the command of Admiral Jacques l'Hermite. Some ships stopped for repairs, and the fleet failed to round the tip of South America at the same time. Finally, in late March 1624 the ships passed into the Pacific and began to reunite on the Juan Fernández Islands off Chile's coast. There they finalized plans to take the port of Arica as the base for mainland operations. Unfortunately for the Dutch, Peru's Viceroy Marquéz de Guadalcázar, learning that the Dutch entered the South Sea, decided on 3 May 1624 to ship the silver to Panama. Simultaneously, the viceroy sent two ships southward to verify the Dutch presence. The Spanish ships mistakenly sailed into the Dutch fleet, and one was captured. After intense interrogation, the Spanish captain convinced the Dutch that the silver fleet had left for Spain long before, but others led the Dutch to believe that a second silver ship remained in Callao. They expected, wrongly, that African slaves in Lima would rise up and help them. The Dutch began their assault on Callao on 10 May and established a blockade lasting several months.

The Dutch base during the blockade was on San Lorenzo Island, near enough to be visible from the port yet large and strong enough to provide the attackers protection. Rather than attempt to expel the Dutch the viceroy decided to wait as their supplies ran out. By mid-August the Dutch abandoned San Lorenzo and sailed northward hoping to take the port of Ancon, establish a position and mount a land force to take Lima and Callao. But the Peruvian forces blocked them. Finally, the Dutch separated and sailed north to New Spain before crossing the Pacific to reach the East Indies. Only one of the ships returned home in June 1626.

The impact of the intrusion of Nassau's fleet, as Peter T. Bradley points out, was multifold. Spanish officials realized the impossibility of controlling access by other powers to the west coast of America, leaving people who lived in coastal communities in a state of dread. It was also evident that adequate defenses could be recruited from the interior if needed, making a permanent position by the foreigners unlikely to be sustainable. The Spanish realized the high costs of maintaining a standing military, and therefore they would need to rely on locals in periods of crisis. They finalized the solidification of the port of Callao and by 1626 they made persistent efforts to ensure that other critical ports were fortified and equipped with armaments and trained men who could lead local resistance until assistance arrived. Chile did not receive the same stimulus for new military investments. Peru's Viceroy Conde de Chinchón in 1629 was convinced that the military in Chile, constantly fighting the Araucanians, was strong enough to hold their own against foreign intruders on Chiloé Island and in Concepción, Valparaíso, and Coquimbo until reinforcements could arrive. The Spanish believed the indigenous people in Chile would see other Europeans as enemies too.[1]

Oré understood the English and French threat and was aware of the growing power of the Dutch. He was well informed of the Dutch interest in the passage to the East Indies around the southern tip of the Americas, as well as their efforts in the Caribbean in the previous decade. His brief residence in Peru before assuming his post in Chile provided an opportunity to secure more local information from both regular and secular clergy and from commercial houses in Lima. Oré also had time for personal conversations with the commander of the fleet he sailed with to Chile, as well as members of the Audiencia of Lima. Oré had complained in his books about foreign enemies threatening Spain's hegemony and he was prepared to face any challenge that might arise in his frontier diocese.

❧ 33 ❧

Beyond Araucania

A PASTORAL INSPECTION

Araucania, the land of the Mapuche, was vast, and the several ethnicities that composed it were among the most adept of any autochthonous group in the Americas at resisting and surviving Spanish settlement. After a brief two-decade period when a large number of Indians were subdued and distributed in encomiendas, the indigenous people began to chafe under the weight of tribute and forced labor, and rose up in revolt. They were quick to adapt to European warfare and became excellent horsemen. Armed with arrows and spears they could outmaneuver and outshoot the Europeans for generations, and even extended their influence far into the Argentine pampas as recently as the mid-nineteenth century. Oré reached his diocese at a most inauspicious moment, when the Araucanians had again scored major victories against the Spanish.

Oré began his tour as the fifth bishop of La Imperial sometime in the first half of 1623. He would supervise the clergy and parishioners of the diocese, but there was also a concern over the relationship between the secular government and the church within the context of the Patronato Real, which was complicated by pressures from Santiago de Chile. Oré was cognizant of the need to extend and improve churches and schools and other religious facilities, always a problem, and especially in an earthquake-prone zone. He also needed to ensure religious revenues were collected. We lack a continuous daily, or even monthly record of Oré's activities as bishop. The remote diocese was at the end of the line of communications and documents were lost to foreigners or storms as ships carried correspondence to Spain. Fires, indigenous attacks, earthquakes, and tidal waves more than once destroyed Concepción and swept away records. Much of the correspondence in and out of the city was prepared and dated to coincide with the royal or merchant ships readying to sail to Callao. Often two or three reports on the same issues were sent, contributing to confusion. Nevertheless, even with limited sources we can glimpse the bishop at work.

A recommendation letter that Oré signed in Concepción on 19 March 1625 indicates some of the normal administrative duties. He wrote that Canon Pablo de Alarcón, who carried the letter, had come from Spain to Chile in 1600. He was "occupied in the wars in this kingdom serving in two military posts, as a soldier, ensign, aide-de-camp, and captain with the approval of the generals.... He became a cleric and because he is a priest of great virtue and example, he was named a canon of this cathedral where I found him engaged in his endeavor." Alarcón asked Oré for authorization to return to Spain to present his service report to the king, hoping to secure a new appointment. Oré's glowing recommendation of the soldier-turned-priest ends with a promise that Alarcón will give the king a "true report informing on the issues relating to peace and war in the service of Your Majesty." The correspondence reached Spain, but Alarcón did not; on the reverse side of the letter was a note that he "died," probably en route to Spain.[1] During these early months in Concepción there was a movement to assign Oré to a larger and more appropriate diocese, one based on his knowledge of Aymara and Quechua speakers. Perhaps as Oré was organizing for his first inspection of the diocese, and perhaps without his knowledge, he was nominated to fill the vacant office of bishop of Tucumán. On 15 December 1624 a report was filed in Madrid detailing his accomplishments and career, but the four votes he received were insufficient.[2]

In 1625 Bishop Oré called a diocesan synod, the second to be convened in southern Chile. The first had been conducted four decades earlier. The purpose of the synod, a meeting of the clergy in the diocese, was to review the work and quality of the religious and their successes and failures, and to recommend steps for improvements. The question of idolatries could be addressed, as well as the indiscretions of clerics. Changes in local jurisdiction could be made, including the establishment of new parishes. The actions taken by the diocesan synod had the force of law. Oré established new parishes in the diocese and set up a seminary for the training of priests at Concepción.[3] Other activities included recognition and greetings for incoming church and state officials. On 15 November 1625 Oré and the Cathedral Chapter of Concepción wrote to the monarch notifying the arrival, presentation, and approval of Mercedarian Friar

Francisco Ponce de León as the chief army chaplain. He had been a lecturer of the general chapter of the order in Lima, had served as visitador and was considered a reformer of his order. The army chaplain arrived in Concepción with the new governor, Luis Fernández de Córdova y Arce, a military man with extensive experience, and the nephew of Peru's viceroy, the Marqués del Guadalcázar.[4]

In a letter to the Crown from Concepción, dated 20 April 1626, read in Spain on 26 June 1627, Oré wrote that he had been at his post for three years and had "twice inspected his province and had celebrated a provincial synod." He sent a separate report on the provincial council meeting. Oré, true to his style, had "embarked to inspect the Chiloé Archipelago where he was well received because it had been forty years since a prelate had gone." During his inspection, "he dealt with what was convenient, and erected new parishes which were needed on those islands." Bishop San Miguel had inspected the then seven curacies of Chiloé between 1571 and 1574. Oré planned the pastoral inspection to examine and confirm both the Indians and Spaniards, stating that he wanted to inspect Chiloé "the year after I arrived" but added "the governor of this kingdom prevented it," because "this South Sea was infested by the Dutch enemy who had reached Lima." Another problem, he wrote, was the distance, one hundred twenty leagues from his seat, and the challenges of navigation. Undeterred by obstacles, Oré reported that after much effort he at last "arrived in the city of Castro, [administrative] center of those islands." The bishop and his company were at sea for seventeen days as they fought the strong current and swells welling up from the south. Oré lamented that unlike the visita conducted by Bishop San Miguel decades earlier, when the land was at peace, the inspection was now extremely difficult to carry out because "almost all the province was in the hands of the enemy."[5]

Founded on the island of Chiloé in 1567, Castro housed some forty vecinos and there were about 3,000 "repartimiento Indians" on the island in the 1620s, according to Antonio Vázquez de Espinosa, who spent months in Chile. He depicted Castro's residents as not rich, but stressed there were ample wheat, chickpeas, corn, and other seed crops. There was a Franciscan monastery with two friars. Chiloé and nearby islands were covered with rugged mountains and tall hardwood trees, excellent for ship timber and other products. It was an ideal place for interlopers to stop to careen and caulk their ships. Vázquez de Espinosa noted the English and Dutch had twice attacked Castro, so to strengthen defenses of the southern route the city and fortress of Valdivia was established. It was an inner port protected by nature as well as by its presidio. Vázquez de Espinosa observed that it was "not only a deterrent against enemies by sea, because the fortification of the port is so good and the land is so abundant and rich, that we may consider that it is the key to all the kingdom, and it would also be a deterrent against enemies by land."[6]

Already in his seventies, Oré was nevertheless determined to reach the Jesuit missions in the Chiloé Archipelago, and set out accompanied by two Jesuits. He reported: "To inspect the said islands the priests of that province experience much danger because they navigate from one island to another in piraguas, which are like long and narrow boats of three planks (*tablas*) sewn together with cords of *coleos,* which are wild canes. Seven or nine people travel in it, rowing with oars they have. In this manner I was inspecting them, in mortal danger, but Our Lord saved me from all that presented itself. Many people have drowned and perished in storms."[7] Oré inspected various other posts, including Carelmapu, Maullin, and points north of the Chacao Channel, and had hoped to reach Osorno and Valdivia but was unsuccessful. He was disappointed as he surveyed the meagre indigenous population and recognized the depth of their resistance to conversion. Oré stated that during the visita he confirmed 7,300 people, both Indians and Spaniards, and established new parishes, placing them under "capable priests for such ministry and the challenges of warfare in this Kingdom of Chile.... I only hope there will be a good result from this, because sixty Indians, their principal caciques and captains, have come to offer peace."[8] Following his inspection Oré convinced royal treasury officials in Santiago to fund four more Jesuits for the Castro mission, an important step to ensure the town's survival. At last, Oré wrote, missionaries reached the Guaytecas and Chonos.[9]

In later correspondence Oré provided additional information on the visitas. He described Chiloé as "an archipelago of populated islands with more than 15,000 Christian Indians, at the latitude of 43° and near the Straits of Magellan." Oré reported that in Castro there were two forts with soldiers, and the province was called Nueva Galicia. He reiterated that he confirmed 7,300 persons and baptized some adults "and I personally married them, celebrated ordinations they had never seen, and I left priests in the parishes." He informed the king that at present (February 1627) he was "visiting for the third time the city of Gamboa and the forts of San Felipe de Austria and of the Estado de Arauco and seven other forts where soldiers are garrisoned, and many estancias, vineyards and grain fields where there are many Spaniards and Indians. Soon I will remedy what needs to be remedied and thus avoid offenses to God, and Your Majesty will be served in all that I will undertake."[10] On 4 March 1627, in fulfillment of a royal order to all bishops (11 July 1625), Oré finished a detailed administrative report on the Royal Treasury revenues of the diocese and their distribution, including payments to the chaplains and parish priests.[11] Oré provided more than just church revenues. The details are related to Oré's ecclesiastical inspections, and he added information on the geography and condition of the human settlement of Chile's south.

Oré's report is organized following the trajectory of his inspections. Starting with the bishopric and the city of Concepción, Oré recorded expenses for himself (1,400 reales), and the deacon, archdeacon, and two canons (350 reales each). There were two parishes in the city of Chillán, and two in Castro. In addition, there was a principal army chaplain who assisted the governor "and goes with him in the incursions into the land of the warring Indians." Oré complained that in spite of the Crown's decree that the governor's chaplains should be seculars, not friars, the order was not observed. There had been successively a Trinitarian, Mercedarian, Franciscan, and presently another Mercedarian, and each one costs the treasury 400 ducats. Oré listed other chaplains in the various forts throughout the region and commented on the good quality of the land for growing wheat near the Fort of San Cristóbal, "for the sustenance of Your Majesty's army."[12]

Oré wrote that chaplains served the soldiers at the forts of Nacimiento and San Rosendo, the Fort of Talcamavida and Santa Juana, the Fort of Lebo "very close to enemy lands," and the Fort of San Pedro and Colquesa. He noted that in the Chiloé province there were two forts seven leagues apart that were served by one priest whose task was difficult. There were also the forts of Carelmapu, and Calbuco. Oré reported that between these forts there were some "settlements of friendly Indians, most of them infidels, and some baptized but poorly converted." In the Indian settlement of San Cristóbal and Talcamavid, two Jesuits "worked with little fruit in the conversion of the friendly pagan Indians, except in baptizing young children," and each received a large stipend of 480 ducats. There was one Indian forced settlement of Arauco with two more Jesuits, paid the same amount. Oré lamented that the Crown "showered on them [Jesuits] a greater salary than all the other curates and chaplains, so that the past governor of this kingdom, Don Pedro Osores de Ulloa wanted to take away such a high salary from them saying that they were not converting the Indians to receive baptism or the Faith." Governor Osores de Ulloa succeeded, and other orders joined in conversion efforts, including a Dominican friar but he stayed only a year. After the governor died, the Jesuits returned with the same stipend. Oré conveyed his concern about the excessive salary in his measured way: "Your Majesty will order whatever is necessary, but although the fathers well deserve it because they are learned men and virtuous and exemplary, it removes the support that should go to the soldiers who suffer from hunger and are fleeced."[13]

Oré described the doctrinas, beginning with Conuco, with many estancias and encomenderos who used indigenous labor, and in theory paid the curate. On the Costa de Colque a Dominican friar served, and in Toquigua on the banks of the Itata River there were two clerics for many estancias surrounded by troublesome marshes. Near Chillán was the doctrina of Perquilauquen y Reynoquelen. In Talgahuano, with numerous separated estancias, there was only one cleric. Oré related that when he inspected Chiloé with its thirty islands and the city of Castro as well as the forts of Carelmapu and Calbuco, he established two parishes and appointed two clerics. Their stipend was low, "because the land was poor, but in the end, they sustain themselves."[14]

It appears Oré, nearing the end of space on his folio, was forced to abbreviate his text as he was concluding his missive. He abruptly returns to the issue of the appointment of Father Francisco de Pereda as church canon. In an earlier letter, 20 April 1626, Oré wrote that Canon Juan López de Tovar is "very old and absent" and recommended appointment of Father Pereda, "an exemplary person and good Christian" who had been carrying out the duties in the elderly canon's absence. In his most current report Oré stressed Pereda's qualifications while pointing out that Canon López de Tovar was absent for four years because he was old and ill and he transferred his post to "a brother of his, a Mercedarian Friar, Commander of the Convent of La Merced." Oré reminded the king that all this time López de Tovar "had been and is in the city of Santiago without wanting to or being able to come because he is very ill with gout and asthma." In addition, "because he holds substantial haciendas worth more than eight to ten thousand pesos, I have named in his absence and by virtue of the Patronato Real, Father Francisco de Pereda as canon." Oré highlighted again Pereda's qualifications but noted that in the meantime the king had named Francisco de Espinoza Caracol as canon. Oré challenges the selection, pointing out that Espinoza Caracol was from Santiago where he had more than 20,000 pesos of haciendas and estates. "Although he took possession of the prebendary he wants to return to his land because it [the climate] is more temperate. I cannot give him license for it, and thus I supplicate Your Majesty to give him a canonry in the church of Santiago; he already serves a chaplaincy of eight hundred pesos in the same church. And Your Majesty orders that to be a canon he renounce whatever benefice [he has]." Oré added that "because this is a simple benefice Your Majesty would be served to instruct me in this and in whatever else is your desire, so that I comply and obey it in all these things."[15] Oré concluded his missive informing that he established two new parishes in Gualque and Leltome with its twelve estancias and many Indians and Spaniards, and "thus all is well ordered and the priests in all parts are moderately competent, but they are very adept in the language of this land to teach the Indians the doctrine and catechism and to preach."[16]

As bishop, Oré had to also address developments in Spain, for example the birth of a royal child. On 5 March 1627 in another letter to Philip IV, he noted receipt of the monarch's announcement from Madrid on 29 December 1625 of the birth of the "most serene infanta [María Eugenia] princess of Spain" to Queen Isabel de Borbón on 21 November 1625.[17] Expressing his joy at the news, Oré related to the king that after contacting Governor Fernández de Córdova y Arce he convoked all the clergy and religious in Concepción, as well as the military officers. They along with the residents "held a most solemn procession on the day of the Purification of Our Lady [2 February]." Oré described the procession in detail. Four priests carried the Holy Sacrament "in its rich monstrance of eighty marks of silver" along with tall ceremonial candles. They also carried the image of Our Lady of the Snows that was originally in the city of La Imperial where she "performed many and clear miracles," before "the war Indians" destroyed the city. Oré compared the devotion to this image to that of the Virgin of Copacabana in Peru "and the sanctuaries in Spain of Guadalupe, Montserrat and Atocha, devotions that in these remote parts are imitated." He concluded, "I said the Pontifical Mass, preached and exhorted all the people to give thanks to Our Lord for this occasion. We supplicated all together, they and I as an unworthy priest between God and the people, to protect for many years Your Majesty and the queen our lady and the most serene infanta our princess." Oré's prayers went unanswered. The princess died on 21 August 1627, probably before the bishop's missive reached the monarch. Only two of Philip and Isabel's eight children survived to adulthood.[18]

The complete turnaround of messages between the metropole and Concepción could take years. Oré received a letter from the king on 2 February 1627 sent two years earlier from Barbastro, Spain, on 1 February 1625. He noted that the letter packet included a royal decree that in all the kingdoms "a solemn festival of the Holy Sacrament should be held forever on 29 November to give thanks to Our Lord for having safely delivered the galleons of the Royal Armada for the guard of the Indies and the fleet of New Spain."[19] Further, the king ordered church officials "to reform the customs [of the people], castigating the public sins that offend God so much." Oré announced the decree and informed the king that "it will be recorded in the book of the Cathedral Chapter of this bishopric where the records of the notable things of its foundation are," including the king's decree for the fiesta and street procession. Perhaps to make it more palatable to the local population, Oré suggested that the monarch send an ambassador to the Vatican to ask the pope to issue a bull declaring a jubilee and indulgences for that day "and for each of the second Sundays of every month of the year that the Confraternity of the Slaves of the Holy Sacrament established in this cathedral conducts a procession of the Sacrament." Regarding improving public morality, Oré assured the king that he had focused on reforms from the time he arrived four years earlier.[20]

❦ 34 ❧

Church and State Conflict

THE *PATRONATO REAL*

The most heated arguments between Governor Fernández de Córdova y Arce and Bishop Oré stemmed from questions of appointment of clergy, be they military chaplains or holders of benefices or doctrinas. The conflict on the frontiers of empire was the consequence of a profound shift of policy under Philip IV and the Count Duke of Olivares, and the church from the papacy downwards. Philip III confirmed in 1609 and 1611 that the Crown held the right to name the *capellán mayor* (chief military chaplain) and the chaplains of the armed forces with the caveat that only the prelates could license the clerics who could administer the Sacraments. Philip IV, active in oversight of church actions, in 1627 and 1628 ordered that viceroys, audiencias and governors could inform themselves extra jurisdictionally of the qualities of those proposed for benefices, but if none were found to be apt for the position, then the prelate could propose them subject to their qualifications.[1]

Oré faced head on challenges over the Patronato Real raised by Governor and Captain General Luis Fernández de Córdova y Arce. The governor claimed the authority to appoint fort chaplains while Oré argued the right of appointment was in church hands.[2] Oré established new parishes in the diocese and founded a seminary in Concepción to train priests. Few candidates for the priesthood were available and many of those who volunteered lacked the desirable attributes. Demands placed on garrison clergymen living among the Indians required special training. Complaints soon surfaced that Oré ordained unfit men and that the seminary was unprepared for its educational role. The bishop defended himself, arguing that most parishes were well attended to spiritually, and that some vacant benefices had been restored. In his report to Philip IV of 4 March 1627 Oré stressed his curates "are very adept in the language of this land to teach the Indians the doctrine and catechism and to preach," something he had always promoted as the most efficient way to convey the Catholic faith.³

Close examination of the correspondence in July 1627 between Oré and the governor reveals growing tension. On 12 July the governor wrote the bishop that when he first arrived at his post two years earlier, he was informed, among other things, about the condition of the army and the clergymen serving at the forts, especially at San Felipe, Estado de Arauco. The governor referred to the unstable and dangerous situation around many posts, including the fort of Lebo, seven leagues from San Felipe, deep in enemy territory. There was not, nor had there been a chaplain stationed there because it was "not possible to go or to come back without a large escort of soldiers." Consequently, several people died without confession, and there was no one to conduct Mass, and the governor was troubled that "the soldiers of the king, our lord, lack such great consolation." As a result, the governor decided to place a chaplain at the fort of Lebo. Part of the problem was inadequate stipend to sustain a priest, and the governor removed part of the salary of the chaplain in Arauco to pay the new chaplain. The hope was to have an earmarked item from the situado so that when the money arrived the stipend could be paid. The governor told Oré that "being unable to find a cleric to serve at that chaplaincy I assigned it to a student I had brought in my company from Peru." He informed the bishop that following his appointment the young man was ordained and "ready to serve." Unfortunately, the student returned to Peru after he was summoned back by his parents, and with Oré's permission.⁴

The governor continued, "at times that I have kissed the hands of Your Excellency I have asked you to provide me some cleric that I might name to go and serve in this chaplaincy, which is so isolated that none of the many that there are wants to go." Despite the governor's entreaties Oré resisted. The governor lamented: "Your Excellency told me many times that Father Feliciano would go, and that Your Excellency had ordered him to approach the government for the dispatches to do it." The governor reminded Oré that because Father Feliciano was poor and it was necessary to provide him an advance of his salary, "I said I would give it to him." Instead, the cleric departed the realm. The governor pointed to another recently arrived cleric with an appointment, "so that I could make the presentation to Your Excellency using the patronage that I have in the name of His Majesty." Oré disapproved of the governor's pretentions and the governor heard about the bishop's displeasure. "They have told me that Your Excellency was very upset" and wished "a ship would come bringing happy news of a governor," that is, a replacement. Governor Fernández de Córdova y Arce insisted that "no one will come who desires more than I to serve Your Excellency."[5] At the same time he defended his actions, writing that "since during my administration nothing similar to this has happened and what my predecessors as governors have permitted cannot prejudice me."

The governor took a firm stance regarding the role of the state, and pointed out to Oré that "until His Majesty orders something else I do not have to allow Your Excellency to make a nomination for the following reasons: First, because yes, since I have done it as all my predecessors have, I can name the *capellán mayor...*" Additionally, he argued that the Royal Patronage did not specifically state that nomination be made to the captains general, only to the governors. He added, "I take this action as captain general, therefore it is not encompassed in the patronage [*patronazgo*]," because the monarch can "temporarily amplify it with the permission that His Holiness has granted him." The governor affirmed that "one should not restrict that which is not expressly stated." He reiterated the need for soldiers in the forts to have clerics qualified to conduct Mass and minister to their spiritual needs. He stressed to Oré that there is no reason to be obstinate and that they should not litigate over the issue of who the priest is so long as he conducts clerical duties.[6]

The governor pleaded: "I supplicate Your Excellency to order the cleric who was ready to go and do what I said because there is no reason to do anything else, being that Your Excellency is such a good pastor. Because of our differences those soldiers are without the consolation of Mass and Confession. I am ready to order him to assume the position and to serve in the office well." As to his stipend, the governor promised he would assure his welfare. He concluded by threatening: "If Your Excellency would not give us this cleric and others, I will search among the religious for friars to be chaplains, and Your Excellency will not deprive them from saying Mass or confessing, as you said that you would do the other day speaking of the topic with your secretary. Something that to me and others seems excessively bad, your Excellency should not act in a way that does not conform to reason and justice, in order to take vengeance."[7] The governor closed his missive firmly. "I am a servant of Your Excellency and in this path, I have the authority [relating to the state] to do so. In the same way Your Excellency has and should have and be master of your authority in all [relating to the church] as I, ordering me that which might be of particular service, and not in any other way until His Majesty orders something else, to whom I will give account of this, as Your Excellency will do also. May God protect your life, as I wish."[8] Such conflict was not new; it existed in La Imperial during the administration of Bishop San Miguel when the governor and jurist, Doctor Luis López de Azoca, issued in 1587 eighteen charges against the prelate for assigning eleven doctrinas to regulars.[9]

Within two days, on 14 July, Oré responded. The aging bishop was displeased by the governor's allegations and plans. His reply was not brief: "I received Your Excellency's message of the twelfth of July and in order to respond with precision to each of the points in it, I wished to first consult the books to see what they instruct us in order to follow the doctrine and avoid errors." Oré quoted "Dr. Navarro, much celebrated in the world,"[10] who concluded that "all the benefices whether of the Patronato Real, or *patrimoniales,* or *prestimoniales,* or of other titles are spiritual rights" that cannot be removed or assigned except by the pope, or someone designated by him and "neither the emperor nor kings or other princes can establish ecclesiastical offices, even the smallest in the world." Oré continued, pointing out that secular officials cannot abolish or take away any either, unless they secure the authority to do so from the pope. Oré stated that the pope should always be obeyed even if there was some detriment to Castilian interests, and quoted Dr. Navarro, "to say the contrary, smells of English heresy."[11]

Oré's position regarding the governor's action is clear: "This can be applied in the present case that Your Excellency has discussed that the chaplaincies and curacies of the forts can be designated solely by you and not by collation or canonical institution as the provision of the royal patronage disposes and orders." The bishop demolished the governor's argument: "Let us presuppose first that such chaplaincies, both that of the *capellán mayor* who resides near the person of Your Excellency as well as the others of the forts require a benefice with ecclesiastical jurisdiction and for that reason are benefices that care for the souls and not chaplaincies or simple benefices to only say Mass. Rather, they are also to administer the sacraments in the presidios and forts where the military reside that are in the garrisons of this kingdom in the state of Arauco, Lebo, Coleura, San Luis de Laraquete, and in San Felipe de Austria, Nuestra Señora de Buena Esperanza, San Rosendo, San Cristóbal, Talcamavida and El Nacimiento."[12] Oré was unequivocal: "In these parishes we have the obligation to provide ministers, appropriate priests who can administer the sacraments, which has been established and has been the pre-existing custom from the time of the erection and foundation of the diocese." He proceeded to name all his predecessors in the bishopric adding "and in my time the same rule has been followed, according to the provision of the royal patronage."[13] The bishop stressed that the monarch and the Council of the Indies, as well as Crown officials elsewhere, had all maintained this policy. Oré returned to Doctor Navarro's text and suggested that the governor's actions were similar to "a schism, or the Anglican heresy from the time of Henry VIII who placed himself at the head of the Church of England." By contrast, according to Oré, the Spanish monarch "as the pillar of the Church defends and sustains it as an invincible arm, in all parts, including this kingdom, by his governors, captains general and the other military officials." Oré again reiterated the need "to be obedient to the laws of the Church" to avoid any suspicion of heresy.[14]

Oré returned to the issue of the fort of Lebo. "I have desired nothing more than to see a priest in Lebo" and told the governor that he had discussed these matters with his predecessors, governors Pedro Osores de Ulloa and Francisco de Alava y Nureña (See table on page 244). He continued, "and at my instance Señor Don Pedro provided a stipend for the priest of El Nacimiento where according to the royal patronage Father Perdomo was placed. Your Excellency supported me in sending Father Toledo to the fort of Carelmapu and Your Excellency knows the times that I have requested sending someone for Lebo." Oré agreed with the governor regarding the young man (Juan Cano) who had come with the governor from Lima, was ordained but then returned to Lima. Oré stated that afterward "I was persuading Father Feliciano de Andrada to assume that post. But he left the kingdom." The bishop also brought up Father Bernardino Ruiz del Canal, whom he had persuaded "more with pleading than violent orders" to take up the post in Lebo, "but I fear that the devil has created obstacles." Father Ruiz "went in the company of Pedro de San Martín who is from his homeland to the estancia of Don Pedro Paez Castillejo in search of sustenance." Oré seemed convinced of the capabilities of Father Ruiz, telling the governor, "it is worth it to work with him again so that he will go gladly." The bishop then changed the tone: "and because of these and other reasons that have been confirmed that Your Excellency put into practice the removal of the priests from the forts and in particular in that of Yumbel and that my *provisor* (a diocesan justice) has told you that you could move him, I left your house to reprimand him for speaking without any foundation." As Oré was leaving he "found at the door the general auditor and Don Antonio Despinosa [the provisor] and told him that some devil of those chained by San Bartolomé must have escaped, because he had advised Your Excellency such a case." Tempers flared, "and about what he responded to me, I said that some ship would come and rid us of all this discord." Oré insisted he was not maliciously attacking the governor, "as the traitor commented who went with the tale and gossip that Your Lordship should not credit."[15] He assured the governor that he had "letters from the *oidores* [justices] of [Royal Audiencia of] Santiago in which they write that no past governor nor one to come will be as competent as Your Excellency by the notice that I have given them of the *malocas*[16] and the successes of Your Excellency and how beleaguered you have the enemy." Oré's flattery continued "no one should be persuaded that having received from Your Excellency so many honors and rewards in the two years we have shared together, that in the first disagreement over jurisdiction, our past concordance should be lost and that I would wish to see Your Excellency out of here, as Your Excellency writes to me and stresses that you wish for it as much as I do."[17]

Despite the mollifying words Oré remained firm. He made use of the documents he carried from Spain and those in the archive of Concepción cathedral. The result is a measured and objective statement of the church's position and continued refutation of the governor's stance that he had a strong case to designate the fort chaplains. Oré stated, "if Your Excellency and past governors have chosen them at your pleasure and without opposition or examination, it was because it was done by absolute power [*absoluta potencia*]." He went on to point out that before the tenure of Governor Ribera, staff chaplains were selected by the opposition's process. Governor Osores "brought with him Father Friar Atanasio" and, he added, "Your Excellency has Father Friar Francisco Ponce." Oré continued: "It is very clear from the decree of His Majesty that there are to be no friars as chaplains, rather clerics, and to please Your Excellency and those in the past, we have tolerated them because it is convenient and has been convenient to please the governors in order to maintain harmony, dissimulating things, even though they are contrary to the orders of His Majesty." He added that "regarding placement of friars in the forts Your Excellency knows very well that they are better off in their monasteries, because from saints they turn into restless gamblers with trades and intrigues." Oré lamented that he would be unable to control or punish them because "it would allow a monstrous fire and not the soft government of the Church." He emphasized that the parishes of the secular clergy could not be given to the regular clergy.[18]

Oré ended on a conciliatory note. "I ask Your Excellency to join together for the good of the souls, and that this cleric goes with my nomination and your Excellency's approval, even if it is for the interim of four months, in order that in the future it will be possible to mediate and everything will be done that Your Excellency orders, so long as it is not prejudicial to ecclesiastic jurisdiction." Oré indicated that "I have not communicated up to now with anyone concerning what Your Excellency wrote to me, because the dean is not here. He is in his estancia and I am suspicious of the archdeacon that in order to gain favors from Your Excellency for Captain Don Miguel de Quiros he will sell me out, as he did in saying that Your Excellency could remove the vicario of Yumbel." In closing, Oré assured the governor that he was "honored to be a greater servant of Your Excellency and your perpetual chaplain praying to Our Lord every day during the Mass to guard your Excellency." Oré signed this letter from his cell in Concepción's Franciscan Monastery on the Day of San Buenaventura, 14 July 1627.[19]

Perhaps the governor expected the bishop to meekly accept his actions. As is evident from Oré's detailed and firm response, that was not the case. Honor and status always lurked as the two men interacted, challenging each other's power and jurisdiction. On 17 July 1627, the governor, undaunted by Oré's arguments and actions, convened a group of religious leaders in Concepción to his residence to provide advice and testimony regarding the two positions. The participants included the Franciscan Provincial Gregorio de Mercado, as well as the past provincial and present guardian of the Franciscan monastery in Concepción, Juan Deca; Dominican Friar Diego de Urbina, the provincial vicario and prior of their monastery in Concepción; Friar Francisco Montes, the Superior of the Dominican monastery; Augustinian Prior and reader of theology Friar Pedro de Enostrossa; Father Francisco Gómez, rector of the Jesuit school; Mercedarian General and visitador, and *capellán mayor* of the royal army, Friar Francisco Ponce de León; and finally, Dr. Andrés Jiménez de Mendoza, general auditor of the army. The governor outlined the issue to the religious authorities and informed them that Bishop Oré had been notified of the meeting and invited to attend "but the bishop had excused himself." The reason why the governor convened the meeting was to seek their support for his actions. He explained to the assembled men that Oré had "sent him a nomination of a cleric" so that he "in conformity with the Patronato Real would order to dispatch the presentation of the chaplaincy of the fort of Lebo." In return, the governor had written to Oré detailing "the strong reasons why the *señor obispo* lacked the authority to name the person who should go and say Mass and give confession at the said fort of Lebo." The governor stressed that the bishop could only, upon being asked, provide him with "an approved cleric" to serve at the fort. The governor noted he had informed Oré that he acted in this instance as captain general and not as governor. To this the bishop had responded using "some texts of Dr. Navarro saying that it was Anglican heresy, and a bull of His Holiness Pío V, and affirming his authority in the naming of the priest for the fort of Lebo." Because this was a serious issue of "competency of jurisdiction" the governor wanted "to assure himself and understand if with lawful and just title of captain general the naming of the priest was within his competency, or the bishop's, and also to know if it was heresy or not or against our Faith." Given the complexity of the dispute the governor stated that he had called them together as "practiced, learned and intelligent persons with experience and Christianity" to resolve the issue "for the service of Our Lord." The governor promised to abide by their verdict.

The friars read the relevant documents and "having thoroughly discussed and conferred about the matter and the pros and cons" of both positions, they unanimously resolved that "the governor as the captain general of this royal army and kingdom, was competent to take this action of naming priests to confess and say mass at the said fort of Lebo." Indeed, the prior of the Dominican monastery in Concepción, Diego de Urbina, ventured to say if the priest has been approved by his prelate, the governor not only had the right to name him without needing the bishop's nomination, but he "would incur in a mortal sin if he did not name the said priest" to the post. The man had ample experience and it was notorious that soldiers had died without confession and they needed someone to say Mass at the fort. In addition to the unanimous declaration in favor of the governor, each member of the junta (special committee meeting) promised to submit their position in greater detail. All attending signed the document.[20] Oré must have been informed of the unanimous finding against him by the religious authorities of Concepción, including two Franciscan friars. The record is silent regarding his immediate reaction. Did he accept it, or did he protest? It is clear from subsequent correspondence between the governor and the bishop, that Oré, undaunted by the verdict, persisted and continued to defend his right to name clergy to serve at the forts.

The issues festered and on 9 December 1627 the governor composed another letter to Oré complaining about the lack of priests at various forts and the scandalous life led by some of the clerics who had been assigned. He informed Oré that he had made scrupulous efforts trying to ensure that the *tercio* (military unit) of San Felipe de Austria was served by a chaplain following the death of Father Diego López Hermoso. He told the bishop that he wanted to send Father Juan Mexía Reynoso—"a creole of this land, virtuous and solid"—but decided "not to do so because he was not approved by Your Excellency." The governor reminded Oré about the conclusions of "all the serious and learned religious of this city" and reiterated "I can place in the name of His Majesty an ecclesiastic to serve as chaplain in any tercio or fort, as long as he is approved." He seemed frustrated as he accused Oré of ignoring his entreaties to send clerics so they could begin service and earn their stipends which the governor was ready to give. He begged Oré to "provide me a desirable cleric who will go in the form I say and I will then make the appointment."[21] The governor raised another matter: "the spiritual and temporal needs of the province of Chiloé require major remedy." He noted that he could deal with the temporal needs but regarding "the other, it is right that Your Excellency attempts to stop the many scandals by the priests there who lead a very bad life" and urged that the situation needed immediate attention. He accused Oré of being too lenient, admonishing "now is the right time to proceed in this and do what is best, because if not, no one knows from year to year what is happening in that province." The governor implored Oré that if they failed to send good clergymen the excesses would continue. He specifically brought up Father Toledo, indicating that he never had much confidence in him. He knew him as someone who "as a soldier and sergeant in the army did not provide a good example and finding myself attending his Mass I was again convinced of his little virtue, letters and sufficiency." The governor told Oré that he found Toledo not just deficient to "commit the souls to him," but "even for the priesthood," because after he became a priest "the scandal happened that occurred in Chillán."[22] The tone of the governor's letter betrays his growing frustration with Oré whom he accuses of neglecting his duties both in failing to fill the forts with chaplains but also in ignoring priestly misconduct and failing to punish and prevent scandals among the clergy. This was not the only dispute between the two men, and as time went on the mutual dislike and distrust only grew.

35

The Struggle for Justice

OFFENSIVE OR DEFENSIVE WAR

O ré's sermon against the enslavement of Indians on 8 December 1627 infuriated the governor and many others present in Concepción's cathedral. The next day the governor countered, emphasizing that the Bishop of Chiapas Bartolomé de las Casas's arguments for defense of the Indians were not relevant in Chile where the indigenous people were constantly at war against the Spanish. Oré's response was measured yet firm in his desire to protect those he considered his flock: "When I see the enemies very harassed, branded and sold and I see them taken away in chains, I remember they also have an angel who defends them, and that I am their bishop and pray to Our Lord to subdue their excessive pride and convert and reduce them into the body of the Holy Church."[1] The contrasting position of how the Europeans should treat indigenous peoples has a long history in America, beginning with the Columbian encounter, and rooted in the millennial history of the struggles in Iberia. Both Bishop Oré and Governor Fernández de Córdova y Arce were well read, and both knew the distinctions between the position of the state and church and the internal philosophical conflicts within each institution. And both knew the impact of Bartolomé de las Casas's defense of the Amerindians.

It was during the long period known as the Reconquista that the justification for conquest and the mode of institutional control over the subjugated was elaborated.[2] The theological and political justification for conquest and control was used in the Canary Islands and later in the Caribbean, and finally on the mainland of the Americas. Once control was established, the conquered were distributed for labor. The immediate impact on the Taino of Hispaniola was appalling, and within a generation most died, falling from overwork, starvation, disease, or outright murder. The religious, first to raise their voices to stop the abuses, were at the forefront challenging the perpetrators and pressing the Crown to protect the indigenous peoples. The Dominican Las Casas became the principal defender of Amerindian rights. Las Casas, born in Seville to a merchant family in 1484, accompanied his father to Hispaniola in 1502 and witnessed some of the worst atrocities the Spanish committed in the Indies, as he later vividly described in the *Brevissima relación*. While on the island, Las Casas, who started out as an encomendero, "moved into a new dimension of his life, motivated by compassion and Scripture" as Lawrence Clayton points out.[3] He was ordained a priest on Hispaniola in 1510. The sermons of Antonio de Montesinos and other Dominican friars on the island stressed the theological reasons why the Spanish treatment of the Tainos was wrong, and Las Casas was inspired to enter the Dominican order.[4]

Oré came across Las Casas's writings in his youth, and must have known his short treatise, the *Brevissima relación*, translated into various languages and widely distributed. Shortly before his death, Las Casas pressed for restitution to the Indians for the crimes committed by the Spanish. His ideas and strong views earned him the admiration of many but also criticism.[5] Oré was certainly influenced by Las Casas and we see his impact in the *Symbolo Catholico Indiano*. The Lascasian thread continues throughout Oré's career in his writings and is evident in his confrontations with Chile's governor. Of all the places Oré served it was on Chile's frontier where debates over justice and Amerindian slavery were most heated.

Indigenous resistance in the shifting and violent border between Araucanian territories and land taken by the Spaniards can be traced to the very beginnings of the European penetration of Chile, starting with Diego de Almagro in the mid-1530s. Pedro de Valdivia set out for Chile in early 1540. He founded Santiago de Chile in 1541, then marched southward leaving Santiago to be ransacked shortly after his departure. The assassination of Francisco Pizarro and the ensuing factional war forced Valdivia to return to Peru. He went back to Chile in 1548, now as adelantado and governor of Chile. Valdivia commanded a series of battles with mixed success, extending Spanish authority south to the Biobío River and setting up a series of poorly equipped forts. They were easy prey for the Mapuche who had improved their strategy based on knowledge of Spanish techniques and weapons. Valdivia was captured and killed after the Battle of Tucapel in 1553. The conflict, the Arauco War, continued with control shifting back and forth and causing a serious drain on the royal treasury.

Some hoped Captain General Martín García Óñez de Loyola could turn the tide, but lacking soldiers and equipment, he was killed in battle in 1598. The Mapuche and their allies destroyed Spanish settlements south of the Biobío to the distant city of Castro on Chiloé Island. For several years the only major post retaken and held was Concepción. The Jesuits and the Franciscans, by founding missions or doctrinas in the south in the subsequent decades, exerted some Spanish influence in the indigenous territory and both orders opposed Indian enslavement.[6]

The Jesuit Luis de Valdivia was mentioned several times in the exchanges between Oré and the governor in 1627. Valdivia, born in Granada in 1560, was sent to Peru in 1589. Adept at languages, after serving in Charcas and Paraguay, he was assigned to the Jesuit school in Juli where he mastered the Mapuche language.[7] Valdivia arrived in Chile in 1593 and became rector of the Jesuit College in Santiago. An advocate for complete conversion of the indigenous groups to Christianity, he initially accepted enslavement of rebellious Indians. Nevertheless, he was also aware of the serious abuses of the Amerindians by the encomenderos. When the vicario general of the diocese of Santiago de Chile, Melchor Calderón, argued in a widely disseminated treatise in 1601 that conquest of Chile was justified, and the rebellious indigenous apostates should be enslaved, Valdivia countered that resistance and rebellion were caused by forced tribute, abusive personal service, and dangerous work in the mines. In 1602 Valdivia was sent to Lima to teach. While there, he rejected Indian slavery and personal service and advocated a policy of "defensive war" rather than "offensive war" as the best route to peace.[8] His position, close to that of Las Casas, led to a short-lived royal policy to protect indigenous Chileans. It seemed that a new Captain General Alonso de Ribera (1601–1605) would be more amenable to work toward a more peaceful relationship with the Mapuche. Governor Ribera strove to assemble a well-trained military to reestablish control over sectors lost. By 1604 he had made significant gains but had alienated enough of the Chilean elite that he was forced to return to Spain.[9]

While in Lima, Valdivia gained the support of Juan de Villela, a justice in Lima's Royal Audiencia, and both men participated in a committee that included the new governor of Chile, Alonso García Ramón. The intent was to formulate a convincing argument for abolition of personal service, a policy they believed would bring peace. Valdivia returned to Chile in 1605 and for months traveled, convincing the Mapuche that if they accepted the policy they would be protected. The Spanish would only go to war against them if they broke the agreement. The Mapuche resisted, wary of trusting the Spanish, and their suspicions proved well-founded. While Valdivia was on his peace mission, Governor García Ramón, pressured by settlers, soldiers, and some clergy, discarded the informal agreement between himself and Valdivia, and with military reinforcements renewed the war.[10]

Undeterred, Valdivia returned to Lima in late April 1606 and convinced Viceroy Marquéz de Montesclaros to promote the concept of defensive war. The viceroy sent Valdivia to Spain to argue for the cause. Simultaneously, Chilean Governor García Ramón and the settlers dispatched Captain Lorenzo del Salto to Spain to advocate for offensive war.[11] In the meantime, the Council of the Indies had presented to Philip III a *memorial* that had approval of "most" of the letrados and theologians in Chile to enslave Indians in rebellious provinces. The Chileans argued that although the Mapuche had been offered peace and accepted it, they abandoned the agreement and rose against the Spanish "capturing and taking away Spanish men, women and children, and continue to hold them in their power."[12] After reviewing the arguments the council recommended that despite prior cédulas prohibiting enslavement of indigenous people, those captured in war in Chile could be enslaved. They also specified that children under 10 ½ years of age should be given to Christians to teach them the Christian faith "as was done with the Moriscos of the kingdom of Granada." The king agreed, emphasizing that only those who rejected Christianity could be enslaved.[13] Philip III's broad cédula, issued on 26 May 1608, provides a foundation for the positions taken by Oré and Governor Fernández de Córdova y Arce two decades later. The king's decree, which overruled all previous cédulas, was clear: rebellious Indians could be enslaved, but "if warring Indians of the Kingdom of Chile return to the obedience of the Church and subject themselves to her, they cease being slaves and no one can take them or have them as such."[14]

Valdivia arrived in Spain about a year after Philip III issued the decree. He argued before the council and the king the value of defensive war and soon published his *Tratado* proposing to end the war in Chile "and make it solely defensive." He pointed out the costs of war to both the Spanish and the Indians.[15] The Council of the Indies accepted Valdivia's plan for "defensive war" with some modifications pressed by Captain Lorenzo del Salto, representing the Chilean settlers, and Governor García Ramón. Personal service was abandoned, prisoners would not be enslaved, but critical defense forts along the frontiers were retained. A type of tribute would be paid directly to the Crown and the Jesuits would supervise much of the conversion work.[16] Philip III named Valdivia visitador of Chile and empowered him to implement defensive war.[17]

Peru's viceroy, the Marquéz de Montesclaros, aided in the distribution of the new cédula ordering that henceforth the war in Chile would be defensive and the Spanish would retreat to the Biobío River. On 29 March 1612, the previous law of 1608 enslaving rebellious Indians was nullified. While Valdivia was in Spain, a new governor had been named: Alonso de Ribera. Valdivia again met with indigenous leaders and as chief negotiator for the Crown guaranteed their protection against settlers and soldiers. The Mapuche were open to negotiation but rejected to be organized into reducciones.[18] Valdivia tried to convince them to reach a comprehensive agreement, but their mistrust of the Spanish was too strong, and negotiations collapsed. Although Mapuche leader Anganamón agreed to free three Spanish captives, he refused to relinquish one of his Spanish captive wives. When she escaped with her children and two other women, Anganamón demanded their return and prepared to act. At the same time Valdivia and the governor were reaching agreements with other indigenous leaders confirming that the Spanish would withdraw from certain forts. Valdivia chose two Jesuit priests and a novice to travel with the Mapuche to Elicura to continue negotiations. In December 1612 they were attacked and killed by Anganamón and his forces, who also killed other Indians who advocated peace. Governor Ribera concluded that defensive war was futile and began to increase the number of soldiers and military equipment entering Chile.[19] From 1614 to 1616 attacks and counterattacks occurred continuously, yet Valdivia persisted and convinced a new supporter, the Jesuit Gabriel Sobrino, to argue for defensive war before the Council of the Indies and the king. He succeeded, and Philip III issued a cédula (21 November 1615) to continue the policy of defensive war. Valdivia, with Sobrino's help, may have succeeded at court, but Chile was far away from Spain and royal decrees and sanctions were frequently ignored or challenged in the distant frontiers.[20]

Father Sobrino was dispatched to Peru with royal orders to continue the policy of defensive war. He arrived in Lima in January 1617 and delivered the documents to the viceroy, Príncipe de Esquilache. Sobrino continued to Chile to report to Luis de Valdivia. Governor Ribera died on 9 March 1617 and to assure that the Crown ruling was enforced, a visitador was sent from Lima. Many indigenous prisoners were freed, Spanish captives were to be released and it seemed briefly that the defensive war policy of leniency and restitution might prevail. But mistrust continued.[21] The new governor, Lope de Ulloa y Lemos, reached Concepción in January 1618 and indicated he intended to work with Valdivia. Encomenderos were angered when they learned that tribute to the king would replace personal service to them and complained. Valdivia's extraordinary powers angered many Jesuits, who attempted to curb his authority. Valdivia returned to Spain in 1620 and sought support at court, but the new Jesuit General Mutius Vitelleschi insisted that he travel to Valladolid to teach at the Jesuit College. Valdivia remained teaching and administering the Jesuit house until his death in 1642.[22]

Valdivia's return to Spain opens the possibility that he and Oré met in Madrid or Valladolid before the bishop-elect set sail to Peru in 1622. The two men were likely familiar with each other's work given their linguistic endeavors. Oré and Valdivia generally agreed on policies regarding conversion and Oré would have benefitted from Valdivia's knowledge of the Chilean situation. Valdivia also might have been interested in promoting defensive war to the incoming bishop. For Oré the Crown's shifting policy between defensive and offensive war proved advantageous in his arguments with Governor Fernández de Córdova y Arce. When Oré reached Concepción, he worked well with the then governor, Pedro Osores de Ulloa, whose views on defensive war caused discontent among the Chilean settlers. The bishop and the governor settled into their administrative duties and worked through the complexities of the Chilean maze. Governor Osores de Ulloa had extensive military experience but followed the viceroy's interest in defensive war. The results seemed initially positive and the number of skirmishes began to stabilize, a tendency Oré desired. The governor's death in September 1624 changed the situation.[23] The next governor, Francisco de Álava y Nureña, served only briefly before he was replaced by Luis Fernández de Córdova y Arce, who began preparations for armed conflict with the Mapuche even before he arrived in Chile. Oré's relationship with the new governor was never smooth and progressively worsened.

It is difficult to imagine two men so different having to negotiate the Chilean experience. The governor, much younger than Oré and of noble ancestry, already boasted an impressive military career. He was just twenty-one years old when he first came to the Indies, accompanying his uncle, Mexico's viceroy, the Marquéz de Guadalcázar. The young man fought against the Dutch as they passed through Acapulco and was named governor of Tlaxcala. In 1618 he sailed to the Philippines as an admiral and fought Dutch privateers in Manila Bay. When he returned to Mexico, he became commander of the fort of San Juan de Ulúa, defending the vital port of Veracruz. After his uncle was appointed viceroy of Peru, he took Luis with him; both arrived in Lima in July 1621.[24]

The Twelve Years' Truce between the Dutch and the Spanish ended the same year, and the need to strengthen defenses in the Americas became a major concern for Spanish authorities. The ascension of Philip IV to the throne in 1621 led to a more aggressive foreign policy under the king's powerful favorite, the Count-Duke of Olivares. It also meant a change in policy regarding the Mapuche in Chile. Governor Fernández de Córdova y Arce arrived in Concepción armed with a new cédula issued by Philip IV on 13 April 1625, ending the policy of defensive war in Chile, and he formally declared its end on 24 January 1626.[25] There was increasing need to guarantee the stability of southern Chile. The coastal topography, the islands and rivers and rough terrain provided the perfect place for foreign enemies to establish a permanent beachhead. If the port of Valdivia fell to enemies it would be a catastrophe for Spain. There was also an increasing preoccupation with the possibility of the Mapuche assisting Spain's enemies. Nataly Cancino Cabello put it bluntly: "What finally propelled the end of defensive war was the Dutch presence in the waters of the Pacific. Under its threat, the abandoned port of Valdivia acquired geopolitical importance, indeed it was an entry way to the continent."[26]

Similar to the Mediterranean basin, coterminous with constant skirmishes there evolved a pattern of capturing enemies and holding them as slaves or as assets to use in exchanges with the enemy. In the Old World the capture and ransoming of enemies had grown into a form of continuous communication between Muslims and Christians, even during periods of war between enemy states. This practice was also common in Chile. On 1 February 1627 Governor Fernández de Córdova y Arce informed the king that several "principal women" had been rescued after being held captive by the Araucanians for some twenty-seven years and "these days two others were ransomed." Furthermore, they had ransomed Captain Marcos Chavarí who was taken and held captive twenty-five years.[27]

Oré was concerned about the indigenous people taken regularly as slaves in the Araucanian wars.[28] In the letter of 9 December 1627 Governor Fernández de Córdova y Arce brought up Oré's sermon, where he invoked Bartolomé de las Casas. The governor disagreed: "regarding what Your Excellency said in yesterday's sermon I judged (as others) some things to be inaccurate. Indeed, what the Bishop of Chiapas wrote defending the natives of the Indies does not apply to the rebels of this kingdom, most of them apostates from our Holy Faith who have negated it using terrible insults." He added, "and regarding slavery, I do not view the one of the Moors as more just than that of these enemies." The governor went further and questioned Las Casas' interpretation and application of canon law. "What the bishop has written is not canonical nor does it have more authority than his own." He continued, "And His Majesty, through others of much learning and expertise as Your Excellency, as he says in the cédula regarding slavery, a copy of which I send with this to Your Excellency, there is today more justification that these rebels should be enslaved than when the cédula was issued, because the mode of defensive warfare was observed for thirteen or fourteen years, which is exceptionally prejudicial to this kingdom, the lives of Spaniards, and the cost to the Royal Treasury."[29]

The following day, 10 December, Oré responded, "Yesterday afternoon I received the text that Your Excellency wrote me, and the cédula of His Majesty regarding Indian slavery." Oré continued later in the letter, "the cédula on slavery is from the year [160]7 and I was pleased to see it, and that one was suspended with the defensive war introduced by Father Valdivia." Oré, well aware of the changing policy, nevertheless asked the governor for more material, adding, "In this subject I am so neutral that when I see some evil occur to ours, I feel it in my soul and I want punishment" but as bishop, he could not accept even enemies being sold into slavery.[30] In the same letter Oré also defended his position regarding naming priests to the forts that the governor had reproached him for at length. He cited the Council of Trent as well as the Second Church Council of Lima regarding who had the right to name and remove priests, insisting that the governor could not act on his own. He warned that "the Second Lima Council orders and says that anyone who dares to place or remove one in an Indian doctrina without a bishop's permission incurs *ipso facto* the sentence of excommunication." Oré insisted that he was acting according to the rules of the church and no matter how much he wished to please the governor, he "was not ready to be forced into something that seems to me to be against [the jurisdiction of] the Church."[31]

The governor responded the same afternoon, stating that he knew full well the cédula regarding the Patronato Real and the rulings of the Council of Trent and the Church Councils of Lima. He added testily "as I have written and told Your Excellency on other occasions," the mandates of the councils were irrelevant here, because they "deal with the curates, and not persons who hold positions of chaplains in the armies or navies." The governor told Oré bluntly that in addition to "the opinions of the learned religious," he had shared the letters exchanged between him and Oré with the justices of the Audiencia of Santiago, "and each one" has read the letters and the finding of the commission of the religious leaders in Concepción supporting the governor's position, "and they feel the same." Therefore, the governor insisted, "I have no need to make further reports to the viceroy or the justices of the Audiencia [of Lima]" or seek their advice.[32] He added pointedly, "Given that it is so just as Your Excellency tells me, to defend the jurisdictions, I ask you not to find it offensive that I defend the royal one for the reasons referred to."

The governor expressed his belief that given the bishop's Christian zeal he should appoint clerics in Chiloé to solve the pressing problems. He then said he had forgotten to include with the cédula regarding enslavement "of these enemies" that he sent the previous day "Your Excellency's letters where you tell me what His Majesty has been served ordering, and in one you put the exact words, as Your Excellency will see from the copies that go with this." The governor added that he was also including a copy of the junta that he had convened, "where the said cédula and letters were read, and Your Excellency was present in all and was served to give your opinion and to sign it." The governor asserted that "thus I believe, that same as I, you must have forgotten this, saying that you were unaware of these documents given that you were there."[33]

The governor's sarcasm and a hint of condescension is evident despite the usual niceties he interspersed throughout the letter. Oré may be a bishop and as such is owed respect, but the governor is a nobleman with an impressive pedigree, and although he sees himself foremost as a soldier, he is well educated, and Oré's insinuation that he may not know the law offends him. Governor Fernández de Córdova y Arce was sent to Chile with a clear mandate from the Crown to conduct an offensive war against a dangerous enemy, and he viewed Oré's position in promoting defensive war as a hindrance to successfully defeating the seemingly indomitable Araucanians. Furthermore, the bishop seems to have been negligent in his duties and the governor did not hesitate to inform the king.

❧ 36 ❧

The Conflict Becomes Ugly

On 16 January 1628 Governor Fernández de Córdova y Arce, who was at the time with his troops in the war zone, wrote the king presenting charges against Bishop Oré that illuminate the depth of the dispute and his growing exasperation. The governor, after reminding the monarch that he had previously written about his difficulties, informed him that he would directly confront the bishop in the firm belief that Oré had taken actions contrary to both church and state strictures. The governor told the king that "in the administration of the sacraments I have warned him also of other things, such as his inordinate excess in ordaining into the sacred orders, and Mass, anyone who wants to be an ecclesiastic, something that the bishop still solicits, and they receive the said ordination." The governor affirmed, "I promise Your Majesty, I take him to be chaste, in spite of telling him he should moderate some of his very frequent inspections, and others of women of little integrity, and in this, I have tried to contain him."[1]

The governor continued: "In regard to the sacraments, there have been times, that having generally confirmed many adults and children, instead of putting chrism oil on them he put the *oleum infirmorum* (oil of the sick) on them." The chrism can be used for baptism or confirmation, but the "oil of the sick" is used to administer the extreme unction, a serious mistake on the bishop's part. According to the governor, when Oré "realized what he had done, he mounted his mule and with a page who carried the chrism for him, he went from house to house (and they even told me, entering kitchens) to put on the chrism." It must have been quite a sight which caused "a major scandal." The governor added that "the said chrism that is always kept clean and used in the baptismal font, no one knows how it was used in each house."

The governor complained that Oré used "some individuals to baptize for him, without authority of what it represents. And in conducting marriages in no way does he follow the rules of the council, rather he conducts them with great ease without any publication of the banns." And there was more. The next charge suggests a laxity in maintaining the sacrament and disregard of the consequences of potential bigamy. "There has been a case in which wanting to marry an Indian with an Indian woman, the *amo* (master) of the said Indian woman, named Captain Hernando Vallejo told me that she was married and that her husband was alive about seven or eight leagues from Concepción and that someone should be sent to find out if it were true because the Indian woman had said he was dead." The governor could not believe what happened next: "The bishop said to go ahead and marry and later if the first husband appeared, she should return and live with him, something that I find astonishing because it is contrary to our law."[2]

The governor's next charge was even more serious and concerned Oré's relaxing the rules for ordination of priests, something that has "scandalized even more." The governor told the king "there are no delinquents, housebreakers, defilers of maidens' honor, or murderers who come to be ordained who fail to succeed." And, most damning, "the said bishop is aware most of the time of the crimes, because they are fleeing from justice." The governor grumbled that the transgressions did not appear to matter, and lamented "it is the greatest shame in the world that in lands so new he ordains into the Holy Order men of lowly occupations, and some who are publicly known to have come as exiled thieves, so ignorant that they barely know how to read or write." Even worse in the governor's opinion, "thus they are ordained to conduct Mass, and for a year or more, they still do not know how to pray the *oficio canónico*, something that breaks the heart and aggrieves many who with just minimal consideration see what is happening." The governor was dismayed that out of "an infinite number of clerics ordained, there are not even two with qualifications or patrimony," and he added "nor do they know the language of the natives."[3] That is indeed a shocking accusation, given Oré's consistent stress in his writings as well as past pronouncements insisting that priests must know indigenous languages to effectively indoctrinate their charges. Was the exasperated governor embellishing his complaints to make a strong case against the troublesome bishop or was Oré showing signs of dementia? Certainly, the careless actions the governor described seem inconsistent with the thoughtful theologian we have been following on these pages. The governor reported that given Oré's laxity, the clerics ordained by him were not given license to conduct Mass in other parts of the archbishopric of Lima, "because they are aware of the lack of qualification." In closing, the governor returned to earlier complaints. "I have repeatedly spoken to and requested the bishop to provide me clergy of good example and to remove others who are found to be very depraved. Because he did not want to do so . . . I have placed in some army forts . . . clergy approved by the said bishop to conduct Mass and to confess." The governor suggested that "many because of threats that he makes do not want to take up their posts, although they wish to, and I have posted some friars of good repute." The governor ended his long missive begging the monarch to intervene, stressing that he needed good curates.[4]

The complaints did not fall on deaf ears. According to a marginal notation on the letter, penned in Madrid on 18 February 1630, "the fiscal says that all in this section [concerning the sacraments and the *crisma*] merits a rapid and efficient remedy; therefore, a very specific order should be immediately dispatched charging the bishop henceforth to proceed with more prudence in such serious things, and adhere to what is prescribed by the canon law and the holy Council of Trent, since many decrees deal with this." Furthermore, a letter should be sent to the archbishop of Lima to inform him of these steps so that he can check and see "how the bishop proceeds and if he is improving, and if he is not, then order what he should and can in conformity with the law and advise the Council of the results. Similarly, the viceroy of Peru and president of Chile should be ordered that if necessary, to proceed to stronger measures . . . and do what is expedient."[5]

There is a subsequent notation in the January letter of 1628, dated Madrid 23 February 1630. "The *fiscal* says that also concerning the contents [the governor naming prelates] the said bishop should be advised to proceed with the care and punctuality required in these nominations and maintain good relations with the governor and have as certain that naming and placing chaplains in the forts and armies does not pertain to the bishop, rather to the governor and that he can remove them at his will and place those he deems suitable without having to go through the process of presentation. It is well known that regarding the doctrinas and benefices it is ordered by the cédulas of this Patronato that it is sufficient that the said bishops or the religious who are thus named as chaplains must be approved and examined in order to be able to administer the holy sacraments."[6] At the core of the Council's clear rebuke of Oré's conduct is the Patronato Real based on earlier papal bulls and royal cédulas that in the Indies the state has precedence in matters of religious assignments.

The argument over appointments in the forts and army was the subject of the governor's *auto* (edict), that he issued on 20 January 1629. On 1 February 1629 the governor wrote a short missive to the king, stating that when he wrote to him a year earlier, he did not include any documentation "because when I wrote it, I was at war," but now he was sending a copy of the edict and other relevant documents.[7] In the edict Luis Fernández de Córdova y Arce as governor and captain general of Chile and as president of the Audiencia Real in Concepción declared "that he has learned and had notice from the Kingdom of Peru that the very reverend Señor Don Friar Luis Gerónimo de Oré, bishop of this diocese of La Imperial of the Council of the King . . ., ordered to prepare a report last year to send to the Royal Council of the Indies and elsewhere, as he had done, saying that the señor president had usurped and deprived him of his ecclesiastical jurisdiction *ex propio motu* and was placing curates in the tercios and forts and war presidios, something the said president has not done in any manner, because he has only filled positions of chaplains in the tercios and forts that the soldiers have needed, without any case of ecclesiastical jurisdiction because the people that he placed have been approved by the said señor bishop to say Mass and to confess and some of the persons the bishop himself had named as curates and vicarios." The governor's declaration also refers to his past correspondence with Oré regarding his right as captain general to name the chaplains as well as the "junta that he had with the most learned, disinterested persons of good conscience of this city and the opinion they issued" supporting him. The governor, who throughout was using his title of president of the Royal Audiencia, was sending the documents to bolster his position and "to inform His Majesty of the truth and justification for doing so, because it is customary that the captains general name, as they do, the staff chaplain. And similarly, as ordered by your royal cédula, that this and the other tercios are paid from the royal situado by order and distribution of the said captain general without the bishop's involvement." The governor assured the king that he will advise Oré of this declaration so that "he is better informed that the señor president did not place priests nor has he deprived him of his ecclesiastic jurisdiction, on the contrary, he has supported and favored him, and he should tell His Majesty about it."[8] Because the governor "was occupied in matters of the war" he delegated the collection of information to Dr. Andrés Jiménez de Mendoza, the general auditor of the royal army.

Five days later, on 25 January 1629, the notary Juan de Ugarte went to Oré's residence and asked permission to inform him of the contents of the governor's edict. The notary stated that "wanting to read it to the bishop, he said, 'stop doing it for now' and so I left."[9] Oré's reaction is surprising and unusual. It is common in such cases that the notary delivers the message and often receives a reply, sometimes short, sometimes quite detailed. Ugarte's attempted presentation of the decision occurred a year before Oré died. Was the bishop already ill when the notary knocked on his door and simply did not have the energy to continue the dispute?

Oré's refusal to hear the edict did not stop the governor, who on 3 February 1629 began to present witnesses supporting his actions, to add to the documentation to send to the king. The first witness, Francisco Gómez, Rector of the Jesuit College of Concepción had heard that Oré prepared a report asserting that the governor was usurping his jurisdiction by "naming priests for the war presidios." Gómez disagreed and said that he was unaware the governor had placed or removed priests from any presidios in Chile. The Jesuit rector confirmed that early in his administration the governor had called together a junta of "serious persons, both learned religious and secular men of the city," and when asked "all participants responded that the custom in this kingdom was for the governors to place chaplains for the soldiers of His Majesty. The bishops when they had ordinary clergy available assigned them the spiritual jurisdiction to administer the sacraments to the soldiers."[10]

Gómez corroborated the governor's complaint that Oré was not designating qualified clerics for the forts forcing the governor to ask the Mercedarians and the Dominicans in Concepción to provide him with "approved" friars and they have served as chaplains in several forts. Gómez lauded the governor's honor and piety, and his knowledge of "all matters particularly moral and ecclesiastical and that he has maintained ecclesiastic jurisdiction without violating it in anything, showing respect to the señor bishop of this city and his general vicario and all the other ecclesiastics." He indicated that the governor is very cognizant of "what belongs to each judge, both ecclesiastical as well as secular" because he has read works of theology and he believed the governor has "never erred in disposing on these matters." Furthermore, if he had some doubt or difficulty regarding an ecclesiastical question, he consulted with Father Gómez "and other theologians of this city," and followed their advice. But the governor had not always acted to the letter of the law and "had covered up many faults of ecclesiastical personnel and tried to remedy them quietly for the honor of the persons." Gómez confirmed that the chaplains in the diocese "were paid for from the royal situado kept in the treasury of this city by order of the said governor without the said bishop having a hand in ordering its payment."[11] The Jesuit rector ended his testimony, insisting that anything "that had been said or written" against the governor "is without foundation and is imagined."[12]

The governor presented other witnesses on 4 February 1629. Friar Mansio de Vega, prior of Concepción's Dominican Monastery verified it was customary for governors to name chaplains. He himself had been named by the earlier Governor Ribera, to serve in the tercio of Yumbel y Cayoguano. The Dominican believed the governor dealt with the bishop's intransigence as correctly as possible under the circumstances. Given that Oré had not named clerics for the forts of Lebos and Buena Esperanza, the governor had done so citing dire need. The bishop various times failed to designate competent clergy, forcing the governor to approach the monasteries to provide him with friars to serve at the forts.[13] The next witness, Dominican Friar Pedro de Aranjuez, provided similar testimony, but added a personal detail: he "served at the post of chaplain at the Fort of Lebos with the salary that was paid to him from the royal situado, and that the bishop gave him a verbal license to administer the holy sacraments when it was opportune and necessary." There were more witnesses, and all confirmed the governor's contention.[14]

The letters and reports reached the king's councils and as we have seen earlier, the officials made recommendations, none favorable to Oré. Philip IV issued an order in 1630 that clarified the matter in favor of the Patronato Real. "The generals of the military forces are the ones who name the chaplains, and the Church prelates are the ones to examine and approve them."[15] Oré did not defend himself well in the arguments against his appointment of unqualified clerics. The ability of the clergy to speak indigenous languages in conversion was insufficient according to the qualified theological members, especially the Jesuits, in the reviewing committee. Oré lost the battle over Royal Patronage. The conflict between state and church became even more heated under the Spanish Bourbon monarchs of the next century and even into the Republican era as several of the new nations of Spanish America tried to secure powers largely exercised by the church over education, hospitals, public cemeteries, civil registration of marriages, births and deaths, and especially to prevent active clergy from holding public office.[16]

VII
Epilogue

37

Bishop Oré's Testament

On 24 April 1630, the Cathedral Chapter of Concepción informed the king that "on the thirtieth of January of the present year Our Lord was served by carrying unto himself Don Luis Gerónimo de Oré, Bishop of La Imperial, a shepherd whose loss has left his flock inconsolable." They praised Oré adding "by the example of his life the loss has been generally felt both for what he brought to the service of Your Majesty as well as for the public good of those who live in such misery and difficulties." In the same letter announcing the bishop's death, Concepción's church authorities asked the king to fill the post as soon as possible, because "livestock without a master is subject to much loss and discomfort."[1]

Three days before Oré died he prepared his will with public notary Fernando de la Concha.[2] His testament was short, suggesting illness and approaching death. He made the standard profession of faith and the notary recorded that he was fully in command of his senses as he dictated his directives. The ailing bishop established a chaplaincy of masses in Concepción's Cathedral dedicated to Saint Louis, King of France. He designated as patron of the chaplaincy the bishop "who would succeed us and in his absence the dean and members of the Cathedral Chapter" to administer it and choose its chaplains. Oré named his nephew, Father Pedro de Serpa, to serve as the first chaplain and directed that he and all future chaplains were to say weekly Masses perpetually every Monday and Saturday for the souls of purgatory "and ours." He bequeathed for its support the income from "our house and lot as known property that we have within this city." During this period there were no street names or numbers, so Oré specified the owners of the contiguous lots; on one side was the residence of Captain Francisco Arias and on the other the lots and houses of Doña Inés de Córdova y Aguilesa, the widow of past governor, Alonso de Ribera. The bishop stipulated that this real estate could never be sold so that its income would perpetually fund his chaplaincy.[3]

In addition to naming his nephew Father Serpa as chaplain, Oré bequeathed him for his devotion and service, all the household goods: tables, chairs, trunks, desks, and other things. But two prized possessions, "the ebony desk with silver hardware, and the holy crucifix that we brought from Spain, should be sent to the Convent of Santa Clara in the city of Huamanga to be placed in the main altar." Oré gave the Cathedral of Concepción a silver Christ to fill a space in the monstrance carried through the city during its religious celebrations. He also directed that "the large silver basin that we have" should be given to the cathedral along with his pontifical robes "in all colors, white, crimson, green, black and purple with the chalice," as well as various receptacles he used during mass, a pectoral, and a ring. Oré bequeathed his personal library–unfortunately neither titles nor number of the volumes appear in the inventory–to the Franciscan Monastery of Concepción, stipulating the books could never leave its walls.

As Oré was preparing his journey to Chile to assume his post as bishop of La Imperial, his brother, Licentiate Francisco de Oré, Archdeacon of Huamanga, had loaned him 3,700 pesos to help pay the expenses for shipment and the accoutrements of his office. Francisco had predeceased him and Oré had only paid him back 1,000 pesos. Thus, in his will he acknowledged that the remaining 2,700 pesos needed to be repaid following Francisco's directives in his testament. Oré stipulated that the money was to come from the "income of our estate" and sent to Huamanga, where it was to be given to the bishop to continue the construction of a chapel in the Convent of Santa Clara.[4] Oré also owed 600 *patacones* (pesos) to Captain Pedro de Recalde, the chief constable of the Real Audiencia of Chile, the same amount "that Doña Inés de Córdova y Aguilesa owes us." As happened in similar cases, Oré directed his executors to collect the money from Doña Inés, his neighbor and the widow of the earlier governor, and pay back Captain Recalde.

Any significant estate needed to be inventoried as soon as possible to avoid fraud and the officials moved expeditiously. Oré's body was barely cold when at 2:30 in the afternoon the city's justices, namely Accountant Diego Martínez de Prado and Treasurer Alonso de Puga y Noboa, along with the cabildo's notary Juan de Ugarte, began to ascertain which goods belonged to the bishop or to His Majesty. Pro forma, the officials first recorded that the bishop died of apparent natural causes and that they saw his body laid out on the bedframe in one of the rooms of the house. After verifying the bishop's death, the officials began the inventory. It appears that even as a bishop, Oré was foremost a Franciscan friar and maintained his order's vow of poverty. Most of his personal items were basic furnishings: a wooden bed, a woolen tent from Chiloé, two small rugs of local straw, eight wooden chairs, a wooden sideboard, and another narrow sideboard that served as an altar. Following the inventory, the goods were placed in deposit in the charge of the Cathedral Dean and Commissioner of the Santa Cruzada Juan López de Fonseca, who promised to release them when the city officials ordered it and as security, he mortgaged his estancia.[5]

Oré left nine religious paintings. One was a scene of Christ's crucifixion. There was another of Saint Gregory and Saint Jerome, and a painting of the Virgin and Child with angels to her sides. The list included an Ecce Homo, the Adoration of the Magi, a Descent from the Cross, Christ at the Column, Santa Ana and the Virgin, and a paper engraving of the Last Judgement. All these Oré donated to Concepción's Cathedral, along with religious ornaments and the engraving plate for prints of the Conversion of Saint Paul that he had stored in his residence. Oré noted in his will that he owed his secretary Father Andrés de Vera 300 pesos "which we have spent in our necessities." Vera had left Spain with Oré in 1621 and remained with him until his death. The bishop stipulated that his secretary should be paid "from what is still owed us in the tithes of this bishopric." He also ordered that his dependent, likely a relative, Domingo de Serpa, should be paid 100 pesos to help with necessities.[6]

Important elements of the testament relate to several Amerindians. The inventory of Oré's property lists two slaves, a Black named Juan Castellano and an Indian *auca* called Pedro de Ylicusa. In his will he did not mention them, but he did name several indigenous *muchachos* captured in war, who had been given to him by various governors, presumably as slaves. Oré specifically stated that in the past Governor Osores de Ulloa gave him a boy captured in the Indian wars, "who at present is called Jerónimo and whom we have indoctrinated and educated" for seven years. Oré asked the current Governor Francisco Laso de la Vega to help young Jerónimo so that he could serve the chaplain of Oré's chaplaincy, and "not to permit anyone to take him away from him by way of placing him in an encomienda or in any other manner." Most Indians captured in the Chilean wars were enslaved and sold to the settlers to work in the mines or fields. Oré also declared in his will that Governor Fernández de Córdova y Arce had given him "an Indian named Pedro Milla Quiñe, native of Tirua who was taken in the war after the publication of the *esclavitud* [decree]." Oré had baptized him and officiated his marriage and instructed that Pedro Milla Quiñe serve his nephew, Father Serpa. The field master Pedro Paes Castillexo had sent Oré from Chiloé another indigenous boy, Antón, in return for fifty Masses for his soul and Oré also designated that he should serve Father Serpa. Oré further said that an Indian named Baltasar who had died in Concepción had left his son Juan to serve him. The bishop in the will provided that Juan also should serve the "chaplain of the said chaplaincy" and he charged his nephew with "giving him the good treatment that I have always done for all."[7]

These words, probably among Oré's last, capture the spirit of the man. He believed that he treated his slaves and servants well and protected them from a worse fate had they ended up laboring in encomiendas and mines. We know Oré spoke up against slavery in his sermons and had heated arguments with the military authorities in Chile. How do we in the present century evaluate his actions? Oré was a Lascasian as early as the execution of Tupac Amaru I, over a half century before he composed his will. Was his holding of slaves hypocrisy? We should use caution before attempting to judge the morality of those of another culture and place four centuries ago. If we condemn Oré we must consider also what would have happened had the friar not accepted the "gift" of slaves. As we saw they were minors. What were their chances of survival had they been distributed to encomenderos, merchants, or miners? Oré considered the theological and moral nature of his situation and throughout his will he insisted that these young men should remain under church protection and were not to be removed. At the same time, there were two slaves listed in the inventory and not mentioned in Oré's will and their fate would be quite different. He could have freed them but did not. The manumission of slaves in testaments was not uncommon and it is surprising that he failed to do so. Oré was a man of his time when holding slaves was common, even among clergy. What to us seems puzzling and repulsive must not have seemed incompatible at the time. Oré could argue against the principle of slavery, while owning slaves himself, because for him good treatment and being brought up in the Catholic faith overshadowed what we view as contradiction.

38

Conclusion

THE LEGACY

Diego de Córdova y Salinas celebrated Oré as "the largest and brightest morning-star of the celestial orb and the sacred Faith. It was illustrated by his doctrine and holiness as he delivered notice of the true God to the innumerable idolatrous gentiles of these vast provinces of Peru."[1] Others viewed Oré differently. The secular doctrineros of the Colca valley found his actions egregious as he attempted to remove some of them from their rich Andean parishes. Various friars of his own order and others ignored his work. The governor of St. Augustine in Florida was displeased by his actions. Oré argued with fellow Franciscans over the nature of the order, and whether one could be a true Franciscan working in the doctrinas. More than once Oré admitted his own failings. The monarchs may have found some of his positions antithetical to those of the Crown. The complaints to the king by Governor Fernández de Córdova y Arce about Oré's ordination practices were heard and acted upon. On 25 March 1632, two years after the bishop's death, Chile's Governor Francisco Laso de la Vega wrote to the king informing him of the state of affairs after Oré's passing. He noted the king's concern regarding how to "repair the excess of the Reverend Bishop of La Imperial in his handling of the ordination of all type of people, as seen in Your Majesty's cédula of 29 August 1630." The governor informed the king that by the time he had received the cédula, on 14 February 1632, "it had been two years since the Reverend Bishop Don Friar Luis Gerónimo de Oré had died and with that the fulfillment of it ceased." The governor praised Oré, "he was a holy man in his customs and will, although I barely knew him" and assured the king that the bishop of Santiago "who today governs his diocese does not have this defect because he is of great rectitude on the subject of ordaining, and in all a perfect pastor. I will make certain that Your Majesty's will is fulfilled."[2] The power of the Patronato Real remained firmly in the hands of the state and would continue so for many decades. Yet despite retaining the authority, none of the governors had much success in bringing peace and stability on Chile's southern frontier.

Oré's legacy is not to be found in the urban center of Concepción, where uprisings and other natural disasters erased the physical presence of this peripatetic friar. Of his burial place, his Cathedral, and the Franciscan monastery in Concepción, or his books and correspondence in his archive and library, nothing is left. A powerful earthquake and tsunami in March 1657 destroyed Concepción. Only the Jesuit residence located on higher ground survived.[3] Oré's legacy lies in his writings. His work, primarily religious in nature, remains a useful source for modern historians. The *Symbolo Catholico Indiano* (1598) is an important contribution to the understanding of the nature of Andean America. Originally designed as a multilingual introduction for new parish priests in the Indian doctrinas, it included a survey of the history and geography of the region and information on indigenous religion. Although the historical pages are imperfect, its use for linguists is recognized, and a modern edition now reaches a growing audience.[4] The *Symbolo Catholico Indiano* was adopted widely in the Andes, and likely had a lasting impact on the "standard" written Quechua and Aymara.

Perhaps more significant is the bishop's massive *Rituale, seu manuale peruanum* (1607), a complete manual for the cleric, with texts of special value for linguists concentrating on the Quechua, Aymara, Mochica, Puquina, Guaraní, and "Brasilica" languages. Much can be gleaned from his work on indigenous religious concepts and marriage practices, particularly in the sections of the text dealing with confession. There is also Oré's interaction with indigenous people. Felipe Guaman Poma knew Oré and found him to be what a good, Christian Spaniard should be. As Rolena Adorno points out, Guaman Poma in general found the Franciscan and Jesuit orders to be the best representatives of the "*buen doctrinero.*" Adorno feels that "Guaman Poma revealed a relationship of a different type in his unmitigated admiration for Friar Luis Jerónimo de Oré . . . Guaman Poma referred to him as 'one of the learned men who composed books.'" She suggests that "Like Oré, Guaman Poma took seriously the type of social action which had the written word as its outcome."[5]

Possibly Oré's two most important contributions are the missing grammars and dictionaries in Quechua and Aymara. Yet these works may not be entirely lost. As he himself did when he compiled his dictionaries and grammars, using a common practice at the time in borrowing from the work of others, other religious with a copy of Oré's manuscripts in hand may have taken their own turn in incorporating words and concepts into theirs. Future linguistic analysis and further archival research may help solve this mystery. We know that several manuscript copies of Oré's texts existed, and numerous church linguists reviewed his dictionaries and grammars, a required process mandated before authorizing publication. Given the wide dissemination of Oré's dictionary and grammar manuscripts to secular clergy and the religious orders it would be a mistake to ignore their legacy. It is possible that sections of Oré's efforts appeared in print under the authorship of another. Modern academics mandate attributions of sources. The lettered of the early modern period were more flexible regarding citing their sources, save for the religious as they dealt with theological issues. The most careful authors cited their references, partly to demonstrate their erudition but more importantly, to avoid error that could lead to facing the questions of Inquisitors. Setting aside the issue of using a Latinized word for certain names and concepts that did not exist in the indigenous languages, the explications needed to be in the autochthonous languages and Oré was adept in translating the core articles of the faith in a simple and understandable Andean vernacular. For dedicated doctrineros propagation of the faith in indigenous languages was paramount, no matter the origin of the tools they used.[6]

Oré's 1614 biographical and hagiographical report on Francisco Solano was a significant historical and religious work that contributed ultimately to the canonization of the humble friar from Montilla. The *Martyrs of Florida* published by Oré in 1619 is an important source for the ecclesiastical history of the late sixteenth and early seventeenth centuries in La Florida's frontier, stretching to the Chesapeake Bay. The book includes valuable ethnohistorical information on indigenous peoples in the missions of Spanish Florida. The text, in its most recent translation, should contribute to a deeper appreciation of the impact of Spain on the history and culture of the United States. Oré's third book, dedicated to the Virgin of Copacabana (1620), is a final nod to the Andean peoples of his homeland. This theological treatise, still largely untouched by specialists, is one of the first composed by a Creole infected by the belief in the immaculate conception of the Virgin Mary. Oré's text is a marvelous, almost poetic, work. It also includes the confessions of its author and provides a window into the inner thoughts of a friar who reveals himself with all his perceived failings.

Oré's love of music, be it singing or playing instruments and teaching, is frequently mentioned in the hagiographies and by many of his contemporaries, yet our knowledge is still clouded, and his legacy deserves investigation by historical musicologists. He frequently mentioned the importance of music in conversion and education. Oré was raised in a musical household, where he and his siblings were taught to play and sing. Not only did Oré play various instruments and sing, he also wrote music as noted in the *Symbolo* and the *Manualum*. Music assisted traveling friars as they encountered "the others" and perhaps transformed hostility into wonderment and calm. Dangerous situations could be tempered by the soft vibrant sound of a flute or a violin and a melody could hold the attention of quieted listeners, enough to convince the assembled that the unarmed friars were not a threat. Franciscans used music in conversion in still-unchristian pockets in medieval Europe, and successfully employed music in the colonies, especially Mexico and then Peru. There are references to Oré's contributions to the Jesuits as they worked the missions in Paraguay and among the Mapuche in Chile.[7]

Luis Gerónimo de Oré, nurtured by Amerindian mothers, understood indigenous languages and culture. He saw and appreciated the beauty and complexity of Andean Quechua and Aymara and recognized their strengths and weaknesses. Throughout his religious career he stressed that successful conversion and indoctrination was predicated on the clergy's fluency in the language of the parishioners. Oré was inquisitive by nature, and though he disagreed with many of the religious concepts of Amerindians, he noted and recorded them as well as what they ate, how they dressed, worked, married, and celebrated. He attempted as best as he could to protect and promote their interest, in Jauja, the Colca Valley, the mines of Potosí, the humid coastal wetlands of La Florida and the frigid frontier of southern Chile. He was a Lascasian. He attempted to check the excesses of the military and promoted peace on the frontiers. By accident or design Oré acted as an intermediary, bridging the two worlds, aided by being bicultural. Oré was firmly rooted in Spanish Catholicism yet at the same time he was wedded to the Andean format as an interpreter and major contributor to the process of transculturation in the Americas.[8]

On 16 April 1630, three months after Bishop Oré died, the bishop of Santiago sent a message to the king lamenting the loss of the posts of Angol, Purren, and Paycaui. He was preoccupied with the extension of the war zone deep into his diocese, and in a most revealing fashion requested not clergy, but two thousand soldiers, preferably fresh men from Spain.[9] Oré's Indian policy in Chile echoed Luis de Valdivia's arguments for defensive war. Had it been consistently followed many lives might have been spared. Oré called for withdrawal of Spanish military forces from Araucanian-claimed territory and advocated that both peoples accept the Biobío River as the natural boundary, to minimize armed conflict. With this, missionary efforts should be increased to bring the Mapuche to the faith and a peaceful existence within the Spanish colonial regime. During Oré's tenure at Concepción, relations between the Amerindians and the Spanish, although tense, were reasonably stable, largely the consequence of the bishop's admonitions to both sides, particularly his attempts to persuade the garrison's military leaders to avoid the excesses of offensive war to maintain peace. Oré's death resulted in a break in this uneasy and informal truce. The complex process of transculturation unfolds in a discrete time and spatial dimension based on individual interactions that lead to broader societal change. To fully understand the nature of change, the ebbs and flows and the speed and impact of transculturation, it is rewarding to examine the process at the lowest level—the personal as in this case Luis Gerónimo de Oré, a go-between, and one of the key figures in the cultural exchanges taking place in the early modern Atlantic world.

Glossary

alcalde: municipal judge
audiencia: court of law
cabildo: city council
cacique: male chief
cacica: female chief
cántico: canticle
canto: liturgical song
canto llano: plainchant
capellán mayor: chief military chaplain
capítulo: meeting of friars to discuss and vote on issues related to their work
capítulo de culpas: meeting to discuss sins or acts of commission or omission
capítulo general: meeting to elect the order's General
capítulo provincial: meeting to elect the order's Provincial
carta: letter
casa de la contratación: house of trade
cédula real: royal decree
censos: mortgages
clarisas: nuns of the Order of St. Claire
cofrade: member of a confraternity
cofradía: confraternity
corregidor: provincial governor
corregimiento: province
custodia: a group of convents not large enough to constitute a province
definidor: member of the governing body
definitorio: assembly or meeting place where members of the governing body make decisions

diezmo: tithe
disciplina: submission to moral canons and practices of the Franciscan order
doctrina: Indian parish
doctrinero: priest or friar charged with a doctrina
encomienda: a grant of tribute-paying Indians
encomendero: holder of an encomienda
fanega: Spanish bushel, or a land measurement equivalent to what can be planted by one fanega
fiscal: Crown prosecutor
guardián: a superior in a Franciscan monastery
huaca: in the Andes any object of veneration
iglesia mayor: principal church or cathedral
justicia mayor: chief justice
kuraka: in the Andes, male chief
maravedí: currency 1/272 of a peso
maestre: ship master
mayorazgo: entailed estate
mayordomo: steward, treasurer
mita: forced paid labor
muchacho: male younger than 18
obraje: cloth factory
oidor: justice in the Real Audiencia
patronato real: royal ecclesiastical patronage
presidio: fort, military outpost
procurador: procurator, solicitor, attorney
real: small unit of currency, at the time 1/8th peso, or 34 maravedís
recogimiento: seclusion
regidor: councilman
residencia: review of an official's term of office
situado: annual royal military payment
soltero: unmarried male
teniente: deputy
tercio: military unit of 3,000 men
tonelada: tonnage
vecino: legal property holding city resident

vicario: person associated with religious administration of the Catholic Church; in the context of a convent, supervisor of the nuns of his order
vicario general: deputy designated by a bishop to officially act on his behalf
visita general: general inspection
visitador: inspector
visitador eclesiástico: religious inspector

Notes

Abbreviations

AAL	Archivo Arzobispal de Lima
ACL	Archivo de la Catedral, Lima
ASFL	Archivo del Convento de San Francisco de Lima
AGI	Archivo General de Indias, Seville
AHN	Archivo Histórico Nacional, Madrid
AHPS	Archivo Histórico Provincial de Sevilla
ANP	Archivo Nacional del Perú, Lima
ASIH	Archivum Sancti Isidori Hibernorum, Rome
BNP	Biblioteca Nacional del Perú, Lima
BNM	Biblioteca Nacional de España, Madrid
CSIC	Consejo Superior de Investigaciones Científicas, Madrid
PUCP	Pontificia Universidad Católica del Perú, Lima
UNMSM	Universidad Nacional Mayor de San Marcos, Lima

Prologue

1. Luis Gerónimo de Oré, *Corona de la sacratissima Virgen Maria madre de Dios nuestra señora, en que se contienen ochenta meditaciones, de los principales misterios de la Fé: que corresponden a setenta y tres Ave Maria y ocho vezes el Pater noster, ofrecidas a los felices años que vivio en el mundo ... Dedicada a la misma virgen sacrosanta, concebida sin pecado original, en su imagen y Santuario de Copacavana* (Madrid: La Viuda de Cosme Delgado, 1619).

2. Atanasio López, ed., *Relación histórica de la Florida, escrito en el siglo XVII* (2 vols., Madrid: Imprenta de Ramona Velasco 1931–1933), and Luis Gerónimo de Oré, *The Martyrs of Florida, 1513–1616*, translated and edited by Maynard Geiger (New York: Joseph F. Wagner, 1936). More recently, Raquel Chang-Rodríguez, ed., *Relación de los mártires de La Florida del P.F. Luis Jerónimo de Oré (c. 1619)* (Lima: PUCP, 2014), and a digitized copy of Oré's original report is available. A modern English version of Luis Gerónimo de Oré's report, *Account of the Martyrs in the Provinces of La Florida*, translated and edited by Raquel Chang-Rodríguez and Nancy Vogeley (Albuquerque: University of New Mexico Press, 2017).

3. Luis Hierónymo de Oré, *Symbolo Catholico Indiano,* facsimile, edited by Antonine Tibesar (Lima: Australis, 1998).

1. Huamanga

1. Pedro de Cieza de León, *Crónica del Perú. Primera Parte* (2nd ed., Lima: PUCP, 1986), 246, 249, reports the word is Victoria, not Frontera, and in a later volume explains the name change. Governor Vaca de Castro was staying in Huamanga following the victory of royalist forces at the battle of Chupas and ordered the cabildo to change the name. *Crónica del Perú. Cuarta Parte* (Lima: PUCP, 1994), 2: 298.

2. *Libro de Cabildo de la Ciudad de San Juan de la Frontera de Huamanga* (Lima: Casa de la Cultura, 1955), 11, cited by María Antonia Durán Montero, *Fundación de ciudades en el Perú durante el siglo XVI* (Seville: Escuela de Estudios Hispanoamericanos, 1978), 108.

3. Marcos Jiménez de la Espada, ed., *Relaciones geográficas de Indias, Perú,* 3 vols. (Madrid: Atlas, 1965), 1: 182.

4. AGI, Patronato 133, ramo 4. Service report of Francisco de Oré, 1598–1603. Miriam Salas de Coloma, *De los obrajes de Canaria y Chincheros a las comunidades indígenas de Vilcashuamán. Siglo XVI* (Lima, 1979). She states that Antonio's father, Jerónimo de Oré, was one of the conquerors of the Canary Islands, but in her later (1998) book, reports it was his great grandfather, 31.

5. Eduardo Aznar Vallejo, *La integración de las Islas Canarias en la Corona de Castilla* (1478–1526) (La Laguna, 1983), analyses the complex nature of the indigenous Guanches, and the difficult process of conquest and integration under the Spanish.

6. I have been unable to identify her first husband; see Salas de Coloma, *Obrajes de Canaria* 1: 33, 63–68, 83, 118; and Noble David Cook, "Viviendo en las márgenes del imperio: Luis Jerónimo de Oré y la exploración del Otro, *Histórica* (Lima) 32, no. 1 (2008): 13. Nicanor Domínguez dates the birth of cleric Francisco de Oré around 1568.

7. José Antonio del Busto Duthurburu, *Diccionario Histórico Biográfico de los Conquistadores del Perú* (Lima: Studium, 1987), 2: 39–40. He established a chaplaincy in the Mercedarian church, and died shortly after 1570, since during Viceroy Toledo's tribute assesment his encomienda was already in the hands of his son, Pedro Díaz de Rojas y de la Cuba; see also James Lockhart, *Men of Cajamarca: A Social and Biographical Study of the First Conquerors of Peru* (Austin: University of Texas Press, 1972), 13, 390, 458–69. For Atahualpa's ransom see Noble David Cook, "Libro de cargos del tesorero Alonso Riquelme con el rescate de Atahualpa," *Humanidades* 2 (1969): 41–88. Thanks to Nicanor Domínguez for sharing his unpublished, "Familia Oré (ca. 1540-ca. 1660)."

8. Rafael Loredo, *Los repartos* (Lima: Miranda, 1954). The unpublished manuscript containing the information on Oré is from the Real Academia de la Historia, 159r, our thanks to Rafael Varón Gabai and Javier Flores Espinosa.

9. Biblioteca Nacional de Lima (BNP), Z328, Z330, Ż336; and Noble David Cook, ed., *Tasa de la visita general de Francisco de Toledo* (Lima: UNMSM, 1975), 276–77, records that Antonio de Oré received the grant from Cristóbal Vaca de Castro following the Battle of Chupas. José de la Puente Brunke, *Encomienda y encomenderos en el Perú. Estudio social y político de una institución colonial* (Seville: Diputación Provincial, 1992), 387, indicates Antonio de Oré received the grant in 1561. For the family's economic holdings see Salas de Coloma, *Obrajes de Canaria.*

10. Pedro de Cieza de León, *Crónica del Perú. Primera Parte,* 2nd ed. (Lima: PUCP, 1986), 249. Huamanga's *iglesia mayor* became a cathedral in 1609 when the diocese was established.

11. Cieza de León, *Crónica del Perú. Primera Parte,* 250.

12. Luis Gerónimo de Oré, *Symbolo Catholico Indiano* (Lima: Ricardo, 1598), 31v–32r.

13. Salas de Coloma, *Obrajes de Canaria,* 35–37. There were regional and chronological variations regarding size of a fanega.

14. Miriam Salas de Coloma, *Estructura colonial del poder español en el Perú. Huamanga (Ayacucho) a través de sus obrajes, siglos xvi–xviii* (3 vols., Lima: PUCP, 1998), 1: 44.

15. Guillermo Lohmann Villena, *Las minas de Huancavelica en los siglos XVI y XVII* (Lima: PUCP, 1998), 27–28. See also, Nicolas A. Robins, *Mercury, Mining and Empire: The Human and Ecological Cost of Colonial Silver Mining in the Andes* (Bloomington: University of Indiana Press, 2011.)

16. Salas de Coloma, *Estructura colonial del poder,* 1: 47–48.

17. Guillermo Lohmann Villena, ed. *Francisco de Toledo. Disposiciones gubernativas para el virreinato del Perú, 1569–80,* 2 vols. (Seville: Escuela de Estudios Hispanoamericanos, 1986–89); John Hemming, *The Conquest of the Incas* (London: Sphere Books, 1972), 391, 505.

18. Salas de Coloma, *Estructura colonial del poder,* 1: 54, 63–68, 83.

19. Jiménez de la Espada, *Relaciones geográficas Perú,* 1: 212–13; and Xavier Pello, "Los últimos días de Luis Jerónimo de Oré (1554–1630): un nuevo documento biográfico," *Bulletin del Instituto Francés de Estudios Andinos* 29:2 (2000), 163.

20. Salas de Coloma, *Estructura colonial del poder,* 1: 63–68, 83, 118. The title of *don* for men was given to those of special merit, in this case Don Gerónimo received the mayorazgo. *Doña* was easier to secure for European women and for the indigenous elite.

21. Steve J. Stern, *Peru's Indian Peoples and the Challenge of Spanish Colonialism. Huamanga to 1640* (Madison: University of Wisconsin Press, 1982), 170, states Gerónimo de Oré married an "Inca noblewoman" by 1574.

22. BNP, Z328, and Z330. For charges of mistreatment see Salas de Coloma, *Obrajes de Canaria,* 37, from BNP, A336. Salas de Coloma also notes, 40, that after Gerónimo's death, the heirs received a pension; see AHN, Residencias 23, c. 62, 34r–v; and BNP, B1485.

23. Salas de Coloma, *Estructura colonial del poder,* 1998, 1: 83–86. By the early seventeenth century there were suits and countersuits between the parties over the properties and income. Salas de Coloma provides details from the ANP, Real Audiencia, Causas Civiles, leg. 6, cuad. 19.

24. AGI, Lima, 136.

25. AGI, Lima, 136.

26. Salas de Coloma, *Estructura colonial del poder,* 1998, 1: 84. Serpa could be spelled with an initial Ç, S, or Z.

27. Thanks to Nicanor Domínguez for bringing this to our attention: "Pidiéndonos que en nombre de todos suplicácemos a Su Magestad": los poderes de los incas cuzqueños al capitán Garcilaso de la Vega, a don Melchor Carlos Ynga, a don Alonso Fernández de Mesa y a fray Jerónimo de Oré, OFM (1604)," in *Garcilasismo creativo y crítico: nueva antología,* eds. Eduardo González Viaña and José Antonio Mazzotti (Salem, Lima, New York: Axiara Editions y Academia Norteamericana de la Lengua Española (ANLE), 2016), 166, ftn 65. Based on Stern, *Huamanga,* 256, ftn. 43. The original dowry document is in the Archivo Regional de Ayacucho, Notariales, Escribano Francisco Navarrete, leg. 41 (1615–30), 209r–13v.

28. Jane E. Mangan, *Transatlantic Obligations: Creating the Bonds of Family in Conquest-era Peru and Spain* (Oxford: Oxford University Press, 2016).

29. *Compendio de los comentarios extendidos por el maestro Antonio Gómez, a las ochenta y tres leyes de Toro* (Madrid: Joseph Deblando, 1785).

2. The First Creole Generation: Youth on the Frontier

1. BNP, C341, 52r–56v. The document was originally in the archive of Lima's Franciscan monastery and was moved to the manuscript collection of Peru's National Library where N. D. Cook encountered it in the 1970s. It has recently been digitized. See Juan López de Velasco, *Geografía y descripción universal de las Indias* (Madrid: Real Academia de la Historia, 1894).

2. Reginaldo de Lizárraga, ed. *Descripción del Perú. Tucumán, Río de la Plata y Chile* [1595–1609], Ignacio Ballesteros (Madrid: Historia 16, 1986), 168. Lizárraga was the immediate predecesor of Oré in the diocese of La Imperial, Concepción; Diego de Córdova y Salinas, *Chronica franciscana de las provincias del Perú* [1651] (Washington, DC: Academy of American Franciscan History, 1957), 346, takes a similar view of the Oré brothers, concluding that the Andean peoples "held them as fathers, mothers and teachers, physicians and nurses."

3. For childhood in the colonial period see Bianca Premo, *Children of the Father King: Youth, Authority and Legal Minority in Colonial Lima* (Chapel Hill: University of North Carolina Press, 2005).

4. Lizárraga, *Descripción del Perú*, 253. See Rebecca Earle, *The Body of the Conquistador: Food, Race and the Colonial Experience in Spanish America, 1492–1700* (Cambridge: Cambridge University Press, 2012), 50–51; Joanne Rappaport, *The Disappearing Mestizo: Configuring Difference in the Colonial New Kingdom of Granada* (Durham: Duke University Press, 2014), 19. Juan de Pineda (1558–1637) was Jesuit theologian and philosopher.

5. Lizárraga, *Descripción del Perú*, 168.

6. There are innumerable works on the movement. See Manuel Burga, *Nacimiento de una utopía. Muerte y resurrección de los incas* (Lima: Instituto de Apoyo Agrario, 1988), 102–16. See also Jeremy Mumford, "The Taki Onquoy and the Andean Nation: Sources and Interpretations," *Latin American Research Review* 33, no. 1 (1998): 150–65; Kenneth Mills, *Idolatry and Its Enemies. Colonial Andean Religion and Extirpation, 1640–1750* (Princeton: Princeton University Press, 1997), 17, 48–52; Juan Carlos Estenssoro Fuchs, *Del paganismo a la santidad. La incorporación de los indios del Perú al Catolicismo, 1532–1750* (Lima: 2003), 130–37; Sabine MacCormack, *Religion in the Andes: Vision and Imagination in Early Colonial Peru* (Princeton: Princeton University Press, 1991), 181–87, and the same author's "Pachacuti: Miracles, Punishments, and Last Judgment. Visionary Past and Prophetic Future in Early Colonial Peru," *American Historical Review* 93 (1988): 960–1006. Stern, *Humanga*, 51–59, views the movement as resistance to the outsiders, while others view it as millenarian, see Marco Curatola, "Mito y milenarismo en los Andes: Taki Onqoy a Inkarrí. La visión de un pueblo invicto," *Allpanchis* 10 (1977): 64–92. See also Franklin Pease G. Y., *Los últimos incas del Cuzco* (Lima: Instituto Nacional de la Cultura, 2004), 225–27.

7. Pedro M. Guibovich Pérez, "Nota preliminar," in *El retorno de las huacas,* ed. Luis Millones (Lima: Instituto de Estudios Peruanos, 1990), 25. See also Juan Ossio, ed., *Ideología mesiánica del mundo andino* (Lima: Ignacio Prado Pastor, 1973).

8. There are a dozen meanings of *vicario* in Spanish associated with religious administration of the Catholic Church. The word used alone, as often occurs in the documents, needs to be understood in context, for example, if in reference to a convent it would be a supervisor of nuns of his order. The *vicario general*, designated by a bishop to officially act on his behalf. Lacking an English equivalent we use the Spanish term.

9. "Información de servicios (Huamanga, 1570)," 29, 93.
10. "Información de servicios (Huamanga, 1570)," 111.
11. Cook, *Tasa de la visita general*, 270.
12. "Información de servicios (Huamanga, 1570)," 157.
13. "Información de servicios (Huamanga, 1570)," 113.
14. "Información de servicios (Huamanga, 1570)," 124.
15. "Información de servicios (Huamanga, 1570)," 131.
16. "Información de servicios (Huamanga, 1570)," 130.
17. "Información de servicios (Huamanga, 1570)," 132.
18. "Información de servicios (Huamanga, 1570)," 130.
19. "Información de servicios (Huamanga, 1570)," 130.
20. Cook, *Tasa de la visita general*, 276–77. There were 778 tributaries and a total of 2,987 Indians during the visita general with 2,000 pesos yearly income.

3. The Oré Family: Mythohistory

1. Oré, *Symbolo Catholico Indiano*, 31v–32r.
2. Lizárraga, *Descripción del Perú*, 168, "A citizen of this city named Sancho [sic.] de Ure . . . , constructed a convent for nuns of Santa Clara."
3. Kathryn Burns, *Colonial Habits: Convents and the Spiritual Economy of Cuzco, Peru* (Durham: Duke University Press, 1999), 2–23. For study of the Andean recogimiento see Nancy E. Van Deusen, *Between the Sacred and the Worldly: The Institutional and Cultural Practice of Recogimiento in Colonial Lima* (Stanford: Stanford University Press, 2001).
4. Burns, *Colonial Habits*, 24–40. Nancy E. Van Deusen, *The Souls of Purgatory: The Spiritual Diary of a Seventeenth Century Afro-Peruvian Mystic, Ursula de Jesús* (Albuquerque: University of New Mexico Press, 2004), 1–77.
5. BNP, Z328, Z330, and C341, 52r–56r.
6. Burns, *Colonial Habits*, 107–109.
7. Salas de Coloma, *Obrajes de Canaria*, 48, states a copy of the document is in BNP, Z316.
8. Antonio San Cristóbal Sebastián, *Esplendor del Barroco en Ayacucho. Retablos y arquitectura religiosa en Huamanga* (Lima: Banco Latino/Ediciones Peisa, 1999), 32. He notes references to Morisco artisans in the city's cabildo records. He contends that the facades of both the church of the monastery of San Francisco (1552) and the convent of Santa Clara (1568) are among a handful of remaining Renaissance facades in Peru, 40–41.
9. Córdova y Salinas, *Crónica franciscana del Perú*, 834. See also Burns, *Colonial Habits*, 33. There was great flexibility in naming children in the early modern Spanish world. Family names could be of either parent, often with preference for the most important of the two families, or of

grandparents, or other relatives. Signatures were inconsistent, as we see Luis Gerónimo de Oré's varied during his lifetime.

10. The Pentecost fluctuates between 10 May and 13 June.

11. Córdova y Salinas, *Crónica franciscana del Perú*, 833–38. Friar Medellín was later Santiago de Chile's bishop.

12. Jiménez de la Espada, *Relaciones geográficas de Indias*, 1: 199.

13. Lizárraga, *Descripción del Perú*, 168–69.

14. BNP, C341, 52r–56r; Córdova y Salinas, *Crónica franciscana del Perú*, 837; Lizárraga, *Descripción del Perú*, 168–69. She died about 1586; see Salas de Coloma, *Estructura colonial del poder*, 1: 63–68, and 118; Cook, "Viviendo en las márgenes del imperio," 13.

15. AGI, Patronato 133, ramo 4. See María Elena Martínez, *Genealogical Fictions. Limpieza de Sangre, Religion, and Gender in Colonial Mexico* (Stanford: Stanford University Press, 2008), especially 173–99 regarding service reports. Lockhart, *Men of Cajamarca*, scrutinized the reports and notarial records and his cautionary warnings are amplified by recent specialists.

16. Evaristo San Cristóval, *Apendice al diccionario histórico-biográfico del Perú*, 4 vols. (Lima: Libreria e Imprenta Gil, 1936) 2: 53–54. San Cristóval took his account from Peruvian educator and feminist Elvira García y García, *La mujer peruana a través de los siglos*, 2 vols., (Lima: Imprenta Americana, 1925–25), 1: 121. The dismissive comment about García y García's work on women in Peru's history by Raúl Porras Barrenechea, *Fuentes históricas peruanas* (Lima: Instituto Raúl Porras Barrenechea, 1963), 326, reflects the pervasive views of women. He questions the text's accuracy, contemptuously characterizing the volumes as an "arsenal of undocumented romantic naivites."

4. Franciscan Novice in the Inca Capital

1. López de Velasco, *Geografía de las Indias*, 477. Cuzco is described also by Balthasar Ramírez, "Descripción del reyno del Pirú [1597]" in *Juicio de límites entre el Perú y Bolivia, prueba peruana*, ed. Victor M. Maúrtua (Barcelona, 1906), 1: 321. Lizárraga, *Descripción del Perú*, 169–71; AGI, Patronato 133, ramo 4. See also the classic novel by Thornton Wilder, *The Bridge of San Luis Rey* (New York: A. & C. Boni, 1928).

2. Cieza de León, *Crónica del Perú. Primera parte*, 316.

3. Victor Angles Vargas, *Historia del Cusco (Cusco Colonial)*, (Lima: Industrial Gráfica, 1983), 435–36, 443–49; Antonine Tibesar, *Franciscan Beginnings in Colonial Peru* (Washington, DC: Academy of American Franciscan History, 1953), 70.

4. López de Velasco, *Geografía de las Indias*, 479–80. There are numerous studies of early Spanish Cuzco, with varying estimates of its autochthonous population, see Noble David Cook, *Demographic Collapse: Indian Peru, 1520–1620* (Cambridge: Cambridge University Press, 1981), 214–15.

5. López de Velasco, *Geografía de las Indias*, 477–78. See Francisco Esteve Barba, *Historiografía indiana* (Madrid: Editorial Gredos, 1964), 113–14; James C. Murray, *Spanish Chronicles of the Indies: Sixteenth Century* (New York: Twayne Publishers, 1994), 117–18.

6. Ramírez, "Descripción del reyno del Pirú," 1: 331; Lizárraga, *Descripción del Perú*, 174.

7. Oré, *Symbolo Catholico Indiano*, 32r–v.
8. Francisco Morales Padrón, *La ciudad del quinientos. Historia de Sevilla*, 2nd ed., corrected. (Seville: Universidad de Sevilla, 1977), 286–88.
9. AGI, Lima, 308.
10. See Carolyn Dean, *Inka bodies and the body of Christ: Corpus Christi in colonial Cuzco, Peru* (Durham: Duke University Press, 1999), for Cuzco's procession.
11. Hemming, *Conquest of the Incas*, 442–49, 505.
12. Baltasar de Ocampo, *An account of the Province of Vilcapampa and a Narrative of the Execution of the Inca Tupac Amaru (1610)*. Translated by Sir Clements Markham, KCB, 1907 (Cambridge, Ontario: Publications, Peruvian Series, 1999).
13. Hemming, *Conquest of the Incas*, 447–50.
14. Oré, *Symbolo Catholico Indiano*, 42r.
15. Oré, *Symbolo Catholico Indiano*, 21r–v.
16. Oré, *Symbolo Catholico Indiano*, 37v.
17. Oré, *Symbolo Catholico Indiano*, 41v. Oré's observation is similar to Pedro de Cieza de León, *The Discovery and Conquest of Peru*, trans. and eds. Alexandra Parma Cook and Noble David Cook (Durham: Duke University Press, 1998), 257.
18. Guillermo Lohmann Villena, "La restitución por conquistadores y encomenderos: un aspecto de la incidencia Lascasiana en el Perú," *Anuario de Estudios Americanos* 23 (1966): 21–89. For a brief life of Las Casas see Lawrence A. Clayton, *Bartolomé de las Casas and the Conquest of the Americas* (Malden, MA: Wiley-Blackwell, 2011), 145–48; for a detailed study see Clayton's *Bartolomé de las Casas: A Biography* (Cambridge: Cambridge University Press, 2012).

5. Preparations for a Religious Life: Lima and the University

1. López de Velasco, *Geografía de las Indias*, 466.
2. See Paul Charney, *Indian Society in the Valley of Lima, Peru 1532–1824* (Landham, MD: University Press of America, 2001); Alejandra B. Osorio, *Inventing Lima: Baroque Modernity in Peru's South Sea Metropolis* (New York: Palgrave Macmillan, 2008); and Noble David Cook, ed., *Padrón de los indios de Lima en 1613* (Lima: UNMSM, 1968).
3. The traditional date of Lima's foundation was 6 January, the feast of the Epiphany, hence the reference to the three Magi. Other evidence points to 18 January as the foundation date, see María Dolores Crespo Rodríguez, *Arquitectura doméstica de la Ciudad de los Reyes (1535–1750)* (Seville: CSIC y Universidad de Sevilla, 2006), 31.
4. Oré, *Symbolo Catholico Indiano*, 28v–29r. There were 14,262 people in Lima in 1600. It grew to about 25,154 according to the 1614 census of Viceroy Marqués de Montesclaros. The religious composed about 7 percent of the population: 894 men and 826 women, see Cook, *Padrón de los indios de Lima*, ii–iii.
5. Ramírez, "Descripción del reyno del Pirú," 1: 313–14.
6. Antonio San Cristóbal Sebastián, *Arquitectura virreynal religiosa de Lima* (Lima: Studium, 1988), 124–29.
7. Benjamin Gento Sanz OFM, *San Francisco de Lima* (Lima: Imprenta Torres Aguirre,

1945), 109–25. See San Cristóbal Sebastián, *Arquitectura religiosa de Lima,* 124–29; and Judith M. Mansilla, "Firm Foundations: Rebuilding the Early Modern State in Lima, Peru after the Earthquake of 1687," (PhD diss., Florida International University, 2016).

8. Lohmann Villena, ed. *Francisco de Toledo. Disposiciones gubernativas.* See also Rubén Vargas Ugarte, *Historia general del Perú,* 10 vols. (Lima: Editor Carlos Milla Batres, 1981), 2: 272.

9. Cobo, *Fundación de Lima,* 231–45; Roberto Levillier, *Don Francisco de Toledo, supremo organizador del Perú* (Madrid: Espasa-Calpe, 1935); and the same author's *Don Francisco de Toledo, supremo organizador del Perú, informaciones sobre los incas (1570–1572)* (Buenos Aires: Imprenta Porter Hnos.," 1940). Luis Antonio Eguiguren, *Historia de la universidad. Tomo I. La universidad en el siglo XVI* (Lima: Imprenta Santa María, 1951), 31–163.

10. Balthasar Ramírez, "Descripción del Pirú," 319. It is near the present Congress building.

11. Pedro Guibovich Pérez, *En defensa de Dios. Estudios y documentos sobre la Inquisición en el Perú* (Lima: Ediciones del Congreso del Perú, 1998), 37; Paulino Castañeda Delgado and Pilar Hernández Aparicio, *La Inquisición de Lima. Tomo I (1570–1635)* (Madrid: Editorial DEIMOS, 1989), 299–306; Rubén Vargas Ugarte, *Historia de la Iglesia en el Perú,* 5 vols. (Lima: Imprenta Santa María, 1954), 1: 386–89; José Toribio Medina, *Historia del Tribunal del Santo Oficio de la Inquisición en Lima (1569–1820),* 2 vols. (Santiago de Chile: Gutenberg, 1887).

12. Harry Kelsey, *Sir Francis Drake: The Queen's Pirate* (New Haven: Yale University Press, 1998), 93–204, is based on primary research in Spanish, English and other archives and documentary collections. Samuel Eliot Morison, *The Great Explorers: The European Discovery of America* (New York: Oxford University Press, 1978), 674–721. John Oxenham, also Oxnam, was executed in Lima on 30 September 1580.

13. *Libros de Cabildos de Lima,* 9: 5–29.

14. *Libros de Cabildos de Lima,* 9: 29–35.

15. Vargas Ugarte, *Historia general del Perú,* 2: 283–84, dates Mogrovejo's arrival on 11 May 1581.

16. Vargas Ugarte, *Historia general del Perú,* 2: 271–72.

17. AHPS, Protocolos 7796, 2132r–2134r; 2150r–60r; 2211r–13v. Notarial documents signed 23 and 29 August 1580 provide the details, including the names of the agents to whom the shipment was entrusted in Seville, Nombre de Dios and Lima.

18. Vargas Ugarte, *Historia general del Perú,* 2: 283–84.

19. José Antonio Benito, ed., *Libro de visitas de Santo Toribio de Mogrovejo (1593–1605)* (Lima: PUCP, 2006).

20. Polo, "Luis Jerónimo de Oré," 74–91.

21. Dionisio was ordained on 14 November 1584. Polo, "Luis Jerónimo de Oré," 74–91; Miguel Angel Espinoza Soria, *La catequesis en Fray Luis Jerónimo de Oré: Un aporte a la nueva evangelización* (Lima: Convento de los Descalzos, 2012), 6.

22. Federico Richter, "Primera Parte: Fray Luis Jerónimo de Oré (biografía) 1554–1630. Segunda parte: Información del oficio en la Real Audiencia de La Plata del Perú, de los méritos del biografiado (3 piezas)," in *Anales de la Provincia de los Doce Apóstoles de Lima* (Huamanga: Imprenta de la Universidad de San Cristóbal de Huamanga, 1986), 1–41.

23. Buenaventura de Salinas y Córdova, *Memorial de las historias de nuevo mundo Piru* (Lima: UNMSM, 1957), 176–77; and Polo, "Luis Jerónimo de Oré," 74–91.

6. Mogrovejo: Third Church Council of Lima and the Translators

1. Raúl Porras Barrenechea, *Los cronistas del Perú (1528–1650) y otros ensayos,* ed. Franklin Pease G. Y. (Lima: Banco del Crédito del Perú, 1986), 347–55, states that Molina, an expert in Quechua, was one of the translators participating in the Council. For an English edition of Molina's work, see *Account of the Fables and Rites of the Incas,* ed. Brian S. Bauer, et al. (Austin: University of Texas Press, 2011).

2. For biographical sketches see José Antonio Benito, "Obispos participantes en el III Limense," in *Tercer Concilio Limense (1583–1591),* ed. Luis Martínez Ferrer (Lima: Facultad Pontificia y Civil de Teología de Lima, 2017), 99–110.

3. Antonio García, "La reforma del Concilio Tercero de Lima," in *Doctrina cristiana y catecismo para instrucción de los indios,* ed. Luciano Pereña (Madrid: CSIC, 1986), 181.

4. Francisco Mateos, "Introducción," *Obras del P. José de Acosta* (Madrid: Atlas, 1954), xiv–xvi.

5. García, "La reforma del Concilio Tercero," 182–91. "Provisión para que en estos reynos no se use de otro Cathecismo ni otro Confessionario . . . y para que todos los que tienen Doctrina tengan el dicho Cathecismo y Confessionario y Sermones." The author of the introduction of the *Tercero cathecismo . . . ,* states that this massive text of about 430 pages was produced by some of the same group that wrote the 1583 catecismo. A copy of this work is in the Biblioteca Nacional de Madrid, Biblioteca Digital Hispánica, accessed 26 October 2020, http://bdh-rd.bne.es/viewer.vm?id=0000012950&page=1

6. Mateos, "Introducción," xvi.

7. Sabine Hyland, *The Jesuits and the Incas: The Extraordinary Life of Padre Blas Valera, S.J.* (Ann Arbor: University of Michigan Press, 2003), 143–48. Sabine Hyland, "Blas Valera (1544–1597)," in *Guide to Documentary Sources for Andean Studies 1530–1900,* ed. Joanne Pillsbury, 3 vols. (Norman: University of Oklahoma Press, 2008), 3: 694–96.

8. Alan Durston, *Pastoral Quechua: A History of Christian Translation in Colonial Peru, 1550–1650* (Notre Dame: University of Notre Dame Press, 2007), 337–38.

9. *Tercero Concilio Limense 1582–1583. Versión castellana original de los decretos con el sumario del Segundo Concilio Limense,* ed. Enrique Bartra, SJ (Lima: Facultad Pontificia y Civil de Teología de Lima, 1982), 186–87. The acts of the council were not immediately published. For the complications prior to final authorizations and printing see *Tercero Concilio Limense (1582–1591). Edición bilingüe de los decretos,* ed. Luis Martínez Ferrer (Lima and Rome: Facultad Pontificia y Civil de Teología de Lima, 2017); see editor Martínez Ferrer's "Estudio histórico documental," 37–126.

10. *Tercero Concilio Limense 1582–1583,* 188–91. Acosta (1540–1600), became a Jesuit novice in 1554 and taught theology in several *colegios* in Castile. He arrived in Lima in 1572 and by 1573 in Cuzco was involved with Viceroy Toledo's general inspection and resettlement project. Acosta studied indigenous languages in Juli and collected information on indigenous peoples, culture, and environment in places he visited. Acosta and Oré coincided various times before the Jesuit's return to Spain. Before leaving Peru in 1586 Acosta completed the core manuscript for the *Historia natural y moral de las Indias,* ed. Fermín del Pino-Díaz (Madrid: CSIC, 2008), and the *De Procuranda Indorum Salute,* ed. Francisco Mateos (Madrid: Atlas, 1952). See Francisco Esteve Barba, *Historiografía indiana* (Madrid: Editorial Gredos, 1964), 102–111, 196–200; Porras

Barrenechea, *Los cronistas del Perú*, 376–87; David A. Brading, *The First America: The Spanish Monarchy, Creole Patriots, and the Liberal State, 1492–1867* (Cambridge: Cambridge University Press, 1991), 184–95; Claudio M. Burgaleta, *José de Acosta, S.J. (1540–1600): His Life and Thought* (Chicago: Jesuit Way, 1999).

11. Rodolfo Cerrón-Palomino, "El Nebrija Indiano," in *Fray Domingo de S. Thomas, Grammatica o Arte de la Lengua General de los Indios de los Reynos del Perú* [1560], ed. Rodolfo Cerrón-Palomino (Madrid: Ediciones de Cultura Hispánica, 1994), i–vi.

12. Cerrón-Palomino, "El Nebrija Indiano," iii–vi.

13. BNP, C341, 28r, 55v; and AGI, Lima 126.

14. *Tercero Concilio Limense 1582–1583*, 55. In a 1586 testimony in an Inquisition case Villacarrillo claimed he was seventy. Archivo Histórico Nacional, Madrid (AHN), Inquisicion 1641, exp. 2.

15. Martínez Ferrer, "Estudio histórico documental," 102–103.

16. Martínez Ferrer, "Estudio histórico documental," 105–106.

17. Rolena Adorno, "Felipe Guaman Poma de Ayala: Native Writer and Litigant in Early Colonial Peru," in *The Human Condition in Colonial Latin America*, ed. Kenneth J. Andrien, 2nd ed. (New York: Rowman & Littlefield, 2013), 184.

18. Durston, *Pastoral Quechua*, 148; Durston adds (338n15): Oré "probably lacked the rank and the institutional backing necessary to have played much of a role in the translation, especially given the marginalization of the mendicant orders in the council."

19. BNP, C341, 60r–v; see Enrique T. Bartra, SJ, "Los autores del Catecismo del Tercer Concilio Limense," *Mercurio Peruano* 470 (1967): 359–72.

20. BNP, C341, 28r. This testimony was taken in Lima about the time that Oré was in Peru prior to his journey to Chile.

21. This confirmation of Oré's presence comes from a document originally in the Archivo Arzobispal de Lima according to Julián Heras, OFM, in correspondence 4 April 1998. Friar Heras encountered notice of it in the paradoxical edition of texts "found" and edited by Augustinian Friar Jesús Viscarra Fabre, *Copacabana de los Incas. Documentos auto-ligüisticos e isografiados del Aymáru-Aymára* (La Paz: Palza Hermanos, 1901). Accessed on 8.8.2021, http://bdigital.bnp.pe/bnp/recursos/2/flippingbook/1000089091/files/assets/basic-html/page-1.html. It included an early seventeenth-century text by Augustinian Friar Baltasar de Salas. Viscarra Fabre's note 40 on pages 28 and 29 provides the text of this document extracted from the Archivo Arzobispal de Lima. The verisimilitude of various assertions in Viscarra's book has been challenged, but there are reasons to validate several of the documentary sources he consulted and transcribed, including this text. Unfortunately, Viscarra failed to provide an archival notation.

22. Licentiate Menacho, was Lima's cathedral canon and interacted with participants regularly. He was secretary for the Third and Fourth (1592) Church Councils of Lima and was active in publication of the decisions of the Fifth Council (1601). He continued as canon into 1631 when he joined others advocating collection of evidence on the life of Archbishop Mogrovejo needed to justify his canonization. See Mendiburu, *Diccionario histórico biográfico*, 7: 297.

23. Luis Arroyo, OFM, *Comisarios Generales del Perú* (Madrid: CSIC y el Instituto Santo Toribio de Mogrovejo, 1950), 55–76; Tibesar, *Franciscan Beginnings*, 29n23.

24. Tibesar, *Franciscan Beginnings*, 31n32. Bishop Trejo established the University of Córdoba

in 1613. José María Liqueno, *Fray Fernando de Trejo y Sanabria, fundador de la universidad* (Córdoba: Bautista Cubas, 1916), accessed 27 October 2020, http://ufdc.ufl.edu/AA00012157/00001/17x. A fourth Franciscan, Bernardino de Cárdenas Ponce, a creole from La Paz, participated in the sessions of the Third Church Council. Pedro de Peralta Barnuevo Rocha y Benavides, author of *Lima Fundada o Conquista del Perú* (Lima 1732), writes that he and Oré were among the important intellects to study in the order's schools. See Tibesar, *Franciscan Beginnings,* 31n33.

25. Regarding Mercedarians, see Ellen G. Friedman, *Spanish Captives in North Africa in the Early Modern Age* (Madison: University of Wisconsin Press, 1983).

26. Accessed 27 July 2015, http://www.catholic-hierarchy.org/bishop/benrta.html. See Salvador Miranda, accessed 3 March 2016, http://www2.fiu.edu/~mirandas/obispos/bio-e.htm. Miranda points out that there has been confusion over the birthplace of Enríques de Almendariz. Note also José Antonio Garí y Siumell, *Biblioteca mercedaria, o sea Escritores de la Celestial, Real y Militar Orden de la Merced Redención de Cautivos* (Madrid: Herederos de la Viuda Pla, 1875), 94. Apparently, he published (1615) a "Carta al R.P. Fr. Alonso Remon," and the following year, *Relación histórica de lo espiritual y temporal de la isla de Cuba.* See also, accessed 3 March 2016, http://www.mcnbiografias.com/app-bio/do/show?key=enriquez-de-armendariz-alonso.

27. AGI, Contratación 5321, No. 2, reg. 10, 8v. For Enríques de Almendariz' career, see *Los Mercedarios en el Perú en el siglo xvi,* ed. Victor M. Barriaga (Arequipa: La Colmena, 1942), 3:190, 208–209, 213, 242, 292–93, 345. See also AGI, Charcas 84.

7. Franciscan Dilemmas

1. Julia McClure, *The Franciscan Invention of the New World* (Cham, Switzerland: Palgrave Macmillan, 2017), 1–30. Martin Nesvig, *Forgotten Franciscans: Writings from an Inquisitional Theorist, a Heretic, and an Inquisitional Deputy* (University Park: Pennsylvania State University Press, 2011) points out variations regarding education and training of the Nahua in central New Spain and differences over translation of religious texts.

2. John Leddy Phelan, *The Millenial Kingdom of the Franciscans in the New World* (Berkeley: University of California Press, 1970) and McClure, *The Franciscan Invention.* For the darker side of the early Franciscans see Inga Clendinnen, *Ambivalent Conquests: Maya and Spaniard in Yucatan, 1517–1570* (Cambridge: Cambridge University Press, 1987). See also Adriaan C. Van Oss, *Catholic Colonialism: A Parish History of Guatemala, 1524–1821* (Cambridge: Cambridge University Press, 1986); and John Frederick Schwaller, *The Church and Clergy in Sixteenth-century Mexico* (Albuquerque: University of New Mexico Press, 1987). The classic survey is Tibesar, *Franciscan beginnings.* Franciscan documentary evidence abounds in *Historia de las misiones franciscanas,* ed. Bernardino Izaguirre, 14 vols. (Lima, 1922–30). Also see Julián Heras, *Aporte de los Franciscanos a la evangelización del Perú* (Lima: Editora Latina, 1992) and his "Los franciscanos en el valle del Colca (Arequipa) dos siglos y medio de evangelización," in *La evangelización del Perú, siglos XVI–XVII* (Arequipa: Actas del Congreso Peruano de Historia Eclesiástica, 1990), 379–449.

3. Fernando de Armas Medina, *Cristianización del Perú (1532–1600)* (Seville: Escuela de Estudios Hispanoamericanos, 1953), 487–518.

4. Tibesar, *Franciscan Beginnings,* 98–99.

5. McClure, *The Franciscan Invention*, 35–39; Bernardino de Sahagún, *Historia general de las cosas de Nueva España*, ed. Ángel María Garibay K. (México: Editorial Porrúa, 1992). Focher was a French Franciscan who traveled to New Spain by 1540. He died in 1572 and his student, Diego Valadés edited and printed his text in Perugia in 1574. Valadés (1533–1582), a Franciscan mestizo, was a linguist, theologian, engraver, and historian. His lavishly illustrated *Rhetorica christiana ad concionandi, et oradi vsum accommodata* (Perugia 1579) was aimed for training doctrineros, like Oré's *Symbolo catholico indiano*.

6. Archivum Sancti Isidori Hibernorum (ASIH, leg. 2/10); Antonine Tibesar generously shared a photocopy of this document in a letter, 16 January 1978, stating that "There is no date on this document, however, it is bound in with other Peruvian documents sent to Rome in 1585 for the General of the Order, Gonzaga, who incorporated same in his volume 'De origine ordinis Seraphici.'" Francesco (Annibalae) Gonzaga (1546–1620), born near Mantua, was at the court of Philip II expecting a military career but was swayed to enter the order. He studied at the Franciscan monastery in Alcalá de Henares and others, and was ordained in Toledo in 1570. He returned to Italy in 1573 and increasingly assumed a role in affairs of church and state, traveling around Europe. From 1583 to 1587 he recruited friars in Spain and Portugal to go to Brazil, the Philippines and China. His four-volume, *De origine Seraphicae Religionis Franciscanae eiusque progressibus, de regularis Observantiae institutione, administrationis form, legibus, eiusque ordinis propagatione*, was published in Rome in 1587. Although there are copies in Germany, I have been unable to see the work. Details accessed 8 April 2016, www.treccani.it/enciclopedia/francesco-gonzaga_res-2e32f583–87ee-11dc-8e9d-0016357eee51_(Dizionario-Biografico)/.

7. Tibesar, *Franciscan Beginnings*, 43; Archivo San Francisco de Lima (ASFL), reg. 15, part 5, "Parecer de las doctrinas de los Collaguas"; Córdova y Salinas, *Chronica franciscana* [1651], 330. Monzón was killed in Africa.

8. BNP, B124, 200r.

9. Tibesar, *Franciscan Beginnings*, 35–40. The incredible beauty of the valley was photographed by Robert Shippee, "A Forgotten Valley of Peru," *The National Geographic Magazine* 65, no. 1 (1934): 110–132.

10. Steven A. Wernke, "La producción y desestabilización del dominio colonial en el proceso reduccional en el Valle del Colca, Perú," in *Reducciones: La concentración forzada de las poblaciones indígenas en el Virreinato del Perú*, Akira Saito and Claudia Rosas Lauro, eds. (Lima: PUCP, 2017), 394–407.

11. ASFL, reg. 15, part 5; Córdova y Salinas, *Chronica franciscana*, 330–31; BNM, 2950; and Diego de Mendoza, *Chronica de la Provincia de San Antonio de los Charcas* [Madrid, 1664] (La Paz: Editorial Casa Municipal de la Cultura Franz Tamayo, 1976), 41–42, 49–51.

12. AGI, Charcas 142.

13. Tibesar, *Franciscan Beginnings*, 65–68.

14. BNP, C341.

15. Garcilaso de la Vega, el Inca, *Royal Commentaries of the Incas, and General History of Peru* [1609], trans. and ed. Harold V. Livermore, 2 vols. (Austin: University of Texas Press, 1966). For the impact of the wars on the Colca Valley see Noble David Cook, with Alexandra Parma Cook, *People of the Volcano: Andean Counterpoint in the Colca Valley, Peru* (Durham: Duke University Press, 2007), 39–46.

16. This complicated story is untangled in Alexandra Parma Cook and Noble David Cook, *Good Faith and Truthful Ignorance: A Case of Transatlantic Bigamy* (Durham: Duke University Press, 1991).

17. For a detailed description of the valley see Cook and Cook, *People of the Volcano*, 3–28.

18. Nicholas Griffiths, *The Cross and the Serpent: Religious Repression and Resurgence in Colonial Peru* (Norman: University of Oklahoma Press, 1996), 6–8; and Mills, *Idolatry and Its Enemies*.

19. AGI, Justicia 471; Tibesar, *Franciscan Beginnings*, 35–50; Heras, *Aporte de los Franciscanos*.

8. Defender of Franciscan Rights

1. ASFL, Registro 9, 375r–77r., Registros 13, 15; Juan de Ulloa Mogollón, "Relación de la provincia de los Collaguas (1586)," in *Relaciones geográficas de Indias, Perú*, ed. Marcos Jiménez de la Espada, 3 vols. (Madrid: Atlas, 1965), 1:332.

2. ASFL, reg. 13, 323r. (quote); AGI, Lima 131; BNM, 2950, 81v–82v. For other examples see Cook and Cook, *People of the Volcano*.

3. ASFL, reg. 13, 220r–22r; AGI, Lima 131; For the Conde del Villar see Alexandra Parma Cook and Noble David Cook, *The Plague Files: Crisis Management in Sixteenth-Century Seville* (Baton Rouge: Louisiana State University Press, 2009), 263–72; Miguel Costa Vigo, "Patronage and Bribery in Sixteenth-Century Peru: the Government of Viceroy Conde del Villar and the Visita of Licenciado Alonso Fernández de Bonilla," (PhD diss., Florida International University, 2005).

4. ASFL, reg. 13, part 3. BNM, 2950, 81v–82v. Villacarrillo died in 1588; see Arroyo, *Comisarios Generales del Perú*, 81. See also María N. Marsilli, *Hábitos perniciosos: religión andina colonial en la diócesis de Arequipa (siglos xvi al xviii)* (Santiago: Centro de Investigaciones Diego Barros Arana, 2014), 43–67; and María N. Marsilli, "'I Heard It Through the Grapevine': Analysis of an Anti-secularization Initiative in the Sixteenth-Century Arequipan Countryside, 1584–1600," *The Americas* 61 (2005): 647–72.

5. ASFL, reg. 13, 220–21; AGI, Lima 131. Cook and Cook, *People of the Volcano*, 192.

6. ASFL, reg. 13, 220r–22r, 451r–81v, 497r–98r, 505r–507v; AGI, Lima 131. See also Noble David Cook, "Tomando posesión: Luis Gerónimo de Oré y el retorno de los franciscanos a las doctrinas del valle del Colca," in *El hombre y los Andes. Homenaje a Franklin Pease*, Rafael Varón Gabai and Javier Flores Espinosa, eds. (Lima: Pontificia Universidad Católica del Perú, 2002), 2: 889–903. See also Marsilli, *Hábitos perniciosos*, 44–45. See also Patricia Seed, *Ceremonies of Possession in Europe's Conquest of the New World, 1492–1640* (Cambridge: Cambridge University Press, 1995).

7. ASFL, reg. 13, 497v.

8. ASFL, reg. 13, 497r–99v; AGI, Lima 131.

9. ASFL, reg. 13, 323r, 497r–500v; AGI, Lima 318; Vargas Ugarte, *Historia general del Perú*, 2: 206; Arroyo, *Comisarios Generales del Perú*, 89–94. ASFL, reg. 13, 618r–v; AGI, Lima 131.

10. The reference is to a ship's cargo space. Each *tonelada* was approximately 2.83 cubic meters of books.

11. AGI, Lima 317. Signatories were Friars Bernardo de Gamarra, the Provincial of Lima, and

definidores Pedro de Oré, Antonio Martínez, Christoval López, Pedro Roman, plus Francisco de Alcoçer, Hernando de Trejo, and Joan de Vega.

12. ASFL, reg. 13, 618r–v.

13. BNM, 2950, 81v.-82v (quote); ASFL, reg. 13, 323r; AGI, Lima 131.

14. Arroyo, *Comisarios Generales del Perú,* 96–98.

15. AGI, Lima 326; Vargas, *Historia del Cusco,* 259, 271; AGI, Contratación 5252, no. 2, reg. 26.

16. Marsilli, *Hábitos perniciosos,* 65–66. Her source is AGI, Lima 36, Cartas del Marqués de Montesclaros, 1611–1615, no. 10.

9. Doctrinero in the Colca Valley

1. Vargas Ugarte, *Concilios Limenses,* 2nd Council, no. 2, 28, 32, 15, 100–110.

2. Oré, *Symbolo Catholico Indiano,* 36–41. See Cook and Cook, *People of the Volcano,* 17–18, 199–211. For links between Spaniards and the Inca elite, see Mangan, *Transatlantic Obligations,* 18–46.

3. The term "transculturation," coined by Fernando Ortiz, was brought into wider usage by anthropologist Melville J. Herskovits, *Man and His Works: The Science of Cultural Anthropology* (New York: Knopf, 1948), 529. For reducciones see Jeremy Mumford, *Vertical Empire: The General Resettlement of Indians in the Colonial Andes* (Durham: Duke University Press, 2012); Steven A. Wernke, *Negotiated Settlements: Andean Communities and Landscapes Under Inka and Spanish Colonialism* (Gainesville: University Press of Florida, 2013); Akira Saito and Claudia Rosas Lauro, eds., *Reducciones: La concentración forzada de las poblaciones indígenas en el Virreinato del Perú* (Lima: PUCP, 2017); Wernke, "Proceso reduccional en el Valle del Colca," in Saito and Rosas Lauro, *Reducciones,* 387–437; and Cook and Cook, *People of the Volcano,* 79–100.

4. AGI, Lima 30; for descriptions of the churches see Luis Enrique Tord, *Templos coloniales del Colca—Arequipa* (Lima: Papelera Atlas, 1983).

5. ANP, Residencias 5, cuad. 9.

6. See Valerie Fraser, *The Architecture of Conquest: Building in the Viceroyalty of Peru, 1535–1635* (Cambridge: Cambridge University Press, 1990). In 1977 all that remained were the church and the chapel. In the late twentieth century the mayor removed the 1565 chapel to provide more seating for a soccer field; personal communications.

7. Oré, *Symbolo Catholico Indiano,* 55v.

8. John Charles, *Allies at Odds: The Andean Church and Its Indigenous Agents, 1583–1671* (Albuquerque: University of New Mexico Press, 2010), 28; Oré, *Symbolo Catholico Indiano,* 55v.

9. Oré, *"Symbolo Catholico Indiano,* 55v. See also Sally Falk Moore, *Power and Property in Inca Peru* (New York: Columbia University Press, 1958).

10. Franklin Pease G. Y., ed., *Collaguas I* (Lima: PUCP, 1977), 343.

11. Oré, *Symbolo Catholico Indiano,* 59v. For Last Rites see Luis Gerónimo de Oré, *Rituale, seu manuale peruanum, et forma brevis administrandi apud Indos sacrosancta Baptismi, Poenitentiae, Eucharistiae, Matrimonij, & Extremae unctionis Sacramenta* (Naples: Appud Io. Iacobum Carlinum & Constantinum Vitalem, 1607), 45–47. See also Gabriela Ramos, *Death and Conversion in the Andes. Lima and Cuzco, 1532–1670* (Notre Dame: Notre Dame University Press, 2010), 152–53.

Notes to Pages 83–91

12. The brief exhortation in Spanish, Quechua, and Aymara is in Oré, *Rituale, seu manuale peruanum,* 248–52, and the long form, 253–71. Oré may have modified the section on the last rites while in Italy as he refers to the Church manual of Turin, *Sacerdotale,* published in Venice, and to a small manual employed by the Capuchines. Regina Harrison, *Sin and Confession in Colonial Peru: Spanish-Quechua Penitential Texts, 1560–1650* (Austin: University of Texas Press, 2014), 223–25, examines Oré's earlier *Symbolo Catholico Indiano* and Diego de Torres Rubio's similar translation as well as Friar Pardo's much later work.

13. Oré, *Rituale, seu manuale peruanum,* 254.

14. Vargas Ugarte, *Concilios Limenses,* First Council, no. 25.

15. AGI, Lima 126; Tibesar, *Franciscan Beginnings,* 66; Ulloa Mogollón, "Relación de los Collaguas," 1: 332; APY. Libros Varios de la Iglesia de Yanque, consulted in 1977. Most of the documentation is now in the Archivo Arzobispal de Arequipa. See Laura Dierksmeier, *Charity for and by the Poor. Franciscan-Indigenous Confraternities in Mexico, 1527–1700* (Norman: University of Oklahoma Press, 2020).

16. ANP, Residencias 5, cuaderno 9; Pease, *Collaguas I,* 343; José Luis Rénique and Efraín Trelles, "Approximación demográfica: Yanque-Collaguas 1591," in Pease, *Collaguas I,* 169–89; Noble David Cook, *People of the Colca Valley: a Population Study* (Boulder: Westview Press, 1982); Cook and Cook, *People of the Volcano,* 208–31.

17. AGI, Lima 326; Mills, *Idolatry and Its Enemies,* provides a fine analysis of the process in mid-seventeenth century Peru.

18. AHN, Inquisition 1641, exp. 1. Thanks to Karoline P. Cook for bringing this case to our attention.

19. AHN, Inquisition 1641, exp.1, 379r, im. 766.

20. AHN, Inquisition 1641, exp.1, 379r, im. 766.

21. AHN, Inquisition 1641, exp.1, 379v, im.767.

22. AHN, Inquisition 1641, exp.1, 379v, im. 767.

23. AHN, Inquisition 1641, exp.1, 380v, im. 769.

24. AHN, Inquisition 1641, exp.1, 380v, im.769.

25. AHN, Inquisition 1641, exp. 1, 381r, im. 770.

26. AHN, Inquisition 1641, exp. 1, 381r, im. 770.

27. AHN, Inquisition 1641, exp. 1, 381r, im. 770.

28. AHN, Inquisition 1641, exp. 1, 374r, im. 756.

29. AHN, Inquisition 1641, exp. 1, 381r, im. 770.

10. Composing the *Symbolo Catholico Indiano*

1. See Miguel Angelo Espinosa Soria, *La Catequesis en Fray Luis Jerónimo de Oré* (Lima: Convento de los Descalzos, 2012); Catalina Andrango-Walker, *El 'Símbolo católico indiano' (1598) de Luis Jerónimo de Oré: Saberes coloniales y los problemas de la evangelización en la región andina* (Madrid: Iberoamericana-Vervuert, Biblioteca Indiana, 2018); Durston, *Pastoral Quechua,* 147–62. Durston views Oré's work (152) "as part of a broader resurgence in mendicant translation programs. This boom seems to have lasted throughout the first thirty or forty years after the council,

a period during which the mendicant orders were locked in conflict with the secular church over their autonomy in the management of their parishes." See also Charles, *Allies at Odds*; Ramos, *Death and Conversion*; and Adorno, "Guaman Poma de Ayala Native Writer."

2. Pease, *Collaguas I*, 132.

3. Cook, "Luis Jerónimo de Oré: una aproximación," 35–39; Jiménez de la Espada, *Relaciones geográficas de Indias*, 1: 326–33; and Vicente Quesada, "Derecho de Patronato," *Anales de la Academia de Filosofía y Letras*, 1 (Buenos Aries, 1910): 22–23. Lettered Andeans such as Don Diego Coro Inga often traveled back and forth to court in Spain; see José Carlos de la Puente Luna, *Andean Cosmopolitans. Seeking Justice and Rewards at the Spanish Royal Court* (Austin: University of Texas Press, 2018); Joanne Rappaport and Tom Cummins, *Beyond the Lettered City. Indigenous Literacies in the Andes* (Durham: Duke University Press, 2012).

4. AGI, Lima 371.

5. Oré, *Symbolo Catholico Indiano*, 76 in Tibesar's facsimile edition (Oré's prologue was unpaginated). Pedro Ordóñez Flores, born in Extremadura, traveled to Peru with Viceroy Toledo and assisted in preparation of the Ordinances. He was inquisitor in Lima, rector of the University of San Marcos (1580–1581) and participated in the Third Church Council as a *letrado jurista*. He returned to Spain and served as the president of the court of the Casa de la Contratación and in the Council of the Indies. He was archbishop of Santa Fe de Bogotá from 1610 until his death in 1614. See Mendiburu, *Diccionario Histórico Biográfico*, 8: 245. Both Pedro and Juan Gutiérrez Flores were government functionaries, and both served as visitadores in the southern Andes in the 1570s, causing some confusion for historians. Oré knew all three, but he knew Pedro Ordóñez Flores as a student at the university and perhaps at the Third Church Council. See Teresa Cañedo-Argüelles Fabrega, *La visita de Juan Gutiérrez Flores al Colesuyo y Pleitos por los cacicazgos de Torata y Moquegua* (Lima: PUCP, 2005), xi–xv.

6. Oré, *Symbolo Catholico Indiano*, in Tibesar's facsimile edition, 64–75.

7. Oré, *Symbolo Catholico Indiano*, 37r–v; José de Acosta, *De natura Noui Orbis libri duo; et De promulgatione Euangelij apud barbaros, siue De procuranda Indorum salute* (Salamanca: Guillelmum Foquel, 1589), and Acosta's *Historia natural y moral de las Indias* (Seville: Juan de Leon, 1590).

8. Oré, *Symbolo Catholico Indiano*, 40r–v. Molina, *Account of the Fables and Rites*, 42.

9. Oré, *Symbolo Catholico Indiano*, 42r; Agustín de Zárate, *Historia del descubrimiento y conquista del Perú* [1555], eds. Franklin Pease G. Y. and Teodoro Hampe Martínez (Lima: PUCP 1995).

10. Felipe Guaman Poma de Ayala, *El primer nueva corónica y buen gobierno*, eds. John V. Murra and Rolena Adorno. 3 vols. (Mexico: Siglo Veintiuno, 1980), 3: 997–98. Guaman Poma's note is in the last pages of his manuscript. He sometimes erred and at one point incorrectly stated the Oré text he consulted was composed by Luis Gerónimo's brother, Pedro.

11. Oré, *Symbolo Catholico Indiano*, 33v.

12. Oré, *Symbolo Catholico Indiano*, 33r–v.

13. Durston, *Pastoral Quechua*, 147; Fray Luis de Granada, *Introducción del Símbolo de la Fe* (Salamanca: Herederos de Matías Gast, 1583), accessed July 12, 2022, https://www.cervantesvirtual.com/obra-visor/introduccion-del-simbolo-de-la-fe-0/html/fedb9048-82b1-11df-acc7-002185ce6064_2.html.

14. Enrique T. Bartra, "Los autores del Catecismo del Tercer Concilio Limense," *Mercurio Peruano* 470 (1967): 359–72; the same author's *Tercer Concilio Limense: 1582–1583* (Lima: Facultad de Teología Pontificia y Civil, 1982), 61; BNP, C 341, 28r, 55v; and AGI, Lima 126.

15. Charles, *Allies at Odds*, 49.

16. Charles, *Allies at Odds*, 48.

17. Garcilaso de la Vega, el Inca, *Obras completas*, 4 vols. (Madrid: Atlas, 1960), 4: 124. Hyland, *Life of Blas Valera*, 168–80, notes Valera's influence in the translations, even as he was under tight restrictions imposed by Jesuit superiors, including José de Acosta. Hyland points out that although Acosta in 1582 voted against mestizos becoming Jesuits, the next year he advocated the ordination of mestizos to work in the doctrinas.

18. Ramos, *Death and Conversion*, 59–60. See *Symbolo Catholico Indiano*, 60v. Regarding priests and indigenous languages see also Acosta's *De Procuranda Indorum Salute* [1588], 2 vols. (Madrid: CSIC, 1984–1987).

19. Harrison, *Sin and Confession*, 64.

20. Harrison, *Sin and Confession*, 67.

21. Oré, *Symbolo Catholico Indiano*, 58r–59r.

22. Oré, *Symbolo Catholico Indiano*, 60r.

23. Martín de Azpilcueta, a theologian and jurist (1492–1586).

24. Oré, *Symbolo Catholico Indiano*, 60v.

25. Oré, *Symbolo Catholico Indiano*, 61r.

26. Oré, *Symbolo Catholico Indiano*, 61v.

27. Oré, *Symbolo Catholico Indiano*, 65v.

28. Oré, *Symbolo Catolico Indiano*, 65v.

29. Oré, *Symbolo Catolico Indiano*, 65v–66r.

30. Oré, *Symbolo Catholico Indiano*, 61v.

31. Martin Lienhard, "Indigenous Texts," in *Guide to Documentary Sources for Andean Studies 1530–1900*, ed. Joanne Pillsbury, 3 vols. (Norman: University of Oklahoma Press, 2008), 1: 94. He cites Julio E. Noriega Bernuy, *Buscando una tradición poética quechua en el Perú* (Coral Gables, FL: University of Miami, Iberian Studies Institute, 1995), 79–86. See also Raquel Chang-Rodríguez, "Luis Jerónimo de Oré y la poesía de su *Símbolo católico indiano* (1598)," *Allpanchis* 44:83–84 (2019): 149–170.

32. Margot Beyersdorff, "Oré, Luis Jerónimo de (1554–1630)," in *Guide to Documentary Sources for Andean Studies 1530–1900*, ed. Joanne Pillsbury, 3 vols. (Norman: University of Oklahoma Press, 2008), 3: 472; see also Margot Beyersdorff, "Rito y verbo en la poesía de fray Luis Jerónimo de Oré," in *Mito y simbolismo en los Andes: La figura y la palabra*, ed. Henrique Urbano (Cusco: Centro de Estudios Regionales Andinos "Bartolomé de las Casas," 1993), 215–37.

33. Oré, *Symbolo Catholico Indiano*, 62r.

34. Oré, *Symbolo Catholico Indiano*, 62r–v. Robert D. Wood, *"Teach Them Good Customs" Colonial Indian Education and Acculturation in the Andes* (Culver City, CA: Labyrinthos, 1986), 106, notes that thanks to Oré the Indians of Jauja were expert by 1598 in "polyphonic singing and could play recorders, shawms, and trumpets."

35. Vargas Ugarte, *La iglesia en el Perú*, 1: 228; Bruca Mannheim, "Juan Pérez Bocanegra (?–1645)," in *Guide to Documentary Sources for Andean Studies 1530–1900*, ed. Joanne Pillsbury, 3 vols. (Norman: University of Oklahoma Press, 2008), 3:516–519.

36. Saint Hilary, fourth-century bishop of Poitier, wrote some of the earliest Christian hymns. Saint Prudentius was born in northern Spain.

37. Oré, *Symbolo Catholico Indiano*, 63r.

38. Oré, *Symbolo Catholico Indiano*, 64v–65r.
39. Oré, *Symbolo Catholico Indiano*, 65r–v.
40. Oré, *Symbolo Catholico Indiano*, 65v.
41. His Italian name was probably Riccardi; see Román Zulaica Gárate, *Los franciscanos y la imprenta en México en el siglo XVI* (Mexico: UNAM, 1991), 277; Vargas Ugarte, *Historia general del Perú*, 2: 293–95; and Antonio Rodríguez-Buckingham, "Monastic Libraries and Early Printing in Sixteenth-Century Spanish America," *Libraries & Culture* 24 (1989): 33–56. Rodríguez-Buckingham states Ricardo's printing shops were located near religious houses, and notes the religious texts being translated required frequent contact between the author and the printer to prevent errors.
42. Salas de Coloma, *Obrajes de Canaria*, 55–57.
43. Salas de Coloma, *Estructura colonial del poder*, 1: 85–86.
44. Oré, *Symbolo Catholico Indiano*, 191v.

11. Doctrinero in Potosí and Cuzco

1. Peter Bakewell, *Silver and Entrepreneurship in Seventeenth-Century Potosí: The Life and Times of Antonio López de Quiroga* (Dallas: Southern Methodist University, 1995), 195, n. 45. See also Jeffrey A. Cole, *The Potosí Mita, 1573–1700: Compulsory Indian Labor in the Andes* (Stanford: Stanford University Press, 1985).
2. Ramírez, "Descripción del reyno del Pirú," 1: 353–55.
3. Oré, *Symbolo Catholico Indiano*, 34r–35r.
4. Kenneth Mills, "Diego de Ocaña, Holy Wanderer," in *The Human Tradition in Colonial Latin America*, ed. Kenneth J. Andrien, 2nd ed. (New York: Roman & Littlefield Publishers, 2013), 151–71. The Virgin of Guadalupe worshipped in Spain is not to be confused with the Virgin of Guadalupe venerated in Mexico.
5. Ocaña, *A través de la América del Sur*, 150–51.
6. Ocaña, *A través de la América del Sur*, 153–54.
7. Ocaña, *A través de la América del Sur*, 155.
8. Ocaña, *A través de la América del Sur*, 158. At the completion of the festival of Saint Jerónimo, Ocaña departed Potosí, reaching Chuquisaca in early November 1601. Beatriz Carolina Peña, "Hermanos de la perdición: Los Pizarros en la memoria colectiva del Perú a inicios del XVII," *Revista de Historia de América* 147 (2012): 77–110, rightly questions the historical accuracy of Ocaña's narrative, especially as he describes earlier events based on his own memory and the collective memory of prior events taken from people he consulted during his travels. But his description of events, people, and places regarding his assignment to spread the cult of the Virgin of Guadalupe his veracity is solid, certainly in Oré's case though he confused his name.
9. Josep M. Barnadas, "Una polémica colonial: Potosí, 1579–1584," *Jahrbuch für Geschichte Latein-amerikas* 10 (1973) 16–70. Pedro de Oré's evaluation is included in Barnadas, Appendix 7, 67–68. One of the Oré brothers was a mine owner. See Harrison, *Sin and Confession*, 218.
10. Vargas, *Historia del Cusco*, 268–73. Antonio de Vega, *Historia del Colegio y Universidad de San Ignacio de Loyola de la Ciudad del Cuzco*, ed. Ruben Vargas Ugarte (Lima: Studium, 1948),

144–47. See chapter 21 of Diego Francisco Altamirano's "Historia de la Provincia del Perú de la Compañía de Jesús." For Alonso Martínez see Durston, *Pastoral Quechua*, 148–49.

11. Córdova y Salinas, *Cronica franciscana del Perú*, 347.

12. Córdova y Salinas, *Cronica franciscana del Perú*, 346.

13. BNP, C341, 28r–v.

14. José Toribio Medina, *Diccionario biográfico colonial de Chile* (Santiago de Chile: Imprenta Elzeviriana, 1906), 613.

15. Oré, *Rituale, seu manuale peruanum*, 7.

16. Nicanor Domínguez, "Pidiéndonos," 165, ftn. 61. Copies of the two documents are on 170–72, and the originals are in the Archivo Regional del Cusco, Sección Notarial, Siglo XVII, Gaspar de Prado 277 (1603–1608), 1604 registro primero, 43r–44r; and reg. segundo, 99v–100r. Domínguez (167) concludes that despite efforts, the Cuzco elite were unable to secure all the privileges they petitioned for.

12. Assignments in Spain and Italy

1. Antonio Vargas, *Historia del Cusco*, 268–73. Bishop Raya died in Cuzco on 28 July 1606. See also Vega, *Historia del Colegio y Universidad de San Ignacio de Loyola*.

2. AGI, Patronato 191, ramo 25.

3. Oré, *Rituale, seu manuale peruanum*, 7.

4. Oré, *Rituale, seu manuale peruanum*, 7–8.

5. Oré, *Rituale, seu manuale peruanum*, 8; Lyle N. McAlister, *Spain & Portugal in the New World, 1492–1700* (Minneapolis: University of Minnesota Press, 1984), 362–63; Roberto Levillier, ed., *Papeles eclesiásticos de Tucumán: documentos originales del Archivo de Indias*, 2 vols. (Madrid, 1926), 2: 377–78.

6. There is a vast literature on Golden Age Seville. For an outline see Noble David Cook, "Sevilla: Una ciudad proto-industrial a base de la economía atlántica?" in *Mirando las dos orillas: intercambios mercantiles, sociales y culturales entre Andalucía y América*, eds. Enriqueta Vila Vilar and Jaime J. Lacueva Muñoz (Sevilla: Fundación Buenas Letras, 2012), 79–104; Cook and Cook, *Plague Files;* Morales Padrón, *La ciudad de los quinientos;* Antonio Domínguez Ortiz, *Historia de Sevilla. La Sevilla del siglo XVII* (Sevilla: Universidad de Sevilla, 1984).

7. AGI, Patronato 133, ramo 4. See Martínez, *Genealogical Fictions*, 173–99 regarding service reports.

8. AHPS, Protocolos 1602, sin fol., 1 June 1590. His agent issued a promissory note to Diego de Mercado, priest in Seville's Magdalena parish.

9. AGI, Escribanía de Cámara 1012A and 1013A. See also Domínguez, "Pidiéndonos," 167, ftn. 62.

10. Oré, *Rituale, seu manuale peruanum*, 8.

11. Oré, *Rituale, seu manuale peruanum*, 8.

12. Arroyo, *Comisarios generales del Perú*, 3–7.

13. Rubén Vargas Ugarte, *Historia del culto de María en Iberoamérica y de sus imágenes y santuarios más celebrados* (Buenos Aires, 1947), 80–83.

14. Rubén Vargas Ugarte, *Impresos peruanos publicados en el extranjero* (Lima, 1949), 6: 12. He too notes the report is in the Vatican Archive.

15. Córdova y Salinas, *Crónica franciscana del Perú*, 1015. Marcello Vestrio di Barbiano (d. 1606) was the secretary of briefs for Popes Clement VIII and Paul V.

16. José Toribio Medina, *Biblioteca Hispano-chilena (1523–1817)*, 3 vols. (Santiago de Chile, 1897–99), 1: 103, 129.

17. Córdova y Salinas, *Crónica franciscana del Perú*, 346.

13. Naples, the *Rituale, seu manuale peruanum*

1. Lucien Marcheix, *Un Parisien à Rome et à Naples en 1632. D'après un manuscrit inédit de J. J. Bouchard* (Paris: Ernest Leroux, nd), 63–65, accessed 23 June 2020, Internet Archive, Getty, https:archive.org/details/unparisienromeetoomarc

2. Oré, *Rituale, seu manuale peruanum*, 11.

3. Oré, *Rituale, seu manuale peruanum*, 9–10.

4. Oré, *Rituale, seu manuale peruanum*, 11.

5. Oré, *Rituale, seu manuale peruanum*, 140.

6. Philip Caraman, *The Lost Paradise, an account of the Jesuits in Paraguay, 1607–1768* (London: Sidgwick and Jackson, 1975), 26–27.

7. Oré, *Rituale, seu manuale peruanum*, 385.

8. Oré, *Rituale, seu manuale peruanum*, 388.

9. Oré, *Rituale, seu manuale peruanum*, 390.

10. Oré, *Rituale, seu manuale peruanum*, 395.

11. Oré, *Rituale, seu manuale peruanum*, 397–418.

12. Oré, *Rituale, seu manuale peruanum*, 400–403.

13. Oré, *Rituale, seu manuale peruanum*, 403–408.

14. Oré, *Rituale, seu manuale peruanum*, 408–12.

15. Oré, *Rituale, seu manuale peruanum*, 412.

16. Oré, *Rituale, seu manuale peruanum*, 412–15. Ernst Schäfer, *El Consejo Real y Supremo de las Indias*, 2 vols. (Seville: Imp. M. Carmona, 1935–47), 2: 567, notes that Bishop Loyola was succeeded (4 October 1609) by Friar Reginaldo de Lizárraga. See Raúl A. Molina, *Fray Martín Ignacio de Loyola: Cuatro obispos del Paraguay y Río de la Plata (1603–1606)*, (Madrid: Ediciones Jura, 1953); and Martín Ignacio de Loyola, *Viaje alrededor del mundo*, ed. José Ignacio Tellechea Idígoras (Madrid: Historia 16, 1989).

17. Oré, *Rituale, seu manuale peruanum*, 412–15, items 1, 2, 5, 6, 8, 15, and 16.

18. Oré, *Rituale, seu manuale peruanum*, 412–15.

19. Medina, *Diccionario biográfico*, 613, calls the *Rituale, seu manuale peruanum* "una joya bibliográfica."

14. Enigma of the Lost Dictionary and Grammar

1. Oré, *Symbolo Catholico Indiano*, 191v.
2. Poma de Ayala, *Nueva corónica y buen gobierno*, 3: 997.
3. Oré, *Rituale, seu manuale peruanum*, 7.
4. Vargas Ugarte, *Historia de la iglesia en el Perú*, 1: 55. Quote from Juan de Betanzos, *Suma y narración de los Incas* (Madrid: Atlas, 1987), 8. Regarding Bocanegra see Harrison, *Sin and Confession*, 65–66.
5. Antonio de Egaña, ed., *Monumenta Peruana* (Rome: Apud "Monumenta historica Soc. Iesu," 1954–), 5: 709; Xavier Albó and Félix Layme, "Introducción," *Vocabulario de la lengua aymara* [1612] by P. Ludovico Bertonio, (fasc. ed. Cochabamba: "El Buítre," 1984), xxvi. For Juli's linguistic school see Jeffrey L. Klaiber, SJ, *The Jesuits in Latin America, 1549–2000* (Saint Luis: Institute of Jesuit Studies, 2009), 47–49.
6. Egaña, *Monumenta Peruana*, 5: 709; Albó and Layme, "Introducción," xxvii.
7. Harrison, *Sin and Confession*, 64–65.
8. Quote from Bertonio, *Vocabulario de la lengua aymara*, 474; see Albó and Layme, "Introducción," xxvii–xxix, and Bertonio, *Segunda parte del vocabulario . . .*, 398–99. Bertonio died in Lima in 1625.
9. Bertonio, *Vocabulario de la lengua aymara* [1612], prologue, npn.
10. Durston, *Pastoral Quechua*, 85–86.
11. González Holguín, *Vocabulario*, 14.
12. Porras Barrenechea, "Prólogo," xiii, xx–xxiii, in González Holguín, *Vocabulario*; From Paraguay he went to Chile, then back to Paraguay and finally to Mendoza where he died in 1618.

15. Recruiting in Spain

1. Luys Hieronymo de Ore, *Relacion de los martires de la Florida, doze Religiosos de la Compañia de IESUS, que padecieron en el Iacan y cinco de la Orden de nuestro Serafico P.S. Francisco, en la Provincia de Guale. Ponese assi mesmo la descripcion de Iacan donde se han fortificado los Ingleses, y de otras cosas tocantes a la conversion de los Indios* (Madrid, 1619?), 29r. This copy is available online. There are flaws in pagination that occured during printing. This is the text used by Raquel Chang-Rodríguez. Our translations generally coincide, although lack of punctuation, incomplete sentences, and several possible definitions of a word led to occasional variations. We rely on Sebastián de Covarrubias Orozco, *Tesoro de la lengua castellana o española* (Madrid: Luis Sánchez, 1611), ed. Felipe C. R. Maldonado (Madrid: Editorial Castalia, 1994), and the *Diccionario de Autoridades* of the Real Academia Española. Juan Fernández de Olivera was appointed governor on 13 May 1609.
2. AGI, Contratación 5538, leg. 2, 125v. There were twenty friars and four servants.
3. Lino Gómez Canedo, *La provincia franciscana de Santa Cruz de Caracas: cuerpo de documentos para la historia, 1513–1837*, 3 vols. (Caracas, 1974), 1: 63–64, 206, 2: 73–76; and Oré, *Relación de la Florida*, 1: 118. Medina, *Biblioteca Hispano-chilena*, 1: 115–17, attempted to prove that Oré failed to reach Florida.

4. See chapters 32 and 35.

5. AGI, Contratación 5538, leg. 2, 125v–26v.

6. Garcilaso de la Vega, *Obras completas*, 4: 124. For Garcilaso as translator and Renaissance scholar see Margarita Zamora, *Language, Authority, and Indigenous History in the Comentarios Reales de los Incas* (Cambridge: Cambridge University Press, 1988).

7. His parents were Pedro de Zerpa and Doña Jerónima del Castillo; Zerpa is alternatively spelled with Z, S or Ç.

8. AGI, Contratación 5539, leg. E, 462v; Contratación 5340, no. 44.

9. AGI, Contratación 5340, no. 44; Contratación 5539, leg. 2, 16r.

10. AGI, Contratación 5539, leg. E, 462v; see also 5340, no. 44.

11. AGI, Contratación 5539, leg. 2, 16r–v; no. 28; no. 90; Contratación 5340, no. 44.

12. AGI, Contratación 5339, no. 41. Joanne Rappaport, *The Disappearing Mestizo*, 171–203, analyzes physiographic descriptions in the colonial period.

13. AGI, Contratación 5339, no. 41.

14. Chang-Rodríguez, *Relación de los mártires*, 197, from AGI, Santo Domingo 25.

15. Chang-Rodríguez, *Relación de los mártires*, 200, from AGI, Santo Domingo 25.

16. AGI, Contratación 5339, no. 41, 6r.

17. AGI, Contratación 5538, leg. 2, 128r–v.

18. AGI, Contratación 5539, leg. 2, 48v. The original was filed in the "Libro de Religiosos a fol. 126."

16. Probing the Youth of a Future Saint, Francisco Solano

1. Luis Julian Plandolit, *El Apostol de América San Francisco Solano* (Madrid: Editorial Cisneros, 1963), 335–36. Friar Plandolit, OFM, provides documentation on the process, much of it from the Archivo Secreto Vaticano, #1328–1340. Testimonies from Trujillo, Ica, and Lima were in Lima's Archivo Arzobispal, *Primera Parte. Legajo sobre el proceso de San Francisco Solano*. Along with the documentation on Solano collected in Peru was the letter by Solicitor Friar Lope Díaz de Navia. The imprint was prepared by Doctor Carrasco de Saz. See Plandolit, *San Francisco Solano*, 35, Doctor Carrasco de Saz, *Allegato juris et Consilium pro examinandis et approbandis miraculis religiosissmi viri Fr. Francisco Solano* (Lima: Francisco Canto, 1612).

2. Díaz de Navia's letter is in AGI, Lima 325. Lima's Cathedral Chapter letter (1 May 1612) to the king is in AGI, Lima 310. Cited by Plandolit, *San Francisco Solano*, 337.

3. The bound volume of testimony of 110 folios is in the Archivo Secreto Vaticano, #1337.

4. Plandolit, *San Francisco Solano*, 336–40. Díaz de Navia's letter 24 April 1612 is in AGI, Lima 325, the 1 May 1612 Lima Cathedral Chapter letter to the king is in AGI, Lima 310. Copies of the original testimonies were in Lima's Franciscan monastery's archive; further testimony, largely on Solano's miracles, was collected in subsequent years and copies of Oré's report on Solano's youth was added. All the material was used by Franciscan chroniclers including Diego de Córdova y Salinas, Buenaventura de Salinas y Córdova, and Friar Alonso de Mendieta. In 1643 Mendieta edited, supplemented, and published in Madrid's Imprenta Real, Friar Diego de Córdova's *Vida, virtudes y milagros del Apostol del Peru del Venerable P[adr]e Fray Francisco Solano de la Serafica*

Orden de los Menores de la Regular Obseruancia . . . / sacada de las declaraciones de quinientos testigos . . . y de otras muchas informaciones . . . por el Padre Fray Diego de Cordoua . . . del Orden de . . . S. Francisco . . . Y en esta segunda edicion añadida por el P[adr]e Fray Alonso de Mendieta de la misma Orden. . . . The first ten chapters were taken almost verbatim from Oré's report on Solano's youth printed in Madrid in 1614, though not cited. Accessed 15 July 2020, http://liburutegibiltegi.biz kaia.eus/handle/20.500.11938/72065.

5. Plandolit, *San Francisco Solano*, 340.

6. Plandolit, *San Francisco Solano*, 25. Plandolit states it is under the rubric "Relaciones diversas" 2/32, and includes (folios 130–36) a title that is only slightly different from the printed version: "Relación breve de la vida, loables costumbres, muerte y milagros del venerable Padre Fray Francisco Solano, sacerdote y predicador de la Orden de San Francisco, sacada de las informaciones y probanzas jurídicas hechas por los ilustrisimos Señores Arzobispos de Sevilla, Granada, Lima, y Obispos de Córdova y Málaga, por el Padre frai. . . ." Here too we find, folios 187–238, the initial manuscript pages of the printed version, the "Información hecha en España en la Provincia de Granada, del Santo Fr. Francisco Solano, hecha por el P. fr. Luis Jerónimo de Oré."

7. Plandolit, *San Francisco Solano*, 15.

8. Luis Gerónimo de Oré, *Relación de la vida i milagros del Venerable Padre Fr. Francisco Solano de la Orden de San Francisco* (Madrid, 1614), 1v.

9. Oré, *Relación de Francisco Solano*, 6r.

10. Ronald J. Morgan, *Spanish American Saints and the Rhetoric of Identity, 1600–1810* (Tucson: University of Arizona Press, 2002).

11. Oré, *Relación de Francisco Solano*, 6v–7r.

12. Oré, *Relación de Francisco Solano*, 9v. San Buenaventura's *Teología* covers specific texts which codify the spiritual goals of the Franciscans.

13. Oré, *Relación de Francisco Solano*, 13v–14v. More documents are published in *Proceso diocesano de San Francisco Solano*, introduction by Fernando Iwasaki Cauti and paleography by María José Acuña (Montilla: Bibliofila Montillana, 1999).

14. Oré, *Relación de Francisco Solano*, 16r.

15. Oré, *Relación de Francisco Solano*, 16v.

16. Oré, *Relación de Francisco Solano*, 23v–25r. See Marjorie Reeves, *Joachim of Fiore and the Prophetic Future* (New York: Harper & Row, 1977), 36–47; Norman Cohn, *The Pursuit of the Millennium*, 2nd ed., rev. (New York: Oxford University Press, 1970), 156–62; Phelan, *The Millennial Kingdom of the Franciscans*; and McClure, *The Franciscan Invention*, 164–79.

17. Oré, *Relación de Francisco Solano*, 28v–32. Oré lists important Franciscans buried in the Lima monastery, including "el Santo Fray Alonso de Alcañizes" who died 43 years earlier, and was esteemed by Viceroy Toledo as saintly, "and he was buried with a similar advocacy of a large multitude of people." Later chroniclers of the order used Oré's list.

18. Peter Burke, "How to be a Counter-Reformation Saint," *Religion and Society in Early Modern Europe, 1500–1800*, ed. Kaspar von Greyerz (London, 1984), 46.

19. Gillian T. W. Ahlgren, *Teresa of Avila and the Politics of Sanctity* (Ithaca: Cornell University Press, 1996), 145–46.

20. Ahlgren, *Teresa of Avila and the Politics of Sanctity*, 150.

21. Plandolit, *San Francisco Solano*, 374.

22. Diego Ortiz de Zúñiga, *Anales eclesiásicos y seculares de la muy noble y leal ciudad de Sevilla* [1796], 5 vols. (Seville: Guadalquivir, 1988), 4: 234–36.

17. Franciscan Province of Santa Elena de La Florida

1. Spanish Florida specialists are familiar with Oré's work as General Commissioner for the Franciscan missions. See Geiger's biographical sketch in his "Introduction" to *The Martyrs of Florida* and Chang-Rodríguez and Vogely, *Account of the Martyrs*. See also John Tate Lanning, *The Spanish Missions of Georgia* (Chapel Hill: University of North Carolina Press, 1935); Michael Gannon, *The Cross in the Sand: The Early Catholic Church in Florida, 1513–1870* (Gainesville: University of Florida Press, 1965). More recent works include Jerald T. Milanich, *The Timucua* (Oxford: Blackwell, 1996); Robert C. Galgano, *Feast of Souls: Indians and Spaniards in the Seventeenth-Century Missions of Florida and New Mexico* (Albuquerque: University of New Mexico Press, 2005). Cristobal Figuero y del Campo, *Franciscan Missions in Florida* (Spain: A R S Magna Ediciones, 1994), devotes a short chapter to Oré. Timothy J. Johnson and Jeffrey M. Burns, eds., *Facing Florida: Essays on Culture and Religion in Early Modern Southeastern America.* (Oceanside, CA: The American Academy of Franciscan History, 2021).

2. Henry F. Dobyns, *Their Number Become Thinned: Native American Population Dynamics in Eastern North America* (Knoxville: University of Tennessee Press, 1983) provides an account of native Floridian food resources.

3. AGI, Santo Domingo 232, 1r–2v.

4. AGI, Santo Domingo 232, 1r–2v. In the period 1600–1602 fish, salt, and olive oil were imported from Havana, fish and meat from San Juan de Ulúa, and *bizcocho* (hard tack), flour, and chickpeas from Veracruz. Further, Mexico supplied copper and Havana iron, likely imported from Spain, AGI, Santo Domingo 232, 948r–50v.

5. AGI, Santo Domingo 232, 1r–2v.

6. AGI, Santo Domingo 232, 22v. For analysis of the revolt see J. Michael Francis and Kathleen M. Kole, *Murder and Martyrdom in Spanish Florida: Don Juan and the Guale Uprising of 1597, Anthropological Papers*, no. 95 (New York: American Museum of Natural History, 2011).

7. AGI, Santo Domingo 232, sf.

8. AGI, Santo Domingo 232, 110r–11v; Oré, *Relación de la Florida*, 14v.

9. AGI, Santo Domingo 232, 553r.

10. AGI, Santo Domingo 232, 555r. The missive was signed by friars Pedro Ruiz, Pedro Bermejo, and Estarian de San Andrés.

18. Cuba, La Florida, and Oré's First Inspection

1. AGI, Contratación 5539, leg. 2, 48v. The exact date of Oré's departure is unknown.

2. *La embajada japonesa de 1614 a la ciudad de Sevilla* (Seville: Ayuntamiento de Sevilla, 1991), 116; and Fernando Iwasaki Cauti, "La embajada de Hasekura Tsunenaga Rokuemon (1613–1620)," *Azotea, Revista de Cultura del Ayuntamiento de Coria del Río* 6/7 (1990), 67–82.

3. Oré, *Relación de la Florida*, following 29r, folio numbers are missing.

4. Oré, *Relación de la Florida*, 27v–28r; foliation skips. See John E. Worth, *The Timucua Chiefdoms of Spanish Florida, Volume 1: Assimilation* (Gainesville: University Press of Florida, 1998), 60–69.

5. Oré, *Relación de la Florida*, foliation skips here. Chang-Rodríguez, *Relación de los mártires*, 180, ft. 439 uses fol. 30r, and provides alternative names of the village as Vitachuco or Villa Apalache.

6. Oré, *Relación de la Florida*, 30 r.

7. Oré, *Relación de la Florida*, 30 v.

8. Oré, *Relación de la Florida*, 30v.

9. Oré, *Relación de la Florida*, 29v.

19. The Cuban Conundrum

1. See Arelis Rivero Cabrera, *Commitment Beyond Rules: Franciscans in Colonial Cuba, 1531–1842* (Berkeley: American Academy of Franciscan History, 2017). In Rivero Cabrera "Missionaries and Moralization for the Franciscan Province of Santa Elena: The Dilemma of an Exported Reform," *The Americas* 61, no. 1 (2005): 673, she points out: "Cuba has been one of the marginalized territories of the American ecclesiastical historiography." She stresses the last third of the seventeenth century, but in her overview of the earlier period, she fails to mention Oré's recruitment of missionaries for Florida and his inspection of the province.

2. Rivero Cabrera, "Franciscan Province of Santa Elena," 673, n. 1; 674.

3. Alejandro de la Fuente, *Havana and the Atlantic in the Sixteenth Century* (Chapel Hill: University of North Carolina Press, 2008), 107, 108–12; Irene A. Wright, *Historia documentada de San Cristóbal de la Habana en el siglo XVI*, 2 vols. (Havana: Imprenta Siglo XX, 1927), 1: 78–81; see also Wright's *Historia documentada de San Cristóbal de la Habana en la primera mitad del siglo XVII* (Havana: Imprenta Siglo XX, 1930). Irene A. Wright, *Cuba* (New York: Macmillan, 1912), 38, states the Franciscan monastery's construction was completed in 1591.

4. Francis and Cole, *Murder and Martyrdom*, 145. For source see AGI, Santo Domingo 232, 974r; AGI, Patronato 19, reg. 30 (7 June 1606), 6r–v; AGI, Santo Domingo 135, 58r–62v. Leonardo Falcon, "Manufacturing Sin on the Frontier of Heresy: Bishops, Franciscans and the Inquisition in Cuba during the Long Sixteenth Century, 1511–1611" PhD diss. (Florida International University, 2019), chapter 5, provides excellent detail on the visitas.

5. Irene A. Wright, *Santiago de Cuba and its district (1607–1640): Written from Documents in the Archive of the Indies, at Seville, Spain* (Madrid: F. Peña Cruz, 1918), 25–26, 30–31, 36–37, 77–83.

6. See Catholic-Hierarchy, accessed 27 July 2015, http://www.catholic-hierarchy.org/bishop/benrta.html. See also Salvador Miranda, accessed 3 March 2016, http://www2.fiu.edu/~mirandas/obispos/bio-e.htm.

7. Wright, *Santiago de Cuba (1607–1640)*, 25–26, 30–31, 36–37, 97–111; and Fuente, *Havana in the Sixteenth Century*, 134–37.

8. Wright, *Santiago de Cuba (1607–1640)*, 97–111. Letter of cabildo to king dated 30 April 1614 notifying that on 5 February 1614 they received his letter of 12 June 1613.

9. Wright, *Habana en la primera mitad del siglo XVII*, 106.

10. Wright, *Habana en en la primera mitad del siglo XVII*, 107–108.

11. Wright, *Habana en en la primera mitad del siglo XVII*, 108–109.

12. Domingo del Monte, "Dos cartas del obispo de Cuba D. Fray Alonso Enríquez Alemendarez, en contestación a una Real Cédula de Felipe III, *Memorias de la Real Sociedad Económica de la Habana*, 2nd Serie, no. 1, January (Havana: Imprenta del Faro Industrial, 1847), 181–186. In 1620 Bishop Enríquez de Almendáriz wrote a "Relación histórica de lo espiritual y temporal de la isla de Cuba" that may provide insight into his relationship with Oré.

13. Norma Roura, "El testamento cerrado de los marqueses de Montesclaros," *Boletín del Archivo Nacional de Cuba* 3 (1989): 56.

14. Roura, "Testamento," 41–57.

20. Second Inspection of the La Florida Missions

1. Oré, *Relación de la Florida*, 29v.
2. Oré, *Relación de la Florida*, 30r.
3. Oré, *Relación de la Florida*, 26r–29r.
4. Oré, *Relación de la Florida*, 29v.
5. Oré, *Relación de la Florida*, 30r.
6. Oré, *Relación de la Florida*, 30r.
7. Oré, *Relación de la Florida*, 30r.
8. Oré, *Relación de la Florida*, 30v. Oré's text has been studied by archaeologists, anthropologists, and ethnohistorians trying to reconstruct his route and the mission towns of the southeastern United States in the early seventeenth century. See John H. Hann, *Apalachee: The Land between the Rivers* (Gainesville: University Press of Florida, 1987); John H. Hann, *History of the Timucua Indians and Missions* (Gainesville: University Press of Florida, 1996); Jerald T. Milanich, *Laboring in the Fields of the Lord: Spanish Missions and Southeastern Indians* (Gainesville: University Press of Florida, 1999); and Jerald T. Milanich and Samuel Proctor, eds., *Tacachale: Essays on the Indians of Florida and Southeastern Georgia during the Historic Period* (Gainesville: University Press of Florida, 1978).
9. Oré, *Relación de la Florida*, 30v.
10. Oré, *Relación de la Florida*, 30v.
11. Oré, *Relación de la Florida*, 31r.
12. Oré, *Relación de la Florida*, 31r.
13. Oré, *Relación de la Florida*, 31r–v.
14. Oré, *Relación de la Florida*, 29r. There are errors in the original pagination in the printed version.
15. Monte, "Dos cartas del obispo Enríquez Alemendarez," 188.
16. Monte, "Dos cartas del obispo Enríquez Alemendarez," 190.

21. Franciscan Martyrs in Oré's Account

1. Carlos M. Gálvez Peña, "Martirios en la tierra de la eterna juventud. A propósito de la Relación de los mártires de la Florida de fray Luis Jerónimo de Oré," *Histórica* 38, no. 1 (2014): 131.

2. Oré, *Relación de la Florida*, 14r–23r.

3. Oré, *Relación de la Florida*, 14v; Chang-Rodríguez, *Relación de los mártires*, 138, n. 289, provides the background material on Friar Montes based on Maynard Geiger, *Biographical Dictionary of the Franciscans in Spanish Florida and Cuba (1528–1841)* Franciscan Studies 21 (Patterson, NJ: Anthony Guild Press, 1940), 77, 34; and for Guardian Bermejo, Chang-Rodríguez, *Relación de los mártires*, 139, n. 295.

4. Chang-Rodríguez, *Relación de los mártires*, 140, n. 301, from Geiger, *Biographical Dictionary*, 52.

5. Oré, *Relación de la Florida*, 15v.

6. Oré, *Relación de la Florida*, 15v. Lisa Noetzel, "Additions, Corrections, and Deletions: A Comparison of the 1612 and 1627 Spanish-Timucuan Catechisms," in *Facing Florida: Essays on Culture and Religion*, 41–50, and George Aaron Broadwell, "The Things They Formerly Worshipped: Timucua Christian Texts on Native Worship," in *Facing Florida: Essays on Culture and Religion*, 51–62.

7. Oré, *Relación de la Florida*, 15v. See Francisco Pareja, *Confessionario en lengua castellana y timuquana* (Mexico: Viuda de Diego López Davalos, 1613). Jerald T. Milanich and William C. Sturtevant, eds. *Francisco Pareja's 1613 Confessionario a documentary source for Timucuan ethnography* (Tallahassee: Florida Division of Archives, 1972). AGI, Santo Domingo 232, 394r–401r.

8. Oré, *Relación de la Florida*, 15v–16r.

9. Oré *Relación de la Florida*, 16r.

10. Oré, *Relación de la Florida*, 16r.

11. Oré, *Relación de la Florida*, 16v.

12. Oré, *Relación de la Florida*, 16r–v; Geiger, *Biographical Dictionary*, 35, and López, *Relación histórica*, 5–10, estimate Marrón's arrival in La Florida around 1574.

13. Oré, *Relación de la Florida*, 16v.

14. Oré, *Relación de la Florida*, 16v–17r; Chang-Rodríguez, *Relación de los mártires*, 146, n. 328, from Geiger, *Biographical Dictionary*, 105–106. For an overview of the evolution of the concept of martyrdom, see Chang-Rodríguez and Vogeley, "Introduction," 41–46.

15. Oré, *Relación de la Florida*, 17r.

16. Francis and Kole, *Murder and Martyrdom*. Chang-Rodríguez and Vogeley agree on the cause of the uprising.

17. Oré, *Relación de la Florida*, 17v.

18. Oré, *Relación de la Florida*, 17v; Francis and Kole, *Murder and Martyrdom*, 52; Chang-Rodríguez, *Relación de los mártires*, 148, n. 338.

19. In present-day Georgia.

20. Cumberland Island in Georgia. Oré, *Relación de la Florida*, 17v.

21. Oré, *Relación de la Florida*, 17v–18r.

22. Oré, *Relación de la Florida*, 18r–v.

23. Jekyll Island off the coast of Georgia.

24. Oré, *Relación de la Florida*, 18v–19r. Chang-Rodriguez, *Relación de los mártires*, 151, n. 345 states the captivity lasted ten months.

25. Oré, *Relación de la Florida*, 19r.

26. Oré, *Relación de la Florida*, 19r. "Relación de los grandes trabajos que passo el padre Avila, en el año y medio en poder de los indios rebelados."

27. Oré, *Relación de la Florida*, 19r–21v.

28. Francis and Kole, *Murder and Martyrdom*, 49.

29. Francis and Kole, *Murder and Martyrdom*, 51.

30. Francis and Kole, *Murder and Martyrdom*, 55.

31. Oré, *Relación de la Florida*, 21v–22r.

32. Oré, *Relación de la Florida*, 21v.

33. Oré, *Relación de la Florida*, 21v–22r. Lima's Inquisition deemed some of Luis de Granada's texts suspect. See Guibovich, "Calificadores de la Inquisición de Lima," 217.

34. Oré, *Relación de la Florida*, 22v–23r. Francis and Kole, *Murder and Martyrdom*, 131.

35. Juan de Silva, *Advertencias importantes acerca del buen govierno y administración de las Indias assi en lo espiritual como en lo temporal repartidas en tres memoriales informativos...* (Madrid: Por la Viuda de Fernando de Corria Montenegro, 1621), 1r–5v. Thanks to Arthur Dunkleman, I have perused this rare book in the Kislak Foundation #623. See Paulino Castañeda Delgado, *Los memoriales del padre Silva sobre predicación pacífica y repartimientos* (Madrid: CSIC: Instituto Gonzalo Fernández de Oviedo Col Tierra Nueva Cielo Nuevo VI., 1983).

36. Silva, *Advertencias importantes*, 6v.

22. Franciscan Democracy: First Provincial General Chapter Meeting

1. Oré, *Relación de la Florida*, 31v.

2. Oré, *Relación de la Florida*, 31v.

3. Oré, *Relación de la Florida*, 31v–32r. Chang-Rodríguez, *Relación de los mártires*, 192.

4. Oré, *Relación de la Florida*, 24r, 32r. Kings I: Chapter 2: 1–9, see Chang-Rodríguez and Vogeley, *Account of the Martyrs*, 157, ftn. 24.

5. Oré, *Relación de la Florida*, 24r–v.

6. Oré, *Relación de la Florida*, 24v.

7. Oré, *Relación de la Florida*, 24v.

8. Oré, *Relación de la Florida*, 24v.

9. Most likely sassafras.

10. Oré, *Relación de la Florida*, 25r–v. See Nicolás Monardes, *Historia medicinal de las cosas que se traen de nuestras Indias occidentales que sirven en medicina...* [1574] (Seville: Padilla Libros, 1988); Gonzalo Fernández de Oviedo y Valdés, *Historia general y natural de las Indias*, ed. Juan Pérez de Tudela Bueso, 5 vols. (Madrid: Atlas, 1959).

11. Monardes, *Historia medicinal*, 51r–64r.

12. Monardes, *Historia medicinal*, 55v.

13. Monardes, *Historia medicinal*, 59r–v.

14. Oré, *Relación de la Florida*, 32r. The Jesuits conducted a similar review and debate at the

local level. See Fabian Fechner, *Entscheidungsprozesse vor Ort. Die Provinzkongregationen der Jesuiten in Paraguay (1608–1762)*, (Regensburg: Verlag Schell & Steiner, 2015).

23. Economic and Spiritual Cost of Empire

1. Paul E. Hoffman, *Spanish Crown and the Defense of the Caribbean, 1535–1585: Precedent, Patrimonialism, and Royal Parsimony* (Baton Rouge: Louisiana State University Press, 1980); Amy T. Bushnell, *The King's Coffer: Proprietors of the Spanish Florida Treasury, 1565–1702* (Gainesville: University Presses of Florida, 1981); and Bushnell, *Situado and Sabana. Spain's Support System for the Presidio and Mission Provinces of Florida* Anthropological Papers, no. 74. (New York: American Museum of Natural History, 1994).

2. Bushnell, *The King's Coffer*, 103, from AGI, Santo Domingo 232.
3. Chang-Rodríguez, *Relación de los mártires*, 199–200, from AGI, Santo Domingo 25.
4. Chang-Rodríguez, *Relación de los mártires*, 200–201, from AGI, Santo Domingo 25.
5. Oré, *Relación de la Florida*, 1: 41–45. Chang-Rodríguez, *Relación de los mártires*, 209–10, from AGI, Santo Domingo 235, 71–72. Signed (14 January 1617) in St. Augustine by Oré, commissioner and visitador; Francisco Pareja, provincial; Friars Pedro Ruiz, Lorenzo Martínez, Alonso Pesquera, Juan de la Cruz, and Francisco Alonso de Jesús.
6. Chang-Rodríguez, *Relación de los mártires*, 203–209, from AGI, Santo Domingo 235, 73–76. Signed in St. Augustine (17 January 1617) by Friars Francisco Pareja, Pedro Ruiz, Lorenzo Martínez, Alonso Pesquera, Juan de la Cruz, Bartolomé Romero, and Francisco Alonso de Jesús.
7. AGI, Santo Domingo 235, 73r, from Chang-Rodríguez, *Relación de los mártires*, 204.
8. AGI, Santo Domingo 235, 73r, in Chang-Rodríguez, *Relación de los mártires*, 204.
9. Chang-Rodríguez, *Relación de los mártires*, 204, from AGI, Santo Domingo 235, 73r–v.
10. Chang-Rodríguez, *Relación de los mártires*, 205, from AGI, Santo Domingo 235, 73v.
11. Chang-Rodríguez, *Relación de los mártires*, 205, from AGI, Santo Domingo 235, 75r.
12. Chang-Rodríguez, *Relación de los mártires*, 206–208, from AGI, Santo Domingo 235, 75r–76r.
13. Chang-Rodríguez, *Relación de los mártires*, 208, from AGI, Santo Domingo 235, 75r.
14. Chang-Rodríguez, *Relación de los mártires*, 208, from AGI, Santo Domingo 235, 76r.
15. Chang-Rodríguez, *Relación de los mártires*, 209, from AGI, Santo Domingo 235, 74v.

24. Compiling the *Verdadera relación de la Florida*

1. Oré, *Relación de la Florida*, 2r.
2. On an earlier expedition Oré organized, he was authorized to transport "ten and a half toneladas of books," AGI, Contratación 5538, leg. 2, 225v–26v.
3. Oré, *Relación de la Florida*, 2v.
4. Garcilaso de la Vega, El Inca, *The Florida of the Inca* [1605], trans. and ed. by John Grier Varner and Jeannette Johnson Varner (Austin: University of Texas Press, 1951), 637–43.
5. Oré, *Relación de la Florida*, 3r; Chang-Rodríguez, *Relación de los mártires*, 103, n. 149.

6. Quotes from Oré, *Relación de la Florida*, 4r. Garcilaso de la Vega, *Florida of the Inca*, 640, 642.

7. Oré, *Relación de la Florida*, 5v. The names of eight of the victims have been uncovered, see Bredan Wolfe, "Juan Baptista de Segura (1529–1571)," in Encyclopedia Virginia, accessed 20 August 2020, http:// EncyclopediaVirginia.org/ Segura_Juan_Baptista_de_1571. Anna Brickhouse, *The Unsettlement of America: Translation, Interpretation, and the Story of Don Luis de Velasco, 1560–1945* (New York: Oxford University Press, 2015) examines the role of Don Luis using literary analysis. Chang-Rodríguez and Vogeley, "Introduction," 25–26, n. 40, point out that Brickhouse's use of Oré's account is second-hand and ignores alternative "Iberian views of settlement."

8. Paul E. Hoffman, *A New Andalucia and a Way to the Orient: The American Southeast during the Sixteenth Century* (Baton Rouge: Louisiana State University Press, 2004), 267, places his arrival in Spain in early summer 1572.

9. Oré, *Relación de la Florida*, 7r.

10. Oré, *Relación de la Florida*, 7v.

11. Oré, *Relación de la Florida*, 8r.

12. Hoffman, *New Andalucia*, 269.

13. Hoffman. *New Andalucia*, 270.

14. Parris Island in South Carolina.

15. Oré, *Relación de la Florida*, 8v.

16. Oré, *Relación de la Florida*, 9r. See Hoffman, *New Andalucia*, 274–82 for French and English actions along the coast north of St. Augustine; see also notes in Chang-Rodríguez, *Relación de los mártires*, 120. Regarding the seafaring Eraso family, see Pérez-Mallaína's *Spain's Men of the Sea*, 30–33.

17. Oré, *Relación de la Florida*, 9r–14r.

18. Oré, *Relación de la Florida*, 9r.

19. Oré, *Relación de la Florida*, 9r.

20. Oré, *Relación de la Florida*, 10r.

21. Oré, *Relación de la Florida*, 10r.

22. Oré, *Relación de la Florida*, 10r. "infieles, por la mayor parte, andan untados y embijados con color bermeja, y a falta se embijan con tizne y carbón en lo cual son semejantes estos de La Florida a los indios infieles y bárbaros que hay en la otra banda de las cordilleras del Pirú. Y los unos y otros son flecheros, pero allá andan vestidos, o menos desnudos que los de acá, y estos se aventajan en ser más guerreros y que carecen del vicio de la embriaguez de que son notados los indios todos, así de la Nueva España como del Pirú." Our translation varies significantly from that of Chang-Rodríguez and Vogely, *Account of the Martyrs*, 100.

23. Oré, *Relación de la Florida*, 10r. Chang-Rodríguez, *Relación de los mártires*, 125, n. 231, from Geiger, "Introduction," 1936, 58, n. 15, identifies this as Charleston Bay, South Carolina. Hoffman, *New Andalucia*, 304, n. 26, states that Oré's is the sole account of this reconaissance.

24. Oré, *Relación de la Florida*, 11r.

25. Oré, *Relación de la Florida*, 12r.

26. Oré, *Relación de la Florida*, 12r.

27. Oré, *Relación de la Florida*, 12r.

28. Oré, *Relación de la Florida*, 12r–v. For background, see Chang-Rodríguez, *Relación de los mártires*, 131, n. 264, 265, based on Geiger, "Introduction," 62, n. 49.

29. Oré, *Relación de la Florida*, 12v–13r.
30. Hoffman, *New Andalucia*, 305.
31. Hoffman, *New Andalucia*, 306–307.
32. Oré, *Relación de la Florida*, 13v.
33. Oré, *Relación de la Florida*, 13v–14r.
34. Oré, *Relación de la Florida*, 14r.

25. Spain Again: Marianism and the Virgin of Copacabana

1. Chang-Rodríguez, *Relación de los mártires*, 37, from AGI, Santo Domingo 235, 235r–v, 77r–78v. Martínez was subsequently sent to New Spain.
2. Ortiz de Zúñiga, *Anales de Sevilla*, 4: 235. For religious impact on culture, particularly the arts, see Amanda Wunder, *Baroque Seville: Sacred Art in a Century of Crisis* (University Park: Pennsylvania State University Press, 2017).
3. We have borrowed Wunder's elegant translation in *Baroque Seville*, 33. The song written by Toro and Cid is in Ortiz de Zúñiga, *Anales de Sevilla*, 4: 235 (*"Todo el mundo en general, A voces Reyna escogida, Diga que sois concebida, Sin pecado original"*).
4. Wunder, *Baroque Seville*, 33–36, 54–55. Ortiz de Zúñiga, *Anales de Sevilla*, 4: 236–38.
5. Ortiz de Zúñiga, *Anales de Sevilla*, 4: 291–95. The concept of Immaculate Conception of Mary became official dogma of the Catholic Church in 1854.
6. *Corona de la sacratissima Virgen Maria madre de Dios nuestra señora, En que se contienen ochenta meditaciones, de los principales misterios de la Fé: que corresponden a setenta y tres Ave Maria y ocho vezes el Pater noster, ofrecidas a los felices años que vivio en el mundo ... Dedicada a la misma virgen sacrosanta, concebida sin pecado original, en su imagen y Santuario de Copacavana*.
7. Oré, *Symbolo Catholico Indiano*, 32v–33r.
8. Verónica Salles-Reese, *From Viracocha to the Virgin of Copacabana. Representation of the Sacred at Lake Titicaca* (Austin: University of Texas Press, 1997), 5–44; Alonso Ramos Gavilán, *Historia del santuario de nuestra señora de Copacabana* [1621] (Lima: Ignacio Prado Pastor, 1988). See Augustinian chronicler Antonio de la Calancha [1584–1654], *Crónicas Agustinas del Perú*, 2 vols. (Madrid: CSIC, 1972), 1: 93–555.
9. A copy exists in the Biblioteca Nacional in Madrid. See Medina, *Biblioteca Hispano Chilena*, 1: 129.
10. Trejo died in 1635. Jorge Nadal Iniesta, "Fray Antonio de Trejo: el primer príncipe conterreformista de la diócesis de Cartagena," Congreso Internacional "Imagen y Apariencia," Fundación Séneca y Departamento de Historia del Arte de la Universidad de Murcia. 19 November 2008, accessed 20 August 2020, https://digitum.um.es/digitum/bitstream/10201/44224/1/CongresoImagen125.pdf.
11. Oré, *Corona de Nuestra Señora*, 1r–2v.
12. Oré, *Corona de Nuestra Señora*, 3r–4r.
13. Oré, *Corona de Nuestra Señora*, 14r.
14. Oré, *Corona de Nuestra Señora*, 15v.
15. Oré, *Corona de Nuestra Señora*, 19v. Early Church specialist Dr. Eduard Iricinschi (email correspondence) examined Saint Epiphanius's *Panarion*, *Ancoratus* and *Treatise on Weights and*

Measures and was unable to find a description of the Virgin Mary as depicted by Oré. In the *Treatise on Weights and Measures* Dr. Iricinschi did find in a passage on *stamnos* and *manna* "that connects Mary's beauty to gold."

    16. Oré, *Corona de Nuestra Señora*, 169r.
    17. Oré, *Corona de Nuestra Señora*, 168v–170r.
    18. Oré, *Corona de Nuestra Señora*, 170r.
    19. Oré, *Corona de Nuestra Señora*, 170v.
    20. About four decades after Oré's printing of *Corona de Nuestra Señora*, dedicated to the Virgin of Copacabana, Spanish playwright Pedro Calderón de la Barca composed a play *La aurora en Copacabana*. It centered on the cult of the Virgin, her miracles and the statue by Francisco Tito Yupanqui. See César García Álvarez, "Las fuentes de La aurora en Copacabana en Calderón de la Barca," *Revista Chilena de Literatura* 16–17 (1980–1981): 179–201.

26. Bishop Oré: Preparations for the Voyage

    1. Chang-Rodríguez, *Relación de los mártires*, 200–201; from AGI, Santo Domingo 25.
    2. Chang-Rodríguez, *Relación de los mártires*, 201–203; from AGI, Santo Domingo 235.
    3. Chang-Rodríguez, *Relación de los mártires*, 200–201; from AGI, Santo Domingo 235, 77v–78r.
    4. Chang-Rodríguez, *Relación de los mártires*, 203, from AGI Santo Domingo 235, 77v–78r.
    5. Levillier, *Papeles eclesiásticos de Tucumán*, 1: 405–406.
    6. Mendiburu, *Diccionario histórico biográfico*, 4: 222–223. Accessed 9/1/2022. https://www.catholic-hierarchy.org/bishop/bcorni.html
    7. Vargas Ugarte, *Historia de la Iglesia en el Perú*, 2: 443; and Medina, *Biblioteca Hispano-chilena*, 1: 129. Egaña, *Monumenta Peruana*, 2: 251, states that Oré was proposed by Philip III on 17 April 1620, and accepted by Pope Paul V; See Vargas Ugarte, *Impresos peruanos publicados en el extranjero*, 6: 12. The procedure is outlined by C. H. Haring, *The Spanish Empire in the New World* (New York: Harcourt, Brace & World, 1963), 167–69; Medina, *Diccionario biográfico colonial de Chile*, 614.
    8. Vargas Ugarte, *Impresos peruanos publicados en el extranjero*, 6: 12.
    9. AGI, Contratación 5378, no. 46. The Casa de la Contratación was established in 1504, and was similar to the English Board of Trade, founded over a century later. See C. H. Haring, *Trade and Navigation between Spain and the Indies in the Time of the Hapsburgs* (Cambridge: Harvard University Press, 1918).
    10. AGI, Contratación 5378, no. 46, 3v.
    11. AGI, Contratación 5378, no. 46, 8r.
    12. AGI, Contratación 5378, no. 46, 9v.
    13. AGI, Contratación 5378, no. 46, 11v.
    14. See Karoline P. Cook, *Forbidden Crossings: Muslims and Moriscos in Colonial Spanish America* (Philadelphia: University of Pennsylvannia Press, 2016); Antonio Domínguez Ortiz and Bernard Vincent, *Historia de los moriscos. Vida y tragedia de una minoría* (Madrid: Alianza Editorial, 1997); and Martínez, *Genealogical Fictions*.

15. AGI, Contratación 5378, no. 46, 19r.
16. AGI, Contratación 5378, no. 46, 21r.
17. AGI, Contratación 5378, no. 46, 21r–28v.
18. AGI, Contratación 5378, no. 46, 37r.
19. AGI, Contratación 5378, no. 46, 21r.
20. AGI, Contratación 5378, no. 46, 45r.
21. AGI, Contratación 5378, no. 46, 41r–44r.
22. AGI, Contratación 5539, leg. 2, 497r–v.
23. AGI, Contratación 5539, leg. 2, 306v.
24. AHPS, Protocolos 7796, 2, 150r–59r.
25. See chapter 37 for the details.

27. Return to the Viceroyalty of Peru

1. AGI, Chile 60.
2. Gerónymo Pallas, *Missión a las Indias: de Roma a Lima, 1619*, ed. by José Jesús Hernández Palomo, (Madrid: CSIC, 2006), 100; biographical details on pp. 11–15. Pallas completed his narrative in 1620.
3. Pallas, *Missión a las Indias*, 102.
4. Pallas, *Missión a las Indias*, 108–11.
5. Pallas, *Missión a las Indias*, 112–113.
6. Pallas, *Missión a las Indias*, 112–113.
7. Alonso de Sandoval, *Treatise on Slavery: Selections from De Instauranda Aethiopum Salute* [1627], ed. and trans., Nicole von Germeten (Indianapolis: Hackett Publishing, 2008); see Alonso de Sandoval, *De instauranda Aethiopum salute. Un tratado sobre la esclavitud*, ed. Enriqueta Vila Vilar (Madrid: Alianza Editorial, 1987).
8. Pallas, *Missión a las Indias*, 119, 124.
9. Christopher Ward, *Imperial Panama: Commerce and Conflict in Isthmian America, 1550–1800* (Albuquerque: University of New Mexico Press, 1993), 29–65; Pallas, *Missión a las Indias*, 120–22.
10. Pallas, *Missión a las Indias*, 124.
11. Pallas, *Missión a las Indias*, 123–27.
12. Pallas, *Missión a las Indias*, 127–29.
13. Pallas, *Missión a las Indias*, 151–53.
14. Pallas, *Missión a las Indias*, 159–60.

28. Consecration in Lima and Preparations for Chile

1. Geoffrey Baker and Tess Knighton, eds., *Music and Urban Society in Colonial Latin America* (Cambridge: Cambridge University Press, 2011), appendix 1, 246–51. Born in Madrid, Fernando de Ocampo served as bishop of Santa Cruz de la Sierra until his death in 1632. Vargas Ugarte,

Impresos peruanos publicados en el extranjero, 12. Vargas Ugarte incorrectly suggests Oré was in Lima by 1621 at the time of Ocampo's consecration.

2. AGI, Lima 308.

3. The ceremony of consecration here described is based on the *Catholic Encyclopedia,* accessed 29 January 2015, http://www.newadvent.org/cathen/04276a.htm.

4. Buenaventura de Salinas y Córdova, *Memorial de las historias del nuevo mundo Peru* (Lima: Gerónimo de Contreras, 1631), image 190 from Biblioteca Digital Hispánica, accessed 15 June 2015, http://bdh.bne.es/bnesearch/detalle/bdh0000092550.

5. Francisco Verdugo Cabrera (1561–1636), born in Spain had extensive experience in both the Indies and Spain. He arrived in Peru in 1600 or 1601 and was appointed Bishop of Huamanga 14 March 1622. He was appointed Archbishop of Mexico the year he died; accessed 26 August 2016, http://www.catholic-hierarchy.org/bishop/bverdc.html.

6. AGI, Lima 308.

7. AGI, Lima 308.

8. AGI, Lima 308.

9. AGI, Lima 308.

10. AGI, Lima 308.

29. Huamanga, the Last Visit

1. For Peru's colonial convents see Burns, *Colonial Habits;* Van Deusen, *The Spiritual Diary.* See also Sergio Ramírez González, "Sacra librería. La Biblioteca del Monasterio de Clarisas de Santa Isabel de Ronda," *Isla de Arriarán* 21 (2003): 293–313.

2. Córdova y Salinas, *Crónica franciscana del Perú,* 840.

3. Córdova y Salinas, *Crónica franciscana del Perú,* 841.

4. Córdova y Salinas, *Crónica franciscana del Perú,* 841.

5. Córdova y Salinas, *Crónica franciscana del Perú,* 841.

6. Nancy E. Van Deusen, *Embodying the Sacred: Women Mystics in Seventeenth-century Lima* (Durham: Duke University Press, 2018), 59.

7. Córdova y Salinas, *Crónica franciscana del Perú,* 838–46.

8. Pedro Rubio Merino, ed. *La monja alférez: Doña Catalina de Erauso. Dos manuscritos autobiográficos inéditos* (Seville: Cabildo Metropolitano de la Catedral de Sevilla, 1995). The English edition, Catalina de Erauso, *Lieutenant Nun: Memoir of a Basque Transvestite in the New World,* trans. by Michele Stepto and Gabriel Stepto. (Boston: Beacon Press, 1996), is based on an eighteenth-century copy by Juan Bautista Muñoz and published in 1829 by Joaquin Ferrer and reprinted in 1918. The translators were clearly unaware of the existence of the two manuscripts discovered by Rubio Merino in the *Archivo Capitular de Sevilla,* when they stated that "Only the Muñoz and Ferrer copies of the original manuscript now exist," xv. The basic story is the same in all three versions, but there are differences in detail. Furthermore, Ferrer embellished the story with descriptions of the places Catalina was in, descriptions that do not appear in the Seville manuscripts.

9. Carvajal died on 19 August 1618.

10. Rubio Merino, *La monja alférez*, 86.
11. Erauso, *Lieutenant Nun*, 66; Rubio Merino, *La monja alférez*, 87.
12. Erauso, *Lieutenant Nun*, 67–68.
13. Rubio Merino, *La monja alférez*, 88.
14. Rubio Merino, *La monja alférez*, 14–16. Erauso, *Lieutenant Nun*, xliii.
15. Córdova y Salinas, *Crónica franciscana del Perú*, 847.
16. Córdova y Salinas, *Crónica franciscana del Perú*, 848–49. According to Bishop Francisco Verdugo she may have died in 1615, though it could have been another sister, since Verdugo only mentions three founding nuns "and the last one died around 1615." There were four, see AGI, Lima 308.
17. ASFL, reg. 10, 29r–31r.
18. AGI, Lima 308. Archdeacon Francisco de Oré was in Huamanga by 1618 (letter on 23 November 1618). Philip III died on 31 March 1621, and the news reached Peru within five months. See John Lynch, *Spain under the Habsburgs* (New York: Oxford University Press, 1969), 2: 62. See Osorio, *Inventing Lima*, 89–93, for description of the Royal Exequies in the Lima Cathedral for Philip III.
19. AGI, Lima 308.
20. AGI, Lima 308.
21. Salas de Coloma, *Obrajes de Canaria*, 48–49.
22. AGI, Lima 308.
23. See Oré's will in Chapter 37.

30. The Changing Face of Lima

1. Gento Sanz, *San Francisco de Lima*, 301–303.
2. Pallas, *Missión a las Indias 1619*, 191.
3. Cobo, *Fundación de Lima*, 263–64. Friar Juan Meléndez, *Verdaderos tesoros de las Indias* (3 vols. Rome, 1683).
4. Cobo, *Fundación de Lima*, 264.
5. Carlos M. Gálvez Peña, "El carro de Ezequiel: la monarquía hispana de fray Buenaventura de Salinas y Córdova," *Histórica* 32, no. 1 (2008): 39–75; and Carlos M. Gálvez Peña, "Writing History to Reform the Empire: Religious Chroniclers in Seventeenth-Century Peru," PhD diss. (Columbia University, 2012), 206–88. The friars' parents were Don Diego de Salinas and Doña Juana de Silva y Córdova. Doña Juana's parents were Don Diego Hernández (or Fernández) de Córdova and Doña Mencia Gutiérrez. The brothers knew their ancestors were of noble lineage.
6. BNP, C341, 1r; Benjamín Gento Sanz, "Semblanza histórica del cronista peruano Fray Diego de Córdova y Salinas (Siglo XVII)," *Revista de Historia de América* 40 (December 1955), 446.
7. Gento Sanz, "Semblanza histórica," 446; BNP, C341, illus. 71 of the recently digitized copy. Juan de Herrera was General Commissioner from 1614–1620; see Arroyo, *Comissarios Generales del Perú*, 111–16. Diego de Córdova y Salinas was guardian of the Lima monastery from 1650 to 1653 and died shortly thereafter. See also Elisa Luque Alcaide, "Córdoba y Salinas, Diego de (1591–ca. 1654)," *Guide to Documentary Sources for Andean Studies 1530–1900*, 2: 165–69.

8. In addition to Gento Sanz see Franklin Pease G. Y., "Salinas y Córdoba, Buenaventura de (ca. 1592–1653)," *Guide to Documentary Sources for Andean Studies, 1530–1900*, 3: 624–26. Brading, *The First America*, 315–22 stresses the impact of Friar Buenaventura noting (315) "few other colonial authors chose to write with such frankness as Salinas, and, if they did, almost invariably failed to publish their works." See also several contributions by Carlos M. Gálvez Peña: "El carro de Ezequiel," 39–75; "Cronistas peregrinos: apuntes sobre ideas y hombres de Iglesia. Conexiones culturales entre México y el Perú durante el siglo XVII," *Iglesia y Sociedad en la Nueva España y el Perú*, eds. José de la Puente Brunke and Alicia Mayer (Madrid: Instituto Riva-Agüero PUCP/Universidad Nacional Autónoma de México/Editorial Analecta, 2015), 193–213; "Historias religiosas como narrativas imperiales en el Perú del siglo XVII," *Literatura y cultura en el virreinato del Perú: apropiación y diferencia (Historia de las Literaturas en el Perú. Tomo II)*, eds. Carlos García-Bedoya and Raquel Chang-Rodríguez, 301–36 (Lima: PUCP, 2017); "El mejor arbitrio, el sermon. Discurso religioso y representación política en el Perú del siglo XVII," *Anuario de Estudios Americanos* 71 (2014): 171–97; "La ciudad letrada y santa: la ciudad de Los Reyes en la historiografía del siglo XVII," *Urbanismo y vida urbana en Iberoamérica colonial* (Bogotá: Archivo de Bogotá. Serie de Memorias de la ciudad de Bogotá, 2008), 71–101.

9. Pallas, *Missión a las Indias 1619*, 194–96.

10. Cobo, *Fundación de Lima*, 248.

11. ASFL, reg. 10, 31v.

31. Chile Fractured: The Diocese of Santiago and La Imperial

1. José Toribio Medina, *Vida de Ercilla* (Mexico, DC: Fondo de Cultura Económica, 1948).

2. H. R. S. Pocock, *The Conquest of Chile* (New York: Stein and Day, 1967), 190, gives January 1552 as the month of foundation and reports its name comes for "a two-headed eagle which appears to have been a usual design found on the roof beams of a number of native houses in the district." More likely Valdivia named it La Imperial in honor of Emperor Charles V.

3. Lizárraga, *Descripción del Perú*, 445–46. Pocock, *Conquest of Chile*, 190, concurring with the Chilean historian Encina, concludes that it was the Araucanian resistance compared to the Pincunches and Huilliches which prevented La Imperial, rather than Santiago, from being the center of the kingdom of Chile. See also Diego Barros Arana, *Historia general de Chile* (16 vols. Santiago, 1884–1902).

4. Lizárraga, *Descripción del Perú*, 451–52.

5. Lizárraga, *Descripción del Perú*, 465.

6. Lizárraga, *Descripción del Perú*, 467.

7. Lizárraga, *Descripción del Perú*, 467.

8. AGI, Chile 63.

9. Antonio de Egaña, *Historia de la Iglesia en la América Española. Hemisferio sur* (Madrid: Biblioteca de Autores Cristianos, 1966), 2: 229, 251.

10. AGI, Chile 63, 27 November 1619. The financial data are from Antonio Vázquez de Espinosa, *Compendio y descripción de las Indias occidentales* [ca. 1621] (Washington, DC: Smithsonian Miscellaneous Collections, vol. 108, 1948), 726.

11. AGI, Chile 63, 25 August 1621. Vargas Ugarte, *Historia General del Perú*, 3: 102.
12. AGI, Chile 63, 24 April 1623. Vázquez de Espinosa, *Compendio y descripción de las Indias*, 712.

32. Foreign Threats on the South Sea

1. Peter T. Bradley, *The Lure of Peru: Maritime Intrusion into the South Sea, 1598–1701* (New York: St. Martin's Press, 1989), 47–71. See also Kris E. Lane, *Pillaging the Empire: Global Piracy on the High Seas, 1500–1750*, 2nd ed. (New York: Routledge, 2016), 57–80.

33. Beyond Araucania: A Pastoral Inspection

1. AGI, Chile 60.
2. Levillier, *Papeles eclesiásticos de Tucumán*, 1: 405–406.
3. Marie Timberlake, "Sínodos diocesanos," in *Fuentes documentales para estudios andinos, 1530–1900*, ed. Joanne Pillsbury, 1: 69–71; Carlos Silva Cotapos, *Historia eclesiástica de Chile* (Santiago de Chile, 1925), 83; and Vargas Ugarte, *Historia de la Iglesia en el Perú*, 2: 443–44.
4. AGI, Chile 63, no. 265. José de Viera y Clavijo, *Noticias de la historia general de las Islas de Canaria* (Madrid: Imprenta de Blas Román, 1776), 3: 227.
5. AGI, Chile 60, ramo 56; Martín Ferrer, "Estudio histórico documental," 103.
6. Vázquez de Espinosa, *Compendio y descripción de las Indias*, 685. Rodrigo Moreno Jeria, "Metodología misional jesuita en la periferia austral de América," in *La misión y los jesuitas en la América Española, 1566–1767: cambios y permanencias*, eds. José Jesús Hernández Palomo and Rodrigo Moreno Jeria (Seville: CSIC, 2005), 239–63.
7. AGI, Chile 60, letter of 4 March 1627.
8. AGI, Chile 60, no. 56, letter of 20 April 1626; Chile 61; Silva Cotapos, *Historia eclesiástica de Chile*, 74–85; Vargas Ugarte, *Historia de la Iglesia en el Perú*, 2: 443–44; and Medina, *Biblioteca Hispano-chilena*, 1: 130. See also Luis Olivares M., O.F.M., *Provincia franciscana de Chile* (Santiago, 1961).
9. AGI, Chile 60, 61; Silva Cotapos, *Historia eclesiástica de Chile*, 74–85; Rodrigo Moreno Jeria, "Entre huilliches, chonos, puelches y poyas: Jesuitas y sueños de reducción en el fin del mundo," *Reducciones. La concentración forzada de las poblaciones indígenas en el Virreinato del Perú*, eds. Akira Saito and Claudia Rosas Lauro (Lima: PUCP, 2017), 639–73.
10. AGI, Chile 60, letter of 28 February 1627. See Pablo E. Pérez-Mallaína and Bibiano Torres Ramírez, *La Armada del Mar del Sur* (Seville: Escuela de Estudios Hispanoamericanos, 1987).
11. AGI, Chile 60, 4 March 1627. "Relación de las rentas eclesiasticas, y como de distribuyr, y otras que se dan de la Hacienda de SM a capellanes y doctrineros."
12. AGI, Chile 60. 4 March 1627, "Relación de las rentas eclesiásticas."
13. AGI, Chile 60, 4 March 1627, "Relación de las rentas eclesiásticas."
14. AGI, Chile 60, 4 March 1627, "Relación de las rentas eclesiásticas."
15. AGI, Chile 60, 4 March 1627, "Relación de las rentas eclesiásticas"; AGI, Chile 60, ramo 56; and Chile 61.

16. AGI, Chile 60. Oré signs in Concepción on 4 March 1627. Silva Cotapos, *Historia eclesiástica de Chile,* 84. Moreno Jeria, "Jesuitas y sueños de reducción," 639–73.

17. AGI, Chile 60. Andrango-Walker, *El Símbolo católico indiano,* 195–224 provides in her appendices transcription of many of the documents from the AGI that we consulted.

18. AGI, Chile 60. John H. Elliott, *The Count-Duke of Olivares: A Statesman in an Age of Decline* (New Haven: Yale University Press, 1986), 309, notes that Philip was also ill during the time.

19. AGI, Chile 60, Oré's letter of 28 February 1627.

20. AGI, Chile 60.

34. Church and State Conflict: The *Patronato Real*

1. Silva Cotapos, *Historia eclesiástica de Chile,* 83; and Vargas Ugarte, *Historia de la Iglesia en el Perú,* 2: 443–44. (Tit. VI [Concerning the Patronato Real], Law 28, p. 29) in Joaquin Aguirre, *Recopilación compendada de las Leyes de Indias aumentada con algunas notas* (Madrid: Ignacio Boix, 1846). Aguirre (Law 50, p. 32) notes that in the Philippines and in similar situations the Captain General had the authority to act in the name of the Crown.

2. AGI, Chile 20, Oré's reply to the governor, 14 July 1627.

3. AGI, Chile 60.

4. AGI, Chile 20. Philip IV in 1623 issued an order (Aguirre, *Recopilación compendada,* Law 48, p. 32), that the prelates should not permit doctrinas to be vacant for more than four months. If there were presentations in this time then temporary curates should not receive a stipend.

5. AGI, Chile 20.
6. AGI, Chile 20.
7. AGI, Chile 20.
8. AGI, Chile 20.
9. Martínez Ferrer, "Estudio histórico documental," 103.
10. Martín de Azpilcueta.
11. AGI, Chile 20.
12. AGI, Chile 20.
13. AGI, Chile 20.
14. AGI, Chile 20.
15. AGI, Chile 20. The Apostle St. Bartholomew is associated with the story of the evils collected and stored in the form of a demon. It was chained by the Saint but at times escaped, causing damage.
16. A Chilean term of Mapuche origin that has two meanings according the dictionary of the RAE: 1. Invasion and pillaging by white men in Indian territory; 2. surprise Indian attacks.
17. AGI, Chile 20.
18. AGI, Chile 20.
19. AGI, Chile 20.
20. AGI, Chile 20.
21. AGI, Chile 20.
22. AGI, Chile 20.

35. The Struggle for Justice: Offensive or Defensive War

1. AGI, Chile 20.
2. Sabine MacCormack, *On the Wings of Time: Rome, the Incas, Spain, and Peru* (Princeton: Princeton University Press, 2007); Seed, *Ceremonies of Possession*; Lewis Hanke, *The Spanish Struggle for Justice in the Conquest of America* (Boston: Little, Brown, 1965), and the same author's *Bartolomé de las Casas: Bookman, Scholar & Propagandist* (Philadelphia: University of Pennsylvania Press, 1952); Clayton, *Bartolomé de las Casas*, and the same author's *Bartolomé de las Casas: A Biography*.
3. Clayton, *Bartolomé de las Casas*, 37.
4. Clayton, *Bartolomé de las Casas*, 19–34, 39–51; Las Casas died in Madrid in 1566. See also Lewis Hanke, *The First Social Experiments in America: A Study in the Development of Spanish Policy in the Sixteenth Century* (Gloucester, Mass: P. Smith, 1964).
5. Lewis Hanke, *All Mankind is One: A Study of the Disputation between Bartolomé de las Casas and Juan Ginés de Sepúlveda in 1550 on the Intellectual and Religious Capacity of the American Indians* (DeKalb: Northern Illinois University Press, 1974). It is unclear if Las Casas was ever in Peru.
6. Moreno Jeria, "Metodología misional jesuita," 241–46; Beatriz Lorraine Blum, "Padre Luis de Valdivia and the Araucanians," MA thesis (Chicago: Loyola University, 1942), 25, n. 35, notes three Franciscans were killed with the Spanish defeat at Curalaba in 1598. Accessed 3 March 2020, https://ecommons.luc_theses/56.
7. Luis de Valdivia published *Arte y Gramática General de la lengua que corre en todo el Reino de Chile, con un Vocabulario y Confesionario compuesto por el Padre Luis de Valdivia de la Compañía de Jesús en la provincia del Pirú* (Lima: Francisco del Canto, 1606), and the *Sermón en lengua de Chile: de los misterios de nuestra santa fe catholica, para predicarla a los indios infieles del reyno de Chile, dividido en nueve partes pequeñas, acomodadas a su capacidad* (Valladolid, 1621).
8. Andrew Redden, "The Best Laid Plans . . .: Jesuit Counsel, Peacebuilding, and Disaster on the Chilean Frontier; The Martyrs Elicura, 1612," *Journal of Jesuit Studies* 4, no. 2 (2017), 252. José Manuel Díaz Blanco, *El alma en la palabra: Escritos inéditos del P. Luis de Valdivia* (Santiago de Chile: Pontificia Universedad de Chile, 2011), 30, provided Redden this important insight. See also Blum, "Valdivia and the Araucanians," 35, n. 27.
9. Blum, "Valdivia and the Araucanians," 83.
10. Blum, "Valdivia and the Araucanians," 31–37.
11. Blum, "Valdivia and the Araucanians," 36.
12. Crescente Errázuriz, *Historia de Chile durante los gobiernos de García Ramón, Merlo de la Fuente y Jaraquemada*, 2 vols. (Santiago: Imprenta Cervantes, 1908), 1: 293–94.
13. Errázuriz, *Los gobiernos de García Ramón, Merlo de la Fuente y Jaraquemada*, 1: 295–96.
14. Errázuriz, *Los gobiernos de García Ramón, Merlo de la Fuente y Jaraquemada*, 1: 300–301.
15. Blum, "Valdivia and the Araucanians," 39, n. 30. The date, printer, and place are questionable. Blum suggests 1610 or 1611. A photostat copy is in the Massachusetts Historical Society, Feb. 1928, no. 264. For the text see Luis de Valdivia, *Tratado de la importancia del medio que el virrey propone de cortar la guerra de Chile y hazerla solamente defensiva*, Google eBook, accessed 8 July 2020. Regarding Valdivia's influence, see also Richard Kagan, "Ante todo, nunca te mientas a ti mismo: Pedro de Valencia, la "Historia de Chile" y la autocensura," *manuScrits.Revista d'Història Mod-*

erna 35 (2017), 83–101, accessed 25 August 2020, https://revistes.uab.cat/manuscrits/article/view/v35-kagan/171-pdf-es.

16. Blum, "Valdivia and the Araucanians," 40–44.

17. Blum, "Valdivia and the Araucanians," 45–47.

18. Redden, "Jesuit Counsel, Peacebuilding, and Disaster on the Chilean Frontier," 259–63.

19. Blum, "Valdivia and the Araucanians," 83.

20. Blum, "Valdivia and the Araucanians," 66–67; Andrew Redden, "Not-So-Good Shepherds: Reluctant Jesuit Martyrs on the Seventeenth-Century Chilean Frontier," *The Frontiers of Mission: Perspectives on Early Modern Missionary Catholicism* (Brill, e-book, 2016), 90–114.

21. Blum, "Valdivia and the Araucanians," 86–92; Antonio Astrain, SJ, *Historia de la Compañía de Jesús en la asistencia de España*, 7 vols. (Madrid: Sucesores de Rivadeneyra, 1905–25), 5: 627; Francisco Enrich, SJ, *Historia de la Compañía de Jesús en Chile*, 2 vols. (Barcelona: Francisco Rosal, 1891), 1: 317.

22. Blum, "Valdivia and the Araucanians," 98–100, 98, n. 44; Diego de Rosales SJ, *Historia general del reino de Chile*, 3 vols. (Valparaíso: Imprenta del Mercurio, 1878), 2: 619 and 100, n. 4–8; Astrain, *Historia de la Compañía*, 5: 642–46; Redden, "Jesuit Counsel, Peacebuilding, and Disaster on the Chilean Frontier," 269, n. 77; Díaz Blanco, *El alma en la palabra*, 43–44.

23. Medina, *Diccionario biográfico colonial de Chile*, 612–15, 627–29; Javiera Jaque Hidalgo, "Misiones jesuitas en la Guerra de Arauco: Resistencia mapuche, negociación y movilidad cultural en la periferia colonial (1593–1641)," *Rocky Mountain Review* 68, no. 2 (2014), 182–83.

24. Much of this biographical information comes from Medina, *Diccionario biográfico colonial de Chile*, 296–301. Medina's source may have been a printed petition by Luis Fernández de Córdova y Arce requesting a noble title and membership in the Order of Santiago, and a position in the Council of War or Council of the Indies. *Señor. Don Luis Fernández de Cordoua y Arze, cuya es la villa del Carpio . . . dize, que don García Fernandez su padre . . . siruio a su costa, como auenturero, quando el ingles entro en Cadiz . . . Suplica . . . le haga V.M. merced de honrar su casa con un título . . . Texto firmado por Lic. Don Francisco de Barreda*. It would have been distributed to the Council and Philip IV around 1630. A digitized copy is available at Biblioteca de la Universidad de Sevilla, Fondo Antiguo, accessed 14 March 2020, https://archive.org/details/A11012511/mode/2up. See also Guillermo Lohmann Villena, "Los Fernández de Córdoba: un linaje preponderante en el Perú en los siglos XVI y XVII," *Anuario de Estudios Americanos* 45 (1988): 167–240.

25. Redden, "Jesuit Counsel, Peacebuilding, and Disaster on the Chilean Frontier," n. 78; Eugene H. Korth, *Spanish Policy in Colonial Chile: The Struggle for Social Justice, 1535–1700* (Stanford: Stanford University Press, 1968), 161. Elliot, *The Count-Duke of Olivares*, 3, 34–45, 50–65, covers in detail this period of transition.

26. Nataly Cancino Cabello, "El (des)conocido impresor de Sermón en lengua de Chile (1621)," *Romance Notes* 56, no. 3 (2016) 497–98; Blum, "Luis de Valdivia and the Araucanians," 103.

27. AGI, Chile 20, letter of Governor Fernández de Córdova y Arce to the king, 1 February 1627; see Daniel Hershenzon, *The Captive Sea: Slavery, Communication, and Commerce in Early Modern Spain and the Mediterranean* (Philadelphia: University of Pennsylvania Press, 2018).

28. For the mistreatment and lack of respect in Spain, see Nancy E. Van Deusen, *Global Indios: The Indigenous Struggle for Justice in Sixteenth-century Spain* (Durham: Duke University Press, 2015).

29. AGI, Chile 20. For arguments regarding enslavement of the Araucanians, Chichimecs,

Chiriguanos, Caribs, and comparison with Moriscos and Muslims taken as slaves, see Cook, *Forbidden Passages*, 180–83.

30. AGI, Chile 20. The 1607 cédula that Oré referenced came with the royal appointment (2 September 1607) for Alonso García Ramón as governor of Chile.

31. AGI, Chile 20.

32. AGI, Chile 20.

33. AGI, Chile 20

36. The Conflict Becomes Ugly

1. AGI, Chile 20, letter to king, 16 January 1628.

2. AGI, Chile 20, letter, 16 January 1628.

3. AGI, Chile 20, letter, 16 January 1628.

4. AGI, Chile 20, letter, 16 January 1628.

5. AGI, Chile 20, Notation in Madrid, 18 February 1630 on the governor's letter to the king of 16 January 1628.

6. AGI, Chile 20, Notation in Madrid, 23 February 1630 on the governor's letter 16 January 1628.

7. AGI, Chile 20, letter to king, 1 February 1629.

8. AGI, Chile 20, letter to king and Council, 20 January 1629.

9. AGI, Chile 20.

10. AGI, Chile 20.

11. AGI, Chile 20.

12. AGI, Chile 20.

13. AGI, Chile 20.

14. AGI, Chile 20. Jesuit Bartolomé Navarro and Mercedarian Rodrigo Lobato testified on 7 February 1629.

15. Aguirre, *Recopilación recomendada . . .*, Libro III, Título 4, Ley 24, 329. Lorenzo Arrazola, *Enciclopedia española de derecho y nuevo teatro universal de la legislación de España e Indias* (Madrid, 1856), 9: Ley 7, Philip IV.

16. J. Lloyd Mecham, *Church and State in Latin America: A History of Politico-Ecclesiastical Relations*, rev. ed. (Chapel Hill: University of North Carolina Press, 1966); W. Eugene Shiels, *King and Church: The Rise and Fall of the Patronato Real* (Chicago: Loyola University Press, 1961); Alfredo Viola, *Real Patronato y obispos del Paraguay colonial* (Asunción: Centro Interdisciplinario de Derecho Social y Económico, 2002).

37. Bishop Oré's Testament

1. AGI, Chile 63.

2. Pello, "Últimos días de Oré," 161–71. Pello found two manuscripts, an inventory of Oré's estate and his will, in the Achivo Histórico de Santiago de Chile (AHSC), Fondo Real Academia (FRA), vol. 1008.

3. Pello, "Últimos días de Oré," FHSC-FRA, vol. 1008, 109v–110r, 112r–v.
4. Pello, "Últimos días de Oré," FHSC-FRA, vol. 1008, 110r–111r.
5. Pello, "Últimos días de Oré," FHSC-FRA, vol. 1008, 77v–79r.
6. Pello, "Últimos días de Oré," FHSC-FRA, vol. 1008, 78r, 110r, 111r–111v.
7. Pello, "Últimos días de Oré," FHSC-FRA, vol. 1008, 111r–112r.

38. Conclusion: The Legacy

1. Córdova y Salinas, *Crónica franciscana del Perú*, 1106–7.
2. AGI, Chile, 20. Governor Francisco Laso de la Vega was appointed on 16 March 1628 (Schäfer, *El Consejo Real de las indias*, 2: 351). Until Oré's replacement arrived, the bishop of Santiago, Francisco de Salcedo (2 April 1623 to 1635) oversaw the diocese (Schäfer, *El Consejo Real de las indias*, 2: 598).
3. See Alfredo Palacios Roa, "Dominio y catástrofe: Los terremotos en Concepción, Chile: 1550–1751," *Anuario de Estudios Americanos* 69, no. 2 (2012), 569–600.
4. See Espinoza Soria, *La Catequesis en Fray Luis Jerónimo de Oré*.
5. Rolena Adorno, "Images of *Indios Ladinos* in Early Colonial Peru," in *Transatlantic Encounters: Europeans and Andeans in the Sixteenth Century*, eds. Kenneth J. Andrien and Rolena Adorno (Berkeley: University of California Press, 1991), 257. Franklin Pease G. Y., in "Chronicles of the Andes in the Sixteenth and Seventeenth Centuries," *Guide to Documentary Sources for Andean Studies, 1530–1900*, 1: 16, wrote that "Oré's books are particularly noteworthy because of his knowledge of indigenous languages and his ample missionary experience."
6. The year after Oré died Juan Pérez de Bocanegra published the *Ritual Formulario, e Institución de Curas . . .* (Lima, 1631). According to Vargas Ugarte, *Historia de la Iglesia en el Perú*, 1: 228, Pérez Bocanegra included some of Oré's material in his text. See also Cipriano Muñoz y Manzano, *Bibliografía Española de lenguas indígenas de América* (Madrid, 1892; reprint, Madrid, 1977), 90.
7. See Baker and Knighton, *Music and Urban Society in Colonial Latin America*; and Ignacio Chuecas-Saldías, *Dueños de la frontera. Terratenientes y sociedad colonial en la periferia chilena, Isla de la Laja (1670–1845)* (Santiago: Ediciones de la Biblioteca Nacional, 2018).
8. Diego Zambrana de Villalobos, named as Oré's successor in 1633, did not reach the diocese until 1638. Andrango-Walker, *Símbolo católico de Oré*, 195–96, notes: "the section where Oré deals with the defense of the natives is not well explained; nevertheless, it constitutes a valuable contribution in order to know more closely the activities of the *letrado* from Huamanga as bishop, as defender of the natives and as champion of the faith."
9. AGI, Chile 60; Medina, *Biblioteca Hispano-chilena*, 1:131.

Bibliography

Published Primary Sources

Acosta, José de. *Historia natural y moral de las Indias* [1590]. Madrid: Historia 16, 1987.

———. *De natura Noui Orbis libri duo; et De promulgatione Euangelij apud barbaros, siue De procuranda Indorum salute.* Salamanca: Guillelmum Foquel, 1589.

———. *De Procuranda Indorum Salute* [1588]. 2 vols. Madrid: CSIC, 1984–87.

Aguirre, Joaquín. *Recopilación compendada de las Leyes de Indias aumentada con algunas notas.* Madrid: Ignacio Boix, 1846.

Arrazola, Lorenzo. *Enciclopedia española de derecho y nuevo teatro universal de la legislación de España e Indias.* Madrid, 1856.

Barco Centenera, Martín del. *La Argentina y Conquista del Río de la Plata.* Lisbon: Pedro Crassbeeck, 1602.

Barriga, Victor M., ed. *Documentos para la historia de Arequipa.* 3 vols. Arequipa: La Colmena, 1939–55.

———, ed. *Memorias para la historia de Arequipa.* 4 vols. Arequipa: La Colmena, 1941–52.

———, ed. *Los Mercedarios en el Perú en el siglo xvi.* Vol. 3. Arequipa: La Colmena, 1942.

Benito, José Antonio, ed. *Libro de visitas de Santo Toribio de Mogrovejo (1593–1605).* Lima: PUCP, 2006.

Bertonio, Ludovico. *Vocabulario de la lengua aymara* [1612]. Facs. edited by Xavier Albó and Félix Layme. Cochabamba: "El Buítre," 1984.

Betanzos, Juan de. *Suma y narración de los Incas* [1551]. Madrid: Atlas, 1987.

Calancha, Antonio de la. *Crónicas Agustinas del Perú.* 2 vols. Madrid: CSIC, 1972.

Cabello de Balboa, Miguel. *Miscelánea antártica: una historia del Perú antiguo* [1586]. Lima: UNMSM, 1951.

Cieza de León, Pedro de. *Crónica del Perú. Primera Parte* [1553], edited by Franklin Pease G. Y. 2nd ed. Lima: PUCP, 1986.

———. *Crónica del Perú. Cuarta Parte, vol. 2. Guerra de Chupas* [1551–54], edited by Gabriela Benavides de Rivero. Lima: PUCP, 1994.

———. *The Discovery and Conquest of Peru*, translated and edited by Alexandra Parma Cook and Noble David Cook. Durham: Duke University Press, 1998.

Cobo, Bernabé. *Historia de la fundación de Lima*. Lima: Imprenta Liberal, 1882.

———. *History of the Inca Empire* [1653], translated and edited by Ronald Hamilton. Austin: University of Texas Press, 1979.

Compendio de los comentarios extendidos por el maestro Antonio Gómez, a las ochenta y tres leyes de Toro. Madrid: Joseph Deblado, 1785.

Constituciones generales para todas las monjas, y religiosas sujetas a la obedencia de la orden de N.P.S. Francisco, en toda esta familia cismontana. Mexico City: Imprenta de la Viuda de Francisco Rodríguez Lupercio, 1689.

Cook, Noble David. "Libro de cargos del tesorero Alonso Riquelme con el rescate de Atahualpa." *Humanidades* 2 (1969): 41–88.

———, ed. *Padrón de los indios de Lima en 1613*. Lima: UNMSM, 1968.

———, ed. *Tasa de la visita general de Francisco de Toledo* [1571–75]. Lima: UNMSM, 1975.

Córdova y Salinas, Diego de. *Chronica franciscana de las provincias del Perú* [1651]. Washington, DC: Academy of American Franciscan History, 1957.

———. *Vida . . . el apóstol del Perú el Venerable P. Fray Francisco Solano*. Madrid: Imprenta Real, 1643.

Covarrubias Orozco, Sebastián de. *Tesoro de la lengua castellana o española* [1611], edited by Felipe C. R. Maldonado. Madrid: Editorial Castalia, 1994.

Cruz, Fray Laureano de la. *Descripción de la América austral o reinos del Perú con particular noticia de lo hecho por los franciscanos*. Lima: PUCP, 1999.

Enríquez Alemendárez, Alonso. "Dos cartas del obispo de Cuba D. Fray Alonso Enríquez Alemendárez, en contestación a una Real Cédula de Felipe III, copiadas de los originales por D. Domingo del Monte." *Memorias de la Real Sociedad Económica de la Habana* 2nd Serie, no. 1, (Janurary 1847): 181–97.

Espinosa Soria, Miguel Angelo. *La Catequesis en Fray Luis Jerónimo de Oré*. Lima: Convento de los Descalzos, 2012.

Fernández, Enríque, ed. *Monumenta Peruana VIII (1603–1604)*. Rome: Institutum Historicum Societatis Iesu, 1986.

Fernández de Oviedo y Valdés, Gonzalo. *Historia general y natural de las Indias* [1535], edited by Juan Pérez de Tudela Bueso. 5 vols. Madrid: Atlas, 1959.

Garcilaso de la Vega, El Inca. *The Florida of the Inca* [1605], translated and edited by John Grier Varner and Jeanette Johnson Varner. Austin: University of Texas Press, 1951.

———. *Obras completas*. 4 vols. Madrid: Atlas, 1960.

———. *Royal Commentaries of the Incas, and General History of Peru* [1609], translated and edited by Harold V. Livermore. 2 vols. Austin: University of Texas Press, 1966.

González Holguin, Diego. *Gramática y arte nveva de la lengva general de todo el Perú, llamada lengua Qquichua, o lengua del Inca*. Lima: Francisco del Canto, 1607.

———. *Vocabulario de la lengua general de todo el Perú llamada Quechua* [1608], edited by Raúl Porras Barrenechea. Lima: UNMSM, 1952.

Loyola, Martín Ignacio de. *Viaje alrededor del mundo,* edited by José Ignacio Tellechea Idígoras. Madrid: Historia 16, 1989.

Izaguirre, Bernardino, ed. *Historia de las misiones franciscanas.* 14 vols. Lima, 1922–30.

Jiménez de la Espada, Marcos, ed. *Relaciones geográficas de Indias. Perú.* 3 vols. Rev. ed. Madrid: Atlas, 1965.

La embajada japonesa de 1614 a la ciudad de Sevilla. Seville: Ayuntamiento de Sevilla, 1991.

Levillier, Roberto, ed. *Papeles eclesiásticos de Tucumán: documentos originales del Archivo de Indias.* 2 vols. Madrid, 1926.

Libro de Cabildo de la Ciudad de San Juan de la Frontera de Huamanga. Lima: Casa de la Cultura, 1955.

Libros de Cabildos de Lima. Libro Noveno (Años 1579–1583). Lima: Torres Aguirre-SanMarti, 1937.

Lizárraga, Reginaldo de. *Descripción del Perú, Tucumán, Río de la Plata y Chile* [1595–1609]. Madrid: Historia 16, 1985.

Lohmann Villena, Guillermo, ed. *Francisco de Toledo. Disposiciones gubernativas para el virreinato del Perú, 1569–80.* 2 vols. Seville: Escuela de Estudios Hispanoamericanos, 1986–89.

López de Velasco, Juan. *Geografía y descripción universal de las Indias* [1571–74]. Madrid: Real Academia de la Historia, 1894.

Loredo, Rafael. *Los repartos.* Lima: Miranda, 1958.

Mateos, Francisco, ed. *Obras del P. José de Acosta.* Madrid: Atlas, 1954.

Maúrtua, Victor M., ed. *Juicio de límites entre el Perú y Bolivia, prueba peruana.* 12 vols. Barcelona, 1906.

Medina, José Toribio. *Biblioteca Hispano-chilena (1523–1817).* 3 vols. Santiago de Chile, 1897–99.

———. *Diccionario biográfico colonial de Chile.* Santiago de Chile: Imprenta Elzeviriana, 1906.

Mendoza, Diego de. *Chronica de la Provincia de San Antonio de los Charcas* [1664]. La Paz: Editorial Casa Municipal de la Cultura Franz Tamayo, 1976.

Milanich, Jerald T., and William C. Sturtevant, eds. *Francisco Pareja's 1613 Confessionario: a documentary source for Timucuan ethnography.* Tallahassee: Florida Division of Archives, History, and Records Management, 1972.

Molina, Cristóbal de. *Account of the Fables and Rites of the Incas.* Translated and edited by Brian S. Bauer, et al. Austin: University of Texas Press, 2011.

Monardes, Nicolás. *Historia medicinal de las cosas que se traen de nuestras Indias occidentales que sirven en medicina* [1574]. Seville: Padilla Libros, 1988.

Monumenta Peruana. Edited by Antonio de Egaña. 8 vols. Rome: Apud "Monumenta Historica Soc. Iesu," 1954.

Ocaña, Diego de. *A través de la América del Sur* [ca. 1605]. Madrid: Historia 16, 1987.

Oré, Luis Hierónymo de. *Symbolo Catholico Indiano, en el qual se declaran los mysterios de la Fe contenidos en los tres Symbolos Catholicos Apostolico, Niceno, y de S. Athanasio. Contiene assi mesmo una descripcion del nuevo orbe, y de los naturales del. Y un orden de enseñarles la doctrina Christiana en las dos lenguas Generales, Quichua y Aymara, con un Confesionario breve y Catechismo de la communion*. Lima: Ricardo, 1598.

Oré, Luis Gerónimo de. *Rituale, seu manuale peruanum, et forma brevis administrandi apud Indos sacrosancta Baptismi, Poenitentiae, Eucharistiae, Matrimonij, & Extremae unctionis Sacramenta* [1607]. Naples: Appud Io. Iacobum Carlinum & Constantinum Vitalem, 1607.

Oré, Luis Gerónimo de. *Corona de la sacratissima Virgen Maria madre de Dios nuestra señora, en que se contienen ochenta meditaciones, de los principales misterios de la Fé: que corresponden a setenta y tres Ave Maria y ocho vezes el Pater noster, ofrecidas a los felices años que vivio en el mundo . . . Dedicada a la misma virgen sacrosanta, concebida sin pecado original, en su imagen y Santuario de Copacavana*. Madrid: La Viuda de Cosme Delgado, 1619.

Oré, Luis Jerónimo de. *Relación de los mártires de la Florida del P. F. Luis Jerónimo de Oré (c. 1619)*, edited by Raquel Chang-Rodríguez. Lima: PUCP, 2014.

Oré, Luys Hieronymo de. *Relacion de los martires de la Florida, doze Religiosos de la Compañia de IESUS, que padecieron en el Iacan y cinco de la Orden de nuestro Serafico P.S. Francisco, en la Provincia de Guale. Ponese assi mesmo la discripcion de Iacan donde se han fortificado los Ingleses, y de otras cosas tocantes a la conversion de los Indios*. Madrid, c. 1619

Oré, Luis Jerónimo de. *Relación histórica de la Florida, escrito en el siglo XVII*, edited by Atanasio López. 2 vols. Madrid: Imprenta de Ramona Velasco, 1931–33.

Oré, Luis Gerónimo de. *The Martyrs of Florida, 1513–1616*, translated and edited by Maynard Geiger. New York: Joseph F. Wagner, 1936.

Oré, Luis Gerónimo de. *Relación de la vida y milagros de San Francisco Solano* [1614], edited by Noble David Cook. Lima: PUCP, 1998.

Oré, Luis Hierónymo de. *Symbolo Catholico Indiano*, facsimile, edited by Antonine Tibesar. Lima: Australis, 1998.

Oré, Luis Jerónimo de. *Account of the Martyrs in the Provinces of La Florida*, translated and edited by Raquel Chang-Rodríguez and Nancy Vogeley. Albuquerque: University of New Mexico Press, 2017.

Ortiz de Zúñiga, Diego. *Anales eclesiásicos y seculares de la muy noble y leal ciudad de Sevilla* [1796]. 5 vols. Seville: Guadalquivir, 1988.

Pallas, Gerónymo. *Missión a las Indias: de Roma a Lima, 1619*, edited by José Jesús Hernández Palomo. Madrid: CSIC, 2006.

Pareja, Francisco. *Confessionario en lengua castellana y timuquana*. Mexico: Viuda de Diego López Davalos, 1613.

Pease G. Y., Franklin, ed. *Collaguas I*. Lima: PUCP, 1977.

Pérez de Bocanegra, Juan. *Ritual Formulario, e Institución de Curas*. . . . Lima, 1631.

Poma de Ayala, Felipe Guaman. *El primer nueva corónica y buen gobierno*, edited by John V. Murra and Rolena Adorno. 3 vols. Mexico: Siglo Veintiuno, 1980.

Proceso diocesano de San Francisco Solano, introduction by Fernando Iwasaki Cauti and paleography by María José Acuña. Montilla: Bibliofíla Montillana, 1999.

Ramírez, Balthasar. "Descripción del reyno del Pirú [1597]. In Victor M. Maúrtua, ed., *Juicio de límites entre el Perú y Bolivia, prueba peruana*. Barcelona, 1906, 1: 281–363.

Ramos Gavilán, Alonso. *Historia del santuario de nuestra señora de Copacabana* [1621]. Lima: Ignacio Prado Pastor, 1988.

Ricardo, Antonio. *Vocabulario y phrasis en la lengua general de los indios del Perú, llamada Quichua* [1586]. Lima: UNMSM, 1951.

Rubio Merino, Pedro, ed. *La monja alférez: Doña Catalina de Erauso. Dos manuscritos autobiográficos inéditos*. Seville: Cabildo Metropolitano de la Catedral de Sevilla, 1995.

Sahagún, Bernardino de. *Historia general de las cosas de Nueva España*, edited by Ángel María Garibay K. Mexico: Editorial Porrúa, 1992.

Salinas y Córdova, Fray Buenaventura de. *Memorial de las historias del Nuevo Mundo Perú*. Lima: Gerónimo de Contreras, 1631, introduction by Luis E. Valcarcel. Lima: UNMSM, 1957.

Sandoval, Alonso de. *De instauranda Aethiopum salute. Un tratado sobre la esclavitud*, edited by Enriqueta Vila Vilar. Madrid: Alianza Editorial, 1987.

———. *Treatise on Slavery: Selections from De Instauranda Aethiopum Salute* [1627], edited and translated by Nicole von Germeten. Indianapolis: Hackett Publishing, 2008.

Santo Tomás, Domingo de. *Gramática o arte de la lengua general de los indios de los reynos del Perú* [1560]. Lima: UNMSM, 1951.

———. *Lexicon o vocabulario de la lengua general de los indios de los reynos del Peru* [1560]. Lima: UNMSM, 1951.

Silva, Juan de. *Advertencias importantes acerca del buen govierno y administración de las Indias assi en lo espiritual como en lo temporal repartidas en tres memoriales informativos*. Madrid: Por la Viuda de Fernando de Corria Montenegro, 1621.

Stepto, Michele and Gabriel Stepto, trans. *Lieutenant Nun: Memoir of a Basque Transvestite in the New World. Catalina de Erauso*. Boston: Beacon Press, 1996.

Tercero Concilio Limense 1582–1583. Version castellana original de los decretos con el suma-

rio del Segundo Concilio Limense, edited by P. Enrique Bartra, S.J. Lima: Facultad Pontificia y Civil de Teología de Lima, 1982.

Tercero Concilio Limense (1582–1591). Edición bilingüe de los decretos, edited by Luis Martínez Ferrer. Lima and Rome: Facultad Pontificia y Civil de Teología de Lima, 2017.

Ulloa Mogollón, Juan de. "Relación de la provincia de los Collaguas (1586)." In *Relaciones geográficas de Indias, Perú*, edited by Marcos Jiménez de la Espada, 1: 326–33. 3 vols. Madrid: Atlas, 1965.

Valdivia, Luis de. *Arte y Gramática General de la lengua que corre en todo el Reino de Chile, con un Vocabulario y Confesionario compuesto por el Padre Luis de Valdivia de la Compañía de Jesús en la provincia del Pirú*. Lima: Francisco del Canto, 1606.

———. *Sermón en lengua de Chile: de los misterios de nuestra santa fe catholica, para predicarla a los indios infieles del reyno de Chile, dividido en nueve partes pequeñas, acomodadas a su capacidad*. Valladolid, 1621.

———. *Tratado de la importancia del medio que el virrey propone de cortar la guerra de Chile y hazerla solamente defensiva*. NP, 1610 or 1611.

Vargas Ugarte, Rubén, ed. *Concilios Limenses*. 3 vols. Lima: Tipografía Peruana, 1954.

Vázquez de Espinosa, Antonio. *Compendio y descripción de las Indias occidentales* [ca. 1621]. Washington, DC: Smithsonian Miscellaneous Collections, vol. 108, 1948.

Vega, Antonio de. "Historia o narración de las cosas sucedidas en este colegio del Cuzco destos Reynos del Perú desde su fundación hasta hoy . . . 1600," Rubén Vargas Ugarte, introducción y notas, *Historia del Colegio y Universidad de San Ignacio de Loyola de la ciudad del Cuzco*, Biblioteca Histórica Peruana, tomo VI. Lima: Studium, 1948.

Viera y Clavijo, José de. *Noticias de la historia general de las Islas de Canaria*. Madrid: Imprenta de Blas Román, 1776.

Villagómez, Pedro de. *Carta pastoral de exhortación e instrucción contra las idolatrías de los indios del arzobispado de Lima*. Lima: Sanmartí, 1919.

Viscarra Fabre, Jesús, ed. *Copacabana de los Incas. Documentos auto-lingüísticos e isografiados del Aymáru-Aymára*. Laz Paz: Palza Hermanos, 1901.

Zárate, Agustín de. *Historia del descubrimiento y conquista del Perú* [1555], edited by Franklin Pease G. Y. and Teodoro Hampe Martínez. Lima: PUCP, 1995.

Secondary Sources

Adorno, Rolena. "Felipe Guaman Poma de Ayala: Native Writer and Litigant in Early Colonial Peru." In *The Human Condition in Colonial Latin America*, edited by Kenneth J. Andrien, 2nd ed., 173–98. New York: Rowman & Littlefield, 2013.

———. "Images of *Indios Ladinos* in Early Colonial Peru." In *Transatlantic Encounters: Europeans and Andeans in the Sixteenth Century*, edited by Kenneth J. Andrien and Rolena Adorno, 232–70. Berkeley: University of California Press, 1991.

Ahlgren, Gillian T. W. *Teresa of Avila and the Politics of Sanctity*. Ithaca: Cornell University Press, 1996.

Albó, Xavier, and Félix Layme. "Introducción." *Vocabulario de la lengua aymara* [1612], by P. Ludovico Bertonio. Fasc. ed., ix–lxxiv. Cochabamba: "El Buítre," 1984.

Andrango-Walker, Catalina. *El 'Símbolo católico indiano' (1598) de Luis Jerónimo de Oré. Sabereres coloniales y los problemas de la evangelización en la región andina*. Madrid: Iberoamericana-Veruert, Biblioteca Indiana, 2018.

Andrien, Kenneth J., ed. *The Human Condition in Colonial Latin America*. 2nd ed. New York: Rowman & Littlefield, 2013.

Andrien, Kenneth J., and Rolena Adorno, eds. *Transatlantic Encounters: Europeans and Andeans in the Sixteenth Century*. Berkeley: University of California Press, 1991.

Armas Medina, Fernando de. *Cristianización del Perú (1532–1600)*. Seville: Escuela de Estudios Hispanoamericanos, 1953.

Arroyo, Luis, OFM, *Comisarios Generales del Perú*. Madrid: CSIC y el Instituto Santo Toribio de Mogrovejo, 1950.

Astrain, SJ, Antonio. *Historia de la Compañía de Jesús en la asistencia de España*. 7 vols. Madrid: Sucesores de Rivadeneyra, 1905–25.

Aznar Vallejo, Eduardo. "The Conquests of the Canary Islands." In *Implicit Understandings: Observing, Reporting, and Reflecting on the Encounters Between Europeans and Other Peoples in the Early Modern Era*, edited by Stuart B. Schwartz, 134–56. Cambridge: Cambridge University Press, 1994.

———. *La integración de las Islas Canarias en la Corona de Castilla (1478–1526)*. La Laguna, 1983.

Baker, Geoffrey, and Tess Knighton, eds. *Music and Urban Society in Colonial Latin America*. Cambridge: Cambridge University Press, 2011.

Bakewell, Peter. *Miners of the Red Mountain. Indian Labor in Potosí, 1545–1650*. Albuquerque: University of New Mexico Press, 1984.

———. *Silver and Entrepreneurship in Seventeenth-Century Potosí: The Life and Times of Antonio López de Quiroga*. Dallas: Southern Methodist University, 1995.

Barba, Francisco Esteve. *Historiografía indiana*. Madrid: Editorial Gredos, 1964.

Barnadas, Josep M. "Una polémica colonial: Potosí, 1579–1584." *Jahrbuch für Geschichte Latein-amerikas* 10 (1973): 16–70.

Barros Arana, Diego. *Historia general de Chile*. 16 vols. Santiago, 1884–1902.

Bartra, Enrique T. "Los autores del Catecismo del Tercer Concilio Limense." *Mercurio Peruano* 470 (1967): 359–72.

Benito, José Antonio. "Obispos participantes en el III Limense." In *Tercer Concilio Li-

mense (1583–1591), edited by Luis Martínez Ferrer, 99–110. Lima: Facultad Pontificia y Civil de Teologia de Lima, 2017.

Beyersdorff, Margot. "Oré, Luis Jerónimo de (1554–1630)." In *Guide to Documentary Sources for Andean Studies 1530–1900*, edited by Joanne Pillsbury, 72–75. 3 vols. Norman: University of Oklahoma Press, 2008.

———. "Rito y verbo en la poesía de fray Luis Jerónimo de Oré." In *Mito y simbolismo en los Andes: La figura y la palabra*, edited by Henrique Urbano, 215–37. Cuzco: Centro de Estudios Regionales Andinos Bartolomé de las Casas, 1993.

Blum, Beatriz Lorraine. "Padre Luis de Valdivia and the Araucanians." MA thesis, Loyola University of Chicago, 1942. Accessed 3 March 2020. https://ecommons.luc_theses/56.

Brading, David A. *The First America. The Spanish Monarchy, Creole Patriots, and the Liberal State, 1492–1867*. Cambridge: Cambridge University Press, 1991.

Bradley, Peter T. *The Lure of Peru: Maritime Intrusion into the South Sea, 1598–1701*. New York: St. Martin's Press, 1989.

Brickhouse, Anna. *The Unsettlement of America: Translation, Interpretation, and the Story of Don Luis de Velasco, 1560–1945*. New York: Oxford University Press, 2015.

Broadwell, George Aaron. "The Things They Formerly Worshipped: Timucua Christian Texts on Native Worship." In *Facing Florida: Essays on Culture and Religion in Early Modern Southeastern America*, edited by Timothy J. Johnson and Jeffrey M. Burns, 51–62. Oceanside, CA: The American Academy of Franciscan History, 2021.

Burga, Manuel. *Nacimiento de una utopía: muerte y resurección de los incas*. Lima: Instituto de Apoyo Agrario, 1988.

Burgaleta, Claudio M. *José de Acosta, S. J. (1540–1600): His Life and Thought*. Chicago: Jesuit Way, 1999.

Burke, Peter. "How to be a Counter-Reformation Saint." In *Religion and Society in Early Modern Europe, 1500–1800*, edited by Kaspar von Greyerz. London, 1984.

Burns, Kathryn. *Colonial Habits: Convents and the Spiritual Economy of Cuzco, Peru*. Durham: Duke University Press, 1999.

Bushnell, Amy T. *The King's Coffer: Proprietors of the Spanish Florida Treasury, 1565–1702*. Gainesville: University Presses of Florida, 1981.

———. *Situado and Sabana: Spain's Support System for the Presidio and Mission Provinces of Florida*. Anthropological Papers, no. 74. New York: American Museum of Natural History, 1994.

Busto Duthurburu, José Antonio del. *Diccionario Histórico Biográfico de los Conquistadores del Perú*. Lima: Studium, 1987.

Cancino Cabello, Nataly. "El (des)conocido impresor de Sermón en lengua de Chile (1621)." *Romance Notes* 56:3 (2016), 495–507.

Cañedo-Argüelles Fabrega, Teresa. *La visita de Juan Gutiérrez Flores al Colesuyo y Pleitos por los cacicazgos de Torata y Moquegua*. Lima: PUCP, 2005.

Caraman, Philip. *The Lost Paradise: an account of the Jesuits in Paraguay, 1607–1768.* London: Sidgwick and Jackson, 1975.

Castañeda Delgado, Paulino. *Los memoriales del padre Silva sobre predicación pacífica y repartimientos.* Madrid: CSIC: Instituto Gonzalo Fernández de Oviedo Col Tierra Nueva Cielo Nuevo VI, 1983.

Castañeda Delgado, Paulino, and Pilar Hernández Aparicio. *La Inquisición de Lima. Tomo I (1570–1635).* Madrid: Editorial DEIMOS, 1989.

Cavallini, Giuliana. *St. Martin de Porres: Apostle of Charity.* St. Louis: B. Herder Book Company, 1963.

Cerrón-Palomino, Rodolfo. "El Nebrija Indiano." In *Fray Domingo de S. Thomas, Grammatica o Arte de la Lengua General de los Indios de los Reynos del Perú* [1560], edited by Rodolfo Cerrón-Palomino, i–lxiii. Madrid: Ediciones de Cultura Hispánica, 1994.

Chang-Rodríguez, Raquel. "Estudio preliminar." In *Relación de los mártires de La Florida del P. F. Luis Jerónimo de Oré (c. 1619)*, edited by Raquel Chang-Rodríguez, 15–76. Lima: PUCP, 2014.

———. "Luis Jerónimo de Oré y la poesía de su *Símbolo católico indiano* (1598)." *Allpanchis* 44: 83–84 (2019): 149–70.

Chang-Rodríguez, Raquel, and Nancy Vogeley, "Introduction." In *Luis Jerónimo de Oré: Account of the Martyrs in the Provinces of La Florida,* translated and edited by Raquel Chang-Rodríguez and Nancy Vogeley, 1–64. Albuquerque: University of New Mexico Press, 2017.

Charles, John. *Allies at Odds: The Andean Church and Its Indigenous Agents, 1583–1671.* Albuquerque: University of New Mexico Press, 2010.

Charney, Paul. *Indian Society in the Valley of Lima, Peru 1532–1824.* Landham, MD: University Press of America, 2001.

Christian, William A. *Local Religion in Sixteenth-Century Spain.* Princeton: Princeton University Press, 1981.

Chuecas-Saldías, Ignacio. *Dueños de la frontera. Terratenientes y sociedad colonial en la periferia chilena, Isla de la Laja (1670–1845).* Santiago: Ediciones de la Biblioteca Nacional, 2018.

Clayton, Lawrence A. *Bartolomé de las Casas and the Conquest of the Americas.* Malden, MA: Wiley-Blackwell, 2011.

———. *Bartolomé de las Casas: A Biography.* Cambridge: Cambridge University Press, 2012.

Clendinnen, Inga. *Ambivalent Conquests: Maya and Spaniard in Yucatan, 1517–1570.* Cambridge: Cambridge University Press, 1987.

Cohn, Norman. *The Pursuit of the Millennium.* 2nd ed., rev. New York: Oxford University Press, 1970.

Cole, Jeffrey A. *The Potosí Mita, 1573–1700: Compulsory Indian Labor in the Andes.* Stanford: Stanford University Press, 1985.

Conover, Cornelius. "Saintly Biography and the Cult of San Felipe de Jesús in Mexico City, 1597–1697." *The Americas* 64:4 (2011): 441–66.
Cook, Alexandra Parma, and Noble David Cook. *Good Faith and Truthful Ignorance: A Case of Transatlantic Bigamy*. Durham: Duke University Press, 1991.
———. *The Plague Files: Crisis Management in Sixteenth-Century Seville*. Baton Rouge: Louisiana State University Press, 2009.
Cook, Karoline P. *Forbidden Crossings: Muslims and Moriscos in Colonial Spanish America*. Philadelphia: University of Pennsylvania Press, 2016.
Cook, Noble David. "Beyond the *Martyrs of Florida:* The Versatile Career of Luis Gerónimo de Oré." *The Florida Historical Quarterly* 71 (1992): 169–87.
———. *Born to Die. Disease and New World Conquest, 1492–1650*. Cambridge: Cambridge University Press, 1998.
———. *Demographic Collapse: Indian Peru, 1520–1620*. Cambridge: Cambridge University Press, 1981.
———. "Luis Jerónimo de Oré: una aproximación." In *Symbolo Catholico Indiano*, by Luis Jerónimo de Oré. Lima: Ricardo, 1598. Facs. ed. by Antonine Tibesar, 35–61. Lima: Australis, 1998.
———. *People of the Colca Valley: A Population Study*. Boulder: Westview Press, 1982.
———. "Sevilla: Una ciudad proto-industrial a base de la economía atlántica?" In *Mirando las dos orillas: intercambios mercantiles, sociales y culturales entre Andalucía y América*, edited by Enriqueta Vila Vilar and Jaime J. Lacueva Muñoz, 79–104. Seville: Fundación Buenas Letras, 2012.
———. "Tomando posesión Luis Gerónimo de Oré y el retorno de los franciscanos a las doctrinas del valle del Colca." In *El hombre y los Andes. Homenaje a Franklin Pease*, edited by Rafael Varón Gabai and Javier Flores Espinosa, 2: 889–903. Lima: Pontificia Universidad Católica del Perú, 2002.
———. "Viviendo en las márgenes del imperio: Luis Jerónimo de Oré y la exploración del otro." *Histórica* [Lima] 32:1 (2008): 11–38.
Cook, Noble David, with Alexandra Parma Cook. *People of the Volcano: Andean Counterpoint in the Colca Valley, Peru*. Durham: Duke University Press, 2007.
Cook, Noble David, and Franklin Pease G. Y. "New Research Opportunities in Los Collaguas, Peru." *Latin American Research Review* 10 (1975): 201–2.
Costa Vigo, Miguel. "Patronage and Bribery in Sixteenth-Century Peru: The Government of Viceroy Conde del Villar and the Visita of Licenciado Alonso Fernández de Bonilla." PhD diss., Florida International University, 2005.
Crespo Rodríguez, María Dolores. *Arquitectura doméstica de la Ciudad de los Reyes (1535–1750)*. Seville: CSIC y Universidad de Sevilla, 2006.
Curatola, Marco. "Mito y milenarismo en los Andes. Taki Onqoy a Inkarrí. La visión de un pueblo invicto." *Allpanchis* 10 (1977): 64–92.

Dean, Carolyn. *Inka Bodies and the Body of Christ: Corpus Christi in Colonial Cuzco, Peru.* Durham: Duke University Press, 1999.

Díaz Blanco, José Manuel. *El alma en la palabra: Escritos inéditos del P. Luis de Valdivia.* Santiago de Chile: Pontificia Universidad de Chile, 2011.

Dierksmeier, Laura. *Charity for and by the Poor: Franciscan-Indigenous Confraternities in Mexico, 1527–1700.* Norman: University of Oklahoma Press, 2020.

Dobyns, Henry F. *Their Number Become Thinned: Native American Population Dynamics in Eastern North America.* Knoxville: University of Tennessee Press, 1983.

Domínguez, Nicanor. "'Pidiéndonos que en nombre de todos suplicácemos a Su Magestad:' los poderes de los incas cuzqueños al capitán Garcilaso de la Vega, a don Melchor Carlos Ynga, a don Alonso Fernández de Mesa y a fray Jerónimo de Oré, OFM (1604)." In *Garcilasismo creativo y crítico: nueva antología,* edited by Eduardo González Viaña and José Antonio Mazzotti, 153–77. Salem, Lima, New York: Axiara Editions y Academia Norteamericana de la Lengua Española, 2016.

Domínguez Ortiz, Antonio. *Historia de Sevilla. La Sevilla del siglo XVII.* Seville: Universidad de Sevilla, 1984.

Durán Montero, María Antonia. *Fundación de ciudades en el Perú durante el siglo XVI.* Seville: Escuela de Estudios Hispanoamericanos, 1978.

Durston, Alan. *Pastoral Quechua: A History of Christian Translation in Colonial Peru, 1550–1650.* Notre Dame: University of Notre Dame Press, 2007.

Earle, Rebecca. *The Body of the Conquistador: Food, Race and the Colonial Experience in Spanish America, 1492–1700.* Cambridge: Cambridge University Press, 2012.

Errázuriz, Crescente. *Historia de Chile durante los gobiernos de García Ramón, Merlo de la Fuente y Jaraquemada.* 2 vols. Santiago: Imprenta Cervantes, 1908.

Egaña, Antonio de. *Historia de la Iglesia en la América Española: Hemisferio sur.* Madrid: Biblioteca de Autores Cristianos, 1966.

Eguiguren, Luis Antonio. *Historia de la universidad: Tomo I. La universidad en el siglo XVI.* Lima: Imprenta Santa María, 1951.

Elliott, John H. *The Count-Duke of Olivares: A Statesman in an Age of Decline.* New Haven: Yale University Press, 1986.

———. *Imperial Spain, 1469–1716.* New York: Mentor Book, 1966.

Enrich, SJ, Francisco. *Historia de la Compañía de Jesús en Chile.* 2 vols. Barcelona: Francisco Rosal, 1891.

Espinoza Soria, Miguel Angel. *La Catequesis en Fray Luis Jerónimo de Oré: Un Aporte a la Nueva Evangelización.* Lima: Convento de los Descalzos, 2012.

Estenssoro Fuchs, Juan Carlos. *Del paganismo a la santidad: La incorporación de los indios del Perú al Catolicismo, 1532–1750.* Lima: Pontificia Universidad Católica del Perú, 2003.

Esteve Barba, Francisco. *Historiografía indiana.* Madrid: Editorial Gredos, 1964.

Falcon, Leonardo. "Manufacturing Sin on the Frontier of Heresy: Bishops, Franciscans and the Inquisition in Cuba during the Long Sixteenth Century, 1511–1611." PhD diss., Florida International University, 2019.

Fechner, Fabian. *Entscheidungsprozesse vor Ort: Die Provinzkongregationen der Jesuiten in Paraguay (1608–1762)*. Regensburg: Verlag Schell & Steiner, 2015.

Fernández-Armesto, Felipe. *The Canary Islands after the Conquest: The Making of a Colonial Society in the Early Sixteenth Century*. Oxford: Oxford University Press, 1982.

Francis, J. Michael, and Kathleen M. Kole. *Murder and Martyrdom in Spanish Florida: Don Juan and the Guale Uprising of 1597*. Anthropological Papers, no. 95. New York: American Museum of Natural History, 2011.

Fraser, Valerie. *The Architecture of Conquest: Building in the Viceroyalty of Peru, 1535–1635*. Cambridge: Cambridge University Press, 1990.

Figuero y del Campo, Cristobal. *Franciscan Missions in Florida*. Spain: A R S Magna Ediciones, 1994.

Fuente, Alejandro de la. *Havana and the Atlantic in the Sixteenth Century*. Chapel Hill: University of North Carolina Press, 2008.

Galgano, Robert C. *Feast of Souls: Indians and Spaniards in the Seventeenth-Century Missions of Florida and New Mexico*. Albuquerque: University of New Mexico Press, 2005.

Gálvez Peña, Carlos M. "El carro de Ezequiel: la monarquía hispana de fray Buenaventura de Salinas y Córdova." *Histórica* 32, no. 1 (2008): 39–75.

———. "La ciudad letrada y santa: la ciudad de Los Reyes en la historiografía del siglo XVII." In *Urbanismo y vida urbana en Iberoamerica colonial,* Serie de Memorias de la ciudad de Bogotá. Bogotá: Archivo de Bogotá, 2008: 71–101.

———. "Historias religiosas como narrativas imperiales en el Perú del siglo XVII." In *Literatura y cultura en el virreinato del Perú: apropiación y diferencia (Historia de las Literaturas en el Perú. Tomo II)*, edited by Carlos García-Bedoya and Raquel Chang-Rodríguez, 301–36. Lima: Pontificia Universidad Católica del Perú, 2017.

———. "Martirios en la tierra de la eterna juventud. A propósito de la *Relación de los mártires de la Florida de fray Luis Jerónimo de Oré.*" *Histórica* 38, no. 1 (2014): 131–8.

———. "El mejor arbitrio, el sermón. Discurso religioso y representación política en el Perú del siglo XVII." *Anuario de Estudios Americanos* 71 (2014): 171–97.

———. "Writing History to Reform the Empire: Religious Chroniclers in Seventeenth-Century Peru." PhD diss., Columbia University, 2012.

Gannon, Michael. *The Cross in the Sand: The Early Catholic Church in Florida, 1513–1870*. Gainesville: University of Florida Press, 1965.

García, Antonio. "La reforma del Concilio Tercero de Lima." In *Doctrina cristiana y catecismo para instrucción de los indios,* edited by Luciano Pereña, 163–226. Madrid: CSIC, 1986.

García Álvarez, César. "Las fuentes de *La aurora en Copacabana* en Calderón de la Barca." *Revista Chilena de Literatura* 16–17 (1980–81): 179–213.
García Rivera, Alex. *St. Martín de Porres. The "Little Stories" and the Semiotics of Culture.* Maryknoll, NY: Orbis Books, 1995.
Garí y Siumell, José Antonio. *Biblioteca mercedaria, o sea Escritores de la Celestial, Real y Militar Orden de la Merced Redención de Cautivos.* Madrid: Herederos de la Viuda Pla, 1875.
Geiger, Maynard. *Biographical Dictionary of the Franciscans in Spanish Florida and Cuba (1528–1841).* Patterson, NJ: Franciscan Studies 21, Anthony Guild Press, 1940.
Gento Sanz, Benjamin. *San Francisco de Lima.* Lima: Imprenta Torres Aguirre, 1945.
———. "Semblanza histórica del cronista peruano Fray Diego de Córdova y Salinas (Siglo XVII)." *Revista de Historia de América* 40 (December 1955): 425–86.
Gómez Canedo, Lino. *La provincia franciscana de Santa Cruz de Caracas: cuerpo de documentos para historia, 1513–1837.* 3 vols. Caracas, 1974.
González, Ondina E., and Bianca Premo, eds. *Raising an Empire: Children in Early Modern Iberia and Colonial Latin America.* Albuquerque: University of New Mexico Press, 2007.
González Viaña, Eduardo, and José Antonio Mazzotti, eds. *Garcilasismo creativo y crítico: nueva antología.* Salem, Lima, and New York: Axiara Editions y Academia Norteamericana de la Lengua Española (ANLE), 2016.
Griffiths, Nicholas. *The Cross and the Serpent: Religious Repression and Resurgence in Colonial Peru.* Norman: University of Oklahoma Press, 1996.
Guibovich Pérez, Pedro. *En defensa de Dios: Estudios y documentos sobre la Inquisición en el Perú.* Lima: Ediciones del Congreso del Perú, 1998.
———. "Custodios de la ortodoxia: los calificadores de la Inquisición de Lima, 1570–1754." *Revista de la Inquisición* 10 (2001): 213–29.
Hanke, Lewis. *All Mankind is One: A Study of the Disputation between Bartolomé de las Casas and Juan Ginés de Sepúlveda in 1550 on the Intellectual and Religious Capacity of the American Indians.* DeKalb: Northern Illinois University Press, 1974.
———. *Bartolomé de las Casas: Bookman, Scholar & Propagandist.* Philadelphia: University of Pennsylvania Press, 1952.
———. *The First Social Experiments in America: A Study in the Development of Spanish Policy in the Sixteenth Century.* Gloucester, MA: P. Smith, 1964.
———. *The Spanish Struggle for Justice in the Conquest of America.* Boston: Little, Brown, 1965.
Hann, John H. *Apalachee: The Land between the Rivers.* Gainesville: University Press of Florida, 1987.
———. *History of the Timucua Indians and Missions.* Gainesville: University Press of Florida, 1996.

Haring, C. H. *The Spanish Empire in the New World*. New York: Harcourt, Brace & World, 1963.

———. *Trade and Navigation between Spain and the Indies in the Time of the Hapsburgs*. Cambridge: Harvard University Press, 1918.

Harrison, Regina. *Signs, Songs, and Memory in the Andes: Translating Quechua Language and Culture*. Austin: University of Texas Press, 1989.

———. *Sin and Confession in Colonial Peru: Spanish-Quechua Penitential Texts, 1560–1650*. Austin: University of Texas Press, 2014.

Hemming, John. *The Conquest of the Incas*. London: Sphere Books, 1972.

Heras, Julián. *Aporte de los Franciscanos a la evangelización del Perú*. Lima: Editora Latina, 1992.

———. "Los franciscanos en el valle del Colca (Arequipa) dos siglos y medio de evangelización." In *La evangelización del Perú, siglos XVI–XVII*. Arequipa: Actas del Congreso Peruano de Historia Eclesiástica, 1990. 379–449.

Hershenzon, Daniel. *The Captive Sea: Slavery, Communication, and Commerce in Early Modern Spain and the Mediterranean*. Philadelphia: University of Pennsylvania Press, 2018.

Herskovits, Melville J. *Man and His Works: The Science of Cultural Anthropology*. New York: Knopf, 1948.

Hoffman, Paul E. *A New Andalucia and a Way to the Orient: The American Southeast during the Sixteenth Century*. Baton Rouge: Louisiana State University Press, 2004.

———. *Spanish Crown and the Defense of the Caribbean, 1535–1585: Precedent, Patrimonialism, and Royal Parsimony*. Baton Rouge: Louisiana State University Press, 1980.

Hyland, Sabine. *The Jesuits and the Incas: The Extraordinary Life of Padre Blas Valera, SJ*. Ann Arbor: University of Michigan Press, 2003.

Iwasaki Cauti, Fernando. *Aplaca, Señor, tu ira! Lo maravilloso y lo imaginario en Lima colonial*. Madrid: Fondo de Cultura Económica, 2018.

———. "La embajada de Hasekura Tsunenaga Rokuemon (1613–1620)," in *Azotea, Revista de Cultura del Ayuntamiento de Coria del Río*. 6/7 (1990): 67–82.

———. "Nota crítica acerca de Francisco del Castillo: el apóstol de Lima y San Martín de Porras." *Histórica* 17 (1993): 297–306.

Jaque Hidalgo, Javiera. "Misiones jesuitas en la Guerra de Arauco: Resistencia mapuche, negociación y movilidad cultural en la periferia colonial (1593–1641)." *Rocky Mountain Review* 68:2 (2014), 177–94.

Johnson, Timothy J. "Are They Damned? Timucuans, Theology, and the Necessity of the Sacraments." In *Facing Florida: Essays on Culture and Religion in Early Modern Southeastern America*. edited by Timothy J. Johnson and Jeffrey M. Burns, 27–40. Oceanside, CA: The American Academy of Franciscan History, 2021.

Johnson, Timothy J. and Jeffrey M. Burns, eds. *Facing Florida: Essays on Culture and Re-*

ligion in Early Modern Southeastern America. Oceanside, CA: The American Academy of Franciscan History, 2021.

Kagan, Richard. "Ante todo, nunca te mientas a ti mismo: Pedro de Valencia, la "Historia de Chile" y la autocensura," manuScrits.Revista d'Història Moderna 35 (2017), 83–101, accessed August 25, 2020, https://revistes.uab.cat/manuscrits/article/view/v35-kagan/171-pdf-es.

Kelsey, Harry. *Sir Francis Drake: The Queen's Pirate*. New Haven: Yale University Press, 1998.

Klaiber, SJ, Jeffrey L. *The Jesuits in Latin America, 1549–2000*. St. Louis, MO: Institute of Jesuit Studies, 2009.

Korth, Eugene H. *Spanish Policy in Colonial Chile: The Struggle for Social Justice, 1535–1700*. Stanford: Stanford University Press, 1968.

Lane, Kris E. *Pillaging the Empire: Global Piracy on the High Seas, 1500–1750*. 2nd ed., New York: Routledge, 2016.

Lanning, John Tate. *The Spanish Missions of Georgia*. Chapel Hill: University of North Carolina Press, 1935.

Levillier, Roberto. *Don Francisco de Toledo, supremo organizador del Perú*. Madrid: Espasa-Calpe, 1935.

———. *Don Francisco de Toledo, supremo organizador del Perú, informaciones sobre los incas (1570–1572)*. Buenos Aires: Imprenta Porter Hnos., 1940.

Lienhard, Martin. "Indigenous Texts," in *Guide to Documentary Sources for Andean Studies 1530–1900*, edited by Joanne Pillsbury, 1: 87–103. 3 vols. Norman: University of Oklahoma Press, 2008.

Liqueno, José María. *Fray Fernando de Trejo y Sanabria, fundador de la universidad*. Córdoba: Bautista Cubas, 1916.

Lissón y Chaves, Emilio. *La Iglesia de España en el Perú*. Seville, 1944.

Lockhart, James. *Men of Cajamarca: A Social and Biographical Study of the First Conquerors of Peru*. Austin: University of Texas Press, 1972.

Lohmann Villena, Guillermo. "Los Fernández de Córdoba: un linaje preponderante en el Perú en los siglos XVI y XVII." *Anuario de Estudios Americanos* 45 (1988): 167–240.

———. *Las minas de Huancavelica en los siglos XVI y XVII*. Seville: Escuela de Estudios Hispanoamericanos, 1949, reprinted Lima: PUCP, 1998.

———. "La restitución por conquistadores y encomenderos: un aspecto de la incidencia Lascasiana en el Perú." *Anuario de Estudios Americanos* 23 (1966): 21–89.

Luque Alcaide, Elisa. "Córdoba y Salinas, Diego de (1591—ca. 1654)." In *Guide to Documentary Sources for Andean Studies 1530–1900* edited by Joanne Pillsbury. 3 vols. Norman: University of Oklahoma Press, 2008, 2: 165–69.

Lynch, John. *Spain under the Habsburgs*. 2 vols. New York: Oxford University Press, 1969.

MacCormack, Sabine. *On the Wings of Time: Rome, the Incas, Spain, and Peru.* Princeton: Princeton University Press, 2007.

———. *Religion in the Andes: Vision and Imagination in Early Colonial Peru.* Princeton: Princeton University Press, 1991.

———. "Pachacuti: Miracles, Punishments, and Last Judgment. Visionary Past and Prophetic Future in Early Colonial Peru." *American Historical Review* 93 (1988): 960–1006.

Mangan, Jane E. *Transatlantic Obligations: Creating the Bonds of Family in Conquest-era Peru and Spain.* Oxford: Oxford University Press, 2016.

Mannheim, Bruca. "Juan Pérez Bocanegra (?-1645)." In *Guide to Documentary Sources for Andean Studies 1530–1900,* edited by Joanne Pillsbury. 3 vols. Norman: University of Oklahoma Press, 2008, 3: 516–19.

Mansilla, Judith M. "Firm Foundations: Rebuilding the Early Modern State in Lima, Peru after the Earthquake of 1687." PhD diss., Florida International University, 2016.

Málaga Medina, Alejandro. *Reducciones toledanas en Arequipa (pueblos tradicionales).* Arequipa: PUBLIUNSA, 1989.

Marcheix, Lucien. *Un Parisien à Rome et à Naples en 1632. D'après un manuscrit inédit de J.-J. Bouchard.* Paris: Ernest Leroux, nd.

Marsilli, María N. *Hábitos perniciosos: religión andina colonial en la diócesis de Arequipa (siglos xvi al xviii).* Santiago: Centro de Investigaciones Diego Barros Arana, 2014.

———. "'I Heard It Through the Grapevine': Analysis of an Anti-secularization Initiative in the Sixteenth-Century Arequipan Countryside, 1584–1600." *The Americas* 61 (2005): 647–72.

Martín, Luis. *Daughters of the Conquistadores: Women of the Viceroyalty of Peru.* Albuquerque: University of New Mexico Press, 1983.

Martínez, María Elena. *Genealogical Fictions: Limpieza de Sangre, Religion, and Gender in Colonial Mexico.* Stanford: Stanford University Press, 2008.

Martínez Ferrer, Luis. "Estudio histórico documental." *Tercero Concilio Limense (1582–1591). Edición bilingüe de los decretos.* Edited by Luis Martínez Ferrer, 37–126. Lima and Rome: Facultad Pontificia y Civil de Teología de Lima, 2017.

Mateos, Francisco. *Obras del P. José de Acosta.* Madrid: Atlas, 1954.

McAlister, Lyle N. *Spain & Portugal in the New World, 1492–1700.* Minneapolis: University of Minnesota Press, 1984.

McClure, Julia. *The Franciscan Invention of the New World.* Cham, Switzerland: Palgrave Macmillan, 2017.

Mecham, J. Lloyd. *Church and State in Latin America: A History of Politico-Ecclesiastical Relations.* Rev. ed., Chapel Hill: University of North Carolina Press, 1966.

Medina, José Toribio. *Biblioteca Hispano-chilena (1523–1817).* 3 vols. Santiago de Chile, 1897–99.

———. *Historia del Tribunal del Santo Oficio de la Inquisición en Lima (1569–1820)*. 2 vols. Santiago de Chile: Imprenta Gutenberg, 1887.

Medina, José Toribio. *Vida de Ercilla*. Mexico, DF: Fondo de Cultura Económica, 1948.

Mendiburu, Manuel. *Diccionario histórico biográfico del Perú*. 12 vols. Lima: Imprenta "Enrique Palacios," 1931–34.

Milanich, Jerald T. *Laboring in the Fields of the Lord: Spanish Missions and Southeastern Indians*. Gainesville: University Press of Florida, 1999.

———. *The Timucua*. Oxford: Blackwell, 1996.

Milanich, Jerald T. and Samuel Proctor, eds. *Tacachale: Essays on the Indians of Florida and Southeastern Georgia during the Historic Period*. Gainesville: University Press of Florida, 1978.

Millones, Luis, ed. *El retorno de las huacas. Estudios y documentos del siglo XVI*. Lima: Instituto de Estudios Peruanos, 1990.

Mills, Kenneth. *Idolatry and Its Enemies. Colonial Andean Religion and Extirpation, 1640–1750*. Princeton: Princeton University Press, 1997.

———. "Diego de Ocaña, Holy Wanderer." In *The Human Tradition in Colonial Latin America*, second edition, edited by Kenneth J. Andrien, 151–71. New York: Roman & Littlefield Publishers, 2013.

Molina, Raúl A. *Fray Martín Ignacio de Loyola: cuarto obispo del Paraguay y Río de la Plata (1603–1606)*. Madrid: Ediciones Jura, 1953.

Moore, Sally Falk. *Power and Property in Inca Peru*. New York: Columbia University Press, 1958.

Morales Padrón, Francisco. *La ciudad del quinientos. Historia de Sevilla*. 2nd edition, corrected. Seville: Universidad de Sevilla, 1977.

———. *Sevilla, Canarias y América*. Spain: Las Palmas, 1970.

Moreno Jeria, Rodrigo. "Entre huilliches, chonos, puelches y poyas: Jesuitas y sueños de reducción en el fin del mundo." In *Reducciones. La concentración forzada de las poblaciones indígenas en el Virreinato del Perú*, edited by Akira Saito and Claudia Rosas Lauro, 639–73. Lima: PUCP, 2017.

———. "Metodología missional jesuita en la periferia austral de América." In *La misión y los jesuitas en la América Española, 1566–1767: cambios y permanencias*, edited by José Jesús Hernández Palomo and Rodrigo Moreno Jeria, 239–63. Seville: CSIC, 2005.

Morgan, Ronald J. *Spanish American Saints and the Rhetoric of Identity, 1600–1810*. Tucson: University of Arizona Press, 2002.

Morison, Samuel Eliot. *The Great Explorers. The European Discovery of America*. New York: Oxford University Press, 1978.

Mumford, Jeremy. "The Taki Onquoy and the Andean Nation: Sources and Interpretations." *Latin American Research Review* 33, no. 1 (1998): 150–65.

———. *Vertical Empire: The General Resettlement of Indians in the Colonial Andes.* Durham: Duke University Press, 2012.
Muñoz y Manzano, Cipriano. *Bibliografía española de lenguas indígenas de América.* Madrid: Atlas, 1977.
Murray, James C. *Spanish Chronicles of the Indies: Sixteenth Century.* New York: Twayne Publishers, 1994.
Navarro Ruiz, Francisco, ed. *Magna Hispalensis: el universo de la iglesia.* Seville: Ayuntamiento de Sevilla, 1992.
Nesvig, Martin Austin, ed. *Forgotten Franciscans: Writings from an Inquisitional Theorist, a Heretic, and an Inquisitional Deputy.* University Park: Pennsylvania State University Press, 2011.
Niles, Susan A. *The Shape of Inca History: Narrative and Architecture in an Andean Empire.* Iowa City: University of Iowa Press, 1999.
Noetzel, Lisa. "Additions, Corrections, and Deletions: A Comparison of the 1612 and 1627 Spanish-Timucuan Catechisms." In *Facing Florida: Essays on Culture and Religion in Early Modern Southeastern America,* edited by Timothy J. Johnson and Jeffrey M. Burns, 41–50. Oceanside, CA: The American Academy of Franciscan History, 2021.
Noriega Bernuy, Julio E. *Buscando una tradición poética quechua en el Perú.* Coral Gables, FL: University of Miami, Iberian Studies Institute, 1995.
Olivares M., Luis, OFM. *Provincia franciscana de Chile.* Santiago, 1961.
Osorio, Alejandra B. *Inventing Lima: Baroque Modernity in Peru's South Sea Metropolis.* New York: Palgrave Macmillan, 2008.
Ossio, Juan, ed. *Ideología mesiánica del mundo andino.* Lima: Ignacio Prado Pastor, 1973.
Palacios Roa, Alfredo. "Dominio y catástrofe. Los terremotos en Concepción, Chile: 1550–1751." *Anuario de Estudios Americanos* 69:2 (2012): 569–600.
Palomero Páramo, Jesús M. "Entre el claustro y el compás." In Francisco Navarro Ruiz, ed., *Magna Hispalensis: el universo de la iglesia.* Seville: Ayuntamiento de Sevilla, 1992, 200–254.
Pease G.Y., Franklin. *Los últimos incas del Cuzco.* Lima: Instituto Nacional de la Cultura, 2004.
———. "Chronicles of the Andes in the Sixteenth and Seventeenth Centuries." In *Guide to Documentary Sources for Andean Studies, 1530–1900,* edited by Joanne Pillsbury. 3 vols. Norman: University of Oklahoma Press, 2008, 1: 11–22.
———. "Salinas y Córdoba, Buenaventura de (ca. 1592–1653)." In Chronicles of the Andes in the Sixteenth and Seventeenth Centuries," in *Guide to Documentary Sources for Andean Studies, 1530–1900,* edited by Joanne Pillsbury. 3 vols. Norman: University of Oklahoma Press, 2008, 3: 624–26.
Pello, Xavier. "Los últimos días de Luis Jerónimo de Oré (1554–1630): un nuevo doc-

umento biográfico." *Bulletin del Instituto Francés de Estudios Andinos* 29/2 (2000): 161–71.

Peña, Beatriz Carolina. "Hermanos de la perdición: Los Pizarros en la memoria colectiva del Perú a inicios del XVII." *Revista de Historia de América* 147 (2012): 77–110.

Pereña, Luciano, ed. *Doctrina cristiana y catecismo para instrucción de los indios.* Madrid: CSIC, 1986.

Pérez-Mallaína, Pablo E. *Spain's Men of the Sea: Daily Life on the Indies Fleets in the Sixteenth Century.* Translated by Carla Rahn Phillips. Baltimore: Johns Hopkins University Press, 1998.

Pérez-Mallaína, Pablo E., and Bibiano Torres Ramírez. *La Armada del Mar del Sur.* Seville: Escuela de Estudios Hispanoamericanos, 1987.

Phelan, John Leddy. *The Millennial Kingdom of the Franciscans in New Spain.* 2nd ed., rev. Berkeley: University of California Press, 1970.

Pillsbury, Joanne, ed. *Fuentes documentales para estudios andinos, 1530–1900.* 3 vols. Lima PUCP, 2016.

———. *Guide to Documentary Sources for Andean Studies 1530–1900.* 3 vols. Norman: University of Oklahoma Press, 2008.

Plandolit, Luis Julian. *El Apostol de América San Francisco Solano.* Madrid: Editorial Cisneros, 1963.

Pocock, H.R.S. *The Conquest of Chile.* New York: Stein and Day, 1967.

Polo, José Toribio. "Luis Gerónimo de Oré." *Revista Histórica* 5 (1913):74–91.

Porras Barrenechea, Raúl. *Los cronistas del Perú (1528–1650) y otros ensayos,* edited by Franklin Pease G. Y. Lima: Banco de Crédito del Perú, 1986.

Porras Barrenechea, Raúl. *Fuentes históricas peruanas.* Lima: Instituto Raúl Porras Barrenechea, 1963.

Premo, Bianca. *Children of the Father King: Youth, Authority and Legal Minority in Colonial Lima.* Chapel Hill: University of North Carolina Press, 2005.

Puente Brunke, José de la. *Encomienda y encomenderos en el Perú. Estudio social y político de una institución colonial.* Seville: Diputación Provincial, 1992.

Puente Luna, José Carlos de la. *Andean Cosmopolitans. Seeking Justice and Rewards at the Spanish Royal Court.* Austin: University of Texas Press, 2018.

Ramírez González, Sergio. "Sacra librería. La Biblioteca del Monasterio de Clarisas de Santa Isabel de Ronda." *Isla de Arriarán* 21 (2003): 293–313.

Ramos, Gabriela. *Death and Conversion in the Andes. Lima and Cuzco, 1532–1670.* Notre Dame: Notre Dame University Press, 2010.

Rappaport, Joanne. *The Disappearing Mestizo: Configuring Difference in the Colonial New Kingdom of Granada.* Durham: Duke University Press, 2014.

Rappaport, Joanne, and Tom Cummins. *Beyond the Lettered City. Indigenous Literacies in the Andes.* Durham: Duke University Press, 2012.

Redden, Andrew. "The Best Laid Plans . . .: Jesuit Counsel, Peacebuilding, and Disaster on the Chilean Frontier; The Martyrs Elicura, 1612." *Journal of Jesuit Studies* 4:2 (2017): 250–69.

———. "Not-So-Good Shepherds: Reluctant Jesuit Martyrs on the Seventeenth-Century Chilean Frontier." In *The Frontiers of Mission. Perspectives on Early Modern Missionary Catholicism*. Brill, E-Book, 2016, 90–114.

Reeves, Marjorie. *Joachim of Fiore and the Prophetic Future*. New York: Harper & Row, 1977.

Rénique, José Luis, and Efraín Trelles. "Approximación demográfica: Yanque-Collaguas 1591." In *Collaguas I*, edited by Franklin Pease G. Y., 169–89. Lima: PUCP, 1977.

Ricard, Robert. *The Spiritual Conquest of Mexico*. Berkeley: University of California Press, 1966.

Richter, Federico. "Primera parte: Fray Luis Jerónimo de Oré (biografía) 1554–1630. Segunda parte: Información del oficio en la Real Audiencia de La Plata del Perú, de los méritos del biografiado (3 piezas)." In *Anales de la Provincia de los Doce Apóstoles de Lima*. Huamanga: Imprenta de la Universidad de San Cristóbal de Huamanga (1986): 1–41.

Rivero Cabrera, Arelis. *Commitment Beyond Rules: Franciscans in Colonial Cuba, 1531–1842*. Berkeley: American Academy of Franciscan History, 2017.

Rivero Cabrera, Arelis. "Missionaries and Moralization for the Franciscan Province of Santa Elena: The Dilemma of an Exported Reform." *The Americas* 61:1(2005): 673–95.

Rodríguez-Buckingham, Antonio. "Monastic Libraries and Early Printing in Sixteenth-Century Spanish America." *Libraries & Culture* 24 (1989): 33–56.

Rosales, S.J., Diego de. *Historia general del reino de Chile*. 3 vols. Valparaíso: Imprenta del Mercurio, 1877–78.

Saito, Akira, and Claudia Rosas Lauro, eds. *Reducciones. La concentración forzada de las poblaciones indígenas en el Virreinato del Perú*. Lima: PUCP, 2017.

Salas de Coloma, Miriam. *Estructura colonial del poder español en el Perú. Huamanga (Ayacucho) a través de sus obrajes, siglos xvi–xviii*. 3 vols., Lima: PUCP, 1998.

———. *De los obrajes de Canaria y Chincheros a las comunidades indígenas de Vilcashuamán. Siglo XVI*. Lima: Sesator, 1979.

Salles-Reese, Verónica. *From Viracocha to the Virgin of Copacabana. Representation of the Sacred at Lake Titicaca*. Austin: University of Texas Press, 1997.

San Cristóbal Sebastián, Antonio. *Arquitectura virreynal religiosa de Lima*. Lima: Studium, 1988.

———. *Esplendor del Barroco en Ayacucho. Retablos y arquitectura religiosa en Huamanga*. Lima: Banco Latino/Ediciones Peisa, 1999.

San Cristóval, Evaristo. *Apendice al diccionario histórico-biográfico del Perú*. 4 vols. Lima: Libreria e Imprenta Gil, 1936.

Schäfer, Ernst. *El Consejo Real y Supremo de las Indias*. 2 vols. Seville: Imp. M. Carmona, 1935–47.

Schwaller, John Frederick. *The Church and Clergy in Sixteenth-century Mexico*. Albuquerque: University of New Mexico Press, 1987.

Schwartz, Stuart B., ed. *Implicit Understandings: Observing, Reporting, and Reflecting on the Encounters Between Europeans and Other Peoples in the Early Modern Era*. Cambridge: Cambridge University Press, 1994.

Seed, Patricia. *Ceremonies of Possession in Europe's Conquest of the New World, 1492–1640*. Cambridge: Cambridge University Press, 1995.

Shiels, W. Eugene. *King and Church: The Rise and Fall of the Patronato Real*. Chicago: Loyola University Press, 1961.

Shippee, Robert. "A Forgotten Valley of Peru." *The National Geographic Magazine* 65:1 (1934): 110–32.

Silva Cotapos, Carlos. *Historia eclesiástica de Chile*. Santiago de Chile, 1925.

Stern, Steve J. *Peru's Indian Peoples and the Challenge of Spanish Colonialism. Huamanga to 1640*. Madison: University of Wisconsin Press, 1982.

Taylor, William. *Magistrates of the Sacred. Priests and Parishioners in Eighteenth-Century Mexico*. Stanford: Stanford University Press, 1996.

Tibesar, OFM, Antonine. *Franciscan Beginnings in Colonial Peru*. Washington, DC: Academy of American Franciscan History, 1953.

Timberlake, Marie. "Sínodos diocesanos." In *Fuentes documentales para estudios andinos, 1530–1900*, edited by Joanne Pillsbury. 3 vols. 1: 369–80. Lima: PUCP, 2016.

Tord, Luis Enrique. *Templos coloniales del Colca-Arequipa*. Lima: Papelera Atlas, 1983.

Urbano, Henrique, ed. *Mito y simbolismo en los Andes: La figura y la palabra*. Cuzco: Centro de Estudios Regionales Andinos "Bartolomé de las Casas," 1993.

Van Deusen, Nancy E. *Between the Sacred and the Worldly: The Institutional and Cultural Practice of Recogimiento in Colonial Lima*. Stanford: Stanford University Press, 2001.

———. *Embodying the Sacred. Women Mystics in Seventeenth-century Lima*. Durham: Duke University Press, 2018.

———. *Global Indios: The Indigenous Struggle for Justice in Sixteenth-century Spain*. Durham: Duke University Press, 2015.

———. *The Souls of Purgatory: The Spiritual Diary of a Seventeenth-century Afro-Peruvian Mystic, Ursula de Jesús*. Albuquerque: University of New Mexico Press, 2004.

Van Oss, Adriaan C. *Catholic Colonialism: A Parish History of Guatemala, 1524–1821*. Cambridge: Cambridge University Press, 1986.

Vargas, Victor Angles. *Historia del Cusco (Cusco Colonial)*. Lima: Industrial Gráfica, 1983.

Vargas Ugarte, Rubén. *Historia del culto de María en Iberoamérica y de sus imágenes y santuarios más celebrados*. Buenos Aires: Editorial Huarpes, 1947.

———. *Historia de la Iglesia en el Perú*. 5 vols. Vol. 1, Lima: Imprenta Santa María, 1954. Vols. 2–5, Burgos: Imprenta de Aldecoa, 1959–62.

———. *Historia general del Perú*. 10 vols. Lima: Editor Carlos Milla Batres, 1981–84.

———. *Impresos peruanos publicados en el extranjero*. Vol. 6. Lima: Biblioteca Peruana, 1949.

Varón Gabai, Rafael. *Francisco Pizarro and His Brothers: The Illusion of Power in Sixteenth-Century Peru*. Norman: University of Oklahoma Press, 1997.

———. "El Taki Onquoy: las raíces andinas de un fenómeno colonial." In *El retorno de las Huacas*, edited by Luis Millones. 332–405. Lima: Instituto de Estudios Peruanos, 1990.

Vergara, Teresa C. "Ursula: the life and times of an aristocratic girl in Santiago, Chile (1666–1678)." In *Raising an Empire: Children in Early Modern Iberia and Colonial Latin America*, edited by Ondina E. González and Bianca Premo. Albuquerque: University of New Mexico Press, 2007.

Vila Vilar, Enriqueta, and Jaime J. Lacueva Muñoz, eds. *Mirando las dos orillas: intercambios mercantiles, sociales y culturales entre Andalucía y América*. Seville: Fundación Buenas Letras, 2012.

Viola, Alfredo. *Real Patronato y obispos del Paraguay colonial*. Asunción: Centro Interdisciplinario de Derecho Social y Económico, 2002.

Ward, Christopher. *Imperial Panama: Commerce and Conflict in Isthmanian America, 1550–1800*. Albuquerque: University of New Mexico Press, 1993.

Weinstein, Donald, and Rudolph M. Bell. *Saints & Society: The Two Worlds of Western Christendom, 1000–1700*. Chicago: University of Chicago Press, 1982.

Wernke, Steven A. "La producción y desestabilización del dominio colonial en el proceso reduccional en el Valle del Colca, Perú." In *Reducciones. La concentración forzada de las poblaciones indígenas en el Virreinato del Perú*, edited by Akira Saito and Claudia Rosas Lauro, 387–437. Lima: PUCP, 2017.

Wilder, Thorton. *The Bridge of San Luis Rey*. New York: A. & C. Boni, 1928.

Wood, Robert D. *"Teach Them Good Customs": Colonial Indian Education and Acculturation in the Andes*. Culver City, CA: Labyrinthos, 1986.

Worth, John E. *The Timucua Chiefdoms of Spanish Florida, Volume 1: Assimilation*. Gainesville: University Press of Florida, 1998.

Wright, Irene A. *Cuba*. New York: Macmillan, 1912.

———. *Historia documentada de San Cristóbal de la Habana en el siglo XVI*. 2 vols., Havana: Imprenta Siglo XX, 1927.

———. *Historia documentada de San Cristóbal de la Habana en la primera mitad del siglo XVII*. Havana: Imprenta Siglo XX, 1930.

———. *Santiago de Cuba and its district (1607–1640): written from documents in the Archive of the Indies, at Seville, Spain*. Madrid: F. Peña Cruz, 1918.

Wunder, Amanda. *Baroque Seville: Sacred Art in a Century of Crisis*. University Park, PA: Pennsylvania State University Press, 2017.

Zamora, Margarita. *Language, Authority, and Indigenous History in the "Comentarios Reales de los Incas."* Cambridge: Cambridge University Press, 1988.

Zulaica Gárate, Román. *Los franciscanos y la imprenta en México en el siglo XVI*. Mexico: UNAM, 1991.

Index

Account of the Martyrs in the Province of La Florida (Oré/Chang-Rodríguez and Vogeley), 173
Acosta, José de, 47, 50–51, 53, 94, 192
Adorno, Rolena, 3, 53, 290
Alamo, Father, 193
Alarcón, Pablo de, 252
Álava y Nureña, Francisco de, 263, 273
Albornoz, Cristóbal de: as *visitador eclesiástico*, 20–22
Alexander VI, Pope, 212–13
Algarves, Pedro de los, 31
Almagro, Diego de, 10, 29
Almagro the Younger, Diego de, 10, 29
Almansa, Martín Enríquez de, 43
Almonacid, Antonio de, 20
Ambrose, Saint, 100
Amerindians: as mentioned in Oré's testament, 287–88; in ongoing conflict with the Spanish, 269–76; Oré's concerns regarding treatment of, 4–5, 268, 273, 274–76, 293
Ampato, cult of, 85
Ana del Espíritu Santo, Sor, 226–227
Andrada, Feliciano de, 263
Andrango-Walker, Catalina, 3
Anganamón, 272
Ánimas del Purgatorio (confraternity), 84
Aquaviva, General, 128
Arana, Andrés de, 71
Aranjuez, Pedro de, 282
Araucanian frontier: and indigenous resistance, 269–70; ongoing conflict on, 239–40, 251. *See also* Chile

Arauco War, 239, 269–70
Argüelles, Bartolomé de, 151–52
Arias, Francisco, 285
Arrigoni, Pompeio, 121
Arte y Vocabulario (Oré), 112
Arteaga, Laureano de, 214, 215, 217
Asperamonte, Adrián de, 71
Atahualpa, 10, 29; execution of, 34, 36
Athanasius, Saint, 100; *Simbolo*, 3
Augustine, Saint, 100
Auñón, Miguel de, 174
Avila, Francisco de, 171, 172, 175–77
Ayacucho. *See* Huamanga
Aymara, 91–92, 94, 95, 292; Bertonio as translator of, 127–30. *See also* indigenous languages of Peru; *Rituale, seu manuale peruanum*
Azevedo y Guevara, Doña Aldonsa de, 14, 15
Azevedo, Doña Aldonsa de, 229

Badajos, Antonio de, 174
Bandera, Damián de la, 12
Barbiano, Vestrio, 117–18
Barrenechea, Raúl Porras, 2
Barrias, Pedro Fernández, 75
Barzana, Alonso de, 49, 96, 122, 128
Bautista de Segura, Juan, 193, 194
Beas, Gerónimo de, 132
Benedict XIII, Pope, 145
Bermejo, Pedro, 170–71
Berrocal, Bartolomé, 20
Bertonio, Ludovico, 44; Aymara dictionary and grammar by, 127–30

Betanzos, Juan de, 78, 127
Beyersdorff, Margot, 98
Bocanegra, Juan Pérez de, 98, 99, 112, 127
Bolaños, Luis de, 123, 143
Bonaventure of Bignoreggio, 59
Bonilla, Francisco de, 172
Bradley, Peter T., 249
breastfeeding: and concerns regarding indigenous wet-nurses, 19
Burke, Peter, 145
Burns, Kathryn, 3, 25

Cabanas: ancient beliefs of, 64; conversion of, 68, 77–78
Cabello, Nataly Cancino, 274
Cabello de Balboa, Miguel, 53
Cabeza de Hierro, Francisco, 214, 217
Cabeza de Vaca, Alvar Núñez, 192
Cabezas Altamirano, Juan de las, 158
Cabrera, Amador de, 13
Cacica, Doña María, 152
Cadabal, Lucas de, 79, 84–85
Cajamarca Indians: conversions among, 63, 64
Calderón (soldier), 194–95
Calderón, Melchor, 270
Callao, Peru: Drake's attack on, 41–43; Dutch assault on, 249; as port city, 37, 38–39
Camargo, Juan de, 71
Campo, Juan del, 27, 54
Cancer, Luis, 192
Cañete, Marqués de, 93–94, 231
Canto, Francisco del, 127
Capitefontium, Cristóbal de, 115
Cárdenas, Francisco de, 21
Cárdenas, Pedro de, 213
Carlinum, Iacobum, 119
Carlist Wars, 116
Carranco, Antonio, 70
Carvajal, Agustín de, 227, 228
Carvajal, Francisco de, 63, 135
Casa de la Contratación, 115, 132, 135, 136, 146, 215
Casa de Recogimiento de San Juan de la Penitencia, 40
Castellano, Juan, 287
Castro, Juan de, 234

Catalina de Erauso, 227–28
Catherine of Aragon, 208
Cepeda, Juan de, 121
Chang-Rodríguez, Raquel, 173
Charles V, 5, 34, 40, 69–70, 113
Charles, John, 80, 96
Chavarí, Marcos, 274
Chaves, Juan de, 63
Chesapeake Bay, 201; Spanish reconnaissance of, 192–93, 198–99
Chile: ongoing conflict between the indigenous people and the Spanish in, 4, 5, 239–46, 251; religious presence in, 243–46, 255–57. *See also* Concepción, diocese of
Chiloé Archipelago: Oré's inspection of, 253–55
Chinchón, Conde de, 249
Christianity: and the concept of duality, 203
Cid, Miguel, 203
Cieza de León, Pedro de, 9, 11–12, 31
Cisneros, Agustín de, 243
Clara of Assisi, Santa, 27
Clayton, Lawrence, 269
Cobo, Bernabé, 128, 231, 234, 235
Colca Valley: burial practices in, 83; and confraternity as part of the conversion process, 83–84; Franciscan presence in, 62–63, 65–68, 78–89; idolatry in, 84–85; Oré as doctrinero in, 1, 18, 56, 62, 65, 70, 74, 75, 76, 77–89, 91–92, 103; principal languages of, 77; resettlement of indigenous people in, 67–68; tensions between the Franciscans and the secular clergy in, 69–76
Colegio de la Compañía de Jesús (Huamanga), 111
Colegio de Maese Rodrigo, 33
Colegio of San Antonio Abad (Cuzco), 111
Collaguas, Los: ancient beliefs of, 63–64; conversion of, 77–78; Franciscan presence among, 63, 68, 70, 73–74, 76, 77–78; Oré in, 65, 70, 91. *See also* Colca Valley
Colmenares, Gaspar de, 82
Concepción, diocese of La Imperial: Cathedral of, 286; challenges inherent in, 240–46; consecration of Oré as bishop of, 223–24; and friction between the dioceses of Santiago and

Index

La Imperial, 239–46; Oré named bishop of, 4, 213, 218, 245–46; Oré's responsibilities as bishop, 251–58
Concepción, María de la, 28
Concha, Fernando de la, 285
Copacabana, peninsula of: as a holy place, 204–5
Coporaque (Colca Valley): Franciscan presence in, 63, 78–82; high mortality in, 82–83; hospital in, 82
Córdova y Aguilesa, Doña Inés de, 285, 286
Córdova y Salinas, Diego de, 18, 28–29, 53, 62, 107, 117, 118, 146, 226, 227, 228; at the Franciscan monastery in Lima, 232–34; on Oré's legacy, 289
Coricancha, the (the Inca Temple of the Sun), 33
Corne, Carlos Marcelo, 213
Corona de la Virgen María (Oré), 202–3, 205–10, 291; Oré's confession as part of, 208–10
Corpa, Pedro de, 172, 173–74, 175
Cortéz, Hernán, 34
Council of the Indies, 73–74, 85, 113, 114–15, 185, 187–88; and Oré's petition for more religious in the Florida missions, 211–12
Council of Trent, 139, 279–80; and conflict between the Franciscans and the secular clergy, 72; on indigenous marriage, 125; and the Third Church Council of Lima, 46–47, 49
Coya, Doña Beatriz Clara, 241
Coya, Doña Clara, 17
Cruz, Baltasar de la, 73
Cruz, Francisco de la, 41
Cuba, 151; challenges faced by Oré in, 158–63; Franciscan presence in, 158, 161–62; Oré's arrival in, 156
Cuenca, Alonso de, 114
Cueva, Juan de, 187
Cuzco: convents for girls and women in, 25–26; Oré as doctrinero in, 107–8; Oré as Franciscan novice in, 31–36; religious celebrations in, 33–34

Dávila, Pedrarias, 10
Deca, Juan, 265

Descobar, Juan, 123
Despinosa, Antonio, 264
Díaz de Navia, Friar, 139–40
Díaz de Rojas y de la Cuba, Pedro, 11, 21
Díaz de Rojas y Rivera, Doña Luisa, 10, 11–12, 24, 25, 28–29, 30; children of, 14; death of, 29
Díaz de Rojas, Pedro, 10–11
Díaz Franco, Pero, 199
Diego Coro Inga, Don, 84–85, 92
Diego de Urrea, Father, 170
Diez de Armendariz, Lope, 136
Domínguez, Nicanor, 16–17, 108
Don Juan: and the Guale uprising, 173–74. 188
Don Luis (indigenous captive), 193
Drake, Francis, 152; and attack on Callao, 41–43
Durán, Sebastián, 84
Durston, Alan, 3, 50, 53, 95, 130
Dutch East India Company: in conflict with the Spanish, 247–48
Dutch West India Company, 247
Dutch, the: Oré's concerns regarding, 250; as threat to Spanish interests in South America, 247–50

Earle, Rebecca, 19
Egaña, Antonio de, 245
Elizabeth I, Queen, 41, 133
Encarnación, Doña Inés de la, 17
Enostrossa, Pedro de, 265
Enríquez de Almendáriz, Alonso: as bishop in Cuba, 159–61; on indigenous people in Cuba, 168–69; at the Third Church Council of Lima, 54, 55–56
Enríquez, Viceroy Martín, 16, 65
Epiphanius, Saint, 208
Eraso, Cristóbal de, 196
Ercilla y Zúñiga, Alonso de, 239
Erenchun, Pedro, 214, 217
Espinoza Caracol, Francisco de, 257
Esquilache, Príncipe de, 272
Estenssoro Fuchs, Juan Carlos, 20
Estrada, Doña Juana de, 15, 229

Fajardo, Cristóbal, 86
Ferdinand: as king of Spain, 115, 119, 212

Fernández de Chozas, Pedro, 171
Fernández de Córdoba, Diego. *See* Guadalcázar, Marqués de
Fernández de Córdova y Arce, Luis, 253, 257, 271, 273; and charges against Oré presented to the king, 277–82, 289; and disagreement with Oré over treatment of indigenous people, 268, 273–76; and ongoing dispute with Oré over appointment of clergy, 259–67
Fernández de Écija, Francisco, 200
Fernández de Mesa, Don Alonso, 108
Fernández de Oviedo y Valdés, Gonzalo, 94, 149, 182
Fernández de Valenzuela, Pedro, 13, 14, 101, 229
Fernández, Diego, 94
Fiore, Joachim de, 144
Flores, Juan Gutiérrez, 93
Flores, Pedro Gutiérrez, 73, 93
Flores, Pedro Ordóñez, 92
Florida: challenges faced by the Franciscans in, 152–53, 184–88; as critical region for the Spanish, 149–50; description of, 151–52; conversion efforts of the Franciscans in, 155–56, 184–88; Guale uprising in, 170–78; indigenous people in, 133, 165–69; indigenous resistance to Franciscan presence in, 150–53; monasteries in, 165–68; Oré's assessment of, as regards recruitment of converts, 177–78; Oré's inspections of missions in, 154, 156, 164–69, 191–201; Oré's request for more friars in, 211–12; Oré's Spanish aspirations in, 132–33; Oré's travel to, 136–38; and tensions between the Spanish monarchy and the friars, 184–88; Timucua communities in, 155. See also *Relación de la Florida* (Oré); Santa Elena, Province of
Focher, Juan: *Itinerario de Misionero en America*, 61–62
Fort Caroline, 150
Francis, J. Michael, 173, 174, 176–78
Francis, Saint: ideals and teachings of, 59–60
Franciscan order: and chapter meeting of the Province of Santa Elena, 179–81; conversion efforts of, 60–61, 63–64, 67–68, 77–89, 95–96; in the Colca Valley, 77–89; in Cuzco, 31–36; divisions within, 59–62; ecclesiastical structure of, 115–16; in Florida, 150–53, 152–53, 155–56, 184–88; history of, in Peru, 18–19, 62–63; indigenous resistance to, 60, 150–53, 173; martyrdom of, in the Guale uprising, 170–78, 194, 196; members of the Oré family as, 14, 17; music as used by, 80; ongoing wars affecting, 116; punishments meted out by, 80–82; and tensions with the secular clergy, 69–76; wealth of, 25. *See also* Colca Valley; Oré, Luis Gerónimo de
Francis Xavier, 145
Frobisher, Martin, 41
Fuente, Alejandro de la, 158
Fuentes, Bernabé de, 54, 107

Gálvez Peña, Carlos, 3, 170
García Ramón, Alonso, 244, 270, 271
García, Andrés, 213
Garcilaso de la Vega, El Inca, 50, 78, 96, 108, 134–35, 141, 149; *La Florida del Inca*, 135, 191, 192, 193
Gavilán, Diego, 21
Geiger, Maynard, 2
Girón, Francisco Hernández, 11, 135
Glavid, David, 199
Golden Hind, the (Drake's ship), 42
Gómez, Francisco, 265, 281–82
Gómez, Luis, 97
Gómez de León, Juan, 93
Gonzaga, Francesco (Annibalae), 62
Gonzáles, Catalina, 136
González, Andrés, 200
González, Vicente, 197–98
González Holguín, Diego, 130, 131
Gose, Peter, 3
Granada, Luis de, 177; *Introducción del símbolo de la fe*, 95; *Vida de Maria*, 95
Granero de Avalos, Alonso, 45
Gregory XV, Pope, 204
Gregory, Saint, 100
Guadalcázar, Marqués de, 223, 228, 249, 253, 274
Guale uprising: Oré's description of, 173–78, 194, 196, 197; and martyrdom of Franciscan friars, 170–78
Guaman Poma de Ayala, Felipe, 53, 89, 92, 94, 123, 127, 129, 290

Guerra, Alfonso, 45
Guibovich, Pedro, 41
Guillén de Mendoza, Hernán, 13
Gutiérrez de Ulloa, Antonio de: investigation into, 86–87

Hanan Chilques, 10, 12, 14, 15, 23
Harrison, Regina, 96
Havana, Cuba: monastery in, 158, 161
Hawkins, John, 41
Henry VIII, 208
Herborn, Nicholas, 61
Hernández, Francisco, 10, 85
Hernández Palmero, Rodrigo, 214
Herrera, Francisco de, 233–34
Herrero, Pedro, 217
Hinojosa, Fernando de, 31
Hinojosa, Gerónimo de, 244
Hoffman, Paul E., 195, 199–200
Hoyo, María del, 214
Huamanga: churches in, 17; convent in, 26–28; description of, 11–12; Oré family in, 11–13, 18–20, 23; as Oré's birthplace, 9–10; Oré's visit to, as bishop, 224, 226–30
Huayna Capac, 94
Huarina, Battle of, 29
Huerta, Alonso de, 127
Huerta, Miguel de, 39
Hurtado, Francisco, 185
Hurtado de Mendoza, García, 16, 70–71, 239
Hyland, Sabine, 50

Ibarra, Pedro de, 155, 200
Immaculate Conception: as church dogma, 146, 203–4, 208, 291
Inca people: in Cuzco, 32–33; subjugation by, 60–61
indigenous languages of Peru, 19; Jesuits' interest in, 126–31; Oré as translator of, 2–3, 19, 47, 77, 91–102, 112, 114–15, 119–23, 290–91; and translations of the religious texts from the Third Church Council of Lima, 47–54, 96. See also *Rituale, seu manuale peruanum*; *Symbolo Catholico Indiano*
indulgences: Oré's treatise on, 116–18
Inga, Don Carlos, 94

Inihayca (Apalachee chieftain), 155–56
Inojosa, Alonso de, 93
Isabel: as queen of Spain, 115, 119, 212
Isabel de Borbón, Queen: children born to, 257–58
Isidro the Laborer, 145
Italy: Oré in, 116–18, 119

James I, King, 133
Jauja missions: Oré as guardian of, 92, 103
Jesuits: in Chile, 254, 255–56; and Oré's *Corona de la Virgen*, 205; Oré's interaction with, 119, 126; presence of, in Florida, 149, 193; in Lima, 101; as translators of indigenous languages, 49, 51, 126, 127–31; and travel from Spain to Peru, 218–22; wealth generated by, 25. See also Acosta José de; Barzana, Alonso de; Valdivia, Luis de; Valera, Blas
Jesús, Francisca de, 26
Jiménez de Mendoza, Andrés, 265
Jofré, Marcos, 52
John XXII, Pope, 60
Juárez y Acevedo, Doña Catalina, 15
Julius II, Pope, 213

Kole, Kathleen M., 173, 174, 176–78

La Gasca, Pedro de, 11, 29, 615
Lara, Alonso de, 193, 195
Lara, Juan de, 193, 195
Lartaún, Sebastián de, 45, 46
Las Casas, Bartolomé de, 41, 51; *Brevíssima relación*, 269; as defender of the Amerindians, 4–5, 36, 62, 125, 268–69; as influence on Oré, 269, 275
Laso de la Vega, Francisco, 287; and praise for Oré after his death, 289–90
las Salinas, Battle of, 10
Lebo, fort of: as issue between Oré and the governor, 260, 263, 266
Ledesma, Bartolomé de, 54
Leonor de Jesús, Sor, 228
Lezo, Bachiller, 72
l'Hermite, Jacques, 248
Lienhard, Martin, 98

Lima, Peru: description of, 37–38; Franciscan monastery in, 39, 231–34; Inquisition in, 41; migrant population in, 38; Oré's education in, 37; university in, 40–41, 234–35. *See also* Third Church Council of Lima

Lizárraga, Reginaldo de, 18–19, 25, 29, 31, 212, 243, 246; Chile as described by, 240–41, 243–44; named bishop of the Rio de la Plata, 244

Loarte, Gabriel de, 34

Loayza, Jerónimo de, 52, 127

Lobo Guerrero, Bartolomé, 139, 145, 223, 228, 233–34

López, Atanasio, 2

López, Baltasar, 198

López de Azoca, Luis, 262

López de Fonseca, Juan, 287

López de Solís, Luis, 54

López de Tovar, Juan, 256

López de Velasco, Juan, 31, 37–38

López Hermoso, Diego, 267

Lorido Flores, Francisco, 75–76

Loyola, Ignatius, 145, 241

Loyola, Martín García Oñez de, 241, 243, 270; death of, 241, 245

Loyola, Martín Ignacio de: instructions issued by, 123–25

MacCormack, Sabine, 20

Magellan, Ferdinand, 41

Mangan, Jane, 17

Mannheim, Bruce, 3

Manual Catholico Romano Peruano y Cuzquense, 121–23

Maravajal, Manuel de, 84

Marrón, Francisco, 172, 173, 175, 176

Martín, Gerónimo, 21–22

Martínez, Alonso, 93, 107

Martínez, Hernando, 70

Martínez, Juan, 93

Martínez, Lorenzo, 70, 153, 180, 183, 185, 202

Martínez, María Elena: *Genealogical Fictions*, 29

Martínez, Miguel, 214, 217

Martínez de Avendaño, Domingo, 173

Martínez de Prado, Diego, 286

Mary. *See* Immaculate Conception; Virgin Mary

Mateos, Francisco, 49

Maurice of Nassau, Count, 248

Mayta Capac, 78

Mazuelos, Cosme Vélez de, 21–22

McClure, Julia, 59, 144

Medel, Hernando, 70

Medellín, Diego de, 28, 45, 52–53

Medina, José Toribio, 2

Menacho, Bartolomé Martínez, 54

Méndez de Canzo, Gonzálo, 171, 177

Mendiburu, Manuel, 2

Mendieta, Alonso de, 144

Mendizabal, Juan Álvarez, 116

Mendoza, Diego de, 63

Mendoza, García de, 234

Mendoza, Rodrigo de, 163, 248

Mendoza y Luna, Juan Manuel de. *See* Montesclaros, Viceroy Marqués de

Menéndez de Avilés, Pedro, 149–50, 192, 195

Menéndez Márquez, Juan, 152, 186, 187, 188, 197–99

Menéndez Márquez, Pedro, 196, 199–200

Mercado, Gregorio de, 265

Mercedarian Order, 55–56

Mesía de Mendoza, Doña Ana, 162–63

Messana, Archangelo de, 121

mestizos: Verdugo's negative views of, 225

Mexía Reynoso, Juan, 267

Mills, Ken, 3

Miranda, Hernando de, 195, 196

Mogrovejo, Archbishop Toribio Alfonso de, 43–44, 65, 107, 127, 217, 234; as convener of the Third Church Council, 45–47, 50, 51, 52, 56

Molina, Antonio de, 54

Molina, Cristóbal de, 45, 94, 107

Monardes, Nicolás, 182–83

Montalvo, Gregorio de, 71–72

Montemayor, Juan de, 75

Monterrey, Conde de, 232

Montes, Blas de, 170; on the challenges facing the friars, 152–53

Montes, Francisco, 265

Montesclaros, Viceroy Marqués de, 140, 145, 162, 163, 231, 232, 248, 271

Montesinos, Fernando de, 50

Index

Montolinia, Toribio de Benavente, 144
Monzón, Juan de, 62–63
Morejón, Pedro, 205
Moreno de Zarato, Alonso, 245
Moriscos, 215
Mullomarca, Doña Luisa, 16
Mumford, Jeremy, 20
Muñiz, Pedro, 74
Muñoz, Lázaro, 214, 215–16, 217
Murder and Martyrdom in Spanish Florida (Francis and Kole), 173, 174, 176–78

Naples: Oré in, 119
Navarrete, Bernardo de, 70
Navarro, Dr., 97, 262, 266
Neri, Felipe de, 145
Nicholas III, Pope, 59
Noguerol de Ulloa, Francisco, 67, 114
Nuestro Señor de los Milagros, 33–34
Núñez, Juan Velásquez Vela, 21

Ocampo, Fernando de: and Oré's consecration as bishop, 223–24
Ocaña, Diego de, 104–6, 203
Oliva, Giovanni Anello, 50, 128
Olivera, Juan Fernández de, 132, 155
Olivera, Luis de, 20
Oré, Alonso de, 229
Oré, Antonio de, 9–10, 17, 18, 100; death of, 28–29; as patron of the convent in Huamanga, 24–25, 26–27; service report on, 29–30; and the Taki Onqoy movement, 21; wealth and status of, 10–14, 25
Oré, Dionisio de, 18, 100–101
Oré, Don Gerónimo de, 14, 24, 101, 229; estate of, 14–16, 17
Oré, Don Jerónimo de, 16–17
Oré, Doña María de, 17
Oré, Francisco de, 20, 24, 113–14, 135, 226, 229, 230, 286; and service report on his late father, 29–30
Oré, Gaspar de, 15
Oré, Luis Gerónimo de, 12, 20, 52, 136; assigned to Spain, 108, 112–15; and the birth of a royal child, 257–58; books and manuscripts by, 2, 89, 112, 116–17, 290–91; charges against, as presented by the governor, 277–82; consecration of, as bishop, 223–25; and consecration of Francisco Verdugo, 224–25; and correspondence with the king, 258; in Cuba, 156, 157–63; death of, 285, 286–87; diverse perceptions of, 289–90; as doctrinero in the Colca Valley, 1, 18, 56, 62, 65, 70, 74, 75, 76, 77–89, 91–92, 103; as doctrinero in Cuzco, 107–8; as doctrinero in Potosí, 103–7; on the English threat, 201; family background of, 9–17; as Franciscan novice in Cuzco, 31–36; in Florida, 154–56, 164–69, 177–78, 185–88, 248; on the Guale uprising, 173–78, 194, 196, 197; as guardian of the Jauja missions, 92, 103; in Huamanga, as bishop, 224, 226–30; impact of Drake's venture on, 42–43; as inspector of missions in Florida, 154, 156, 164–69, 191–201; and the investigation into Gutiérrez de Ulloa, 86–89; as investigator of Solano, 133–34; in Italy, 116–18; last testament of, 285–88; legacy of, 290 lost manuscripts of, 126–27; and the martyrdom of Franciscans in Florida, 170–78; at the monastery in Lima, 37, 38, 39, 42–44; music as important to, 292; named bishop of Concepción, 4, 213, 214–17, 218; and ongoing dispute with the governor over appointment of clergy, 259–67; oratorical skills of, 132; ordination of, as deacon, 44; and possible connection to translations by Jesuit scholars, 130–31; as recruiter for the Florida missions, 132, 135–36; as religious leader on many levels, 3–4; religious paintings owned by, 287; responsibilities of, as bishop of, 251–58; retinue of, as bishop, 214–17; scholarly interest in, 1–5; slavery as concern of, 4–5; in Spain, 108, 112–15; and Viceroy Toledo, 40–41; as translator at the Third Church Council, 47, 53–54, 56; as translator of religious doctrine, 2–3, 91–102, 112, 114–15, 119–23, 290, 292; traveling to Florida, 136–38; treatise on indulgences by, 116–18; at the University of San Marcos, 44. *See also Corona de la Virgen María; Manual Catholico Romano Peruano y Cuzquense; Relación de la Florida; Relación de los mártires de la Florida; Rituale, seu manuale peruanum; Symbolo Catholico Indiano; Tratado sobre las indulgencias*

Oré, Pedro de, 18, 73, 75, 93, 100, 114; Luis Gerónimo's differences with, 106
Oré, Sor Catalina de, 15, 229
Oré de la Purificación, Doña María de, 28
Oré family: mythohistory of, 24–30; as part of the first creole generation, 23; sisters as members of the Huamanga convent, 28
Oré y Azevedo, Cristóval de, 229
Orobio, Pedro, 70
Ortiz, Antonio, 72–73, 210
Ortiz, Fernando, 79
Ortiz de Ayala, Francisca, 26
Ortiz de Zúñiga, Diego, 146, 203
Osores de Ulloa, Pedro, 256, 263, 264, 273, 287
Osorio, Alonso de, 70, 86, 88
Oxnam, John, 42

Pachacuti, the, 22
Pachacamac, 3, 37
Paez Castillejo, Pedro, 263, 288
Pallas, Gerónymo, 231, 234; journey of, to Peru, 218–22
Pánfilo de Narváez, 192
Paredes, Pedro de, 114–15
Pareja, Francisco, 172; as provincial of Santa Elena, 180–82; and the Timucua people, 171, 181–82
Patronato Real, 46, 54, 115, 213, 256, 289; and ongoing dispute between Oré and Governor Fernández de Córdova y Arce, 259–67, 280, 282
Paul V, Pope, 76, 116, 117, 204, 219
Peña, Pedro de la, 45
Pereda, Francisco de, 256
Perelli de Montalto, Alejandro, 50
Pérez, Simon, 215
Pérez Chacón, Hernán, 215
Pérez de Espinosa, Juan, 218, 245
Phelan, John L., 144
Philip II, 5, 14, 34, 43–44, 51, 53, 84, 92, 115, 133, 159, 170, 241, 247; on the conflict between the Franciscans and the secular clergy, 73–74
Philip III, 5, 115, 137, 157, 160, 204, 205, 229, 259; decree on slavery issued by, 271, 272
Philip IV, 5, 204, 225, 229, 259, 274, 282; daughter of, 257–58

Picado, Martín de, 71
Piñas, Baltasar de, 54, 234
Pineda, Juan de, 19
Pinzón, Ginés, 197–98
Pissaro de Orellana, Doña Mariana, 15
Pizarro, Francisco, 9, 10–11, 23, 34, 65, 78, 217, 231, 269
Pizarro, Gonzalo, 11, 29, 53, 65, 67, 114, 135
Pizarro, Hernando, 78
Polo Ondegardo, 49
Ponce de León, Francisco, 253, 265
Ponce de León, Juan, 151, 191
Portugués, Pedro, 31
Potosí: description of, 103–4; Oré as doctrinero in, 103–7
Prado, Martín de, 70
Prado, Pedro del, 21, 96, 98
Prieto, Martín de, 154–56
Prudentius, 100
Puga y Noboa, Alonso de, 286

Quechua, 91–92, 94–95, 96, 292. *See also* indigenous languages of Peru; *Rituale, seu manuale peruanum*
Quiñe, Pedro Paes, 288
Quiros, Miguel de, 265

Ramírez, Balthasar, 39, 40–41, 103
Ramón, Pedro, 70
Ramos Gavilán, Alonso, 205
Ramos, Gabriela, 96
Ramos, Sebastián, 112
Rappaport, Joanne, 19
Raya Navarrete, Antonio de, 75, 107–8, 115, 116; as advocate for Oré and his work, 111–12, 119; background of, 111
Recalde, Matheo de, 72, 73–74, 92
Recalde, Pedro de, 286
Reconquista: and justification for conquest, 268
Relación de la Florida (Oré), 132, 154–56, 176, 190, 191–201; inconsistencies in, 192–93; publication of, 202; sources for, 191, 192, 200
Relación de los mártires de la Florida (Oré), 171, 178, 190, 291
Revenga, Juan de, 64
Reynoso, Alonso de, 172, 197

Ribera, Alonso de, 243–44, 248, 264, 270, 272, 282, 285
Ricardo, Antonio, 47–49, 74, 101, 127
Ríos, Pedro de los, 63
Rituale, seu manuale peruanum (Oré), 3, 92, 99, 118, 122, 143, 203, 218, 290; authorized for publication, 113, 119; Bishop Loyola's instructions relating to, 123–25; as manual for administration of church sacraments, 119–23; publication of, 119–21; title page of, 120
Rivera, Diego de, 214–15, 217
Roca, Miguel, 139
Rodríguez, Blas, 174–75
Rojas, Cristóval de, 229
Rojas, Diego de, 229
Roldán, Francisco, 142
Ruiz, Antonio, 70, 71
Ruiz, Pedro, 151, 171
Ruiz de Canal, Bernardino, 263
Ruiz de Pereda, Gaspar, 158, 159–61

Sahagún, Bernardino de, 62
St. Augustine (Florida): description of, 151–52; Oré's inspections of, 154, 164–65; Prieto's conversion efforts in, 154–55; as Spanish territory, 133, 150, 151
Salado, Mateo, 41
Salas de Coloma, Miriam, 10, 101
Salinas, Juan de, 186, 212
Salinas y Córdova, Buenaventura de, 44, 146, 224, 232, 234
Salles-Reese, Verónica, 205
Salto, Lorenzo del, 271
San Antonio de Enacape convent, 165–66
San Buenaventura, Alonso de, 143, 144, 145; *Teología*, 143, 144
San Buenaventura, Francisco de, 137, 154
San Buenaventura de Guadalquini monastery, 166–67, 179
San Cristóbal Sebastián, Antonio, 27
San Cristóval, Evaristo, 30
San Francisco de Potano monastery, 166
San Gil, Luis de, 70
San Gil, Pedro de, 86–89
San José de Zapala, monastery of, 179
San Juan de Guacara, Mission of, 167

San Marcos (fort), 196–97
San Marcos, University of, 40–41; Oré as student at, 44
San Martín, Pedro de, 263
San Martín, Tomás de, 40
San Martin Timucua monastery, 166
San Miguel, Antonio de, 45, 46, 52, 243, 253, 262
San Nicolás, Juan de, 172–73
Sánchez, Diego, 18, 29, 53–54
Sánchez de Moya, Francisco, 159, 160–61
Sánchez de San Juan, Gaspar, 213
Sandoval, Alonso de, 219
Sandoval, Juan de, 215–16
Santa Catalina (Arequipa), Convent of, 111
Santa Clara, Convent of, 235, 286; and Catalina de Erauso, 227–28; establishment of, 26–27; financial struggles of, 229–30; Oré's sisters and nieces at, 15, 24, 226, 229
Santa Clara, Order of (convent), 24, 25, 26–28
Santa Cruz, Alonso de, 32
Santa Cruz, Province of, 151
Santa Cruz de Tarihica, Mission of, 167
Santa Elena, Province of, 151, 153; chapter meetings of, 179–81, 183; Oré's preparation for inspection of, 149; Oré's visitas to, 154, 156, 179–81, 183
Santa Isabel de Utinahica, Mission of, 167–68
Santiago de Cuba, monastery of, 157, 158, 160
Santiago, Bartolome de, 49
Santíssimo Sacramento (confraternity), 84
Santo Tomás, Domingo de, 51–52, 127
Sanz, Gento, 232, 233–34
sassafras: medicinal benefits of, 182–83
Sebastián, Juan, 128
Second Church Council of Lima, 77
Sermoniario de las Dominicas y fiestas del año (Oré), 112
Serpa, Cristóbal de, 16, 229
Serpa, Doña Ana de, 17, 28
Serpa, Pedro de, 285, 286, 288
Serrano, Alonso, 156
Serrano, Gerónimo, 235
Seville, Spain: Oré in, 113; Franciscan compound in, 117; and the dogma of Immaculate Conception, 203

Silva, Juan de, 173, 178
Sixtus VI, Pope, 50
slavery: Oré's concerns regarding, 4–5, 288
Sobrino, Gabriel, 272
Solano, Francisco, 46, 60, 154, 232, 234; canonization of, 139–40, 145–46, 291; early years of, 141–42; Oré's research and report on, 133–34, 139–46, 170, 291; and *Relación de la vida i milagros de Francisco Solano*, 141, 146; in South America, 143–44
Soler, Francisco, 214, 215–16, 217
Solís, Pedro Baptista, 93
Sorés, Jacques de, 158
Soria, Miguel Angel Espinosa, 3
Sotelo, Friar, 154
Soto, Hernando de, 155
Spain: Japanese diplomatic mission to, 154; Oré's assignment in, 108, 112–15
Spanish Civil War, 116
Spanish empire: the Dutch as threat to, 247–50, 274; Florida as financial strain on, 184; and Oré's concerns regarding the English threat, 200–201; and the value of the religious orders, 132–33
Spanish monarchs: and the Christian mission in the Indies, 212–13. *See also* Ferdinand; Isabel
Symbolo Catholico Indiano (Oré), 2, 24–25, 32, 35–36, 76, 80, 85, 112, 118, 126, 135, 191, 203, 229, 269, 290; on the administration of the sacraments, 96–97; approval of, 93; composing of, 91–102; praise for, 93–94, 99; printing of, 100–101; religious poetry as part of, 98–101; sources used for, 94; title page of, 90; and the Virgin of Copacabana, 204

Taki Onqoy movement, 20–23, 77
Tapia, Jerónimo de, 70
Tejada, Doña Leonor de, 17, 28
Tejada, Inés de, 28
Tello, Juan, 214, 217
Teresa of Avila, 145
Third Church Council of Lima, 106; convening of, 45–47; Oré as translator at, 47, 53–54; participants in, 54–56; principal focus of, 46–47, 96; published religious texts resulting from, 47–54, 101, 116; and translations of religious texts into indigenous languages, 47–54, 96
Tibesar, Antonine, 2
Timucua people: conversion of, 155, 166, 171, 181–82
Tito Yupanqui, Francisco, 205
Tobar, Juan de, 243
Toledo, Viceroy Francisco de, 13–14, 32, 34, 35, 39–40, 54, 64, 67, 74, 78, 108, 128, 156, 168, 204, 267; achievements of, 40; and Francis Drake, 42–43; in Lima, 40–41; and the Third Church Council, 46
Toro, Bernardo, 203, 204
Toro, Laws of, 17
Torre, Ynés de la, 216
Torres Bollo, Diego de, 129
Torres Rubio, Diego de, 128
transculturation: as manifested by the assimilation between the Spanish and the Inca cultures, 77–80, 293
Tratado sobre las indulgencias (Oré), 116–18
Trejo, Antonio de, 132, 139–40, 205
Trejo de Sanabria, Hernando, 54–55, 72, 93
Treviño y Guillamas, Juan de, 164, 186, 211; and tensions with the Franciscans, 184–85
Trinidad, Leonor de la, 27–28
Tundidor Sánchez, Juan, 136, 137–38, 154
Tupac Amaru I, 241; execution of, 34–35
Twelve Years' Truce, 274

Ugarte, Juan de, 281, 286
Ulloa Mogollón, Juan de, 70, 86, 87
Ulloa y Lemos, Lope de, 273
Urban VIII, Pope, 145
Urbina, Diego de, 265
Urbina, Martín de, 70

Vaca de Castro, Cristóbal, 10, 29
Valadés, Diego, 61
Valdivia, Luis de, 5; as advocate of "defensive war," 270–73, 293
Valdivia, Pedro de, 240, 243, 269
Valencia, Alonso de, 86–89
Valenzuela, Gerónimo de, 93
Valenzuela, Juan de, 106

Index

Valera, Blas, 49–50, 96, 127
Valladolid, Spain: Oré in, 114–15
Vallejo, Hernando, 278
Van Deusen, Nancy E., 3, 227
Vargas Ugarte, Rubén, 2, 99, 116
Varona, Juan, 216
Vázquez, Juan, 130
Vazquez de Ayllón, Luis, 191
Vázquez de Coronado, Francisco, 192
Vázquez de Espinosa, Antonio, 253–54
Vázquez de Leca, Mateo, 203, 204
Vega, Juan de, 93
Vega, Mansio de, 282
Vega y Fonseca, Fernando de, 50–51
Vela de la Cuba, Doña Antonia, 228
Velasco, Antonio de, 205
Velasco, Diego de, 194, 195
Velasco, Luis de, 94, 232
Venezuela, 151
Venido, Juan de, 121, 287
Vera, Andrés de, 214, 215, 216, 217
Vera, Francisco de, 216
Verdugo, Diego, 229
Verdugo, Francisco, 33, 223, 229–30; consecration of, as bishop, 224–25
Verdugo, Gaspar, 70
Victoria, Francisco de, 45
Villacarrillo, Jerónimo de, 52, 63, 64–65, 78; and the conflict between the Franciscans and the secular clergy, 69, 72, 74
Villafañe, Angel, 192
Villalobos, Juan Rodríguez de, 31
Villar, Conde de, 16, 70, 72, 101
Villaverde Ureta, Juan de, 158–59

Villavicencio, Hernando de, 214, 217
Villela, Juan de, 270
Viniegra, Pedro de, 171–72
Viracocha, 3, 50, 94
Virgin Mary: Oré's book in praise of, 202–3, 205–10; Oré's description of, 208; songs praising, 203–4; statue of, in Lima, 232
Virgin of Copacabana, 204–5, 291
Virgin of Guadalupe: celebration of, 104–6
Vitalem, Constantinum, 119
Vitelleschi, Mutius, 273
Vivanco, Juan de, 136–37, 185
Vives, Juan Luis: *The Education of a Christian Woman*, 208
Vogeley, Nancy, 173

War of the Spanish Succession, 116
Wernke, Steven, 63
Wilder, Thornton, 31

Yanque Collaguas: Franciscan presence in, 63, 68, 69, 79, 91
Ylicusa, Pedro de, 287
Ynga, Don Carlos Melchor, 108
Yupanqui, Manco Inga, 29

Zamora, Francisco de, 20, 21, 28, 70
Zannetti, Luis, 129
Zapata, Luis, 64
Zárate, Agustín de, 94
Zavallos, Alonso de, 86, 87, 88
Zerpa, Pedro de, 136
Zerpa y Padilla, Anton de, 135–36
Zerpa y Padilla, Francisco de, 135–36

Printed in the USA
CPSIA information can be obtained
at www.ICGtesting.com
LVHW051458101123
763510LV00018B/347/J